A·N·N·U·A·L E·D·I·T·I·O·N·S

Early Childhood Education

Twenty-Third Edition

02/03

EDITORS

Karen Menke Paciorek
Eastern Michigan University

Karen Menke Paciorek is a professor of early childhood education and coordinator of graduate education at Eastern Michigan University in Ypsilanti. Her degrees in early childhood education include a B.A. from the University of Pittsburgh, an M.A. from George Washington University, and a Ph.D. from Peabody College of Vanderbilt University. She is the coeditor, with Joyce Huth Munro, of *Sources: Notable Selections in Early Childhood Education* (McGraw-Hill/Dushkin) and the editor of *Taking Sides: Clashing Views on Controversial Issues in Early Childhood Education.* (McGraw-Hill/Dushkin). She has served as president of the Michigan Association for the Education of Young Children and the Michigan Early Childhood Education Consortium. She presents at local, state, and national conferences on curriculum planning, guiding behavior, preparing the learning environment, and working with families.

Joyce Huth Munro
American Association of Colleges for Teacher Education

Joyce Huth Munro is Associate for Professional Issues and Liaison at the American Association of Colleges for Teacher Education in Washington, D.C. She has been an administrator and professor at colleges in Kentucky, South Carolina, and New Jersey. Her current writing and research focuses on discovering what makes quality teacher education programs. She is coeditor, with Karen Menke Paciorek, of *Sources: Notable Selections in Early Childhood Education* (McGraw-Hill/Dushkin). At regional and national conferences, she presents seminars on innovative methods of teacher education and curriculum design. Dr. Munro holds an M.Ed. from the University of South Carolina and a Ph.D. from Peabody College at Vanderbilt University.

McGraw-Hill/Dushkin
530 Old Whitfield Street, Guilford, Connecticut 06437

Visit us on the Internet
http://www.dushkin.com

Credits

1. **Perspectives**
   Unit photo—United Nations photo by John Isaac.
2. **Child Development and Families**
   Unit photo—United Nations photo.
3. **Care and Educational Practices**
   Unit photo—New York Times photo by John J. P. Coleman.
4. **Guiding and Supporting Young Children**
   Unit photo—AP photo by Carlos Osorio.
5. **Curricular Issues**
   Unit photo—Shore Line Times photo by John Ferraro.
6. **Trends**
   Unit photo—The Image Works photo by Bob Daemmrich.

Copyright

Cataloging in Publication Data
Main entry under title: Annual Editions: Early Childhood Education. 2002/2003.
1. Early Childhood Education—Periodicals. I. Paciorek, Karen M. II. Munro, Joyce H. Title: Early childhood education.
ISBN 0–07–250676–8   658'.05   ISSN 1092–4876

Twenty-Third Edition

Cover image © 2002 PhotoDisc, Inc.
Printed in the United States of America   1234567890BAHBAH5432   Printed on Recycled Paper

Editors/Advisory Board

Members of the Advisory Board are instrumental in the final selection of articles for each edition of ANNUAL EDITIONS. Their review of articles for content, level, currentness, and appropriateness provides critical direction to the editor and staff. We think that you will find their careful consideration well reflected in this volume.

To the Reader

In publishing ANNUAL EDITIONS we recognize the enormous role played by the magazines, newspapers, and journals of the public press in providing current, first-rate educational information in a broad spectrum of interest areas. Many of these articles are appropriate for students, researchers, and professionals seeking accurate, current material to help bridge the gap between principles and theories and the real world. These articles, however, become more useful for study when those of lasting value are carefully collected, organized, indexed, and reproduced in a low-cost format, which provides easy and permanent access when the material is needed. That is the role played by ANNUAL EDITIONS.

Early childhood education is an interdisciplinary field that includes child development, family issues, educational practices, behavior guidance, and curriculum. *Annual Editions: Early Childhood Education 02/03* brings you the latest information in the field from a wide variety of recent journals, newspapers, and magazines. In selecting articles for this edition we were careful to provide you with a well-balanced look at the issues and concerns facing teachers, families, society, and children. There are four themes found in readings chosen for this twenty-third edition of Annual Editions: Early Childhood Education. They are: (1) with appropriate adult guidance, children can overcome the obstacles of trauma, (2) the importance of parents and family in the success and academic achievement of children in school and the concerted effort to provide universal preschool for all, (3) key findings that stress the need for early literacy experiences for young children and, (4) the ongoing battle to provide an appropriate balance of extracurricular activities for all children. It is especially gratifying to see issues affecting children and families covered in magazines other than professional association journals. The general public needs to be aware of the impact of positive early learning and family experiences on the growth and development of children.

Continuing in this edition of *Annual Editions: Early Childhood Education* are selected World Wide Web sites that can be used to further explore topics addressed in the articles. We have chosen to include only a few high-quality sites. Students are encouraged to explore these sites on their own, or in collaboration with others, for extended learning opportunities.

Given the wide range of topics included, *Annual Editions: Early Childhood Education 02/03* may be used by various groups: undergraduate or graduate students studying early childhood education, professionals pursuing further development, parents seeking to improve their skills, or administrators new to early childhood education who want to develop an understanding of the critical issues in the field.

The selection of readings for this edition has been a cooperative effort between the two editors and the advisory board members. We appreciate the time the advisory board members have taken to provide suggestions for improvement and possible articles for consideration. We couldn't produce this book without the assistance of many. The production and editorial staff of McGraw-Hill/Dushkin ably support and coordinate our efforts. This book is used at over 550 colleges and universities throughout the country. We realize that this is a tremendous opportunity to provide a thorough review of the current literature. This is a responsibility we take seriously. Our job is to provide the reader with a snapshot of the critical issues facing professionals in early childhood education.

To the instructor or reader interested in the history of early childhood care and education programs throughout the years, we invite you to view our other book, also published by McGraw-Hill/Dushkin. *Sources: Notable Selections in Early Childhood Education*, 2nd edition (1999) is a collection of 46 writings of enduring historical value by influential people in the field. All of the selections are primary sources that allow you to experience firsthand the thoughts and views of these important educators. Available this year is the first edition of *Taking Sides: Clashing Views on Controversial Issues in Early Childhood Education*. This book is also published by McGraw-Hill/Dushkin and is edited by Karen Menke Paciorek. Twenty controversial issues facing early childhood professionals or parents have been selected. A pro and a con article are presented for each issue along with background information on the issue and a list of additional readings. The book can be used in a seminar or issues course.

We are grateful to readers who have corresponded with us about the selection and organization of previous editions. Your comments and articles sent for consideration are welcomed and will serve to modify future volumes. Take time to fill out and return the postage-paid *article rating form* on the last page. You may also contact either of us at karen.paciorek@emich.edu or jmunro@aacte.org.

We look forward to hearing from you.

Karen Menke Paciorek
Editor

Joyce Huth Munro
Editor

Contents

UNIT 1
Perspectives

Six selections consider developments in early childhood education.

Unit Overview   xviii

The concepts in bold italics are developed in the article. For further expansion, please refer to the Topic Guide and the Index.

UNIT 2
Child Development and Families

Nine selections consider the effects of family life on the growing child and the importance of parent education.

The concepts in bold italics are developed in the article. For further expansion, please refer to the Topic Guide and the Index.

UNIT 3
Care and Educational Practices

Fourteen selections examine various educational programs, assess the effectiveness of a few teaching methods, and consider some of the problems faced by students with special needs.

The concepts in bold italics are developed in the article. For further expansion, please refer to the Topic Guide and the Index.

The concepts in bold italics are developed in the article. For further expansion, please refer to the Topic Guide and the Index.

UNIT 4
Guiding and Supporting Young Children

Five selections examine the importance of establishing self-esteem and motivation in the child and consider the effects of stressors such as violence on behavior.

UNIT 5
Curricular Issues

Eight selections consider various curricular choices. The areas covered include play, authentic learning, emergent literacy, motor development, technology, and conceptualizing curriculum.

The concepts in bold italics are developed in the article. For further expansion, please refer to the Topic Guide and the Index.

UNIT 6
Trends

Seven selections consider the present and future of early childhood education.

Unit Overview   192

The concepts in bold italics are developed in the article. For further expansion, please refer to the Topic Guide and the Index.

The concepts in bold italics are developed in the article. For further expansion, please refer to the Topic Guide and the Index.

Topic Guide

This topic guide suggests how the selections in this book relate to the subjects covered in your course. You may want to use the topics listed on these pages to search the Web more easily.

On the following pages a number of Web sites have been gathered specifically for this book. They are arranged to reflect the units of this *Annual Edition*. You can link to these sites by going to the DUSHKIN ONLINE support site at *http://www.dushkin.com/online/*.

ALL THE ARTICLES THAT RELATE TO EACH TOPIC ARE LISTED BELOW THE BOLD-FACED TERM.

World Wide Web Sites

The following World Wide Web sites have been carefully researched and selected to support the articles found in this reader. The easiest way to access these selected sites is to go to our DUSHKIN ONLINE support site at *http://www.dushkin.com/online/*.

AE: Early Childhood Education 02/03

The following sites were available at the time of publication. Visit our Web site—we update DUSHKIN ONLINE regularly to reflect any changes.

General Sources

Children's Defense Fund (CDF)
http://www.childrensdefense.org

At this site of the CDF, an organization that seeks to ensure that every child is treated fairly, there are reports and resources regarding current issues facing today's youth, along with national statistics on various subjects.

Connect for Kids
http://www.connectforkids.org

This nonprofit site provides news and information on issues affecting children and families, with over 1,500 helpful links to national and local resources.

Eric Clearing House on Elementary and Early Childhood Education
http://www.ericeece.org

This invaluable site provides links to all ERIC system sites: clearinghouses, support components, and publishers of ERIC materials. You can search the massive ERIC database and find out what is new in early childhood education.

National Association for the Education of Young Children
http://www.naeyc.org

The NAEYC Web site is a valuable tool for anyone working with young children. Also see the National Education Association site: *http://www.nea.org.*

National Institute on Early Childhood Development and Education (ECI)
http://www.ed.gov/offices/OERI/ECI/

ECI was created by the U.S. Department of Education to provide programs of research, development, and dissemination to improve early childhood development and education. Access to grants, publications, presentations, on-line conferencing, and networking are available.

U.S. Department of Education
http://www.ed.gov/pubs/TeachersGuide/

Government goals, projects, grants, and other educational programs are listed here as well as many links to teacher services and resources.

UNIT 1: Perspectives

Child Care Directory: Careguide
http://www.careguide.net

Find licensed/registered child care by state, city, region, or age of child at this site. Site contains providers' pages, parents' pages, and many links.

Early Childhood Care and Development
http://www.ecdgroup.com

This site concerns international resources in support of children to age 8 and their families. It includes research and evaluation, policy matters, programming matters, and related Web sites.

Goals 2000: A Progress Report
http://www.ed.gov/pubs/goals/progrpt/index.html

Open this site to survey a progress report by the U.S. Department of Education on the Goals 2000 reform initiative. It provides a sense of educators' future goals.

UNIT 2: Child Development and Families

Administration for Children and Families
http://www.acf.dhhs.gov

This site provides information on federally funded programs that promote the economic and social well-being of families, children, and communities.

Global SchoolNet Foundation
http://www.gsn.org

Access this site for multicultural education information. The site includes news for teachers, students, and parents as well as chat rooms, links to educational resources, programs, and contests and competitions.

I Am Your Child
http://www.iamyourchild.org

Rob Reiner's I Am Your Child Foundation features excellent information on child development.

Internet Resources for Education
http://web.hamline.edu/personal/kfmeyer/cla_education.html#hamline

This site, which aims for "educational collaboration," takes you to Internet links that examine virtual classrooms, trends, policy, and infrastructure development. It leads to information about school reform, multiculturalism, technology in education, and much more.

The National Academy for Child Development
http://www.nacd.org

The NACD, an international organization, is dedicated to helping children and adults reach their full potential. Its home page presents links to various programs, research, and resources into such topics as learning disabilities, ADD/ADHD, brain injuries, autism, accelerated and gifted, and other similar topic areas.

National Parent Information Network/ERIC
http://npin.org

This clearinghouse of elementary, early childhood, and urban education data has information for parents and for people who work with parents.

National Safe Kids Campaign
http://www.babycenter.com

This site includes an easy-to-follow milestone chart and advice on when to call the doctor.

www.dushkin.com/online/

Parent Center

http://www.parentcenter.com/general/34754.html

Parenting resources can be found at this site as well as information for assisting children who are facing stressful situations as a result of terrorism.

Zero to Three

http://www.zerotothree.org

Find here developmental information on the first 3 years of life—an excellent site for both parents and professionals.

UNIT 3: Care and Educational Practices

Canada's Schoolnet Staff Room

http://www.schoolnet.ca/home/e/

Here is a resource and link site for anyone involved in education, including special-needs educators, teachers, parents, volunteers, and administrators.

Classroom Connect

http://www.classroom.net

A major Web site for K–12 teachers and students, this site provides links to schools, teachers, and resources online. It includes discussion of the use of technology in the classroom.

The Council for Exceptional Children

http://www.cec.sped.org/index.html

Information on identifying and teaching gifted children, attention deficit disorders, and other topics in disabilities and gifted education may be accessed at this site.

National Resource Center for Health and Safety in Child Care

http://nrc.uchsc.edu

Search through this site's extensive links to find information on health and safety in child care. Health and safety tips are provided, as are other child-care information resources.

Online Innovation Institute

http://oii.org

A collaborative project among Internet-using educators, proponents of systemic reform, content-area experts, and teachers who desire professional growth, this site provides a learning environment for integrating the Internet into educators' individual teaching styles.

UNIT 4: Guiding and Supporting Young Children

Child Welfare League of America (CWLA)

http://www.cwla.org

The CWLA is the United States' oldest and largest organization devoted entirely to the well-being of vulnerable children and their families. Its Web site provides links to information about issues related to morality and values in education.

National Network for Family Resiliency

http://www.nnfr.org

This organization's home page will lead you to a number of resource areas of interest in learning about resiliency, including General Family Resiliency, Violence Prevention, and Family Economics.

UNIT 5: Curricular Issues

Association for Childhood Education International (ACEI)

http://www.udel.edu/bateman/acei/

This site, established by the oldest professional early childhood education organization, describes the association, its programs, and the services it offers to both teachers and families.

California Reading Initiative

http://www.sdcoe.k12.ca.us/score/promising/prreading/prreadin.html

The California Reading Initiative site provides valuable insight into topics related to emergent literacy. Many resources for teachers and staff developers are provided.

Early Childhood Education Online

http://www.ume.maine.edu/ECEOL-L/

This site gives information on developmental guidelines, presents issues in the field, gives tips for observation and assessment, and information on advocacy.

International Reading Association

http://www.reading.org

This organization for professionals who are interested in literacy contains information about the reading process and assists teachers in dealing with literacy issues.

Kathy Schrock's Guide for Educators

http://www.discoveryschool.com/schrockguide/

This is a classified list of sites on the Internet found to be useful for enhancing curriculum and teacher professional growth. It is updated daily.

Phi Delta Kappa

http://www.pdkintl.org

This important organization publishes articles about all facets of education. By clicking on the links in this site, for example, you can check out the journal's online archive, which has resources such as articles having to do with assessment.

Reggio Emilia

http://ericps.ed.uiuc.edu/eece/reggio.html

Through ERIC, you can link to publications related to the Reggio Emilia approach and to resources, videos, and contact information.

Teachers Helping Teachers

http://www.pacificnet.net/~mandel/

Basic teaching tips, new teaching methodology ideas, and forums for teachers to share their experiences are provided on this Web site. Download software and participate in chat sessions. It features educational resources on the Web, with new ones added each week.

Tech Learning

http://www.techlearning.com

An award-winning K–12 educational technology resource, this site offers thousands of classroom and administrative tools, case studies, curricular resources, and solutions.

UNIT 6: Trends

Awesome Library for Teachers

http://www.neat-schoolhouse.org/teacher.html

Open this page for links and access to teacher information on everything from educational assessment to general child development topics.

EdWeb/Andy Carvin

http://edweb.gsn.org

The purpose of EdWeb is to explore the worlds of educational reform and information technology. Access educational resources

www.dushkin.com/online/

around the world, learn about trends in education policy and information infrastructure development, and examine success stories of computers in the classroom.

Future of Children
http://www.futureofchildren.org

Produced by the David and Lucille Packard Foundation, the primary purpose of this page is to disseminate timely information on major issues related to children's well-being.

National Institute on the Education of At-Risk Students
http://www.ed.gov/offices/OERI/At-Risk/

The At-Risk Institute supports a range of research and development activities designed to improve the education of students at risk of educational failure due to limited English proficiency, race, geographic location, or economic disadvantage. Access numerous links and summaries of the Institute's work at this site.

Prospects: The Congressionally Mandated Study of Educational Growth and Opportunity
http://www.ed.gov/pubs/Prospects/index.html

This report analyzes cross-sectional data on language-minority and LEP students in the United States and outlines what actions are needed to improve their educational performance. Family and economic situations are addressed. Information on related reports and sites is provided.

We highly recommend that you review our Web site for expanded information and our other product lines. We are continually updating and adding links to our Web site in order to offer you the most usable and useful information that will support and expand the value of your Annual Editions. You can reach us at: *http://www.dushkin.com/annualeditions/*.

UNIT 1
Perspectives

Unit Selections

1. **The Mission of the Movement to Leave No Child Behind. What You Can Do**, *Children's Defense Fund*
2. **Eager to Learn—Educating Our Preschoolers: Executive Summary**, Barbara Bowman, M. Suzanne Donovan, and M. Susan Burns
3. **Preschool Perspective, Èn Français**, Linda Jacobson
4. **How Do Education and Experience Affect Teachers of Young Children?** Susan Kontos and Amanda Wilcox-Herzog
5. **Wired for Thought**, Sharon Begley
6. **The 20th Century's Best and Worst Education Ideas**, James W. Guthrie

Key Points to Consider

- To effect real change in education, what are three key recommendations that should be enacted, according to the National Research Council?

- How does the French system of preschool education differ from what is available for families of preschoolers in the United States? What aspects of the French system would be most adaptable to the United States?

- Describe the post-secondary education and experience that is most beneficial in bringing about change in the educational system?

- What educational practices of the past are good enough to keep around for this century? Which ones were poor choices that have not benefited children?

 **Links: www.dushkin.com/online/**
These sites are annotated in the World Wide Web pages.

Child Care Directory: Careguide
http://www.careguide.net

Early Childhood Care and Development
http://www.ecdgroup.com

Goals 2000: A Progress Report
http://www.ed.gov/pubs/goals/progrpt/index.html

As we provide a perspective of what has happened in the past year and what is to come for young children and their families, we cannot help but be affected by the events of September 11, 2001. The act of terrorism against America as well as the world has mobilized citizens to a new resolve—to focus more on what is important in life. Friendships and family interactions have taken center stage and people are valuing opportunities to be with children, relive old memories, and plan for the future.

Marian Wright Edelman keeps us focused on what is best and just for all children. She has become the spokesperson for millions of children living in poverty, without access to medical care, adequate food and shelter, and quality educational experiences.

We include the introduction from *The State of America's Children 2001 Yearbook* from the Children's Defense Fund. As always, Edelman includes the statistics and facts vital for any child advocate to use when stating a case for resources to be invested on young children.

The 2000 release of *Eager to Learn—Educating our Preschoolers: Executive Summary* by the National Research Council (NRC) has been widely cited. Never have we known so much about the importance of young children's participation in appropriate educational experiences. In the last article in this edition, "Time to Talk of Early Childhood," author Anne Lewis makes reference to the *Eager to Learn Executive Summary.* She states that the NRC provides standards for preschool programs and urges state and local educators to follow the recommendations of the council. The executive summary, Lewis states, reports the importance of children being involved in quality early childhood programs and curricula where they are given opportunities to reflect, predict, and question. This will lay a strong foundation for the skills that will be most needed as they progress through the education system. It will cause those teachers who use a canned, or predetermined, curriculum to rethink their approach to providing educational experiences for young children. Children need a learning atmosphere in which they are given responsibility for being active participants in the development of the learning experiences, not merely passive bystanders who do what the teacher has carefully planned and prepared. This is what the editors call the "pot luck" versus "dinner party" approach to planning and teaching. At a pot luck, everyone contributes something to the meal, whereas at a dinner party, one person creates the menu and prepares the meal. Children deserve learning experiences that reflect a pot-luck approach over the teacher-directed dinner-party method. Children can contribute to their learning when given opportunities to do so.

We all need to be aware of best practices in early childhood education from other countries. The French system of child-care centers for infants and toddlers called *crèches* and preschoolers called *école maternelle* is described in "Preschool Perspective, En Francais." Learning from others may offer Americans some ideas for revamping our beleaguered early childhood system. In France, teachers must have a college degree plus 2 years of a teacher training program in order to teach preschool children. In many American states, the requirements for adults wanting to work in programs prior to public school entry age do not include required hours in child growth and development or any post–secondary education but only a criminal background check involving crimes against children. Requirements for teachers vary greatly from state to state. As a people, we are willing to accept

no formal preparation for teachers of children under the age of 5, but want teachers in kindergarten through 12th grade to hold college degrees and teacher certification. On this front, much improvement is needed. Along these lines, Susan Kontos and Amanda Wilcox-Herzog reviewed the literature on teacher preparation and experience and its effects on learning opportunities made available for the children in their care. Their findings are reviewed in "How Do Education and Experience Affect Teachers of Young Children?" Not surprisingly, they found that teachers who have had more formal preparation work in classrooms received high-quality ratings. There is a relationship between specialized education for teachers of young children and the quality of educational experiences they are able to provide.

In the next article, "Wired for Thought," Sharon Begley explains the knowledge now known on the development of the human brain. This information was unknown just 10 short years ago, but is now changing the way parents interact with their children.

This unit on Perspectives ends with "The 20th Century's Best and Worst Education Ideas." The ideas were compiled by the faculty of Peabody College of Vanderbilt University in Nashville, one of the nation's most respected institutions in the field of education. The panel chose best ideas such as the 1954 Supreme Court ruling in *Brown v. Board of Education,* which struck down segregation; allocation of resources for students with disabilities; and implementation of alternative forms of education. Among the list of worst ideas were the federal funding formulas for school districts and the blending of small districts into large impersonal districts that make it difficult for families to participate in their children's education. Enjoy reading this section, which provides a view of important issues facing early childhood education today.

Foreword: It's Time

The Mission of the Movement to Leave No Child Behind. What You Can Do

Never has the time been riper to set forth a big moral and policy vision for children. Never has the time been riper for child advocates to seize the mantle of leadership to build a nation fit for children. Never has the time been riper to transform America's shameful child neglect and poverty into a bounty of hope and opportunity for the world to see and emulate.

The real challenge is not *what* to do for children but *how* to build the spiritual and civic will to achieve what all children need for all children. How do we build a broad-based movement to Leave No Child Behind that has the transforming power of the civil rights, anti-war, and environmental movements of the 1960s and 1970s? How do we evoke in the American people the same deep ingrained national commitment to voteless children that existed to protect elderly Americans from poverty, hunger, and social isolation? How do we move children's needs to the top of community, state, and national agendas regardless of who is in office? How do we mobilize and organize a critical mass of Americans to demand concrete major actions from policy makers and then hold them accountable? How do we present a bold, visionary, and comprehensive agenda that covers all of children's needs, rather than piecemeal, fragmented incremental steps that do not resonate beyond the beltway, state capitals, or policy wonks? How do we bring together disparate child advocates and service providers (child care, child welfare, child health, education, youth development, juvenile justice, and violence prevention) with powerful mainstream networks (faith, women, parents and grandparents, youths, and health professionals) to support, strengthen, and achieve an inspiring big vision to protect the whole child and family and to rebuild community and a sense of common space and purpose as a nation?

It's time. It's time to assure every child a *Healthy Start*, a *Head Start*, a *Fair Start*, a *Safe Start*, and a *Moral Start* and successful passage to adulthood. It's time to withdraw our permission from America's official child neglect and abuse and to sow seeds of hope and empowerment in communities, schools, congregations, and homes all across America until they grow into a mighty torrent of demand for justice. We *can* stop our leaders from investing in prisons and death and start them investing in life—in health care, early childhood and parent training and support, and education. We *can* stop them investing in what we know does not work—missile defense systems, F22s, juvenile detention centers, and boot camps—and start them investing in what does work: Head Start, immunizations, after-school programs, and parental jobs with decent wages that lift them from poverty. We *can* stop our leaders from passing another round of unjust tax cuts and increased welfare for rich corporations and

individuals and start them closing the fairness gap by investing in targeted tax policies which offer middle- and low-income families relief.

That is what this movement to Leave No Child Behind will do with your help.

The Vision: As we enter the 21st century, America's strength reflects our courage, our compassion, our hard work, our moral values, and our commitment to justice. Today, we can extend the American dream of our forefathers and foremothers to every child and family. We have the know-how, the experience, the tools, and the resources. And we have the responsibility as mothers, fathers, grandparents—concerned and sensible people across the country.

We Cannot Afford Not to Invest in Our Children...

- A dollar invested in good early childhood programs for low-income children saves $7.00.
- A dollar invested in immunizations against diphtheria, tetanus, and whooping cough saves $23.00.
- A dollar spent in the Women, Infants and Children (WIC) nutritional program saves $3.07 during a baby's first year.
- The average cost of providing a year of Head Start for one child is $5,043.
- The average cost of keeping a person in prison for a year is $20,000.
- Every year we allow a child to grow up in poverty costs $9,000 in lost future productivity over his or her working life.

We can build a nation where families have the support they need to make it at work and at home; where every child enters school ready to learn and leaves on the path to a productive future; where babies are likely to be born healthy, and sick children have the health care they need; where no child has to grow up in poverty; where all children are safe in their communities and every child has a place to call home—and all Americans can proudly say "We Leave No Child Behind."

Our mission and vision in the months ahead is to do what it takes to meet the needs of children and their parents by building on the strengths and sense of fairness of the American people, learning from the best public and private ideas and successes, and moving forward to a renewed commitment to all our children.

How America Stands Among Industrialized Countries

The United States ranks:

1st	in military technology
1st	in military exports
1st	in Gross Domestic Product
1st	in the number of millionaires and billionaires
1st	in health technology
1st	in defense expenditures
10th	in eighth grade science scores
11th	in the proportion of children in poverty
16th	in efforts to lift children out of poverty
16th	in living standards among our poorest one-fifth of children
17th	in low birthweight rates
18th	in the gap between rich and poor children
21st	in eighth grade math scores
23rd	in infant mortality
Last	in protecting our children against gun violence

According to the Centers for Disease Control and Prevention, U.S. children under age 15 are:

9	times more likely to die in a firearm accident
11	times more likely to commit suicide with a gun
12	times more likely to die from gunfire, and
16	times more likely to be murdered with a gun

than children in 25 other industrialized countries *combined*.

Of the 154 members of the United Nations, the United States and Somalia (which has no legally constituted government) are the only two nations that have failed to ratify the U.N. Convention on the Rights of the Child.

A Key Policy Pathway: Working with a range of national, state, and local child advocacy networks and members of Congress, CDF has developed the comprehensive Act to Leave No Child Behind as a key way to embody this vision and to move forward for children. Any state or local community should feel free to adopt such a comprehensive approach. The Act gives the President, Congress, and all Americans the opportunity to:

- Ensure every child and their parents health insurance.
- Lift every child from poverty—half by 2004; all by 2010.
- End child hunger through the expansion of food programs.
- Get every child ready for school through full funding of quality Head Start, child care, and preschool programs.
- Make sure every child can read by fourth grade and can graduate from school able to succeed at work and in life.
- Provide every child safe, quality after-school and summer programs so children can learn, serve, work, and stay out of trouble.
- Ensure every child a place called home and decent affordable housing.
- Protect all children from neglect, abuse, and violence and ensure them the care they need.
- Ensure families leaving welfare the supports needed to be successful in the workplace, including health care, child care, and transportation.

The twelve titles of the Act to Leave No Child Behind add up to a comprehensive whole because children do not come in pieces. They live in families and communities who need the capacity to support them. The Act is achievable because it builds on the best ideas for helping children and because we have all the resources we need to provide them. The Act is timely because our nation is at a pivotal point as we debate what kind of moral, community, policy, and political choices we are prepared to make at this turn of century and millennium to realize a more just and compassionate society—one where no child is left behind.

How Will We Achieve Our Vision? *By building a powerful grassroots and grasstops movement across America through Wednesdays in Washington and Back Home and other public awareness and engagement efforts.* In 1964, interracial teams of women with a variety of talents and skills went to Mississippi to bear witness every Wednesday for racial justice and to build bridges between White and Black women across income and racial lines. Each was required to get training and to commit to work back home to inform and mobilize their communities about what they saw and what could be done. On Wednesdays—in Washington and Back Home—we are calling on women (especially mothers, grandmothers, and all those with a mothering spirit), people of faith, youths, senior citizens, child advocates, and concerned citizens from all walks of life to take action for children in this new era until the words Leave No Child Behind and the Act to Leave No Child Behind become reality for every child. Everybody can be a part of the movement who shares our mission.

In addition to Wednesdays in Washington and Back Home we will use every means possible to raise public awareness about children's needs and what can be done, including Stand For Children Day events in all 50 states on June 1st; Child Watch visits to expose community leaders and policy makers to children's needs and what they can do; television, radio, and print media campaigns; town meetings; prayer vigils; study circles; and house parties. Coalition building, nonviolence, media skills and organizing training to build a critical mass of effective advocates will be an ongoing and integral part of our movement building in Washington, at Haley farm, and in states and regions.…

An American slave woman, Harriet Tubman, ushered slaves to freedom on the Underground Railroad. Another slave woman, Sojourner Truth, consistently spoke out against slavery and unjust treatment of women and vowed to keep her enslavers "scratching." South African women fought and helped win an end to murderous apartheid policies. Dorothy Day, co-founder of the Catholic Worker Movement, dedicated her work and her life to the poor and homeless and speaking boldly about the duty one owed to one's neighbor—"anyone in need." Sister Katherine Drexel used her fortune to educate Black and Native American youths and helped found Xavier University in New Orleans. Jane Addams and other prominent women "settlers" started settlement houses and worked for the poor and for peace. Poor women in India struggling to feed their children and families walked with empty plates and spoons to protest rising food prices. Rachel Carson's groundbreaking book *Silent Spring* launched the modern environmental movement in the United States. Hundreds of years earlier, courageous environmental pioneer Amrita Devi gave her life to protect the trees in her village because she believe them sacred. Her sacrifice inspired others who repeated her sacrifice and saved the trees and sparked the Chipko Movement in India. Thousands of Chilean women faced death and demonstrated in the streets to demand the resignation of a military junta leader. Black women were the backbone of the American civil rights movement: Mrs. Rosa Parks, Septima Clark, Ella Baker, Fannie Lou Hamer, Mae Bertha Carter, Diane Nash, Victoria Gray, and little girls and boys like Ruby Bridges, the Little Rock Nine, and the Carter children who walked through taunting crowds and sat in hostile classrooms to get a better education. And there are so many more stories to tell and so much more history being made each day right now by ordinary people doing extraordinary things across America and the world. To bring all these growing voices together into a mighty demand to Leave No Child Behind is the challenge before us.…

A 2001 Action Agenda to Leave No Child Behind®
And to Ensure Every Child a Healthy Start, a Head Start,
a Fair Start, a Safe Start, and a Moral Start in Life
and Successful Passage to Adulthood

With federal budget experts projecting a $5.6 trillion federal budget surplus over the next decade, and billions of tobacco settlement dollars available in a post-Cold War era, now is the time to end immoral and preventable child poverty, hunger, homelessness, sickness, and illiteracy in the richest nation on earth. Now is the time to stand up and show our children we truly value them. Now is the time to build a more just and compassionate and less violent society—one where no child is left behind. Together the nation, states, communities, employers, parents, and citizens must:

I. Ensure Every Child a Healthy Start. **There are 10.8 million uninsured children in America; nearly 90 percent of them live in working families. About six million are currently eligible for health care under the Children's Health Insurance Program (CHIP) and Medicaid. Nearly five million lack any health coverage. We must:**

- Mount a massive and urgent campaign to reach and enroll every one of the six million children now eligible for CHIP and Medicaid.
- Simplify and unify application and eligibility procedures in every state to make it easier rather than harder for children to get health care.
- Expand health coverage to every uninsured child and their parents.
- Encourage employers to expand coverage for employees and their children and to stop dropping dependent coverage.
- Urge every community network—religious, child care, health care, parents, senior citizens, education, grassroots, youths, and corporations—to join a massive and persistent public awareness and enrollment campaign until every child is provided appropriate health care.

II. Ensure Every Child a Head Start. **Only three out of five children eligible for Head Start and only 12 percent of children eligible for federal child care assistance receive it. Nearly seven million school-age children are home alone after school and are at risk of tobacco, alcohol, and drug use, teen pregnancy, and violence. Quality preschool, child care, after-school, and summer programs, and public school systems are essential to getting all children ready to learn and achieve and keeping them safe when parents are in the workforce.**

- Head start should be increased so that every eligible child can participate by 2005 and 40 percent of eligible infants and toddlers can participate in Early Head Start.
- The Child Care and Development Block Grant should be increased to serve all eligible children by 2005 and investments should be made to strengthen the quality of child care.

(continued)

(continued)

- Congress should increase funding for the new Early Learning Initiative for very young children and significantly increase investments in 21st Century Community Learning Centers and other quality after-school and summer programs.
- Every state should provide a high quality comprehensive prekindergarten program for all families who wish to participate and invest more state dollars in quality child care and Head Start programs.
- Every business should offer affordable quality child care, flex-time, and paid parental leave options to help employees balance work and family responsibilities.
- Federal and state family and medical leave laws should be expanded and strengthened to include paid leave.
- As a nation, we need to make sure that every child can read by fourth grade and can graduate from school able to succeed at work and in life.

III. Ensure Every Child a Fair Start. **Over 12 million children are poor; 78 percent of them live in working families; 5.8 million of them live in extreme poverty in families with incomes below $6,600. They often suffer hunger, homelessness, and lack other basic necessities. Our nation must commit to doing whatever is necessary to reduce child poverty in America by half by 2004 and end it by 2010. Children should get a fair share of the federal and state budget surpluses, tobacco settlement monies, and be guaranteed the same income and health security as senior citizens. We must:**

- Ensure work at a decent wage and education and training for parents to improve their earnings.
- Make the Child Tax Credit refundable, increase and make refundable the Dependent Care Tax Credit (DCTC) for lower-income families, and expand the Earned Income Tax Credit (EITC) for families with three or more children.
- Make sure that every poor family with children currently eligible for nutrition, health, housing, child care, and other assistance gets them. States should immediately use rather than hoard dollars intended to help parents work and become more self-sufficient, reduce their bureaucracies, and create a culture of service among their employees.
- Strengthen child support enforcement.

IV. Ensure Every Child a Safe Start and Successful Transition to Adulthood. **American children under 15 are 12 times more likely to die from guns than children in 25 other industrialized nations combined. A child is reported abused or neglected every 11 minutes. Children are exposed to relentless glorification of violence in toys and on movie, television, video game, and Internet screens. All children need positive role models in their homes and communities and positive alternatives to the streets.**

- Parents should be educated about the dangers of owning a gun and be required to store guns locked and unloaded. Manufacturers, sellers, and other adults should be held liable for guns that get into the hands of criminals and children.
- Congress should support legislation that will help communities provide positive developmental activities for all youths.
- Youth involved in criminal activity should be held accountable for their behavior, but also should be provided appropriate treatment and rehabilitative services to give them the opportunity to turn their lives around to become productive law-abiding adults. And we must invest in children before they get into trouble.
- Nonviolence training, conflict resolution, peer mediation, and other activities to prevent all forms of family and community violence should be instilled in our homes, congregations, schools, and communities.
- Investments should be made in services and activities to prevent child abuse and neglect, assist families in crisis and offer ongoing support for birth, adoptive, and kinship care families to assure permanent homes for children leaving foster care.
- Partnerships between child protection and substance abuse agencies should be encouraged to expand comprehensive treatment for families with alcohol and drug problems to promote safety and permanent homes for children and recovery for their parents.
- Community-based supports for kinship caregivers should be expanded so that they can get help for their children, including ongoing assistance when they commit to care permanently for children who have been in foster care.

V. Ensure Every Child a Moral Start. **It is time for American adults to stop our moral hypocrisy and to live the values we want our children to learn. If we want them to stop being violent, then we should stop being violent. If we want them to be honest, then we should be honest. Parents, preachers, teachers, and all public officials must conduct themselves as they would want their own children or any child to emulate. Our children need consistent love, time, attention, discipline, family stability, and limits at home and in school, and they need to see that adults in their nation, private sector, and communities value and care for them—not as consumers and future customers to be exploited or as a non-voting group to be ignored—but as the heirs of America's institutions and values. It is time for all adults to accept their responsibility to be good protectors of and mentors for the next generation.**

*Most of these and other proposals are included in the Act to Leave No Child Behind—which lays out CDF's comprehensive policy vision of what a great and sensible nation could provide all its children.

Reprinted by permission. From *Children's Defense Fund,* The State of America's Children Yearbook 2001, pp. xvi-xxvii. Washington, D.C.: Children's Defense Fund, 2001.

Eager to Learn—
Educating Our Preschoolers:
Executive Summary

Children come into the world eager to learn. The first five years of life are a time of enormous growth of linguistic, conceptual, social, emotional, and motor competence. Right from birth a healthy child is an active participant in that growth, exploring the environment, learning to communicate and, in relatively short order, beginning to construct ideas and theories about how things work in the surrounding world. The pace of learning, however, will depend on whether and to what extent the child's inclinations to learn encounter and engage supporting environments. There can be no question that the environment in which a child grows up has a powerful impact on how the child develops and what the child learns.

Eager to Learn: Educating Our Preschoolers is about the education of children ages 2 to 5. It focuses on programs provided outside the home, such as preschool, Head Start, and child care centers. At this, the threshold of a new century, there can be little doubt that something approaching voluntary universal early childhood education, a feature of other wealthy industrialized nations, is also on the horizon here. Three major trends have focused public attention on children's education and care in the preschool years:

1. the unprecedented labor force participation of women with young children, which is creating a pressing demand for child care;
2. an emerging consensus among professionals and, to an ever greater extent, among parents that young children should be provided with educational experiences; and
3. the accumulation of convincing evidence from research that young children are more capable learners than current practices reflect, and that good educational experiences in the preschool years can have a positive impact on school learning.

The growing consensus regarding the importance of early education stands in stark contrast to the disparate system of care and education available to children in the United States in the preschool years. America's programs for preschoolers vary widely in quality, content, organization, sponsorship, source of funding, relationship to the public schools, and government regulation.

Historically, there have been two separate and at times conflicting traditions in the United States that can be encapsulated in the terms *child care* and *preschool*. A central premise of this report, one that grows directly from the research literature, is that *care and education cannot be thought of as separate entities in dealing with young children*. Adequate care involves providing quality cognitive stimulation, rich language environments, and the facilitation of social, emotional and motor development. Likewise, adequate education for young children can occur only in the context of good physical care and of warm affective relationships. Indeed, research suggests that secure attachment improves social and intellectual competence and the ability to exploit learning opportunities. Neither loving children nor teaching them is, in and of itself, sufficient for optimal development; thinking and feeling work in tandem.

Learning, moreover, is not a matter of simply assimilating a store of facts and skills. Children construct knowledge actively, integrating new concepts and ideas into their existing understandings. Educators have an opportunity and an obligation to facilitate this propensity to learn and to develop a receptivity to learning that will prepare children for active engagement in the learning enterprise throughout their lives. This report argues, therefore, that promoting young children's growth calls for early childhood settings (half day or full day, public or private, child care or preschool) that support the development of the full range of capacities that will serve as a foundation for school learning. As the child is assimilated into the culture of education in a setting outside the home, early childhood programs must be sensitive and responsive to the cultural contexts that define the child's world outside the school or center, and they must build on the strengths and supports that those contexts provide.

CONTEXT OF THE REPORT AND COMMITTEE CHARGE

As Americans grapple with decisions about early childhood education that many European countries have already made, we can draw on certain advantages. We have a strong research community investigating early childhood learning and development and production evidence on which to base the design, implementation and evaluation of programs. And we have a tradition of experimentation and observation in preschools that gives us access to a wealth of experience in early childhood education.

The Committee on Early Childhood Pedagogy was established by the National Research Council in 1997 to study a broad range of behavioral and social science research on early learning and development and to explore the implications of that research for the education and care of young children ages 2 to 5. More specifically, the committee was asked to undertake the following:

- Review and synthesize theory, research, and applications in the social, behavioral, and biological sciences that contribute to our understanding of early childhood pedagogy.
- Review the literature and synthesize the research on early childhood pedagogy.
- Review research concerning special populations, such as children living in poverty, children with limited English proficiency, or children with disabilities, and highlight early childhood education practices that enhance the development of these children.
- Produce a coherent distillation of the knowledge base and develop its implications for practice in early childhood education programs, the training of teachers and child care professionals, and future research directions.
- Draw out the major policy implications of the research findings.

The study was carried out at the request of the U.S. Department of Education's Office of Educational Research and Improvement (Early Childhood Institute) and the Office of Special Education Programs, the Spencer Foundation, and the Foundation for Child Development. An important motivation for sponsors of the study is to help public discussion of these issues move away from ideology and toward evidence, so that educators, parents, and policy makers will be able to make better decisions about programs for the education and care of young children....

RECOMMENDATIONS

What is now known about the potential of the early years, and of the promise of high-quality preschool programs to help realize that potential for all children, stands in stark contrast to practice in many—perhaps most—early childhood settings. In the committee's view, bringing what is known to bear on what is done in early childhood education will require efforts in four areas: (1) professional development of teachers, (2) develop-

ment of teaching materials that reflect research-based understandings of children's learning, (3) development of public policies that support—through standards and appropriate assessment, regulations, and funding—the provision of quality preschool experiences, and (4) efforts to make more recent understandings of development in the preschool years common public knowledge. The committee proposes recommendations in each of these areas.

Professional Development

At the heart of the effort to promote quality early childhood programs, from the committee's perspective, is a substantial investment in the education and training of those who work with your children.

Recommendation 1: Each group of children in an early childhood education and care program should be assigned a teacher who has a bachelors' degree with specialized education related to early childhood (e.g., developmental psychology, early childhood education, early childhood special education). Achieving this goal will require a significant public investment in the professional development of current and new teachers.

Sadly, there is a great disjunction between what is optimal pedagogically for children's learning and development and the level of preparation that currently typifies early childhood educators. Progress toward a high-quality teaching force will require substantial public and private support and incentive systems, including innovative educational programs, scholarship and loan programs, and compensation commensurate with the expectations of college graduates.

Recommendation 2: Education programs for teachers should provide them with a stronger and more specific foundational knowledge of the development of children's social and affective behavior, thinking, and language.

Few programs currently do. This foundation should be linked to teachers' knowledge of mathematics, science, linguistics, literature, etc., as well as to instructional practices for young children.

Recommendation 3: Teacher education programs should require mastery of information on the pedagogy of teaching preschool-aged children, including:

- Knowledge of teaching and learning and child development and how to integrate them into practice.
- Information about how to provide rich conceptual experiences that promote growth in specific content areas, as well as particular areas of development, such as language (vocabulary) and cognition (reasoning).
- Knowledge of effective teaching strategies, including organizing the environment and routines so as to promote activities that build social-emotional relationships in the classroom.
- Knowledge of subject-matter content appropriate for preschool children and knowledge of professional standards in specific content areas.

- Knowledge of assessment procedures (observation/performance records, work sampling, interview methods) that can be used to inform instruction.
- Knowledge of the variability among children, in terms of teaching methods and strategies that may be required, including teaching children who do not speak English, children from various economic and regional contexts, and children with identified disabilities.
- Ability to work with teams of professionals.
- Appreciation of the parents' role and knowledge of methods of collaboration with parents and families.
- Appreciation of the need for appropriate strategies for accountability.

Recommendation 4: A critical component of preservice preparation should be a supervised, relevant student teaching or internship experience in which new teachers receive ongoing guidance and feedback from a qualified supervisor.

There are a number of models (e.g., National Council for Accreditation of Teacher Education) that suggest the value of this sort of supervised student teaching experience.

Recommendation 5: All early childhood education and child care programs should have access to a qualified supervisor of early childhood education.

Teachers should be provided with opportunities to reflect on practice with qualified supervisors.

Recommendation 6: Federal and state departments of education, human services, and other agencies interested in young children and their families should initiate programs of research and development aimed at learning more about effective preparation of early childhood teachers.

Recommendation 7: The committee recommends the development of demonstration schools for professional development.

The U.S. Department of Education should collaborate with universities in developing the demonstration schools and in using them as sites for ongoing research:

- on the efficacy of various models, including pairing demonstration schools as partners with community programs, and pairing researchers and in-service teachers with exemplary community-based programs;
- to identify conditions under which the gains of mentoring, placement of preservice teachers in demonstration schools, and supervised student teaching can be sustained once teachers move into community-based programs.

Educational Materials

Recommendation 8: The committee recommends that the U.S. Department of Education, the U.S. Department of Health and Human Services, and their equivalents at the state level fund efforts to develop, design, field test, and evaluate curricula that incorporate what is known about learning and thinking in the early years, with companion assessment tools and teacher guides.

Each curriculum should emphasize what is known from research about children's thinking and learning in the area it addresses. Activities should be included that enable children with different learning styles and strengths to learn.

Each curriculum should include a companion guide for teachers that explains the teaching goals, alerts the teacher to common misconceptions, and suggests ways in which the curriculum can be used flexibly for students at different developmental levels. In the teacher's guide, the description of methods of assessment should be linked to instructional planning so that the information acquired in the process of assessment can be used as a basis for making pedagogical decisions at the level of both the group and the individual child.

Recommendation 9: The committee recommends that the U.S. Department of Education and the U.S. Department of Health and Human Services support the use of effective technology, including videodiscs for preschool teachers and Internet communication groups.

The process of early childhood education is one in which interaction between the adult/teacher and the child/student is the most critical feature. Opportunities to see curriculum and pedagogy in action are likely to promote understanding of complexity and nuance not easily communicated in the written word. Internet communication groups could provide information on curricula, results of field tests, and opportunities for teachers using a common curriculum to discuss experiences, query each other, and share ideas.

Policy

States can play a significant role in promoting program quality with respect to both teacher preparation and curriculum and pedagogy.

Recommendation 10: All states should develop *program* standards for early childhood programs and monitor their implementation.

These standards should recognize the variability in the development of young children and adapt kindergarten and primary programs, as well as preschool programs, to this diversity. This means, for instance, that kindergartens must be readied for children. In some schools, this will require smaller class sizes and professional development for teachers and administrators regarding appropriate teaching practice, so that teachers can meet the needs of individual children, rather than teaching to the "average" child. The standards should outline essential components and should include, but not be limited to, the following categories:

- School-home relationships,
- Class size and teacher-student ratios,
- Specification of pedagogical goals, content, and methods,
- Assessment for instructional improvement,
- Educational requirements for early childhood educators, and
- Monitoring quality/external accountability

Recommendation 11: Because research has identified content that is appropriate and important for inclusion in

early childhood programs, *content* standards should be developed and evaluated regularly to ascertain whether they adhere to current scientific understanding of children's learning.

The content standards should ensure that children have access to rich and varied opportunities to learn in areas that are now omitted from many curricula—such as phonological awareness, number concepts, methods of scientific investigation, cultural knowledge, and language.

Recommendation 12: A single career ladder for early childhood teachers, with differentiated pay levels, should be specified by each state.

This career ladder should include at a minimum, teaching assistants (with child development associate certification), teachers (with bachelor's degrees), and supervisors.

Recommendation 13: The committee recommends that the federal government fund well-planned, high-quality center-based preschool programs for all children at high risk of school failure.

Such programs can prevent school failure and significantly enhance learning and development in ways that benefit the entire society.

The Public

Recommendation 14: Organizations and government bodies concerned with the education of young children should actively promote public understanding of early childhood education and care.

Beliefs that are at odds with scientific understanding—that maturation automatically accounts for learning, for example, or that children can learn concrete skills only through drill and practice—must be challenged. Systematic and widespread public education should be undertaken to increase public awareness of the importance of providing stimulating educational experiences in the lives of all young children. The message that the quality of children's relationships with adult teachers and child care providers is critical in preparation for elementary school should be featured prominently in communication efforts. Parents and other caregivers, as well as the public, should be the targets of such efforts.

Recommendation 15: Early childhood programs and centers should build alliances with parents to cultivate complementary and mutually reinforcing environments for young children at home and at the center.

FUTURE RESEARCH NEEDS

Research on child development and education can and has influenced the development of early childhood curriculum and pedagogy. But the influences are mutual. By evaluating outcomes of early childhood programs we have come to understand more about children's development and capacities. The committee believes that continued research efforts along both these lines can expand understanding of early childhood education and care, and the ability to influence them for the better.

Research on Early Childhood Learning and Development

Although it is apparent that early experiences affect later ones, there are a number of important developmental questions to be studied regarding how, when, and which early experiences support development and learning.

Recommendation 16: The committee recommends a broad empirical research program to better understand:

- The range of inputs that can contribute to supporting environments that nurture young children's eagerness to learn;
- Development of children's capacities in the variety of cognitive and socioemotional areas of importance in the preschool years, and the contexts that enhance that development;
- The components of adult-child relationships that enhance the child's development during the preschool years, and experiences affecting that development for good or for ill;
- Variation in brain development, and its implications for sensory processing, attention, and regulation, are particularly relevant;
- The implications of developmental disabilities for learning and development and effective approaches for working with children who have disabilities;
- With regard to children whose home language is not English, the age and level of native language mastery that is desirable before a second language is introduced and the trajectory of second language development.

Research on Programs, Curricula, and Assessment

Recommendation 17: The next generation of research must examine more rigorously the characteristics of programs that produce beneficial outcomes for all children. In addition, research is needed on how programs can provide more helpful structures, curricula, and methods for children at high risk of educational difficulties, including children from low-income homes and communities, children whose home language is not English, and children with developmental and learning disabilities.

Research on programs for any population of children should examine such program variations as age groupings, adult-child ratios, curricula, class size, and program duration. These questions can best be answered through longitudinal studies employing random assignment. In developing and assessing curricula, new research must also continue to consider the interplay between an individual child's characteristics, the immediate contexts of the home and classroom, and the larger contexts of the formal school environment.

Recommendation 18: A broad program of research and development should be undertaken to advance the state of the art of assessment in three areas: (1) classroom-based assessment to support learning (including studies of the impact of methods of instructional assessment on pedagogical technique and children's learning); (2) assessment for diagnostic purposes; and (3) assessment of program quality for accountability and other reasons of public policy.

Research on Ways to Create Universal High Quality

Recommendation 19: Research to fully develop and evaluate alternatives for organizing, regulating, supporting, and financing early childhood programs should be conducted to provide an empirical base for the decisions being made.

The current early childhood system is fragmented, lacks uniform standards, and provides uneven access to all children. Numerous policy choices have been proposed. This research would inform public policy decision making.

CONCLUSION

At a time when the importance of education to individual fulfillment and economic success has focused attention on the need to better prepare children for academic achievement, the research literature suggests ways to make gains toward that end. Parents are relying on child care and preschool programs in ever larger numbers. We know that the quality of the programs in which they leave their children matters. If there is a single critical component to quality, it rests in the relationship between the child and the teacher/caregiver, and in the ability of the adult to be responsive to the child. But responsiveness extends in many directions: to the child's cognitive, social, emotional, and physical characteristics and development.

Much research still needs to be done. But from the committee's perspective, the case for a substantial investment in a high-quality system of child care and preschool on the basis of what is already known is persuasive. Moreover, the considerable lead by other developed countries in the provision of quality preschool programs suggests that it can, indeed, be done on a large scale.

From *National Research Council,* 2000, pp. 1-3, 10-17. © 2000 by National Research Council.

Preschool Perspective, *En Français*

A growing number of early-childhood specialists in the U.S. are visiting France to observe its preschools, or *écoles maternelles*, to gather ideas to take back home.

BY LINDA JACOBSON

Paris

On the side of a hill just off a freeway in a suburb about 20 minutes southeast of this historic city sits an eye-catching building designed for some of France's youngest citizens.

The structure—which looks almost like three separate buildings linked on top of each other by staggered stairways—serves as a child-care center, preschool, and elementary school, with the youngest children in the bottom building and the oldest ones on the top.

At the child-care center, called a *crèche*, and the preschool—or *école maternelle*—heavy doors feature flexible rubber trim to keep small fingers from getting crunched. Windows in the classrooms are often placed at knee level to allow little ones to watch the activity in the hallway or peer into adjacent classrooms; other windows that stretch from the floor to the ceiling brighten the environment with a regular flow of natural light, enhancing the multicolored artwork hanging on classroom walls and in hallways.

"We consider our preschools a success," boasts Jean-Pierre Villain, an adviser to Jack Lang, France's education minister.

Inside the main entrance, puzzles and other learning games for preschoolers are intentionally placed in hallways for children to use while their parents are meeting with administrators or teachers. And in the crèche, a room sports a shallow wading pool with floating toys for youngsters to use. Meanwhile, in a cafeteria, where women wearing white caps and smocks serve hot meals, children eat off real china and use full-size knives and forks.

Showpiece facilities like these in the town of Créteil, French officials say, provide proof of this nation's commitment to young children. "We consider our preschools a success," boasts Jean-Pierre Villain, an adviser to Jack Lang, France's education minister.

Last month, Villain and other French education officials welcomed a group of Americans—most of them early-childhood-education advocates—who were touring several child-care and preschool facilities in France. For the Americans, the purpose of the trip was to see how France cares for and educates its infants, toddlers, and preschoolers, and whether some of the early-childhood programs and services in this Western European nation are worth copying.

Even though French education officials are unabashedly proud that their system of early-childhood education is receiving international recognition, they are honest about some of the challenging issues they face. And, by and large, the Americans who went on the trip recognized some of those problems and left France with definite opinions about what they would like to replicate and what they'd just as soon leave behind.

After touring the facilities in Créteil, Mark Ginsberg, the president of the Washington-based National Association for the Education of Young Children, emphasized that the purpose of the trip was not to learn how to adopt the French model, but to answer the question "What can we adapt that fits our model?"

At the center of France's broad and often innovative services for children stands the école maternelle—roughly translated as a maternal school. Americans familiar with the program often describe it as universal preschool. But in many ways, it is more accurate to say that in France, children enter public school at age 3. And some children, depending on where they live, begin as early as age 2.

The preschool program is part of the same national Ministry of Education that runs the compulsory education system for children ages 6 and older. Teachers in the preschools are highly trained, carrying not only a college degree, but also two years of education training. Their lessons are guided by a national curriculum that focuses heavily on building oral-language skills, but also includes art, music, physical education, and pre-mathematics.

Participation rates of children, however, hide the fact that it is a voluntary program for parents. One hundred percent of the nation's 4- and 5-year-olds attend the schools, which are often attached to, or located near, a neighborhood elementary school. Ninety-five percent of 3-year-olds attend the full-day programs, and about 35 percent of older 2-year-olds, most between 2½ and 3 years old, are now enrolled.

The école maternelle, Villain emphasizes, is a "school that doesn't want to be a school," because while it is technically the first level of public education for the children of France, it is also intended in part to preserve the early-childhood years as a distinct and important period. "There is plenty of time for children to have exams, to get marks," he says in French to the American visitors, who wear battery-powered headphones throughout the trip to receive simultaneous translation. "We want them to play, to learn through games. It's a time for waiting, not for pushing."

Though it is receiving increasing attention from American educators, the école maternelle is not a new educational phenomenon. It has a history dating back to the late 19th century. And similar "day nurseries," run mostly by Catholic nuns, even existed during the Napoleonic era. As a result, French people can't remember a time when little children didn't attend these kinds of schools—a cultural memory that stands in stark contrast to the relatively recent emphasis on child-care issues and preschool education in the United States.

The écoles maternelles and the nation's subsidized crèche system of day-care centers are also part of a broader agenda that took shape at the end of World War II. Because France lost so many men during the war, its leaders instituted policies and programs to encourage families to have children.

"There's a greater social goal," says Susan B. Watts, who formed an early-childhood-education project at the French-American Foundation in New York City and now works as a consultant. "They realized that to rebuild their country, they needed to start with pregnant women. They see children as a joy."

Indeed, members of the American delegation of early-childhood-education advocates and experts on the June 3–9 trip, which was sponsored by the Washington-based Children's Defense Fund, were, at times, more stunned by the public support for the programs than they were by the services themselves.

Support for early-childhood education is "embedded in the culture, in the society here," says Ginsberg, the NAEYC president, while touring the école maternelle in Créteil.

In Catherine Partaix's classroom, 3-year-olds crowd onto wooden benches as they gather to sing a song about a green mouse for their American visitors.

In French, the teacher tells the children, "Mr. Quiet wants to be listened to," as she tries to draw her students' curious eyes away from the observers in the room.

The classroom features some of the same activity areas, or "centers," as those in good early-childhood programs in the United States—such as a book corner, an easel for painting, and play kitchen tools. But there are many ways in which the practices in French preschool classrooms differ from what American teachers and parents have come to expect.

The first and most obvious difference is the number of children per classroom. Today, Partaix has roughly 20 pupils, but the average class size in écoles maternelles is 26 students, and some classes have as many as 28 to 30 children.

In contrast, the NAEYC recommends no more than 14 2½-year-olds in a class with two teachers and a maximum of 20 preschoolers in a class of 3- to 5-year-olds.

In fairness, it's worth noting that teachers in the French preschools have assistants. Still, the directors of those schools often have to spread three or four assistants over several classes. And even when the assistants are in the classrooms, French education officials concede, they are usually there to handle non-educational tasks, such as taking children to the bathroom or preparing materials for an activity.

Invariably, the difficulties of dealing with such large groups of children mean teachers often engage students in whole-group lessons, such as singing songs, leading everyone in counting activities, and reading stories that call for group participation.

Even when children disperse to work in smaller groups, the choices appear to be made more by the teacher than by the pupils. The teacher usually directs students to specific workstations rather than allowing them to choose what they would like to do.

Depending on the day's activity, teachers might move quickly from station to station, or spend most of their time with younger students who might need more help. As a consequence, a majority of pupils do not receive a great deal of individual attention, something early-childhood educators in the United States say is especially important for preschoolers.

"I work a great deal at making the children learn to be independent because I can't do everything," explains Partaix, who is also the headmistress at the school.

Nevertheless, the teachers are able to handle such large groups, French officials say, because they are so well trained.

"When teachers know their job, it's not a problem," says Guy Blandino, the director of the école maternelle affiliated with the Institut Universitaire de Formation des Maîtres, a teacher-training college in Paris.

To ensure that the large numbers of children do not overwhelm them, French preschool teachers say they make sure every lesson or task the children do has a clear educational purpose, which is different from some of the looser, "child-centered" lessons seen in many American preschools.

For instance, the American visitors saw organized groups of French children practice counting to the beat of musical rhythms. One teacher described a lesson in which she sends children with a "shopping list" through the classroom to collect objects of specific shapes and colors, and another task in which she had students draw fishnets to learn the concept of "upright lines and lying-down lines," or vertical and horizontal.

Similar to the practices in many preschools in the United States, children throughout France collect the best examples of their work into personal books to show their parents. And much like in American programs, many parents simply don't understand the educational theories undergirding many of the lessons used by French preschool teachers.

"Parents don't always properly understand what we're doing with the children," Partaix says. And, echoing an oft-heard complaint of preschool teachers in the United States that they are more than day-care workers, she told the visitors that her school is "not just a crèche."

Unlike in the United States—where the requirements to teach young children vary from program to program and from state to state—anyone who wants to teach in an école maternelle must have a college degree, plus two years of additional preparation at the teacher-training institute.

More than half the teacher candidates already have a degree in French literature or the social sciences, and some have even more education than that. Then, if they pass the institute's entrance exam, they begin a series of required education courses that include French, mathematics, and philosophy. Students also study child development and the process of learning to read and write. Beyond that, teachers-in-training spend time observing classroom teachers and working in classrooms themselves before they graduate. Additional courses focusing specifically on young children are optional.

Some of the American visitors on this trip were surprised by the lack of emphasis on early-childhood education at the institute. In fact, even though they can express a preference, graduates of the program don't always know whether they plan to work in a preschool or an elementary school.

That may be why officials at the teacher-training university note that teachers in the écoles maternelles probably need some additional training, but many professors simply don't consider such extra preparation a priority.

"A lot of my colleagues say, '[Young children] don't learn anything in école maternelle,'" says Dominique Delomier, a professor at the institute and an expert in language acquisition who trains future preschool teachers.

Even so, Deborah Phillips, a child-development expert who is the chairwoman of the psychology department at Georgetown University in Washington, was impressed by the high level of training these future teachers receive after she heard Ms. Delomier's comments during last month's tour of the French system. "It's not just how to manage children and do activities," Phillips says. "Here you have someone with a Ph.D. in linguistics and language acquisition teaching preschool teachers. That is amazing."

And she points out that because many teachers in France move from teaching one age level to another, they probably have a better sense of how the subject matter they are covering relates to what children learn before and after that point.

In the United States, on the other hand, states are just beginning to connect the guidelines they have for preschool programs—at least in places where such guidelines exist—with their K-12 academic standards. As the American system heads

in that direction, though, it might benefit from examining a paradox that stands out about the French system: The same ministry that sets down strict rules about curriculum and teacher training apparently gives teachers a lot of freedom in how they use that curriculum and training in the classroom. "I have official guidelines," says teacher Partaix. "But how I apply those I am 100 percent free to define."

Even though French educators stress that the preschool years are a treasured time for children in which they should learn how to play and enjoy life, many of the écoles maternelles feel very much like regular elementary schools. They have enrollments of about 200 or more students—and children often sit at desks and tables instead of doing work on the floor, as is often the practice in American preschools.

For some members of the U.S. delegation, this was most obvious at lunchtime, when about half the pupils at the school in Créteil gathered en masse around tables in a large school cafeteria to eat. In American preschools, eating is usually a more intimate affair, with children eating in their classrooms. In many Head Start programs, for example, hot meals are served in classrooms, and children eat at the same tables where they draw, paint, or do other activities.

"This [French style of feeding youngsters] is not the best way for children to share a meal experience at this age. It's not intimate enough," says Carol Brunson Day, the president of the Council for Professional Recognition, a Washington organization that works to improve the training of people who work with preschool-age children.

Beyond serving meals, much of what Day saw on the trip to France makes her wonder whether the United States can have "a universal system—spaces for all kids—without it resulting in an institutional model."

And Americans such as Day are not the only ones who are expressing such concerns. Because of the highly structured nature of the French preschool classrooms, a debate in France is heating up over whether the écoles maternelles are appropriate environments for 2-year-olds.

"We don't have any special treatment for children this young," says Blandino, who is increasingly worried about how the system is dealing with its youngest children. "We treat a child who is two like a child who is ten," he told the American delegation, although he pointed out that 2-year-olds are still allowed to take naps during the day.

Still, French parents have come to rely more and more on services for 2-year-olds.

An increasing number of 2-year-olds began entering the schools when the Education Ministry formed what are known as Zone d'Education Prioritaires, or ZEPs, in the 1980s. Similar in some ways to the U.S. government's Title I program for disadvantaged students, the ZEPs are France's first attempt to direct additional funding to areas with high percentages of low-income families. More than 500 areas throughout the country are now designated as ZEPs. Schools can use the extra money to lower class sizes, buy additional materials, or address other needs.

Many communities initially resisted the label because they were afraid it would "ghettoize" the neighborhood, education officials say. The concept of treating any one group in a different way runs counter to French values, according to French officials.

But studies showed that when children from such homes entered the écolcs maternelles earlier—at age 2 instead of 3—they were more likely to perform at a higher level in elementary school.

"In the ZEPs, I think it's good" to bring in 2-year-olds, says Partaix from the école maternelle in Créteil. She adds that in the ZEPs, the preschool teachers "represent hope to people that their children will become something."

The policy, however, has not been used quite the way French officials had intended.

Parents in wealthier areas—either because they want "free child care," as one teacher in Paris says, or because they want to give their children an academic advantage in elementary school—are also asking their local city halls to create additional space so they can enroll their 2- year-olds at no cost.

Another roadblock to making the programs work for those who need them the most is that some immigrants are reluctant to bring their young children to the local école maternelle because "they think they are going to lose their children," says Villain, the adviser to the education minister, apparently suggesting that the parents believe the children should be home with their mothers, where they will get the best care and be able to learn the customs and language of their primary culture.

The French approach to ethnic and racial differences contrasts with the thinking of many American educators.

Villain frets: "We would like to concentrate our 2-year-old policy in poorer areas, but it is difficult to implement."

One of the biggest differences, and drawbacks, of the French system noted by the American visitors was how this European nation approaches racial and ethnic differences—an aspect of the culture that has generated discussion among many U.S. educators and policymakers who have toured the écoles maternelles.

To the French, language is an obsession. And teachers and education officials here emphasize again and again that poor language skills are what prevent children from doing well in school. Therefore, the goal in the écoles maternelles is for non-French-speaking youngsters to master the language as quickly as possible. That's one of the reasons why the government wants 2-year-olds in the ZEPs, where many immigrants live, to start school earlier.

Some visitors from the States, though, left with the impression that teachers in the ZEPs—who didn't necessarily choose to work in those neighborhoods—are not well prepared to under-stand the needs of immigrant children or to work with parents whose primary language is not French.

In fact, some French preschool teachers simply express frustration with immigrant parents. "The majority" of immigrant parents "doesn't care" about how their preschool-age children do in school, complains Nathalie Bertin, a young teacher at Ville de Paris École Maternelle, a Paris preschool where 98 percent of the enrollment is from Africa. For instance, the booklets filled with students' work that she sends home to parents, she says, often come back to her without any evidence that the parents examined them. "I think people put their children here because it's free child care," Bertin says.

This is one area—reaching out to poor and minority communities—in which the United States has a much longer history and much more experience than France does, members of the American delegation point out, citing programs such as Head Start and Title I. "We do have something to offer," says Helen Blank, the director of the child-care and development division at the Children's Defense Fund.

Evelyn Moore, the president of the Washington-based National Black Child Development Institute—who has now observed the system here twice—says that the French "have made a clear decision that they want French citizens."

"Even though we want people to become American citizens," Moore adds, "we do not want to disconnect them from their culture, and that is the beauty of our system."

Some participants in the Children's Defense Fund trip also point out how the education of French children with disabilities differs from that of their counterparts in the U.S., where districts and government agencies are mandated by federal law to serve children with disabilities beginning when the youngsters are age 3.

Throughout France, many children with special needs at all age levels don't even attend the public schools.

The école maternelle in Créteil offers a *classe d'intégration scolaire*—or an integrated class—in which children with physical disabilities are blended with typical children for part of the day. The reality, however, is that such classes are not common.

At Ville de Paris École Maternelle, the American visitors talked about watching a young boy, whom the teacher identified as having a mental disability, wander out of the gym during a physical education class without his teacher's knowledge.

Again, the large number of children in the classes can make it hard to meet the individual needs of children without disabilities as well as those with special needs.

In another class at Ville de Paris École Maternelle, a teaching assistant brought a preschooler, who had been left out on the playground, back to his class several minutes after his classmates had returned. When he returned, the little boy went to sit by himself.

"We clap to tell them to come back in [from the playground], but it's difficult for some of the younger ones," says Karine Boiteux, the little boy's teacher.

This difficulty inherent in the French system is something that is a major drawback for students with special needs, the American visitors say. And the teachers lack of knowledge about how to work with special-needs children can lead to high levels of frustration.

"They're trained to handle the average [French] child," says Sheri Steisel of the Denver-based National Conference of State Legislatures.

"I saw burned-out, very new teachers," says Sheri Steisel, the senior director of human services at the National Conference of State Legislatures, based in Denver, who took part in the trip. "They're all trained the same way. They're trained to handle the average French child."

Some efforts are in place, however, to address the mental-health needs of children before they enter the écoles maternelles. Enfant Présent, for instance, is a nonprofit organization in Paris that offers round-the-clock child care for children who are at risk of abuse and neglect.

Child care in France, which is run by the Ministry of Health, began as a medically oriented service to reduce infant mortality. But as public-health problems began to disappear, "psychological problems were increasing," says Philippe Pruja, the director of one of Enfant Présent's two centers.

The organization offers care in a family child-care setting and counseling to parents who are having trouble raising their children because of drug abuse, mental-health problems, or other difficulties. Working in cooperation with family-court judges and social service agencies, Enfant Présent aims to step in before a crisis occurs that would result in a child's removal from the home.

Enfant Présent's centers are also used to bring the providers and children together for group activities. The organization is currently meeting just one-tenth of the demand, but the city has asked the directors to open another center in Paris and a fourth in the suburbs.

Even though this crèche is designed to care for children only until they are 3, the staff sometimes keeps children about six months longer, "so when the child goes into preschool, it's not going to be a complete disaster," Pruja says.

But services like these are still unusual in France. "People think you can do without prevention," Pruja says.

François Gerber, the director of the other center, said they would like to set up similar services in the public schools, but they don't think the Ministry of Education would be too receptive to the idea. "We have to wait for political will," she says. "Then they'll find the money."

After touring the écoles maternelle's, some Americans were surprised to learn that even with significant national spending, funding at the local level varies widely from city to city.

The Education Ministry spends about $1,700 per child each year for teachers' salaries and training. The rest comes from the cities, with larger municipalities spending roughly $1,300 to $1,600 per child annually, while smaller cities spend about $700 to $800.

Some cities offer more before- and after-school services than others do. And not all municipalities have modern facilities.

"We saw playgrounds that were bare," says W. Steven Barnett, a professor of education and public policy at Rutgers University in New Brunswick, N.J., who toured écoles maternelles outside Paris earlier this year with a group sponsored by the American Federation of Teachers.

French education officials counter that while there may be some disparities, they are relatively small.

"You don't find preschools in the basement," says Olga Baudelot, a senior researcher with the National Institute of Pedagogical Research, a division of the Education Ministry, hinting at where many preschools are located in the United States.

Of course, such tours of French preschools give outsiders only a limited view of how the system actually works.

"I have a real problem when people buzz in for 15 minutes and say, 'That's my observation,'" says Linda Bevilacqua, who developed the early-childhood-education program for the Core Knowledge Foundation in Charlottesville, Va., and has made repeated trips to France to study the écoles maternelles.

But even when visitors detect differences in the appearance of the buildings and the skills of the teachers, most leave with a sense of something greater.

While high-quality preschool classrooms with well-trained teachers and organized, stimulating activities certainly exist throughout the United States, France has made such programs a national priority.

"There is clearly a floor here below which these classrooms are not falling," Phillips of Georgetown University says on the final day of the trip.

Moore, from the National Black Child Development Institute, adds that—good or bad—the French "have a system that is universal, publicly supported, and financed. It's the national will of the people."

From *Education Week*, July 11, 2001, pp. 40-46. © 2001 by Education Week. Reprinted by permission.

How Do Education and Experience Affect Teachers of Young Children?

Susan Kontos and Amanda Wilcox-Herzog

How do teachers excel at their "craft?" Can we teach individuals to be experts, or are good teachers" genetically predisposed" to their abilities via personality or some other factor? Perhaps teaching is learned on the job, by experience, rather than through educational programs. Or perhaps the answer is all of the above.

Early childhood educators continue to discuss teacher/caregiver qualifications and ways to encourage best practice across groups of professionals who bring a variety of qualifications to their work (Johnson & McCracken 1994). It is crucial to inform those discussions with relevant research as support for, if not a counterbalance to, expert informed opinions. This Research in Review synthesizes what we know from research about how general education, specialized education, and experience relate to early childhood professionals' practices in teaching young children.

Education

Education refers to the level of formal schooling an early childhood professional has attained, regardless of the content. For example, an early childhood teacher with a bachelor's degree in business has more formal schooling (though less specialized education) than a teacher with an associate's degree in early childhood education. Because many early childhood educators enter the field with little or no specialized education, researchers have been interested in whether level of education, independent of content, is related to teachers' teaching practices. In other words, researchers have attempted to determine if teachers with more education exhibit behaviors that better exemplify best practice.

This article divides practice into two components: teachers' interactions with children and the overall quality of the classroom learning environment. Note that we often use the term *teacher* for the sake of simplicity, while acknowledging the importance of the caregiving function in early childhood education as well as the respect due to those early childhood professionals who prefer the term *caregiver* and/or *family child care provider.*

Teachers' interactions with children

A classic study conducted by Berk (1985) focused on the relationship between teacher education and teacher behavior toward children in child care settings. She found that teachers with college degrees were more likely than those without a degree to encourage children, make suggestions to them, and promote their verbal skills.

These three studies demonstrate that not only are specialized education and quality associated, but there may also be a causal relationship between them (that is, a change that can be attributed to education).

Another classic study, the National Day Care Study (Ruopp et al. 1979), demonstrated that caregiver education was positively associated with social interaction, cognitive/language stimulation, and conversation with children. The National Child Care Staffing Study (Whitebook, Howes, & Phillips 1990), a large, multisite study, found that education was the caregiver background variable that best predicted caregiver behavior (sensitivity, harshness, detachment). On the other hand, a more recent large, multisite study of infant/toddler care (NICHD Early Child Care Research Network [ECCRN] 1996) found no relationship between teachers' education and the frequency or ratings of positive caregiving.

Kontos and colleagues (1995) demonstrated similar relationships between interactions and formal education for family child care providers and for teachers in centers. In this study, level of formal schooling was significantly positively related to observer ratings of provider sensitivity and observations of responsive involvement with children but negatively related to observer ratings of detachment and providers' self-ratings of restrictiveness.

The learning environment

The Staffing Study (Whitebook, Howes, & Phillips 1990) revealed that teacher education was positively associated with "appropriate caregiving," a subscore of the

Early Childhood Environment Rating Scale (ECERS—Harms & Clifford 1980), which is a frequently used measure of overall classroom quality. Consistent with the Staffing Study, three other studies demonstrated a relationship between teachers' general education and the quality of the learning environment. Scarr, Eisenberg, and Deater-Deckard (1994), Phillipsen et al. (1997), and Epstein (1993) all found statistically significant associations between general education and scores on the ECERS (Harms & Clifford 1980) and /or the ITERS (Infant/Toddler Environment Rating Scale—Harms, Cryer, & Clifford 1990). A study of family child care providers produced similar results; provider education and global family child care quality as measured by the Family Day Care Rating Scale (FDCRS) (Harms & Clifford 1989) were significantly related.

Taken together, these studies demonstrate that better educated teachers and family child care providers work in classrooms or homes with higher quality ratings than do those with less education. It is tempting, but not valid, to assume that educated teachers create higher quality classrooms. These correlational studies do not allow us to determine the direction of effects, even though it may make intuitive sense that teachers with more education create higher quality classrooms. Maybe it is simply that better quality centers are able to hire staff with more education.

Specialized education

Teachers' formal schooling may or may not focus on child development and/or early childhood education. Specialized education may also take place outside of formal schooling (via workshops and other means). Many states allow teachers to do their work with little if any specialized education (Phillips, Lande, & Goldberg 1990). Thus, it is important to know if specialized education is related to how well they are likely to do their job. We turn now to that issue.

The learning environment

Studies examining the relationship between specialized education and the quality of the classroom or home child care learning environment (Whitebook, Howes, & Phillips 1990; Epstein 1993; Scarr, Eisenberg, & Deater-Deckard 1994; Cost, Quality, and Child Outcomes Study Team 1995; Kontos et al. 1995) have found consistent positive correlations using such instruments to measure quality as the ECERS (Harms & Clifford 1980), FDCRS (Harms & Clifford 1989), or the ITERS (Harms, Cryer, & Clifford 1990). One study (Scarr, Eisenberg, & Deater-Deckard 1994) also included the Assessment Profile (Abbott-Shim & Sibley 1987). The small to moderate but statistically significant correlations indicated that teachers' specialized education accounts for some, but not all, of the variation in the quality of learning environments they provide.

Taken together, these studies demonstrate that better educated teachers and family child care providers work in classrooms or homes with higher quality ratings than do those with less education.

Three studies measured quality before and after training with comparison or control groups (quasi-experimental designs). DeBord and Sawyers (1996) examined the impact of specialized education on the quality of care provided by 22 family child care providers, some of whom were affiliated with a child care association. They found that providers unaffiliated with a child care association initially displayed lower quality ("minimal," on average, according to the FDCRS) but increased to "good" following training. Affiliated providers were rated as "god" to start with and did not change following training. In a second study conducted by Cassidy and her colleagues (Cassidy et al. 1995; Cassidy & Buell 1996), teachers who obtained 15–20 credit hours of course work at the junior college level had higher quality ECERS scores at post-test than the control group that did not receive the course work. Finally, quality of family child care, as measured by the FDCRS, increased significantly following Family to Family training (offered to family child care providers in 40 U.S. communities as part of Dayton Hudson Foundation's quality child care initiative) and was higher than that of a comparison group of regulated providers who did not participate in this training program (Kontos, Howes, & Galinsky 1997). These three studies demonstrate that not only are specialized education and quality associated, but there may also be a causal relationship between them (that is, a change that can be attributed to education).

Teachers' interactions with children

The studies that we review next examined the relationship between teachers' behaviors with children and their specialized education. A follow-up analysis of Staffing Study data (Howes, Whitebook, & Phillips 1992) indicated that specialized education at the college level was important for teachers' competent interactions with infants and toddlers (as measured by the appropriate caregiving subscale of the ITERS), in contrast to preschool teachers who seemed to do well with a college degree in *any* subject *or* specialized education at the college level. Howes (1983) demonstrated that center-based caregivers with more specialized education played more with children and were less restrictive. In addition, family child care provider with more specialized education also played more with children and showed more responsivity, results consistent with those reported by Kontos and colleagues (1995). Kaplan and Conn (1984) reported that, following 20 clock hours of training in child development distributed across an average of seven sessions, teachers used more activities than before to facilitate social-emotional development, had better arranged and more plentiful materials, and spent more time in "physical child care" (not defined, but considered positive). Their study had no control group, however, so it is not possible to infer that the observed changes can be attributed to the intervention.

These data suggest that coherent teacher preparation programs (regardless of length or cost of the program) are more effective in preparing teachers than are more ad hoc educational experiences.

Arnett (1989) observed the behavior of 159 child care teachers in Bermuda with four different levels of specialized education ranging from no training to extensive training (a college degree in early childhood education). Results demonstrated that teachers with degrees were more warm and less punitive and detached in their interactions with children than teachers in the other three groups. Teachers with mid-range training consisting of two or four courses in child development were more positive and less punitive and detached than teachers with no training. Thus, Arnett demonstrated that some specialized education is good for the quality of teachers' interactions with children but more is even better.

Several studies were unable to show a relation between specialized education and teacher interactions with children. Cassidy and Buell (1996) reported that, in spite of increased ECERS scores following specialized education, there was no change in the amount of responsive language used by teachers/caregivers. In other words, the course work appears to have influenced overall classroom quality but not the quality of teacher's verbalizations with children. Family to Family training did not change providers' sensitivity or responsivity of the caregivers' interaction with the children, although quality was enhanced (Kontos, Howes, & Galinsky 1997). Thus, results regarding the association between specialized education and teacher interactions with children are mixed in studies using quasi-experimental designs.

One problem with research examining the effects or correlates of teacher education and specialized education is that the two factors tend to be intertwined. In other words, teachers with more formal education were also more likely to have more specialized education. Berk (1985), for instance, demonstrated differences in teacher interactions with children between teachers with specialized education and those with high school diplomas (in favor of the former). However, she was unable to show that specialized education was superior to a degree in a non-child-related field.

Another problem is that amount of formal and specialized education tends to be calculated as continuous variables (that is, actual years of education) rather than categorized into groups such as teachers with a high school diploma, teachers with an associate degree, teachers with a bachelor's degree, and so on. As a result, we can use these studies to investigate relationships between teachers' education and other variables, but we cannot get from them policy-relevant information telling us which category of education (formal or specialized) makes a significant difference to practice.

Howes (1997) conducted a study that attempted to address both of these two research problems. Using data from two large investigations of child care, Howes classified teachers into five categories by crossing categories of formal education with categories of specialized education and including in the study only teachers who fit into those predetermined categories. These categories were high school diploma with workshops. Child Development Associate (CDA) training, some college with some early childhood education courses, associate degree (AA) in early childhood, and an undergraduate or graduate degree in early childhood. Groups were compared for teacher sensitivity (Arnett 1989) and involvement (Howes & Stewart 1987). Results from both studies indicated that teachers with bachelor's degrees in early childhood education or higher were the most sensitive and involved teachers compared to all other groups. Teachers with AA degrees and CDA credentials were more sensitive and involved than teachers with some college or high school plus workshops, however. These data suggest that coherent teacher preparation programs (regardless of length or cost of the program) are more effective in preparing teachers than are more ad hoc educational experiences.

One study reported results contrary to the studies above. The National Institute of Child Health and Human Development (NICHD) Study of Early Child Care (1996) examined predictors of positive caregiving in settings with infants and toddlers. Specialized education was not among the statistically significant predictors for that age group. Instead, positive caregiving was predicted by group size and child-adult ratio.

There is a considerable amount of evidence that specialized training is related to the quality of the learning environment for children and to the quality of teachers' interactions with children.

Summary

There is a considerable amount of evidence that specialized training is related to the quality of the learning environment for children and to the quality of teachers' interactions with children. Two studies (Cassidy et al. 1995; Kontos et al. 1997) used quasi-experimental designs that allow us to infer causality between specialized education and practice. These two studies indicate that global indicators of quality may change somewhat (at least statistically, if not observably), but that observations of teachers' interactions with children revealed no change as a function of specialized education. It may be that researchers are not observing the kinds of behaviors that are likely to change as a function of specialized education. Two studies (Howes, Whitebook, & Phillips 1992; NICHD/ECCRN 1996) found different results for infants/toddlers compared to preschoolers; Howes found specialized education most important for work with infants, whereas the NICHD/ECCRN study found specialized education more important for work with preschoolers.

Experience

Some people believe that education, either general or specialized, is unrelated to effective teaching of young children. In the opinion of many, practical experience is the key to good teaching (Berk 1985). Experts in the early childhood field have described stages of teacher development, focusing essentially on level of experience (Katz 1972). What do research findings point to regarding the relationship between teaching experience and abilities?

Practices

Evidence from research on the relationship between teacher experience and practices appears to be mixed. For example, in Arnett's Bermuda study (1989), experience was unrelated to the sensitivity of teachers' interactions with children. The Staffing Study (Whitebook, Howes, & Phillips 1990; Howes, Whitebook, & Phillips 1992) found that experience failed to predict the quality of the learning environment or teacher behavior. Similarly, experience was not a predictor of positive caregiving in child care settings with infants and toddlers, according to the NICHD ECCRN study (1996).

Howes (1983), on the other hand, found that more experienced teachers in both family child care and center-based care were more likely to exhibit developmentally appropriate caregiving behaviors. Family child care providers with more experience were more likely to restrict toddlers and display negative affect with them. Center caregivers with more experience were more likely to play with toddlers and less likely to ignore their requests. Thus, some positive correlates of experience have been demonstrated.

Less positive results for experience were reported by the Family Child Care and Relative Care study (Kontos et al. 1995). A small negative but statistically significant association ($r = -.17$) was found between family child care providers' years of experience and the quality of care provided (as measured by the FDCRS). In addition, providers with more experience were rated by observers as more harsh and detached, and they rated themselves as

more restrictive. In this study, experience was related to less desirable characteristics in family child care providers.

Evidence from research on the relationship between teacher experience and practices appears to be mixed.

In Epstein's (1993) study of High/Scope training, experience was a highly significant predictor of overall classroom quality, as measured by the ECERS. However, both groups of teachers in her study—those receiving inservice training and the comparison group—were highly educated, had received a lot of specialized education and were highly experienced, which makes it impossible to disentangle the unique effects of experience. Although confounding education and specialized education is an across-the-board problem, the Epstein sample is unique in that it added experience to the mix.

The complexity of the issue is apparent when we examine another study in which moderate experience appears to be the key (Phillipsen et al. 1997). In this case, results indicated that when teachers had less than three years of experience, they were more sensitive with children and worked in classrooms of high quality; and when teachers had more than three years of experience, classroom quality and teacher sensitivity were lower. According to this study, there may be an optimum level of experience beyond which its effectiveness becomes questionable.

In general, the results relating experience to practice are mixed and rather weak.

Summary and implications: What does research tell us?

In a nutshell, our review of the research can be summarized in three sentences:

- Teachers' formal education correlates with overall classroom quality and, less often, with effective teacher behavior.
- Specialized education may be causally related to overall classroom quality, and it is correlated with effective teacher behavior.
- Teachers' experience cannot be consistently linked to overall classroom quality or effective teacher behavior.

What does this mean for the field of early childhood education and for teachers working in that field?

The research reviewed here essentially supports the concept behind the career lattice developed as part of NAEYC's professional development program (see Johnson & McCracken 1994). Although the research does not support experience as an important influence on practice, it does show how relating increased job responsibilities to educational background (general and specialized) is a sound approach. As the career lattice concept illustrates, specialized education *and* experience provide opportunities for early childhood professionals to add breadth to their expertise and also move up in responsibility and pay.

Family child care providers with more experience were more likely to respond positively to toddlers' social bids and were less likely to restrict toddlers and display negative affect with them. Center caregivers with more experience were more likely to play with toddlers and less likely to ignore their requests.

Education and specialized education are considered to be "regulatable" variables in the child care world. In other words, they represent aspects of the child care environment that can be regulated by states. In most states, however, teachers in early childhood settings not affiliated with public schools are subject to little or no regulation regarding their educational qualifications. In some states the standards utilize education and experiential requirements. For instance, teachers in California can get child development permits to work based on a mix of experience and education. Teachers and aides are not required to hold specialized degrees if they have the right blend of experience and course work. Research does not support this approach.

In light of research demonstrating that education and specialized education are linked to program quality, it makes sense for states to upgrade regulations regarding teachers' educational background. For this to happen, teachers, administrators, and other child advocates (including parents) need to make known to state policymakers the positive impact of teacher education on the learning potential of early childhood classrooms (as measured by overall classroom quality and teacher behavior). Advocacy for teacher qualifications will go a long way toward enhancing the educational background of the early childhood teacher workforce. At issue are specialized education experiences as well as credentials that may go along with these experiences, such as specialized licensure that documents the merits of the educational experiences.

Advocacy takes time, however. In the interim, it is crucial for teachers and administrators to put in place temporary voluntary standards for teacher educational qualifications that go beyond the current state regulatory requirements. Even though states may not require early childhood teachers to have postsecondary education or specialized education, teachers and administrators can recognize their value and seek out education for themselves as well as promote the hiring of staff with more ed-

ucation than is required. Moreover, according to Howes's study (1997), seeking out teacher preparation programs of various types (CDA training, associate degree, bachelor degree) is a better strategy than simply taking a hodgepodge of relevant courses and workshops as they become available.

One problem in the field is recruiting and retaining qualified teachers (Johnson & McCracken 1994). Even if teachers and administrators value and seek out education, the poor wages typical in early childhood education lead to high turnover, especially among educated teachers who have other work alternatives that pay better. Some administrators are even hesitant to hire teachers with specialized education and/or licensure for fear they will ultimately lose them to a better paying job (for example, teaching in public school). Thus, qualifications are compromised for the potential of greater continuity among staff. Advocacy for worthy wages is therefore a crucial strategy for obtaining and maintaining a qualified early childhood workforce. NAEYC and the Center for the Child Care Workforce both have ongoing advocacy activities that early childhood educators can join.

Even though states may not require early childhood teachers to have postsecondary education or specialized education, teachers and administrators can recognize their value and seek out education for themselves as well as promote the hiring of staff with more education than is required.

Another problem is providing access to specialized education for early childhood professionals who cannot afford and/or do not choose to quit their jobs to upgrade their education. To meet the needs of inservice professionals, the field will need to rely more and more on distance education strategies. Some distance programs have already begun to appear. For instance, using distance techniques. Pacific Oaks College in Pasadena, California, offers a master's degree in early childhood education and Ivy Tech State College in Indiana offers an associate's degree in child development. These programs are not the correspondence courses that we have been familiar with in the past. These new programs utilize new technology, including the Internet and the World Wide Web, in addition to print, occasional classroom meetings, and other strategies. It will not be long before there are accessible, affordable programs for early childhood educators to obtain specialized education.

Finally, we should point out that, although research tells us that specialized education is important, it tells us nothing about what content is most important and needed, who (administrators, head teachers, assistant teachers, or aides) is most likely to benefit from education, and what pedagogical methods are most effective in changing beliefs and behaviors of teachers (Kagan &

Neuman 1996). These are concerns toward which future research must be directed.

To meet the needs of inservice professionals, the field will need to rely more and more on distance education strategies. These new programs utilize new technology, including the Internet and the World Wide Web, in addition to print, occasional classroom meetings, and other strategies.

References

Abbott-Shim, M., & A. Sibley. 1987. *Assessment profile for early childhood programs.* Atlanta, GA: Quality Assist.

Arnett, J. 1989. Caregivers in day-care centers: Does training matter? *Journal of Applied Developmental Psychology* 10: 541–52.

Berk, L. 1985. Relationship of caregiver education to child-oriented attitudes, job satisfaction, and behaviors toward children. *Child Care Quarterly* 14: 103–29.

Cassidy, D., & M. Buell. 1996. Accentuating the positive? An analysis of teacher verbalizations with young children. *Child and Youth Care Forum* 25: 403–14.

Cassidy, D., M. Buell, S. Pugh-Hoese, & S. Russell. 1995. The effect of education on child care teachers' beliefs and classroom quality: Year one evaluation of the TEACH early childhood associate degree scholarship program. *Early Childhood Research Quarterly* 10: 171–83.

Cost, Quality, and Child Outcomes Study Team. 1995. *Cost, quality, and child outcomes in child care centers: Technical report.* Denver: Economics Department, University of Colorado, Denver.

DeBord, K., & J. Sawyers. 1996. The effects of training on the quality of family child care for those associated with and not associated with professional child care organizations. *Child and Youth Care Forum* 25: 7–15.

Epstein, A. 1993. *Training for quality: Improving early childhood programs through systematic inservice training.* Monographs of the High/Scope Educational Research Foundation. Ypsilanti, MI: High/Scope.

Harms, T., & R. Clifford. 1980. *Early Childhood Environment Rating Scale.* New York: Teachers College Press.

Harms, T., & R. Clifford, 1989. *Family Day Care Rating Scale.* New York: Teachers College Press.

Harms, T., D. Cryer, & R. Clifford. 1990. *Infant/toddler Environment Rating Scale.* New York: Teachers College Press.

Howes, C. 1983. Caregiver behavior in center and family day care. *Journal of Applied Developmental Psychology* 4: 99–107.

Howes, C. 1997. Children's experiences in center-based child care as a function of teacher background and adult : child ratio. *Merrill-Palmer Quarterly* 43: 404–25.

Howes, C., & P. Stewart. 1987. Child's play with adults, toys, and peers: An examination of family and child care influences. *Developmental Psychology* 23: 423–30.

Howes, C., M. Whitebook, & D. Phillips. 1992. Teacher characteristics and effective teaching in child care: Findings from the National Child Care Staffing Study. *Child and Youth Care Forum* 21: 399–414.

Johnson, J., & J. McCracken, eds. 1994. *The early childhood career lattice: Perspectives on professional development.* Washington, DC: NAEYC.

Kagan, S.L., & K.M. Neuman. 1996. The relationship between staff education and training and quality in child care programs. *Child Care Information Exchange* (January): 65–70.

Kaplan, M., & J. Conn. 1984. The effects of caregiver training on classroom setting and caregiver performance in eight community day care centers. *Child Study Journal* 14: 79–93.

Katz, L. 1972. Developmental stages of preschool teachers. *Elementary School Journal* 73: 50–54.

Kontos, S., C. Howes, & E. Galinsky. 1997. Does training make a difference to quality in family child care? *Early Childhood Research Quarterly* 11: 427–45.

Kontos, S., C. Howes, M. Shinn, & E. Galinsky. 1995. *Quality in family child care and relative care.* New York: Teachers College Press.

NICHD (National Institute of Child Health and Human Development) Early Child Care Research Network. 1996. Characteristics of Infant child care: Factors contributing to positive caregiving. *Early Childhood Research Quarterly* 11: 269–306.

Phillips, D., J. Lande, & M. Goldberg. 1990. The state of child care regulation: A comparative analysis. *Early Childhood Research Quarterly* 5: 151–79.

Phillipsen, L., M. Burchinal, C. Howes, & D. Cryer. 1997. The prediction of process quality from structural features of child care. *Early Childhood Research Quarterly* 12: 281–303.

Ruopp, R., J. Travers, F. Glantz, & C. Coelen. 1979. *Children at the center: Final report of the National Day Care Study.* Cambridge, MA: Abt Associates.

Scarr, S., M. Eisenberg, & K. Deater-Deckard. 1994. Measurement of quality in child care centers. *Early Childhood Research Quarterly* 9: 131–51.

Whitebook, M., C. Howes, & D. Phillips. 1990. *Who cares? Child care teachers and the quality of care in America. Final report of the National Child Care Staffing Study.* Oakland, CA: Child Care Employee Project.

Susan Kontos, Ph.D., *is professor of child development and family studies at Purdue University in West Lafayette, Indiana. Susan teaches in the undergraduate and graduate programs and conducts research on the developmental outcomes of classroom processes for young children.*

Amanda Wilcox-Herzog, Ph.D., *is an assistant professor of human development/psychology at California State University at San Bernardino. Amanda primarily teaches human development and early childhood education classes and has taught children ranging in age from birth through eight.*

Wired for Thought

Babies know more, and know it sooner, than researchers ever suspected. There is a mind in the crib, requiring stimulation to thrive.

By Sharon Begley

WHEN ALISON GOPNIK GOT HOME from the lab one day, she was overcome with the feeling that she was a lousy teacher, an incompetent scientist and a bad mother. A student had argued with a grade, a grant proposal had been rejected and the chicken legs she'd planned for dinner were still in the freezer. So the University of California, Berkeley, developmental psychologist collapsed on the couch and started to cry. Her son, almost 2, sized up the situation like a little pro. He dashed to the bathroom, fumbled around for what he needed and returned with Band-Aids—which he proceeded to stick all over his sobbing (and now startled) mother, figuring that eventually he would find the place that needed patching. Like most 2-year-olds, the little boy had just reached the point where he could not only exhibit empathy (even babies bawl when they hear another baby cry), but also try to soothe another's pain.

For decades scientists studying the blossoming of children's minds had been pretty much blind to this and other talents of the sandbox set. That's changing: researchers today have a lot more respect for what a child's mind is capable of. Babies know more, and know it earlier, than

the founders of the field of child development ever guessed. Even 1-month-olds learn whether their parents respond to them quickly or slowly. From 4 to 6 months, babies come to understand that some things (Dad's clothes) change, but others (his face) do not. Between 7 and 10 months they may learn to carry out sequences of actions to reach a goal, like piling up pillows so they can clamber up and see onto Mom and Dad's bed. By 18 months they can form intentions and understand the intentions of others.

Pint-size scientists
Babies actively seek out information through observations and experiments, changing their brains

---

How children come to achieve these and other cognitive milestones has proved the real revelation. The sequence of brain development is genetically programmed, with the brain stem coming online first to control basic bodily func-

tions like respiration. The cerebellum and basal ganglia follow, to control movement. The limbic system, for emotion and memory, comes next, and the cerebral cortex, for higher-order thinking, matures last. "The *quality* of neural development, however, is shaped by a child's experiences," says neurobiologist Lise Eliot of Chicago Medical School. Like miniature scientists, babies are sponges for information, learning through "mini-experiments with pots and pans, and by playing peekaboo and other everyday games," says developmental psychologist Andrew Meltzoff of the University of Washington. "A baby doesn't just grow into a 3-year-old without external stimulation, like a caterpillar into a butterfly. A baby contributes to cognitive growth by actively seeking information, through observations, play and baby-size experiments. This information changes the baby's mind."

Literally. Brains change as a result of the experiences they live. At birth the brain is packed with an estimated 100 billion neurons. But newborn brains should be labeled SOME ASSEMBLY REQUIRED. Although genes rough out where the brain's visual centers will be and where the auditory centers will nestle, where the regions that govern emotion will lie and where the center of higher thought will sit, the fine details are left to experience. This discovery of the importance of experience led in the 1990s to a proliferation of products and services offering "brain stimulation" for babies, marketed to parents frantic that failing to introduce number concepts in infancy will doom their child to a 400 on the SAT. But the formative experiences scientists have in mind don't involve flashcards. A new report from the National Academy of Sciences called "The Science of Early Childhood Development" puts it this way: "Given the drive of young children to master their world... the full range of early childhood competencies can be achieved in typical, everyday environments. A cabinet with pots and pans... seems to serve the same purpose as a fancy, 'made for baby' musical instrument."

How powerful are everyday interactions? Scientists have recently found that the way a parent talks to children can make them better at some tasks than others. It is a peculiarity of the Korean language that verb endings convey so much information that a mother can talk about the world to her baby without using many nouns. English, in contrast, uses comparatively more nouns and fewer verbs. The result? Korean babies use more verbs in their speech, and English-speaking babies more nouns. But the effects go beyond language. Korean babies, scientists at UC, Berkeley, found in a recent study, learn to solve action problems, like using a long-handled rake to retrieve out-of-reach objects, months before English-speaking kids do. But English hearers learn the concept of categories before Korean-speaking children do, apparently reflecting a language that emphasizes objects. The difference between the languages that babies hear seems to make one kind of problem easier than another.

No one is suggesting that parents adopt a different language depending on how they want their child to think: playing to children's strengths is enough to nurture little minds. Scientists learned how badly they had underestimated babies when Meltzoff discovered that just

40 minutes after birth, babies can imitate facial expressions. That might not seem like such a big deal, but it's actually pretty impressive. A newborn has never seen her own face, yet still knows that she has cheeks she can raise to mimic Dad's smile, and a tongue she can poke out to match what her brother is doing. From the first, babies know that they are like other people, an insight they will build on as they play imitating games with you.

36% of parents of young children say they plan to start sending their child to school by the age of 3; an additional **29%** say they'll do so at 4

It is babies' capacity for "abstract mental representation," as Eliot calls it, that has really taken scientists by surprise. At the tender age of 4 weeks, many babies can transfer data taken in by one sense over to another sense. After they have been sucking on a nubby pacifier, for instance, they can pick it out of a lineup: shown a smooth one and the nubby one, they look longer at the nubby one, an indication that they recognize how something should look from how it feels. Their capacity for abstract thinking extends even to physics. When scientists rig things so a block appears suspended in midair, even 3-month-olds stare at it as if in disbelief that the law of gravity has been repealed. Perhaps the most dramatic evidence of infants' capacity for abstract thinking comes from a 1992 experiment in which 5-month-olds watched scientists place dolls one by one behind a screen. If six dolls went in, but the screen was raised to reveal only four, the babies appeared startled. The kid can't sit, but she's caught you in a mathematical error.

Babies have an innate understanding of the world of things that the simplest games can encourage. A 5-month-old will follow a ball with his eyes as it rolls behind a screen, then scan ahead to the far edge, expecting the ball to emerge.

But his grasp of where and when an object should be found has limits. If you show a 6-month-old a little toy, then cover it with a cloth, his face is a mask of befuddlement. A 9-month-old, though, can find the toy, and loves playing hide-and-seek games with objects.

When babies turn 1, they begin to look where people point. This suggests that their minds grasp not only the physical world but other minds. "Like imitation, pointing implies a deep understanding of yourself and other people," says Gopnik, coauthor with Meltzoff and Patricia Kuhl of the 1999 book "The Scientist in the Crib." The baby now grasps that two minds can share an intention—to turn the eyes in the indicated direction. At this age, pointing games are not only a blast but a way to encourage the neural connections underlying this nascent understanding.

Also by their 1st birthday, babies begin to grasp the idea of shared feelings. If Mom peeks into one box and looks disgusted, then peeks into another box and looks delighted, and next pushes the two boxes toward her baby, the child will shun the first box but gleefully reach into the second. He is learning to judge what is good and bad in the world by others' reactions, which means that a look of disgust when your in-laws arrive can leave a lasting impression. Even a 9-month-old can learn how the world works by watching how others make it work. When Meltzoff ran an experiment in which he touched his forehead to a box rigged to light up when touched, babies were mesmerized. When the kids returned to the lab a week later, they immediately touched their own foreheads to the box and turned the lights on.

This is not just a "stupid baby trick." It shows, rather, that "babies can use other people to figure out the world," says Meltzoff. This is the age when they are adept little mimics, an age when parents have a clear shot at teaching babies how the world works by holding books, hugging older siblings and otherwise acting as they hope their children will.

Before they are 1, most babies can grasp only broad categories. If a blue ball rolls behind a screen and a yellow truck comes out, they're not surprised: the category "rolling object" covers both ball and truck. Once children reach their 1st birthday, though, a blue truck's turning into a yellow duck elicits definite surprise. This is about the age when kids sort objects into sensible groups, like grouping toy horses with toy horses and pencils with pencils. At 2 or 3, children go beyond superficial appearances. They know that baby tigers, though they look like kittens, belong to the same category as grown tigers. And, showing that they are ready for the era of the genome, they seem to know about heredity: ask a preschooler if a pig raised by cows will have a curly tail or a straight one, and he doesn't hesitate to answer curly. Young children take to category games like pigs to pokes.

Fun with physics
Even a 3-month-old stares in disbelief at objects that defy gravity, like balls dangling in midair

It was only a generation ago that psychologists proclaimed that newborns have no cortex, the thinking part of the brain. They thought of babies as slightly mobile vegetables—"carrots that cry." Now we know that babies come prewired to learn. Although many parents (and marketers) have interpreted that as a clarion call to bombard them

with "stimulation," in fact the best science we have today says that children learn about causes and categories, self and other, through listening and watching, and through games no fancier than hide-and-seek and peekaboo. "If you make a child feel loved, connected, purposeful and inquisitive, brain development will follow," says Peter Gorski of Harvard Medical School. "Our role as parents is not to perfect brain circuitry, but to foster the development of healthy, sane and caring human beings." We are a social species. Our babies learn in social environments, from people who love them, who delight in their little triumphs and pick them up when they slip, who recognize the mind behind the brain.

The 20th Century's **Best** and **Worst** Education Ideas

A panel of experts debates hits and misses in education

by James W. Guthrie

For every endeavor of mankind, the 20th century represented a time of rapid change and new discovery. Advancements in science and medicine eclipsed those made during all previous centuries combined. We flew to the moon, constructed 100-story buildings, and survived two world wars. Technology and communication became industries, and human rights became a movement.

The American education landscape during the past century certainly saw its share of hills and valleys, too— great successes as well as failures. But what were those successes? What were the failures? And what is the state of American education today as we enter a new century?

Last fall a panel of Peabody College faculty members and other education policy experts convened on campus to discuss and debate these questions. The spirited conversation ranged widely, and some of the people, policies, and practices that did *not* make the century's "best dressed" list of education ideas are as significant for their exclusion as several that did.

Of course, these being academics, agreement was far from complete regarding any particular idea. Still, a general consensus of opinion emerged among these experts regarding the 20th century's education strengths and weaknesses.

Education for All

Participants concluded that the 1954 *Brown v. Board of Education* U. S. Supreme Court decision desegregating the nation's once racially separated schools may well have been the most significant education event of the century. Indeed, it may even have been the century's most impor-

tant domestic policy decision for the entire society, let alone for our schools.

The *Brown* decision triggered other significant efforts to make the nation's schools more democratic. Prior to the last quarter of the 20th century, most students did not graduate from high school and only an elite few went to college. Kindergarten and preschool were rarities, and if you were physically or mentally disabled or did not speak English well, public schools may not have held a place for you at all.

Today our schools are free from legally enforced racial segregation, kindergarten has become universal, and pre-schooling is headed in the same direction. More than 90 percent of students graduate from high school. Disabled students are guaranteed places in classrooms. Federal and state programs assist financially in the schooling of recent immigrants. Community colleges have been created to bring higher education closer to home. College and university enrollments have vastly expanded, and public loan programs now financially enfranchise many more college students than ever before.

But opening our schools and colleges to all citizens was not the only high point of the century's education efforts. Great strides also have been made in the theories underlying the measurement of human ability and in the technical practices of testing. Much of the fundamental understanding of scientific measurement of human abilities occurred in connection with World Wars I and II and thereafter. Performance testing programs, now used by more than 40 states and in most school districts and classrooms—as well as increasing use of computer technology to instruct and appraise student performance—are grounded in these measurement developments.

BEST

Desegregation of the nation's once racially separated schools with the landmark Brown v. Board of Education ruling of 1954

Provision of equal education resources for students with disabilities

Assessment of student progress through standardized performance tests

Efforts to equalize funding among school districts and states

The Elementary and Secondary Education Act of 1965, which created programs such as Project Head Start to improve the schooling of children from low-income families

New forms of schooling (charter and magnet schools, "whole school reforms") that are injecting variety into public school systems

Publication of 1983 report A Nation at Risk, which, despite its flawed thesis, sparked societal demand for higher levels of academic achievement

Participants were quick to assert that efforts during the past 25 years to equalize finances available to support students in school districts and states were another significant development. Earlier in the century, some districts had more than 20 times the dollars per pupil to spend than did neighboring schools in the same state. In the last quarter of the century, governors, legislatures, and courts vastly narrowed, although not yet eliminated, these resource gaps. Today, two-thirds of the nation's per-pupil spending differences occur among states rather than among local districts, an inequity that really only the federal government is in a position to redress.

Demand for Higher Achievement

The 20th century is also notable for the firm recognition that out-of-school factors influence a student's academic performance. Perhaps the most symbolic crystallization of this idea resides in the 1965 enactment of the Elementary and Secondary Education Act, which authorizes federal funds for improving the schooling of youngsters from low-income households.

A result of that act, for example, is Project Head Start, the federal preschool child development program for children and families who live below the poverty level. The program, which has served more than 13 million children since 1965, was inspired by the celebrated research of the late Peabody psychology professor Susan Gray.

The recognition of out-of-school influences on learning is not a one-sided blessing. Some school critics contend that such knowledge too easily provides educators with excuses for not succeeding with low-income and non-English-speaking students. Texas Governor George W. Bush, for example, refers to "the soft bigotry of low expectations" in criticizing this phenomenon.

Panel participants contended that the recent evolution of new forms of schooling such as magnet schools and charter schools, and "whole school reforms" such as Success for All, Roots and Wings, Waldorf Schools, Edison Schools, the Modern Red Schoolhouse, and possibly even voucher plans were hopeful because they may inject great variety into what is, in too many places, a moribund public school system.

Finally, on the positive side, the panelists unanimously claimed that the 1983 publication of the bombastic report A Nation at Risk was a good thing for the United States. We now see in retrospect that the report had a flawed thesis, in that it claimed a flabby school system was placing the nation at risk in terms of international economic competition. Today, with the benefit of hindsight and with the United States' occupying the top rung on the world's economic ladder, we can see that it was sloppy management far more than inept schooling that was hampering U. S. trade efforts.

Still, seminar participants believed A Nation at Risk was a significant and valuable publication because it spurred societal demand for higher levels of achievement. It fueled today's concern for measuring schooling outcomes, for assessing the academic performance of pupils, and for legislative calls for more effective schools. And it stimulated the historic 1989 Charlottesville Summit at which the president and the nation's governors specified the first-ever set of national education performance goals. Thus, even if wrongheaded analytically, A Nation at Risk was influential in the evolution of better schools.

Red Tape and School Closures

The negative side of the education reform ledger also garnered plenty of attention by the Peabody panelists. High on the list of detrimental ideas was the invention of the Carnegie Unit with which most schools and colleges today measure student progress. This measure counts time spent in a class, rather than performance, as the *numeraire* of schooling. Participants collectively lamented that the nation is so willing to accept the number of "units" or hours in subjects, rather than measures of knowledge, as the coin of educational success.

The federal government, or at least the manner in which it has chosen to structure financial aid to schools, also came in for a substantial share of criticism. Many participants blamed federal funding programs for eviscerating the fundamental integrity of the instructional process by intrusive accounting procedures and unjustifiable regulatory measures.

The massive "consolidation" effort at the turn of the century, which eliminated literally tens of thousands of the nation's small and rural schools and combined them into larger schools and school districts, was seen by many panelists as a bad idea. Consolidation was the beginning of the end for intimate neighborhood schools that closely linked teachers to parents. And early 20th-century "Progressive Era" reforms were the beginning of dysfunctionally large city schools and insensitive school bureaucracies as the nation gathered its burgeoning numbers of pupils into ever-larger, big-city systems.

Finally, on the negative side, seminar participants expressed disappointment in the widespread abandonment, in schools of education and many college academic departments, of rigorous intellectual procedures for discovering and verifying knowledge. Acceptance by academics of so-called "critical theory"—which purports that the biases of a researcher can never be overcome and doubts the utility of the scientific method—was seen as a major impediment to gathering useful knowledge for practitioners about how students learn and how teachers might effectively instruct.

The Century Ahead of Us

What about the current hot-button issues in education today? Not many of them held up when subjected to the perspective of an entire century of significant developments.

For example, panelists omitted school violence from serious consideration because, despite television and newspaper hype over incidents such as the Columbine High School tragedy in Colorado, schools are actually safer now than they have been in half a century. Interest in school uniforms comes and goes and, whatever the current concern, no real evidence yet supports the claim that uniforms influence student learning.

Teaching methods, such as phonics versus whole-language approaches to reading, are a tempest in a teapot that excites lawmakers and some parents. However, good teachers have long known that a blend of instructional methods, tailored to the needs of the individual student, is always the right approach. It is difficult to find an elementary teacher who is not an eclectic when it comes to phonics and whole language.

What about growing private-school enrollments? They aren't. Private-school enrollments are actually declining nationally. What about taxpayer revolts in paying for schools? They aren't. Education now costs the nation nearly $2 billion per day, with the trajectory climbing.

So what lies ahead? Participant Joseph Murphy observed that the 19th century was characterized by a na-

WORST

Creation of the Carnegie Unit as a measure of student progress

Arcane structuring of federal financial aid to schools

Intrusive government red tape and regulatory measures

Consolidation of small, rural schools into dysfunctionally large districts

with impersonal bureaucracies

Acceptance of critical theory by academics, which has led to loss of rigorous intellectual procedures for discovering knowledge

Miscommunication regarding the state of public education in the United States

tionwide effort to make our schools public while the 20th century was spent making our schools accessible. (This is the "democratization" effort for which the Brown decision was so crucial.) When seminar participants turned to their crystal balls, they concluded that the 21st century, or at least the early part of it, would be concerned with efforts to render the nation's schools effective and more productive.

This is the legacy of *A Nation at Risk*, the Charlottesville Summit, and the actions of literally dozens of states in setting student performance standards, implementing statewide testing systems, and designing accountability plans.

And what about technology and the Internet? This is a difficult topic to address because it is still too early to predict the impact. Students are certainly learning from computers and the Internet, but they may be learning more on their own and more at home than they are at school. Although exciting instructional software relying upon the Internet is emerging rapidly, teachers are not yet being trained appropriately in the use of technology for instruction. Peabody is leading the way in technology training for tomorrow's teachers, and the impact could be dramatic, but a reassessment of these developments is needed a bit further downstream.

In response, the participants agreed to convene in 2099 to undertake a similar conversation.

Author James W. Guthrie is chairman of Peabody's Department of Leadership and Organizations, professor of public policy and education, and director of the Peabody Center for Education Policy.

UNIT 2

Child Development and Families

Unit Selections

Key Points to Consider

- How does language develop in young children?

- What are the seven needs as described by Brazelton and Greenspan?

- What role do parents and the media play in gender identification?

- Identify some of the pressures imposed on children today that were not evident a generation ago.

- How do children benefit by having their fathers involved in their school?

- What can parents and teachers do to help children develop tolerance for people of races and cultures different from their own?

 **Links: www.dushkin.com/online/**
These sites are annotated in the World Wide Web pages.

Administration for Children and Families
http://www.acf.dhhs.gov
Global SchoolNet Foundation
http://www.gsn.org
I Am Your Child
http://www.iamyourchild.org
Internet Resources for Education
http://web.hamline.edu/personal/kfmeyer/cla_education.html#hamline
The National Academy for Child Development
http://www.nacd.org
National Parent Information Network/ERIC
http://npin.org
National Safe Kids Campaign
http://www.babycenter.com
Parent Center
http://www.parentcenter.com/general/34754.html
Zero to Three
http://www.zerotothree.org

The practical and comforting advice of Drs. T. Berry Brazelton and Stanley Greenspan in "Our Window to the Future" encourages the reader to provide for the many needs of young children. They stress the fact that the early childhood years are the most critical and most vulnerable time in a person's life. Early childhood professionals find it difficult to comprehend that parents choose a place for the care and education of their children by the same criteria that they would use to choose a new home—location and the outward appearance of the building. We must continue to educate parents about the importance of selecting a program for their child that is based on the preparation and competency of the caregiver or teacher. All studies point to the educational preparation of the staff as the strongest predictor of quality in early childhood programs. Strong, trusting relationships must be developed between all involved in the caregiving triad of family, child, and caregiver. In addition, there is the critical need for caregivers to be compensated for their work at a level that will encourage them to remain in the field and to continue their education in the area of child development and early childhood education. Well-compensated teachers will stay in a job and will be there to develop lasting relationships with children in their care.

Often the editors find themes emerging from the hundreds of articles we read each year, both in professional journals and magazines aimed at the general public. From these readings we find similar topics in many articles, as was the case this year. Unfortunately, it took us back 20 years to the publication of David Elkind's *The Hurried Child* in 1981. Elkind reported on the practice in the early 1980s of parents pushing their children to grow up too quickly, missing childhood. Three of the articles chosen for this unit report a similar theme. "No Time for Fun," "Too Sexy Too Soon," and "The New Summer Break" all have as their theme parents pushing their children to do more, achieve more, and grow up more quickly. Children are increasingly being denied the chance to participate in what many adults remember as their fondest childhood memories. Leisurely passing away the hours while attempting to dam up a little stream and float leaves and sticks, finding secret hiding places for games of hide-and-go-seek, or using every available cushion, pillow, and blanket to make a fort are memories many adults have of childhood. What will be your children's memories of their play experiences? Asking parents that question can cause some serious reflection on their part related to their hectic lifestyle and heavy reliance on technology for their children's leisure activity. As early childhood educators we must work with families to help them find the balance of appropriate extracurricular activities that will enable their children to live a rich and fulfilling life while still enjoying the period known as childhood. They will have years to engage in focused study but the fleeting years of childhood pass quickly. It is appropriate for teachers of young children to provide opportunities for families to explore their role in helping their children achieve in the future as well as fully participate in childhood. Articles, such as those included in this edition, can be summarized for parents and posted on a bulletin board or included in a newsletter. Parent discussion groups can have out-of-school activities as a discussion topic. Teachers can use their knowledge about child development to guide parents in making appropriate decisions regarding their children. Often parents, caught up in the frenzy of competing with other families, lose perspective on what is best for their own child. As a parent it is perfectly acceptable to say to a child, "No," "You're too young," or "Not in our family." Parents can also ask themselves why they are pushing their children to engage in activities that were never a part of their own childhood 20 or so years ago.

The terrorist attacks of September 11, 2001, caused the entire country to examine personal practices of discrimination based on peoples' skin color, race, dress, or cultural identity. Adults can help children develop healthy attitudes about people different from themselves by seeking experiences that expose their children to ethnic and cultural diversity. Helpful suggestions for beginning conversations with children about race are included in "Talking to Kids About Race."

Finally, after years of schools having "helping moms" or "room mothers," teachers are realizing the benefit of working to encourage dads to participate in their child's education. "Fathers' Involvement in Programs for Young Children" describes how fathers can become integral contributors to childhood education. In one Chevy Chase, Md., school, Lena is envied by her peers for her father's active participation in her school. Her dad will accompany the class on trips, document learning opportunities with photographs, or share art with the class. His contributions are greatly appreciated by a teaching staff that recognizes the importance of fathers in the classroom. Lena's father is encouraged by the teacher's use of "moms or dads" in her conversations about families helping in the classroom. The most striking evidence for supporting dads in their child's education comes in the form of a 1997 study from the U.S. Department of Education. The researchers recognized the contributions mothers make as essential to the social and emotional well-being of children, but found that the involvement by the fathers may be critical to academic achievement. Although this study was done with 6th- through 12th-grade students, it is important to note that parent participation in the later grades hinges on their involvement in their child's preschool and primary education. Our job as early childhood educators is to encourage all parents, but mostly fathers, to come into the classroom and to feel comfortable and useful during their visit. By getting parents off to a positive start with their initial school volunteer experience, we are doing our colleagues who work with older children a huge favor. By the time they have the chance to work with those fathers, they will be used to contributing to their child's education.

We end this unit with, "Children of Divorce: 25 Years Later," which examines Judith Wallerstein's landmark study of children whose parents divorced when they were young. Teachers who recognize that children feel the impact of a divorce can work to assist those children to deal with their emotions in the classroom. We encourage teachers to share these discussion topics with parents of young children.

Look Who's Listening

New research shows babies employ many tricks to pick up language

BY RICHARD MONASTERSKY

Sitting in a dim laboratory at the Johns Hopkins University, David Wiggs peers at a flashing red light and listens intently to a series of sentences playing over a loud-speaker.

"Fluid ice is a difficult concept to grasp. Merchants used to trade ice for water. Weird ice no longer surprises anyone. The experts soon detected that it was flawed ice."

The words could be the rantings of a glaciologist on acid, but David doesn't raise an eyebrow. For this blue-eyed infant, the strange passage is just one small drop in a river of gibberish flowing past his ears every day.

In the nine months since his birth, David Wiggs (not his real name) has been wading through that stream of largely un-intelligible sound. Now he is starting to navigate its pools and eddies. Succeeding in a task that no computer could tackle, the plump little boy has learned how to break the continuous flow of speech he hears from any person into discrete chunks—what we call words—even though he has no idea what most of the chunks mean.

And that's only his latest success. David has been picking up clues about how to pull apart and understand his native language ever since he floated in the womb. From the day he gulped his first breath, he could distinguish the rhythms of English from many other languages, simply from the memory of the muffled sounds that had filtered though his mom's belly.

Now the scientists studying language acquisition are growing up right along with

David. Even as the youngster starts to cob-ble together an understanding of English, researchers are teasing apart the complex process of how children pick up language. Their discoveries challenge the work of earlier investigators, who tended to see the problem in stark terms of nature or nurture. Though that conflict still smolders, most scientists now recognize that both genes and environment must play a role. So re-searchers today concentrate on determin-ing which abilities are bred into humans and which ones they develop through lis-tening to the babble that surrounds them.

"We are starting to get a clearer picture about when things develop and about how they're developing," says Peter W. Jusczyk, a professor of psychology at Johns Hopkins. "So I do think there's a coherent middle ground that's forming here. Maybe we are moving more into a kind of a maturity."

A WAR IS OVER WORDS

Although philosophers have argued for centuries about innate knowledge, the modern debate over language started in 1957, when B. F. Skinner pushed his the-ory of stimulus response, or S.R., into the linguistic realm and published Verbal Be-havior. In that work, the famous psycholo-gist asserted that language parallels other types of behavior: Children are born as blank slates and learn language from their environment, through direct reinforcement from parents and others.

At that time, rival theories of psycho-logical development couldn't gain a toe-

hold in the United States, says Mr. Jusczyk. "You had Skinner beating every-body over the head, and all the S.R. theo-rists for a long time held sway in this country."

Their grip started to loosen in 1959, when Noam Chomsky, a professor of lin-guistics at the Massachusetts Institute of Technology, published a review of *Verbal Behavior* that aired his competing theory of language as an innate ability, a theory he expanded on in later writings. Infants are born with a universal grammar, he wrote, and the language heard early in life plays only a limited role, setting the cognitive switches inside the brain and tuning the universal grammar to a particular lan-guage—for instance, specifying that ob-jects come after verbs in English but before verbs in Japanese.

Peter D. Eimas, now an emeritus pro-fessor of cognitive and linguistic science at Brown University, extended the "nativist" theory when he posited that children are born with a "phonetic feature detector" that is unique to humans and has evolved the specialized task of picking out pho-nemes—the building blocks of words—from speech.

The debate over learned versus innate faculties raged through the 1960's and 1970's. "There was a war here," says Mr. Jusczyk, who was an undergraduate student of Mr. Eimas at the time. But eventually the Chomskian revolution swept over the field of language research. "A lot of people jumped on the bandwagon," Mr. Jusczyk says, "and it was because, in some sense, the S.R. view was so extreme before."

In recent years, the pendulum of theory has swung again: not back to behaviorism, but toward a new position that examines how both innate abilities and subsequent learning play specific roles. The skirmish still flares up in scientific journals, though, revealing a deeply ingrained—if not innate—polarization.

Steven Pinker, a professor of psychology at M.I.T. who aligns himself with nativist theory, says researchers must move beyond the simplified form of the nature-nurture debate. "What we should be doing is figuring out what is innate, and not arguing whether innate stuff is important or unimportant and whether learning is important or unimportant. There has to be something innate—otherwise house cats would learn language the same way that children do. But a whole language can't be innate."

Jeffrey L. Elman, a professor of cognitive science at the University of California at San Diego, agrees, even though he lives on the other side of the theoretical divide. Many aspects of linguistic ability stem from our genes, he grants, but he wonders what the specific innate mechanisms are that make language possible, and whether they are unique to humans. "The road from the genome to relative clauses is very long, shrouded in clouds, and not at all an obvious one."

BORN LISTENERS

That road takes many twists in the first year of life, as infants pass through a series of stages and employ several techniques for dealing with the sounds coming out of their parents' mouths.

From their earliest moments of life, children seem tuned into the rhythms of language, the patterns of stress and pacing that make English distinct from, say, Russian. Studies by French researchers in 1998 showed that newborns have a knack—manifested by how frequently they sucked on a pacifier—for telling the difference between languages with different rhythms, although they have a harder time with ones that share a rhythmic pattern, like English and Dutch.

And newborns are born listeners, with an ability to hear differences between sounds that adults can't hope to match, says Patricia K. Kuhl, a professor of speech and hearing sciences at the University of Washington. She calls them "citi-zens of the world," because they can perceive phonemes from all languages.

Adults, by contrast, have selective hearing. In experiments conducted over the past four years, Ms. Kuhl and her colleagues have documented that native Japanese speakers, for example, cannot distinguish between the phonemes "ra" and "la." English speakers, on the other hand, have a hard time telling the Mandarin Chinese phoneme "qi," which starts with something akin to a "ch" sound, from the phoneme "xi," which begins with a sound closer to "sh."

Young infants can hear them all, but that ability soon disappears, Ms. Kuhl and her graduate student, Feng-Ming Tsao, found in a study last year. The incessant speech that babies hear early on actually warps their ability to distinguish among sounds later. For babies raised by English speakers, Ms. Kuhl says, "by the time they get to their first birthday, their brains are quite strongly committed to the English way of listening."

Even as they are acclimating to their mother tongue, infants are also starting to take their first steps toward comprehending language. The key to that process involves learning how to pick out words from the rapidly flowing stream of normal speech.

GIVE HIM A BREAK

For the first few months of a baby's life, every day is like wandering around in a foreign country where the inhabitants jabber away in some unknown dialect. "If you're listening to a foreign language, it's very difficult to figure out where one word ends and another begins. If you're a baby, you have to cope with this same problem of segmenting the input," says Mr. Jusczyk.

Only after accomplishing that feat can infants start to associate meanings with individual words.

A decade ago, nobody knew when infants began to break the speech stream into individual words. Then, in 1995, Mr. Jusczyk and Richard N. Aslin, of the University of Rochester, perfected a technique for testing whether children could perform that task. They sat babies in a darkened room and had them listen to individual words, like "cup," "dog," and "bike."

Then the researchers played passages of speech, some of which contained the previously heard words. They measured how interested the babies were in the words by how long they gazed at a light that flashed repeatedly as each passage was played.

Six-month-old infants showed no preference for passages containing the previously heard words. But infants only seven weeks older than that listened significantly longer to those passages, indicating that they could distinguish words like "bike" within strings of speech, even though they may not have known their meaning.

"I never would have suspected that they could have picked up that information as rapidly as they did," says Mr. Jusczyk. "After I got the data, I was forced to deal with that fact."

Using the same method, cognitive psychologists set out to determine how babies could perform such preverbal tricks. The recent experiments have "really changed the landscape for what we think is going on inside infants' heads," says Jenny R. Saffran, an assistant professor of psychology at the University of Wisconsin at Madison.

Among babies' tools for decoding speech, one technique apparently involves a subconcious form of statistics. Simply put, babies can keep track of how many times they hear a sound. For example, when presented with the phrase "funny puppy," infants are more likely to group "fun" with "ny" rather than "ny" with "pup," because they have heard the combination "fun-ny" more often than they have heard "ny-pup."

Ms. Saffran and her colleagues demonstrated that capacity when they exposed infants to an artificial language consisting of words like "pabiku" and "tibudo" strung together randomly, without breaks. After only two minutes of listening, the babies had learned to segment the words from each other, simply because those combinations of phonemes appeared more frequently than did combinations that cut across words.

"Learners may behave somewhat like sponges," says Ms. Saffran. "If there are certain things that recur, you are just going to suck them up. You can't help it."

She and San Diego's Mr. Elman and others say such results argue against the nativist concept of infants as poor learners. But the nativists, including M.I.T.'s Mr. Pinker, say that interpretation is too simple.

In any case, infants can't live by statistics alone, because that would lead them astray quite often, says Mr. Jusczyk. In one example documented by a researcher, a mother urged her toddler to "behave," and the child shot back, "I am have." Because the word "be" often occurs on its own, the child had used that pattern to segment "behave" into two words.

Infants appear to have a whole range of other tricks, as Mr. Jusczyk has shown in recent experiments, including the one that young David participated in. That study, published last month in the *Journal of Experimental Psychology: Human Perception and Performance,* examined how infants regard sentences that include such phrases as "cold ice," "weird ice," and "fluid ice."

If the babies were simply keeping track of repetitions, then they should have reacted to the word "dice" as familiar, because each of the examples contained "d" followed by "ice." But in the study, eight-and-a-half-month-old infants did not exhibit any familiarity with "dice," reported Mr. Jusczyk and Sven L. Mattys, a lecturer in experimental psychology at the University of Bristol, in Britain. The babies' brains had latched onto some other aspect of language that overrode the circuits monitoring phoneme repetition. For instance, the "i" in "ice" sounds slightly different from the "i" in "dice," because speakers close off their windpipes before voicing the vowel in "ice."

ALGEBRA AT 7 MONTHS

If statistics won't get babies everywhere with language, they may try a little algebra. At least that's the way Gary F. Marcus describes the results of his study of seven-month-old infants.

An associate professor of psychology at New York University, Mr. Marcus let the babies listen to a repeating pattern of syllables that obeyed either an A-B-A or an A-B-B grammar, such as "ga ti ga" or "li na na." Then he played different syllables arranged in both patterns, such as "wo fe wo" and "wo fe fe." The infants reacted to the patterns they had heard before as if they were familiar, even though the syllables were completely new.

Such results, he says, show that infants develop algebra-like rules and can plug different sounds into the patterns they hear. Mr. Chomsky argues for the same type of "generalization" ability to explain how we can create, and also comprehend, completely novel combinations of words.

"Chomsky illustrated this with the now-famous sentence 'Colorless green ideas sleep furiously.' You can understand the syntax of that even if you've never heard it before," says Mr. Marcus.

While his research shows that infants have that ability early on, if not from birth, other studies challenge the nativist view that many of the language tools of infants are evolved specifically for that purpose.

Marc D. Hauser, a professor of psychology at Harvard University, has found that adult monkeys can match young infants in many of their cognitive abilities. In the March issue of *Cognition*, Mr. Hauser and his colleagues showed that a species called the cotton-top tamarin can perform the same statistical processing that infants

displayed in Ms. Saffran's test. More recently, tamarins have accomplished the pattern-identification task mastered by babies in Mr. Marcus's algebra study, says Mr. Hauser, who has yet to publish those data.

"Every time there's been a question raised and people have bothered to do the experiments, the animal data showed that the mechanism is similar," he says. The implication is that infants use general auditory tools for listening to and understanding speech—tools that we inherited from our primate ancestors and later co-opted for language. "They are not special to speech," says Mr. Hauser.

Researchers are now investigating how far they can push those general tools. Can tamarins actually learn more-complex grammatical patterns, the kinds that most interested Mr. Chomsky? asks Mr. Hauser. Ms. Saffran, meanwhile, has started to test whether simple statistical procedures can help in grammar acquisition, a point pushed by the anti-nativists.

In the laboratory at Johns Hopkins, all those issues are playing out beneath David's blond curls. He finishes the "weird ice" experiment without much fidgeting, and the tester rewards him by holding up a cuddly monkey puppet, which makes the baby scream. Too young for words, David sobs for a few minutes as the adults around him struggle in vain, trying to figure out what is going on inside his head.

Our Window to The Future

A pediatrician and a psychiatrist join forces in an attempt
to get parents to pay more attention to the critical early years.

BY DRS. T. BERRY BRAZELTON & STANLEY GREENSPAN

As A PEDIATRICIAN AND A CHILD PSYCHIATRIST
caring for the families in our practices and studying child
development on a broader scale, we have become deeply
concerned about the unmet needs of children in this
country and abroad. While there have been admirable initiatives in public health, education, pediatrics and the
law to improve the lot of children, there have been few efforts to catalog the fundamental requirements of a
healthy childhood. For this reason, we have set out to
identify the irreducible needs of children and to describe
the care they need to grow, learn and thrive.

Early childhood is both the most critical and the most
vulnerable time in any child's development. Our research
and that of others demonstrates that in the first few years,
the ingredients for intellectual and moral growth must be
laid down. Children who don't get this nurturing are
likely to be two or three steps behind, no matter how hard
we try to help them catch up.

Parents cannot underestimate the importance of their
role in these early years. Each child is born with a unique
biology but that doesn't mean his or her future is preor-
dained. The way a parent nurtures a baby has a profound
effect on how the child develops. Recent research on the
way genes work in the body suggests that their expression
or influence depends on interactions with many different
environments, including those in the cell, the body, and in
the social and physical world. These interactions in part
determine how we function. Nature and nurture thus appear to act together seamlessly, in a developmental duet.

In spite of the considerable evidence for the importance
of the early years, some researchers argue that later experiences are equally important in shaping a child. They say it
is peers—not parents—who are the biggest influence.
However, these scientists are not distinguishing early essential experiences that help children to relate, read social
cues and think from attitudes, values and academic skills,
which are acquired throughout life. Although peer relationships are important, they build on the relationship that

a child has with his parents. Children who haven't had the
benefit of nurturing adults early on have trouble even
forming friendships, let alone negotiating the inevitable
ups and downs of these relationships.

Human beings have to be able to work cooperatively,
compassionately and empathetically with others in a
group in all aspects of life. It takes cooperation and organization for family, community or societal groups to function. This requires the capacity for empathy and
compassion, for understanding and for coping with feelings in constructive and mature ways. New generations
of children will be able to carry out these functions only if
they are reared in nurturing empathetic families.

> ## "Every baby needs a warm, intimate relationship with a primary caregiver over a period of years, not months or weeks"

The seven needs we have identified provide the fundamental building blocks for our higher-level emotional, social and intellectual abilities (sidebar). The first and most
basic of these is the need for consistent nurturing care
with one or a few caregivers. Most recent studies have
found that family patterns that undermine this ongoing
nurturing care may lead to significant cognitive and emotional problems, while even the simplest interactions help
a child grow. Listening to the human voice, for example,
helps babies learn to distinguish sounds and develop language. Interactive experiences can result in brain cells' being recruited for particular purposes—such as extra ones
for hearing rather than seeing. Exchanging emotional
gestures helps babies learn to perceive and respond to
emotional cues and form a sense of self. Without these experiences, the child suffers. Just as early interference with

vision can lead to functional blindness or lifelong problems with depth perception and spatial comprehension, emotional deprivation or stress is associated with changes in brain physiology.

Relationships also teach communication. For infants who can't yet speak, that means gestures and emotional cues (smiles, assertive glances, frowns, pointing, taking and giving back, negotiating and the like). From these simple exchanges, a child develops a complex system of problem-solving and dealing with others. Even though this nonverbal system eventually works in conjunction with symbols and words, the basic structure stays the same. (For example, we tend to trust someone's nonverbal nod or look of approval more than words of praise, which are sometimes misleading; and we shy away from a person with a hostile look even if the person says, "You can trust me.")

When there are secure, empathetic, nurturing relationships, children learn to be intimate and empathetic and eventually to communicate about their own feelings, reflect on their own wishes and develop their own relationships with peers and adults. Relationships also teach children which behaviors are appropriate and which are not. As children's behavior becomes more complex in the second year of life, they learn from their caregivers' facial expressions, tone of voice, gestures and words what kinds of behavior lead to approval or disapproval.

The give-and-take between children and caregivers creates patterns of behavior. The child is also developing emotions, wishes and self-image. The emotional tone and subtle interactions in relationships are vital to who we are and what we learn. Relationships enable a child to learn to think. In his interactions, the child goes from desiring Mom and grabbing her to saying "Mom" and looking lovingly. He goes from acting out or behaving his desires or wishes to picturing them in his mind and labeling them with a word. This transformation heralds the beginning of symbols for thinking.

Pretend or imaginative play involving emotional human dramas (for example, making dolls hug or fight) helps the child learn to connect an image or picture. He can then use this image to think, "If I'm nice to Mom, she will let me stay up late." Later on, he'll be able to figure out the motives of a character in a story as well as important quantitative issues, like the difference between 10 cookies and three cookies.

The ability to create mental pictures leads to more advanced thinking. For instance, a key element essential for future learning and coping is the child's ability for self-observation, his capacity to look at how his behavior appears to others. This ability is essential for self-monitoring of activities as simple as matching pictures with words or numbers. Self-observation also helps a person label rather than act out feelings. He can say, "I'm angry or upset," rather than hitting the object of his ire. It helps him to empathize with others and meet expectations.

Emotions are actually the internal architects, conductors or organizers of our minds. They tell us how and

'All Young Children Have Seven Irreducible Needs'

1. ONGOING NURTURING RELATIONSHIPS

Every baby needs a warm, intimate relationship with a primary caregiver over a period of years, not months or weeks. This is far more important to emotional and intellectual development than early cognitive training or educational games. If this relationship is absent or interrupted, a child can develop disorders of reasoning, motivation and attachment. Infants, toddlers and preschoolers need these nurturing interactions most of their waking hours.

2. PHYSICAL PROTECTION, SAFETY AND REGULATION

Both in the womb and in infancy, children need an environment that provides protection from physical and psychological harm, chemical toxins and exposure to violence.

3. EXPERIENCES TAILORED TO INDIVIDUAL DIFFERENCES

Every child has a unique temperament. Tailoring early experience to nurture a child's individual nature prevents learning and behavioral problems and enables a child to develop his or her full potential.

4. DEVELOPMENTALLY APPROPRIATE EXPERIENCES

Children of different ages need care tailored to their stage of development. Unrealistic expectations can hinder a child's development.

5. LIMIT-SETTING, STRUCTURE AND EXPECTATIONS

Children need structure and discipline. They need discipline that leads to internal limit-setting, channeling of aggression and peaceful problem-solving. To reach this goal, they need adults who empathize as well as set limits. They need expectations rather than labels, and adults who believe in their potential but understand their weaknesses. They need incentive systems, not failure models.

6. STABLE, SUPPORTIVE COMMUNITIES AND CULTURE

To feel whole and integrated, children need to grow up in a stable community. This means a continuity of values in family, peer groups, religion and culture, as well as exposure to diversity.

7. PROTECTING THE FUTURE

Meeting all these needs should be our highest priority. If we fail, we will jeopardize our children's future.

what to think, what to say and when to say it, and what to do. We "know" things through our emotional interactions and then apply that knowledge to the cognitive world. For instance, when a toddler is learning who to say "hello" to, he doesn't do this by memorizing lists of appropriate people. Experience leads him to connect the greeting with a warm, friendly feeling in his gut that leads him to reach out to other people's welcoming faces with a verbalized "Hi!" If he looks at them and has a different feeling inside, perhaps wariness, he's more likely to turn his head or hide behind your legs.

We encourage this kind of "discrimination" or ability to see beyond surface appearances because we don't want our children to say "Hi!" to strangers. We want them to say hello to nice people like Grandpa. If a child learns to greet those people in this way, he will quickly say "Hi!" to a friendly teacher or to a new playmate. He carries his emotions inside him, helping him to generalize from known situations to new ones, as well as to discriminate or decide when and what to say. Even something as purely academic and cognitive as a concept of quantity is based on early emotional experiences. "A lot" to a 3-year-old is more than he wants; "a little" is less than he expects. Later on, numbers can systematize this feel for quantity. Similarly, a child learns the concepts of time and space by the emotional experience of waiting for Mom, or of looking for her car pulling into the driveway.

Early emotional interactions also form the foundation of morality, a person's sense of right and wrong. Morality comes from empathy, the ability to understand another person's feelings and to care about how he or she feels. And empathy is developed through nurturing interactions with caregivers and parents. We can feel empathy only if someone has been empathetic and caring with us. Children can learn altruistic behaviors, to do "the right thing," but truly caring for another human being comes only through experiencing that feeling of compassion oneself in an ongoing relationship. We can't experience the consistency and intimacy of ongoing love unless we've had that experience with someone in our lives. For some it may be a grandmother or an aunt, or it may even be a neighbor, but it must be there. There are no shortcuts.

The basic feature of caring relationships between a baby and a caregiver who really knows her over the long haul is responsible for a surprisingly large number of vital mental capacities. These "reciprocal interactions" teach babies how to take the initiative. They do something and it makes something happen. This is also the beginning of a sense of self and of learning how to think purposefully and logically, of understanding cause and effect.

In the first months of life, a baby and her parent will have been through three levels of learning with each other. In the first stage, from birth through 3 weeks, the parent learns how to help the newborn infant maintain an alert state. In stage two, from 3 to 8 weeks, the baby produces smiles and sounds and the adult responds. In the third stage, from about 8 to 16 weeks, these signals are reproduced in sets of four or more—what researchers call "games." These games teach rhythm and reciprocity. By 4 months, the baby will have learned to take control of the game and to lead the parent in it. This is the beginning of autonomy.

Something else is also occurring. Through these reciprocal interactions, the child is learning to control or modulate his behavior and his feelings. The difference between children who can regulate their behavior and children who can't lies in the degree to which the child masters the capacity for the rapid exchange of feelings and gestures. When a child is capable of rapid interactions with his parents or another important caregiver, he is able to negotiate how he feels. If he is annoyed, he can make an annoyed look or sound or hand gesture and he knows that his mother or father will understand what he means. He learns that he can regulate his emotions through the responses he gets.

By the time a child is talking at 2 or 2 ½, he should already have the capacity to be involved in long chains of interaction involving his different emotions, feelings and behaviors. Children without this capacity have meltdowns or tantrums or get carried away with their excitement or joy, or anger or sadness, or even depression. Often, these extreme reactions are out of proportion to the events of the moment. They suggest that some parts of the child's feelings, mood and behavior didn't have a chance to become regulated through reciprocal interactions.

Addressing this need for consistent nurturing care and the other irreducible needs of childhood will take us all on a journey that should radically alter our attitudes and policies toward children and families. We must re-evaluate our convictions and our daily practices in child care and family functioning, in education, health care, social services and in our legal system.

But the first steps on this journey must be in the home. What parents should take away from all this research is that everything they do for their children in these early years is vital. Emotionally vibrant experiences set the stage for a happy and independent life.

BRAZELTON *is a professor emeritus at Harvard Medical School and author of many best-selling books, including "Infants and Mothers" and "Touchpoints."* GREENSPAN *is a clinical professor of pediatrics and psychiatry at George Washington University School of Medicine and author of numerous books, including "Building Healthy Minds" and "The Child With Special Needs." Their new book is "The Irreducible Needs of Children"* (224 pages. Perseus Publishing/A Merloyd Lawrence Book. $24).

GENDER EXPECTATIONS OF YOUNG CHILDREN AND THEIR BEHAVIOR

BY RAE PICA

Is it nature (biology) or nurture (environment) that determines personality and behavior? Are boys naturally more aggressive than girls? Are girls naturally more nurturing than boys? Or do the expectations of parents and society impose these behaviors, and others, on children of one gender or the other?

NATURE VERSUS NURTURE

There are, of course, inherent differences between girls and boys. We now know that male fetuses are a bit more active than female fetuses (Blum, 1999)—perhaps due to the extra dose they receive of the hormone called androgen, which has been linked to excitability (ASU Research, 1998). Also, human males can produce as much as 10 times more testosterone than females. Both of these hormones are associated with a stronger drive for rough-and-tumble play and competitiveness. In fact, when a baby girl's adrenal gland inadvertently elevates testosterone levels (a condition known as congenital adrenal hyperplasia), the girl also prefers cars and trucks and aggressive play (Blum, 1999).

Researchers have also found that just one year after birth, boys and girls show distinct toy preferences, with boys attracted to more mechanical or structural toys and girls gravitating toward toys that have faces and can be cuddled (Blum, 1999). Similarly, one study showed that when a barrier is placed between one-year-olds and something they want, the boys tend to try to knock down the barrier, while the girls look to their mothers for help.

Does this indicate that girls are naturally more passive and boys naturally more active? There are experts who disagree on the issue. It was Freud's belief that the answer lay exclusively with biology. That belief held strong until the 1960s and 1970s, when many academics (including John Money, a renowned sex researcher) began promoting the idea that *nurture* was the stronger influence in an individual's developing sexual identity (Anselmo & Franz, 1995).

Katz (1986) has written that adults in all cultures respond differently to boys and girls from the time of birth, and that differences in behavior cannot be attributed to biological factors affecting gender. Gurian (1997), on the other hand, believes it is first biological differences that affect behavior and then cultural responses to that behavior that influence development. Most experts do agree, however, that it is difficult to determine how much of behavior is due to biology and how much to perceptions and expectations—and that "gender-specific behavior is a complicated mix of both nature and nurture" (Bryant & Check, 2000, p. 64).

PARENTAL INFLUENCE

It is true that, from birth, parents display very different expectations of each gender. A study conducted in 1974 showed that parents—especially fathers—described newborn girls as "softer, finer-featured, smaller, weaker, and more delicate" than boys. A follow-up study in 1995 showed similar results. And other studies in the 1970s and 1980s, in which infants were "disguised" in cross-gender clothing, demonstrated that parents brought trucks to the supposed boy babies and dolls to those they considered girls (Bryant & Check, 2000, p. 65). Gurian (1997) also tells us parents talk to, cuddle, and breastfeed their boy infants significantly less than their girl infants.

As children get older, parents tend to talk more to their daughters, encourage them to help others, and discourage autonomy. Boys, on the other hand, are encouraged to be fearless. One study used videotapes of children on a playground to determine parental responses. The results showed that mothers of daughters were more likely to see danger in their activity, and they intervened more quickly and more often than did mothers of sons (Morrongiello & Dawber, 2000). Mothers of daughters also issued more statements of caution, while mothers of sons offered more words encouraging risk-taking.

Strickland (1999) further points out that, when a baby boy falls down, parents make light of it, encouraging the child to get up and try again. On the other hand, when a baby girl takes a tumble, we "run over and scoop her up and make sure she's all right" (p.40).

Throughout childhood, boys tend to have more interaction with their fathers than girls, with vigorous physical activity predominant in that interaction (Beveridge & Scruggs, 2000). Boys also receive more encouragement from both parents and society to participate in physical activity.

ADVERTISING, MARKETING, AND TELEVISION

Parents, of course, are not the only ones in our society promoting gender stereotyping and inequality. Children are bombarded daily with television images promoting what they conceive to be the "norm": boys playing with cars, trucks, and action figures and girls playing with dolls. "Pink" aisles in the toy stores feature dolls, makeup, and miniature appliances, while "blue" aisles offer vehicles and war toys. Even modeling clay and building blocks are sold in different colors—bold for boys and pastels for girls (Kutner, 1998).

An examination of "boys'" toys and games shows they tend to promote problem solving and exploration—"key ingredients for gaining a sense of mastery and competence" (Giuliano, 2000). "Girls'" toys, on the other hand, limit exploration and discourage independence and problem solving.

One result of this media pressure is that, regardless of what they may have asked for, boys more often receive activity-oriented toys and games, while girls are given stuffed animals, toy houses, kitchen sets, and dress-up outfits. Researchers have found that despite what toys may be on their lists, children receive gender-specific toys (Zhumkhawala, 1997). Girls are then praised when playing with dolls. On the other hand, boys are ignored when they display nurturing behavior. Additionally, one study demonstrated that a high number of boys felt their fathers would think cross-gender play was "bad"; thus their toy choices were more stereotypical (Raag & Rackliff, 1998).

RESULTING BEHAVIOR

There is evidence that childhood play socializes and prepares children for different adult roles. Even before adulthood, however, the impact of early socialization is apparent. Though no one is sure why, children begin segregating by sex at about two-and-a-half-years-old, with girls pulling away first (Macoby, 1999). By age four, children play with others of the same sex about three times more often; by six, they play with same-sex friends about 11 times more often (Woolfolk, 2001).

Because researchers in such places as India, Mexico, Africa, and the Philippines have found the same pattern occurs in their

areas—and because it is even seen among certain animals—there is reason to believe the phenomena is at least partly due to biology. However, research also shows that children as young as four begin presuming there are similarities within each gender (i.e., stereotyping). And even at such a young age, they already have very strong beliefs about what is and is not gender-appropriate; and they have no qualms about pressuring others to conform. Boys, especially, worry about being teased for having a girl as a friend.

Play styles, too, are drastically different. Girls play in small groups, closer to teachers, with cooperation and verbal interaction prevalent. Boys play in large, unstructured groups, spread out, with body contact and competition reigning. The result of all this is an increasingly stronger separation between "boy" activities and "girl" activities. And this separation can eventually impact adult behavior because they grow up with different habits, social skills, and expectations (Martin & Fabes, 2001).

How much can be attributed to androgen and testosterone isn't known. However, girls are often noticeably upset by the aggressive nature of boys' play. Might they be less upset—and more inclined to join in—had their parents and society encouraged them to be greater risk-takers, or if their toys had encouraged problem solving and adventure?

Research has shown that playing with boys and "their" toys—i.e., being considered a tomboy—distinguished between women who later became college athletes and those who didn't (Giuliano, 2000). These women, as girls, had also received more encouragement from all family members than did women who were not very involved in sports.

Lever (1976) contends that boys' play promotes business or professional careers for males, while girls' play promotes family careers for females. Along these same lines, Toyama (1977) found that successful female administrators were more likely to have played football and other team activities in childhood. Williams and McCullers (1983) determined that successful professional women with atypical careers (e.g., doctors and lawyers) were more likely to have had "masculine" play styles than those who took on the more gender-typical careers of nurses and court reporters. Coats and Overman (1992) looked at the childhood play styles of women in traditional occupations (e.g., teachers and librarians), somewhat nontraditional occupations (e.g., insurance agents or research associates), and highly nontraditional occupations (e.g., lawyers or doctors). Consistent with the other studies, they found that the women in nontraditional roles were more likely to have taken part in male play activities as children.

Potential is lost in other ways, too, as a result of perceptions and stereotypes. Because boys are louder and seem to possess more energy, society has assumed they have more emotional stamina. Science tells us the opposite is true. As it turns out, boys require a lot of emotional support and that, without it, lower IQs may result (Blum, 1999). By the same token, confinement seems to bring down IQ in girls.

WHAT TEACHERS AND PARENTS CAN DO

While we certainly do not want males and females to be alike in every way, we can try to provide equal opportunity for both girls and boys to reach their full potential as human beings. Some differences are biologically driven, but stereotypes are culturally imposed. Parents and teachers, therefore, must monitor their actions and words so as not to promote gender bias.

For example, parents can introduce gender-stereotypical toys, like trucks and dolls, to their children of both sexes. They should dress both their sons and daughters for active, outdoor play. Arranging play dates where boys and girls interact in structured activities seems to encourage more cooperative play between the sexes (Martin & Fabes, 2001).

Early childhood teachers can place stuffed animals and dolls of both genders in the housekeeping area and in the block area. Also, parents and teachers should avoid even such seemingly innocuous messages as use of words like snowman, when snowperson displays more gender equity (Zhumkhawala, 1997).

Role-playing activities in which children of both genders demonstrate the actions of police officers, hairstylists, chefs, homemakers, and other occupations traditionally associated with one gender or the other may be subtle but will make an impression on young children. Additionally, both parents and teachers can ensure boys and girls are praised equally—for achievement, not appearance—and that both girls and boys have equal opportunity and encouragement for physical play.

CONCLUSION

These solutions may seem too understated to make a difference. However, by playing with blocks, girls will gain experience and confidence in their math and science skills (Zhumkhawala, 1997). By participating more in physical activity, girls will gain greater confidence in their physical skills and will be better equipped to take risks. Boys who are encouraged to take part in "girl" activities are more likely to fully develop their nurturing and verbal skills, as well as fine motor coordination. When boys and girls play together (games like tee ball and jump rope can easily cross "gender lines"), girls learn assertiveness and boys learn to better cooperate and control their impulses (ASU Research, 1998). And we can help ensure the IQ of both genders remains at its full potential by encouraging autonomy in girls and by offering boys greater affection.

Teachers especially have opportunities to offer support to boys faced with teasing or rejection by other boys should they choose to engage in activities normally preferred by girls. And teachers can do much to educate and reassure parents, beginning perhaps by sharing this article with them. For teachers and parents, awareness is the first step toward eliminating gender bias.

REFERENCES

Anselmo, S., & Franz, W. (1995). *Early childhood development*, 2nd ed. Englewood Cliffs NJ: Prentice-Hall. ASU Research. (1998). Social structure on the playground. *ASU Research E-Magazine*.

Beveridge, S., & Scruggs, P. (2000). TLC for better PE: Girls and elementary physical education. *Journal of Physical Education, Recreation and Dance*, 71(8), 22–25.

Blum, D. (1999). What's the difference between boys and girls? *Life*, 22(8), 44–50.

Bryant, A., & Check, E. (2000). How parents raise boys and girls. *Newsweek* Special Issue, 64–65.

Coats, P.B., & Overman, S.J. (1992). Childhood play experiences of women in traditional and nontraditional professions. *Sex Roles*, 26, 261–71.

Giuliano, T.A. (2000). Footballs versus Barbies: Childhood play activities as predictors of sport participation by women. *Sex Roles*, 52, 134–42.

Gurian, M. (1997). *The wonder of boys: What parents, mentors, and educators can do to shape boys into exceptional men. NY: J.P. Tracher.*

Katz, L.G. (1986). Boys will be boys and other myths. *Parents*, March issue, p. 176.

Kutner, L. (1998). The gender divide. *Parents*, 73(4), 112–14.

Lever, J. (1976). Sex differences in the games children play. *Social Problems*, 23, 478–87.

Macoby, E. (1999). *The two sexes: Growing up apart and coming together*. Cambridge MA: Harvard University Press.

Martin, C.L., & Fabes, R.A. (2001). The stability and consequences of young children's same-sex peer interactions. *Developmental Psychology*, 37(3), 431–446.

Morrongiello, B.A., & Dawber, T. (2000). Mothers' responses to sons and daughters engaging in injury-risk behaviors on a playground: Implications for sex differences in injury rates. *Journal of Experimental Child Psychology*, 76(2), 89–103.

Raag, T., & Rackliff, C.L. (1998). Preschoolers' awareness of social expectations of gender: Relationships to toy choices. *Sex Roles*, 38 (9/10), 685–700.

Strickland, E. (1999). How to build confidence through outdoor play. *Early Childhood Today*, 13(7), 39–40.

Toyama, J.S. (1977). Selected socio-psychological factors as related to the childhood games of successful women. In M.L. Krotee (Ed.), *The Dimensions of Sport Sociology* (pp. 52–59). West Point NY: Leisure Press.

Williams, S., & McCullers, J. (1983). Personal factors related to typicalness of career and success in active professional women. *Psychology of Women Quarterly*, 7, 343–57.

Woolfolk, A. (2001). *Educational psychology*, 8th ed. Boston: Allyn & Bacon.

Zhumkhawala, S. (1997). Dolls, trucks, and identity: Educators help young children grow beyond gender. *Children's Advocate*, Nov/Dec, 6–7.

Rae Pica is a movement education consultant and an adjunct instructor with the University of New Hampshire. She is the author of 13 books, including the text *Experiences in Movement, the Moving & Learning Series*, and the recently-released *Wiggle, Giggle, and Shake: 200 Ways to Move & Learn*. Rae is nationally known for her workshops and keynotes and has shared her expertise with such groups as Children's Television Workshop, the Head Start Bureau, Centers for Disease Control, and Nickelodeon's *Blue's Clues*.

NO TIME FOR FUN

HOMEWORK IN KINDERGARTEN? PERSONAL COACHES FOR LITTLE LEAGUE? THE PRESSURES FACING CHILDREN TODAY ARE ENORMOUS. HERE'S HOW YOU CAN LIGHTEN THE LOAD—AND RESTORE FUN TO CHILDHOOD.

By Susan Garland

Last year, my daughter Kristina brought a note home from kindergarten telling parents that each child was expected to learn to recognize 150 words, 5 each night, by the end of the year. But whenever I sat down to help her study, she'd start to cry and flail, "I can't do it," she would sob.

I eased up, figuring there was no need to push her. After all, I didn't read until I was in first grade. Kristina, however, wouldn't let go. She worried that her classmates were moving ahead of her and that everyone would tease her if she fell behind. Her competitive drive motivated her to make some progress, but Kristina still didn't finish the project by June —a fact that bothered her even after her summer vacation began.

WE LIKE TO THINK OF CHILDHOOD AS AN IDYLLIC, CAREFREE TIME. BUT IN TODAY'S FAST-PACED, HIGH-ENERGY WORLD, CHILDREN FEEL PRESSURED AT EVER-YOUNGER AGES.

Stressed-out over kindergarten?

Parents may love to think of childhood as an idyllic, carefree time. But child-development experts report that today's com-petitive, high-energy society is forcing kids to cope with stress and pressure at younger ages. Academic demands aren't the only source of tension. Well-meaning parents, eager to give their children every advantage, enroll even the youngest kids in so many activities that they need their own Palm Pilots to keep track. Moms and dads are so busy themselves that they often rush their children through everyday tasks, such as getting dressed and eating. Time for relaxed talk or play is at a premium in many American households.

What's more, children are relentlessly bombarded with information that unsettles them. Television news about school shootings, neighborhood violence, and environmental decay delivers the message that the world is a dangerous place. Meanwhile, the entertainment industry continues to target younger kids with sophisticated content that they're not ready to handle. And hours spent at fast-paced computer games can overwhelm even the best-adjusted child.

The resulting stimulation, frenetic pace, and demands to master so much so soon can leave kids overpowered by feelings of helplessness, child-development experts say. "When a child's sense of control over his world goes down, his level of stress goes up," says Georgia Witkin, Ph.D., an assistant clinical professor of psychiatry at the Mt. Sinai School of Medicine, in New York City, and author of *KidStress: What It Is, How It Feels, How to Help* (Penguin Paperback, 2000).

For some kids, the results are particularly disturbing: A study last June by the American Academy of Pediatrics found that 18.7 percent of children who visited pediatricians' offices in 1996 were identified as having psychological problems related to their social environment—up from 6.8 percent in 1979. And a 1999 Surgeon General's report found that 13 percent of children ages 9 to 17 suffered from anxiety disorders.

Researchers report that kids are showing the same symptoms of chronic stress as adults, including headaches, stomachaches, insomnia, and irritability. In some cases, stress is worsening such childhood health conditions as asthma and allergies. Landmark research by Bruce E. Compas, Ph.D., a professor of psychology, medicine, and pediatrics at the University of Vermont, in Burlington, has found links between stress and emotional and behavioral problems, including aggression and difficulties at school. Though researchers don't know for sure whether stress contributes to depression and anxiety disorders, they suspect that a link exists.

Some cases of childhood stress, of course, can be tied to divorce or to a parent's death or illness. But it's not just traumatic situations that send a child into a tailspin. Dr. Compas's research indicates that the cumulative effect of many smaller stresses—pressure to achieve academically, feelings of being excluded by peers, conflicts at home—can be just as harmful. "Little things are chronic," he says. "They keep coming back. They're more psychologically immediate."

Sources of Stress

In today's 24/7 world, the pressures on children are pervasive. To help kids get an edge in an increasingly competitive labor market, well-meaning parents are pushing children to learn more at earlier ages. School systems are trying to boost test scores in order to get more recognition and funding. Some parents even hire tutors so their 5-year-olds can keep up with the kindergarten curriculum.

Ted Feinberg, Ph.D., a former senior psychologist for a school district outside Albany, New York, recalls one worried mother who called him before her preschooler was to meet with education specialists at the elementary school that her son was to attend in the fall. All preschoolers in New York are screened for special needs and other issues. The mother wanted a copy of the screening test so she could prepare her child. "I told her that this was not entrance to college and not something to be anxious about," says Dr. Feinberg, who is now assistant executive director of the National Association of School Psychologists, in Bethesda, Maryland. The problem for her child, he says, is that "if a parent is anxious, there is a strong potential that the child will be anxious by association."

In a study of elementary-school children, Louis A. Chandler, Ph.D., an associate professor of educational and developmental psychology at the University of Pittsburgh, diagnosed many as suffering from stress, which was manifested in such ways as frequent temper outbursts and impulsive and stubborn behavior.

Dr. Chandler says he found that in most cases, the parents and the schools were pushing too much responsibility and decision making on the children. What appeared to be missing, he says, were sufficient stability, routine, and guidance from adults. The trend in the schools, says Dr. Chandler, is for "cooperative learning," in which even the youngest children work in teams to help each other learn, with the teacher often relegated to sideline monitor. Removing the teacher from a central authority role, Dr. Chandler says, can increase insecurity and anxiety, because "children are being forced to make choices without the strong guidance of adults."

Too Busy to Play

The pressures on kids continue after school. Many are being shuttled from ballet class to soccer practice, from religious school to violin lessons, with adrenaline pumping and meals grabbed on the go. Organized sports have replaced the casual neighborhood pickup game, so winning has become ever more important.

What's more, kids are increasingly exposed to unsettling news from around the world—about violence, wars, air pollution. Concerns about such dangers heighten their feelings of a lack of control over their life. "Television news scares the hell out of them," says Scott Poland, Ph.D., president of the National Association of School Psychologists. "They pick up a sense of fearfulness. It adds a bit of pessimism." A Montclair, New Jersey, mother recalls how her daughter "went through a period when she asked me every night before she went to sleep whether I thought acid rain was going to kill all the fish."

SIGNS OF STRESS

• Typical symptoms in kids include stomachaches, headaches, nervous behavior, irritability, frequent crying, fear of insomnia and going to bed alone, and bed-wetting. Extreme shyness could also be an indication.
• Changes in behavior can also signal stress. Is your usually outgoing and talkative child now quiet and sullen? Is a child who normally plays nicely with other kids now shoving and arguing? Is a child who used to head off to school happily refusing to go now?
• Experts suggest consulting a doctor if the behavior lasts more than two weeks or is affecting your child's diet or sleep. The physician can refer you to a mental-health specialist if needed.

Even in the safest communities, young kids worry about violence. When Patti Raber Max's son was 7, he was one such worrier. "On several occasions, as he went to bed, he told me in a very soft voice, 'I'm afraid of being shot,' " says Raber Max, of Potomac, Maryland. She suspects that he'd heard something on the radio news. "It's not as if we live in a crime-ridden neighborhood or he knew of any particular incident. I told him, 'I would never let anything happen to you. I will always protect you.' That seemed to help."

Coping Skills

Just as adults do, children have varying abilities to handle stress. Hereditary factors and environment both play a role. Some kids may be born with an inherent disposition toward fearfulness, though such a temperament at birth doesn't mean they'll always be timid.

A study by Jerome Kagan, Ph.D., a professor of psychology at Harvard University, found that about 20 percent of more than 450 infants reacted to stimulation with agitated limb movements and crying. By the time these "high reactive" children were 4 ½, 87 percent of them seemed to resemble typical children, though they were less extroverted. Dr. Kagan concluded that the environment can play a part in reducing anxiety. The children who showed high fear at all ages were most likely to develop anxious symptoms by the time they were 7.

Research by W. Thomas Boyce, M.D., a professor of epidemiology and child development at the University of California at Berkeley, arrived at similar conclusions. Over the course of several studies, Dr. Boyce found that between 15 and 20 percent of several hundred children ages 3 to 8 had "exaggerated biological responses" to various stressful events. Stressors included changes in the drop-off routine for children attending day care. Responses included higher-than-normal changes in blood pressure and heart rates and higher secretion levels of stress-related hormones. These children also had higher rates of respiratory illnesses and behavioral problems.

The good news, Dr. Boyce says, is that the evidence shows that these sensitive children can thrive in supportive conditions. His studies show that the stress-prone kids actually showed a lower rate of illness and behavior problems than other children when placed in low-stress settings.

Time to Chill

Obviously, parents can't protect their children from all stress, nor would they want to. But they can reduce the amount of stress as well as help kids manage the unavoidable pressures. The best thing parents can do is allocate regular quiet time to talk to their children. Discussing their day and their feelings can automatically reduce children's stress level.

Dr. Compas says parents should teach their kids problem-solving skills to handle stressful situations head-on. Dozens of academic studies, he says, show that children who "try to avoid the stress and suppress their feelings will do worse psychologically than those who confront the stress and face their feelings."

So a child who is being picked on at school, Dr. Compas says, will do better if he is able to talk about the situation with his parents, who can then help him figure out what to do about it. A child who seems preoccupied with pollution can be shown that she can do something to help the environment, perhaps signing up for a park-cleanup day with a parent.

IT'S BEST TO LIMIT AFTER-SCHOOL ACTIVITIES TO TWO A WEEK; AT THE VERY LEAST, THEY SHOULD BE SCHEDULED SO CHILDREN AREN'T RUSHED FROM PLACE TO PLACE.

Bettie B. Youngs, Ph.D., author of *Stress and Your Child* (Fawcett, 1995), says that parents can give their child a sense of control by helping her develop problem-solving skills: Identify the problem, brainstorm alternative solutions, evaluate possible consequences, and come up with a game plan. She also suggests that parents ask children at bedtime to discuss the best part of their day, which allows them to "focus on the positive and to stop

feeling anxious about things that didn't work."

Another important step: slowing the pace of your child's life. Some experts suggest that most children shouldn't participate in more than two extracurricular activities a week. At the very least, activities should be scheduled so children aren't rushed from place to place. Parents who need to place their children in after-school programs should be careful about piling on more activities in the evenings and on weekends.

Children should also be given lots of unstructured time, either by themselves or with friends at home. Downtime gives children a chance not only to relax but also to work out problems through play. "Kids need time to think, to be creative, to use their imagination," says Sheila Ribordy, Ph.D., a child psychologist in Chicago. "They need to learn how to entertain themselves."

Also, parents should help their youngsters choose a sport or another activity in which they can feel competent. Competitive baseball for an uncoordinated child is sure to raise frustration levels and hurt self-esteem. And lay off the pressure to excel. Instead of focusing on grades, parents should praise a child for persevering. "Parents should say, 'We don't expect you to be the best student in your class. You please us by being a loving son,'" Dr. Poland says. Turbo-charged parents don't do their kids any favors by turning them into

miniatures of themselves, he warns. "Kids who are very competitive in their early years often burn out by the time they reach high school," he says.

TOO MUCH PRESSURE CAN LEAVE A CHILD OVERWHELMED BY FEELINGS OF HELPLESSNESS.

Finally, it's important to become role models for our children. Stress levels can soar when parents are too busy for their children. Obviously, parents can't always avoid distractions, but a regularly short-tempered and harried parent can leave a child with a sense of helplessness. Not surprisingly, a child's stress level will soar if the parent is frantic. "Children are not getting a chance to learn from example how to de-stress," Dr. Witkin says.

So let your child see you at the kitchen table calmly pondering a crossword puzzle. Put away your briefcase in the evening, and read a novel. Go out with your kids after dinner for a long, leisurely walk. Not only will such measures help your child reduce the stress of contemporary life but they could do wonders for your stress levels as well.

From *Parents* magazine, April 2001, pp. 144-150.

TOO SEXY TOO SOON

Between sultry pop stars and suggestive prime-time TV, children encounter sexual language and images at very young ages. Here's how to protect your kids. A special must-read report.

By Dianne Hales

For many years, children at one Chicago nursery school have enjoyed playing with big cardboard boxes, transforming them into trucks, spaceships, castles, and forts. Lately, though, the preschool staff has been watching a little more closely when kids disappear into the cartons. The reason? Teachers recently found a 4-year-old boy lying on top of a female classmate, trying to kiss her.

In the past, educators would have thought such behavior was an indication that a child had been sexually abused. But these days, they're just as likely to suspect that kids are merely mimicking something they've seen on TV. "Children always react to what they're exposed to in the media," says Diane Levin, a former teacher and author of *Remote Control Childhood? Combating the Hazards of Media Culture* (National Association for the Education of Young Children, 1998). "Play often in-volves issues children are trying to under-stand, and one of those issues is sex."

Although violence in the media has provoked major public controversy, con-cern is growing about the impact of expo-sure to sexualized language and situations, especially on the very young. There's no consensus among experts on the short- or long-term effects our sex-heavy pop cul-ture has on kids. But parents of young chil-dren seem to agree that the media's obsession with sex is prodding kids to look and act precociously sexual. "My 3-year-old stands in front of the mirror and belts out words from a Britney Spears song—'I'm not that inn-o-cent,' " says Molly Gordy, a mother of two girls in New York City. "We sure hope that's not true."

What's coming out of the mouths of babes hardly *sounds* innocent—even though it usually is. Driving a car pool of 5-year-olds, a California mother was dumbfounded when her daughter asked, "What's a blow job?"

Sex-saturated culture

The first response of startled parents is to wonder where their youngsters are picking up such words and ideas. But the answer is simple: everywhere. Long before they can read, today's kids are bombarded with sex-ual imagery—on magazine covers, in TV commercials, in movie trailers, and on bill-boards. "Advertisers increasingly use sex to capture a consumer's attention," says Gail Dines, Ph.D., a professor of sociology at Wheelock College, in Boston.

At home, television has turned up the sexual heat. More than half of all television programs—56 percent—contain some sexual material, according to a recent study by the Parents Television Council, a nonpartisan advocacy group. From 1989 to 1999, the frequency of sexual interactions, verbal and physical, more than tripled during prime-time viewing hours. References to genitalia occurred more than seven times as often, while foul language increased more than five and a half times.

Even movies geared toward young children aren't as tame as they were a generation ago. Pocahontas, with her strapless dress and exposed cleavage, is far sexier than Cinderella ever was. Remakes of *The Adventures of Rocky and Bullwinkle* and Dr. Seuss' *How the Grinch Stole Christmas*, unlike the originals, are sprinkled with double entendres and sexual references.

Many parents assume that sexual sizzle goes over the heads of kids barely old enough to tie their shoes. But that's not necessarily the case, says clinical psychologist Ben Allen, Psy.D., of Northbrook, Illinois. "Children are sponges," he says. "They don't respond to suggestive material by becoming sexually stimulated in the way that adults do, but they do find it intriguing."

Certainly, young children are curious and impressionable. "My 6-year-old picks up on everything he sees in ads, on billboards, and on magazine covers," says Mary Kay Turner, of San Ramon, California. "He'll ask questions like 'Why are they kissing that way?' I find myself having conversations that I don't think he's ready for." A Washington, D.C., mother, certain that her preschooler wasn't even paying attention to a commercial for Viagra that came on during a game show, said she was amazed when the 4-year-old asked her what *erectile dysfunction* meant. "I told him it was a medical problem, and that was enough information to keep him satisfied," she said. "I'm glad he wasn't watching television with his 12-year-old cousin. Who knows how he would have explained it."

Some experts say that the barrage of sexual material can be baffling to young children. "Kids have always been interested in each other's bodies, but now they're puzzled because they're seeing things that are far more complex than what they would naturally be curious about," says Levin. Worse, a precocious interest in sexuality may distract 4- and 5-year-olds from more important developmental tasks, such as learning to negotiate with friends, use language precisely, and play creatively.

Peering into the future, parents wonder where the bombardment of sexual messages and images will lead. "What parents fear most is the impact on later behavior and sexual experimentation," observes Debra Haffner, former president of the Sexuality Information and Education Council of the United States and author of *From Diapers to Dating: A Parent's Guide to Raising Sexually Healthy Children* (Newmarket, 2000). "But there's no evidence at all to suggest that learning to roll your hips to a music video at age 6 means you're more likely to have sex when you're in ninth grade," Haffner says.

Nonetheless, sexual experimentation is beginning at surprisingly early ages. According to the Alan Guttmacher Institute, a nonprofit reproductive-health research organization, two out of ten girls and three out of ten boys have had sexual experience by age 15. What's more, there are widespread reports of increased sexual activity, including oral sex, among middle-school students—although reliable statistics are hard to come by.

Talking About SEX

Here's advice on how to handle potentially awkward moments:

THINK AHEAD

Sexual attitudes and values are highly personal. What do you most want to communicate to your child about sex?

FOCUS ON HOW YOU SOUND

Tone is as important as content. Be straightforward and matter-of-fact. If you're nervous, make it clear that it's because you want to get everything right, not because sex is shameful.

CHOOSE A PRIVATE SETTING

If youngsters bring up something embarrassing in the supermarket line or a crowded restaurant, let them know that you will discuss it just as soon as you get to the car or arrive home—and be sure to do so.

Even at younger ages, though, children have an awareness of sexuality and sexual terms. One mom described taking her 5-year-old to a birthday party where little girls were gyrating their hips while lip-synching the lyrics of a suggestive song.

"They looked like a bunch of little Lolitas," she says.

Fashion feeds into the trend as well. Though little girls have always delighted in dressing up in grown-up clothes, some kids' styles are even sexier than what's inside Mom's closet. Stores sell tube tops, belly-baring hip-hugger skirts, even bras and bikini panties for girls as young as 6 or 7. "They all want to look and dress just like the sexiest pop stars," one New York City mom complains.

How do the sexually charged images of pop music affect children? Experts disagree. "Young girls don't comprehend that people can view a pop singer as a sex symbol," says Dr. Allen. "But at the same time, they know that looking and acting like Christina Aguilera grabs attention. The danger is that girls may think they need to be like her to have a sense of self-worth."

However, others believe that children find harmless comfort in contemporary music. "Young kids get into a hypnotic state that's somewhat erotic when they watch music videos or listen to pop songs," says psychiatrist Lynn Ponton, M.D., of the University of California at San Francisco, an expert on child sexuality and author of *The Sex Lives of Teenagers* (Dutton, 2000). "It's one of the ways they feel safe having their first sexual feelings. The songs give them permission to feel excited in a harmless way."

Curbing the sleaze

Most parents say they can largely control what movies, television, and music their children are exposed to. Nonetheless, even the most vigilant parent can't completely shield a child from the sexual material that's so much a part of contemporary culture. Sooner or later, every youngster is going to see an inappropriate video or listen to a song with obscene lyrics. "We live in an age when sexuality is freely accepted and exposed," Dr. Allen says. "Trying to insulate a child from sexual material is like fighting a tornado. You need to think of it as junk food. Once in a while, it's not really a threat, but you want to avoid a steady diet."

Parents should make an effort to help a child understand what he'll inevitably encounter. The best way to do that is by talking openly with your child about sex and being available and willing to answer any questions that come up. For preschool kids, it's wise to teach correct anatomical terms for body parts and functions. If a child hears (or uses) slang, parents may want to explain that such words are inappropriate.

Opinions vary on when parents should talk to their children about the birds and the bees; some experts say that explaining sex to a child at about age 5 or 6 can help ensure that he'll get the message from you, not his friends. With kids this age, keep conversations simple and brief. Ask kids what they already know to gauge how much they've heard. Listen carefully to their responses, and clarify any mistaken impressions. Provide only the information they want at the moment.

When it comes to a child's using sexual language or mimicking sexual behavior, the way parents respond makes a lasting impression. It's important not to scold or punish a child or make him feel ashamed. "Remember that sexual curiosity and experimentation, like playing doctor, are normal for 4- and 5-year-olds," Haffner says. However, children who engage in behaviors such as oral-genital contact or simulated intercourse may well have been victims of sexual abuse, so that possibility should be investigated. It's also possible, however, that these kids may have come across inappropriate materials in the media.

If parents find that young children are venturing into adults-only territory, they should explain why the material isn't suitable for kids. "It's not fair for adults to make children feel bad for their fascination with material that we expose them to," says media expert Levin. "If you say,

'Don't do that' without explaining why, children conclude that they can't go to adults for help figuring this stuff out."

Rather, your goal should be to put what your children see and hear into context. Here are some ways to begin:

•**TAKE CHARGE.** In the same way that you wouldn't give preschoolers free rein over what they wear or eat, carefully choose the videos, CDs, and television shows that your youngsters listen to and watch. If your kids complain that their friends get to see other programs, explain that your family has made a different choice.

•**KEEP TVS AND COMPUTERS IN FAMILY SPACES** rather than in children's rooms. Whenever you can, watch with your child and discuss what you see. Monitor their Internet use, and use filtering software (available from most Internet service providers) to keep them away from inappropriate Websites.

•**MAKE SURE YOUR TELEVISION HAS A V-CHIP**, a device that prevents kids from accessing certain channels. Particularly useful if older siblings or baby-sitters may flip to inappropriate shows when you're not around, the V-chip will keep out explicit sexual language and behavior.

•**DON'T ASSUME ANYTHING GOES OVER A CHILD'S HEAD.** By ages 5 and 6, children pick up the sexual undercurrents in prime-time programs like *Friends* and *Will & Grace*. Some experts say that kids may actually pay closer attention than

adults, who have been desensitized to sexual innuendo in the media.

•**DON'T ENCOURAGE SEXUAL PRECOCIOUSNESS.** You may be sending your child the wrong messages if you buy skin-baring clothing or applaud sexy dancing as cute. Encourage children to appreciate their bodies for the many things they can do rather than for how they appear.

•**TAKE ADVANTAGE OF TEACHABLE MOMENTS.** When sexual subjects come up on a TV program that you're watching with your kids, ask open-ended questions, such as "What do you think about that?" or "How would you feel if someone treated you like that?" This is a good opportunity to communicate your values about sex and sexuality.

•**EMPHASIZE RESPECT FOR ONESELF AND OTHERS.** "Boys need to know that being a man is not about sexual conquests, which is what the media tell them," Dr. Dines says. "Girls should know that they weren't put on earth to please boys—which is what they see in the media—but to live a full, happy, and successful life."

•**KEEP THE CONVERSATION GOING.** Try to help make your child feel comfortable approaching you to discuss issues of sex and sexuality. Never dismiss his questions and concerns as silly or trite. Children who learn early on that they can talk with their parents about these subjects without fear of ridicule or rebuke develop a trust that can endure into adolescence and beyond.

THE NEW SUMMER BREAK

Today, kids of all socioeconomic and ethnic backgrounds boast nonstop scheduling all summer long—a trend fueled by the rising numbers and financial clout of Generation Y, the 71 million people born between 1977 and 1994. Recognizing the potential power of Gen Ys, an army of camp directors, travel agents and corporate executives has begun to target this growing and lucrative market.

By Michael J. Weiss

Daniel Ryan, a 14-year-old honors student from Arlington, Va., has a vision of his ideal summer vacation: He'd be a bum. He'd kick back on the couch, cling to a remote and watch lots of MTV videos and *Simpsons* reruns. If he felt energetic, he might drag himself to the computer and chat online with some buddies, or head for the refrigerator to scarf down a slice of cold pizza. Otherwise, he'd worship at the altar of Bart Simpson, sleep for 12 hours straight and then repeat the routine the next day. "Yeah, that would be cool," Daniel says cheerfully.

Better luck next year, kid. This summer, the lanky and soft-spoken teenager finds himself engaged in a different kind of teen sport: structured programming. He's enrolled in a series of summer camps and organized activities designed to keep him physically and intellectually fit from June through August. His summer began with a counseling stint at a 4-H camp, followed by theater instruction at Camp Shakespeare, then a family vacation at the Atlan-

tic shore and, to round it all out, this month he attends high school football practice geared to prep him for fall tryouts. Unlike previous summers that were completely structured, he lined up two unscheduled weeks this year in exchange for agreeing to attend what he calls "that Shakespeare thing." As he puts it: "There's no time for boredom."

Forget the hazy, lazy days of summer. Summer break, a three-month tradition that dates back to agrarian times, is changing. Your father's summer vacation may have involved afternoons playing sandlot baseball or dropping a fishing line into a creek. Today's American children are more likely to attend a series of camps and classes that have them traveling abroad, rebuilding dilapidated housing in inner cities and volunteering for internships in research areas just shy of human cloning. Kids who used to complain of ennui during drowsy summer afternoons now identify stress as their biggest concern, according to several survey firms. "The days of kids

just going out into the yard and playing are disappearing," says Chris Wilson, president of Simmons Market Research Bureau. "In many ways, they're just as busy as their parents."

The over-programming of American children is hardly a new story. Many affluent kids race from school to violin lesson to chess club during the academic year, leaving them a weary mess. What's changing is that kids of all socioeconomic and ethnic backgrounds now boast nonstop scheduling all summer long, fueled by their rising numbers and financial clout. Generation Y, the bulge of 71 million Americans under the age of 18, rose by 14 percent between 1990 and 2000—a growth spurt rivaling the Baby Boom. Recognizing the economic power of Gen Y families, an army of camp directors, travel agents and corporate executives has recently targeted this growing and lucrative market. Summer camp, once dominated by mom-and-pop operations, has become an $11 billion industry with a host of mega-corporations providing catered meals and trendy crafts to discerning campers.

With 62 percent of mothers in the U.S. in the work force, the old tradition of stay-at-home moms watching over their vacationing kids has gone the way of black-and-white TV. Haunted by the prevalence of violence, sexual promiscuity and drug abuse among today's youth, some adults look to organized programs as a safe haven for their children. Others feel guilty that they don't spend more time at home and compensate by sending their kids to pricey summer programs—a pattern children's marketing expert James McNeal terms DWI, or "deal with it," spending. In an era when many children spend their free time alone, glued to TV sets and computer screens, parents are more than willing to open their wallets to get their kids out of the house and into group activities. "Parents still wag the dog during the summer," says Rena Karl, publisher of *Marketing to Kids Report*. "Kids would just as soon do nothing all summer long, but there's that problem with child care. So parents fill up their time."

Which leaves little time for kids to become couch potatoes, a trend that Daniel Ryan's father finds comforting. "We trust our son completely, but kids at 14 still need structure," says Don Ryan, an environmental health advocate. This summer, *The Simpsons* will have to wait.

The Hot Selling Season

The new summer break is altering recreational patterns that have endured for over a century. When Simmons recently surveyed 6- to 11-year-olds as part of its annual Youth Poll, the kids named soccer, Rollerblading and bowling among their favorite leisure activities. Fewer than a quarter enjoyed going fishing—about the same percentage as those who play miniature golf or go skateboarding. Of the 12- to 17-year-old respondents, volleyball and weight training increased by double-digit rates in the past two years and now rank higher than camping and hiking. Only swimming, a hot weather essential, attracts a majority of teens and children. The rest of their time seems to be spent multitasking among athletic, entertainment and intellectual pursuits. "The data we're seeing shows that kids today are just more active in more activities than those in the past," says Simmons' Chris Wilson. "Their days are just filled up."

Free time at summer camp also seems to be on the endangered list. Whereas some kids once spent an entire summer roasting s'mores at mountaintop retreats, they now flit between weeklong specialty camps, which may be housed at suburban malls. The number of camps has increased from 9,000 to 10,000 over the past decade, reports the National Camp Association (NCA). Attendance has zoomed from 4 million to 5 million youngsters in the past two years alone. Part of the growth is attributed to kids from other countries who want to experience the uniquely American summer camp experience; inquiries from overseas have increased by approximately 50 percent over the past five years, reveals the NCA. But the boom in summer campers is also credited to facilities now catering to a wide age range of kids—from those as young as 3 years old to 18-year-old high school seniors. Previously, those older teenagers used to work in the summer. But these days, many parents and children recognize that camp programs in computers and rocketry may prove more beneficial than having kids hone their grocery-bagging skills.

In most major metros, summer camps begin filling up in winter for specialty programs in musical theater, fencing, gourmet cooking and mountain biking. The recreation-minded bureaucrats of Montgomery County, Md., a suburb of Washington, D.C., offer local children summer sessions devoted to Japanese culture, cartooning, the Internet and soccer goal-tending (as opposed to another program targeted specifically for soccer strikers). Other capital-area camps feature $1,000 journeys to Native American ruins in Colorado and whale watching off the California coast. "There's so much competition that they want to use summer break as a constructive way to prepare for the future," says Michael Wood, vice president of Teenage Research Unlimited (TRU) in Northbrook, Ill. "They'll do almost anything that will look good on a college application."

The glut of new summer activities has prompted old-school camp administrators—and, frequently, their new corporate owners—to upgrade their facilities in an effort to lure discriminating consumers. NASCO, which delivers arts and crafts supplies to 7,000 camps, notes that campers demand more than lanyard and key chain projects these days; the current trend is making masks and flags à la *Survivor*. Sports staffs now call on country club pros to serve as tennis instructors. And in some camp kitchens, where Army surplus fare

used to be prepared, professional caterers and food service corporations now provide a more wholesome cuisine. Sodexho Marriott, which began serving campers in 1987, currently offers vegetarian entrees and deli bars at 25 camps around the country. At some, "bug juice" has been replaced by fresh-squeezed orange juice and Starbucks coffee. At several facilities in New England, waiters serve steak or lobster on fine china. "The choices have expanded because the kids' tastes have expanded at home," explains Dan Eusebio, a district manager for Sodexho Marriott. "They expect the same variety when they go away to camp'"....

The Summer Break Backlash

The emphasis on structured summers hasn't come without a price. Some youth-oriented researchers detect a growing backlash against the nonstop, year-round programming. According to the 2000 Roper Youth Report, one-quarter of 6- to 17-year-olds feel they don't have enough free time. Surveys by TRU have found that the biggest complaint among U.S. teens is anxiety from their overbooked lives. "We're hearing a lot of complaints from teenagers who recognize that they don't have as much time for fun as they used to," says TRU's Michael Wood. Although numbers are sketchy, some parents of Gen Ys have begun to reject the scheduled activities and let their kids go free of organized programs during the summer. "The focus of the summer should be fun," says Norman Friedman, a camp safety expert. "And not enough of that is happening."

One repercussion of the structured summer break may be the rise of individual sports over team athletics. In the past, baseball dominated summer play. But the under-18 set can now choose from Nintendo 64 or Pokemon as well as extreme sports like mountain biking or rock climbing. Slower-moving sports no longer capture the attention of sensory-overloaded teens weaned on instant messaging and screeching video games. The top five sports for children, according to an online survey by research company Element, are swimming, bicycling, basketball, in-line skating and baseball. And analysts say that basketball and baseball made the list only because kids could play pickup games without having to drum up two complete teams. "Today's kids want self-expression," says Mike May of the Sporting Goods Manufacturers Association, "where they can make up their own rules and can participate at their pleasure, not tied to other people.''…

"Today's kids are tired of being programmed," says Karl. "Getting on bikes and scooters lets kids experience some freedom away from the confines of organization." It also doesn't hurt that more communities are building skateboard parks and bike areas to provide kids with a safe place to enjoy such freedom.

Despite such individual pursuits, the number of kids in structured summer programs shows little sign of peaking. Even with the sagging economy, experts predict more group travel abroad and more structured activities sponsored by corporations. "The days of hanging out at the schoolyard are over," says Karl. As incomes rise in minority communities, the rate of participation for Hispanic and Asian American youth in summer classes is only expected

to grow. The future of summer camp looks promising. "Camp is rapidly becoming a serious educational business serving as a transition from high school to college," says Jeffrey Solomon, executive director of the NCA. And the search for increasingly specialized programs continues. "If humans started inhabiting Mars, I wouldn't be surprised if some camp starts offering trips there," says Solomon, his tongue somewhat planted in cheek.…

Talking to Kids About Race

Children are quick to pick up racial biases from family members, friends, and TV. That's why it's so crucial to talk about issues like skin color and to dispel myths about race at an early age. Here's how to get started.

By Lori Miller Kase

When it came to race, Jennifer Seavey and her husband, who are white, had always tried to instill a sense of color blindness in their three children. "If we met someone who is black, our focus was 'Pretend you don't see any difference,'" says the Atlanta mom. But one day while she was driving, something her 6-year-old son, Drew, said to a black friend made Seavey rethink this philosophy. "You know what I used to think when I was little?" Drew asked his friend. "I used to think that God put us all in the oven, and you came out burned and we came out perfect."

Though Drew's friend didn't say anything, Seavey was mortified. "My stomach jumped into my throat, and I said, 'It's funny that you used to think that when you were little, but isn't it great that we know now that God makes people in all different colors?'" Then she quickly changed the subject. "I realized that because I had never talked to Drew about racial differences or given him an accurate explanation, he felt that he needed to explain it to himself," Seavey says.

Though very young children's queries about race are born of curiosity rather than prejudice, that racial innocence is short-lived. Kids are quick to absorb the biases around them and, when they enter school, those of society in general. "If you don't talk about race with young children, your kids may ascribe greater importance to the differences they see in people than you want them to," says Phyllis Katz, Ph.D., director of the Institute for Research on Social Problems, in Denver. When Dr. Katz tracked the development of racial attitudes in children, she found that almost half of the 200 children had racial biases by age 6.

That's why it's crucial for parents of all races to respond openly and honestly to their young children's questions and misperceptions about skin color and other ethnic differences, no matter how awkward it may seem—and to continue to bring up these issues as their kids grow. You can't always control the racial stereotypes that children pick up from TV, movies, or classmates; if you don't live in a diverse community, it may also be difficult to expose your child to kids of other races. But by talking to your child early and often about racial differences—teaching him why prejudice is wrong and setting a good example yourself—you can raise him to be an accepting, tolerant person.

How Kids Learn Racial Attitudes

The preschool period is a key time for parents to nurture children's natural inclination to see people as individuals rather than as stereotypes. By age 3 or 4, kids can identify skin color but still have little understanding of the concept of race, says Marguerite A. Wright, Ed.D., author of *I'm Chocolate, You're Vanilla* (Jossey-Bass, 1998). In fact, preschoolers are more likely to describe themselves as pink and peach or brown and chocolate than they are to use the terms black or white. "Children often learn about negative attitudes attached to other people's skin color before they can actually identify who is black and who is white," Dr. Wright says. Usually, it's because of conversations they've overheard in their home—among parents, older siblings, or others who spend time around them.

Dr. Wright recalls one black preschooler she interviewed named Josie, who had a surprisingly negative attitude toward white people for someone so young. Her hostility toward whites also encompassed light-skinned blacks: Because she was too young to understand racial categories, she simply grouped together those with similar skin color. Dr. Wright discovered that Josie's mother frequently portrayed whites as intent on mistreating blacks. Unfortunately, attitudes like this, when ingrained in a child early in life, are hard to shake later on.

Between the ages of 5 and 7, kids begin to pick up on the social meanings attached to skin color, says Dr. Wright, and start to become aware of other kinds of physical differences, such as eye shape and hair texture as well. They also start to adopt the prejudices of family members and friends, not to mention those depicted on television and in movies and popular music. In a study by psychologists Darlene Powell Hopson, Ph.D., and Derek S. Hopson, Ph.D., which used black and white dolls to assess the racial attitudes of young children, 65 percent of black children preferred to play with the white dolls—and more than three quarters of both black and white kids said that the black dolls "looked bad" to them.

An Honest Conversation

Answering your child's questions honestly and without embarrassment is the first step toward teaching tolerance. Here are a few basic principles.

Don't deny differences. "If your white child asks, 'Why does that kid have brown skin and I have light skin?' parents should not say 'There's really no difference.' Kids aren't color-blind, and they won't believe you," Dr. Katz says. "They're just trying to find out whether these differences mean anything." Instead, you could simply respond, "Because his mommy and daddy have brown skin" or "Skin color is passed down from parents and grandparents, and people are different colors depending on which part of the world their ancestors came from." You should also tell your child that people think and feel and enjoy a lot of the same things, even if they look different.

While researching their book *40 Ways to Raise a Nonracist Child* (HarperPerennial, 1996), Barbara Mathias and Mary Ann French found that black families tended to talk to their children much earlier in life about race than their white counterparts—probably because race is a much more salient issue for minorities. "I can't tell you how many white parents say to me, 'My child doesn't notice racial differences—why should I bring them up if he doesn't notice?'" Mathias says. "You should bring it up because they live in a society that does notice. And this society has a very powerful effect on a child."

Give straight answers. Never make a young child feel ashamed for bringing up racial issues or pointing out differences in skin color. By responding to kids' questions and comments in a matter-of-fact fashion, parents can pave the way for future candid conversations about race. For example, if your child points to a black woman at the grocery store and says, "Look, Mom, that lady's face is brown," don't be embarrassed and hush him up—take the opportunity to educate your child and explain why.

Similarly, if your child notices that Asian children have "different eyes," as my daughter once put it, you can explain that eyes come in many colors and shapes and that parents pass on something to their children that makes their eyes look like their own. "There's no need to bring in race if the child is just talking about a person's eyes," Dr. Wright says. "Adults think race, but children just think eyes or skin or whatever other characteristic. Keep your answers specific but truthful." Tailor your explanations to your child's questions and to his particular age and comprehension level.

Start early. Kappel Clarke, who is African-American, and his wife, Mabeline, who is Hispanic, anticipated how they would talk to their children about race before they even had their first daughter, Dánia, now age 8. "We knew that there are real issues that affect children born to biracial couples, so we decided to discuss as much about her background as possible during the early years so we would have a platform to stand on, one that she could be really proud of," says Clarke, a personal trainer at the Equinox Health Club, in New York City.

Clarke says that from the time Dánia was 3 years old, he and his wife have tried to make race a regular part of their conversation. "We wanted to avoid waiting until an incident happened before confronting these topics," Clarke says. But though he and his wife have told Dánia that some people will judge her by the way she looks, they try not to make race the biggest issue. "We try to develop her confidence in all aspects of her life."

Be reassuring. Sometimes children simply need to hear that it's okay to be different, especially if they are in the minority. Charlotte Wade, and African-American who is raising her niece Starkiesha in a predominantly Asian section of Oakland, California, recalls the day her niece came home from second grade and said, "There are only two students in the class who look like me." "We had never talked about race until this happened—in fact, it took me a while to understand what she was talking about," Wade remembers. "I said, 'You mean two little girls who have ponytails?' and she said, 'No, I mean little girls who are black like me.' I responded, 'That's okay. There don't have to be any students in your class who look like you so long as your teacher is teaching everybody.' Then Starkiesha asked, 'So it's okay that there's only three of us?' and I said, 'Yes, it is.'"

Don't overdo it. Maintaining a balance is important, says Dr. Wright, especially if you're a minority. Minority parents who dwell too much on race, particularly with very young children who can't yet process the information, may be doing them a disservice. For example, Dr. Wright says, she knows black parents who tell their children that they'll have to work twice as hard as white students do to succeed in school. "Some of them grow up thinking that they are destined to be treated unfairly and don't even bother trying," she says. "It handicaps a child, it really does."

Dealing With Prejudice

Despite our best efforts, we can't protect our children from the reality of prejudice and bigotry. Nor can we shield them from the stereotypes that are so prevalent in our society. Rachelle Ashour, a Virginia grammar-school teacher, recalls the eye-opening experience she had while teaching a predominantly black third- and fourth-grade class in Washington, D.C. "If you go into the gift shop of a museum with the kids, for instance, they really are watched more than other children are—it used to make me so angry," she says. "And the kids would pick up on it. They'd say, 'They're following me in the store because they think I'm going to steal something.' I'd say, 'They're just prejudiced.'" By acknowledging the racism, Ashour says, it gave her the opportunity to discuss with her students ways in which they might handle such situations.

According to experts, parents can help make children proud of who they are—and thus less affected by others' views of them—by giving them an understanding and appreciation of their heritage. Those of us who are minorities should surround our children with positive images of people who resemble them—both family portraits and pictures of our cultures' admirable achievers, says Drs. Darlene and Derek Hopson. But white parents, too, should explore their family's history, suggests

Reuel Jordan, dean of children's programs at the Bank Street College School for Children, in New York City. "Many white families think they don't have an ethnicity, that they are just American. But we encourage all families to get in touch with their heritage, which can help them understand other people's ethnicity."

Unfortunately, many families find themselves living in communities in which their kids are surrounded only by people who look just like them. "Young kids begin to develop attitudes toward people who are different from them very early on if they're not exposed to people from other environments and cultures," says Alvin F. Poussaint, M.D., a professor of psychiatry at Harvard Medical School and coauthor of *Raising Black Children* (Plume, 1992). Experts say they can easily develop an "us-them" mentality. Here's what you can do to help.

Monitor the media. When kids don't encounter people of other races in their day-to-day lives, their images of racial groups come mostly from television and movies. "What often happens is that white kids think that all blacks are athletes, because they see so many on TV, or that most black kids are comedians, because they've seen the black sitcoms," Dr. Poussaint says. Even the evening news, he says, which often shows policemen handcuffing blacks and Latinos, perpetuates stereotypes. It's up to parents to point these out to their children—and to counter such images by highlighting the many different ways in which people of all backgrounds have contributed to society.

Expose kids to various cultures. Dr. Poussaint says it is especially important for parents to expose their kids to other cultures through the books they read together, by attending shows or movies featuring musicians or actors of different races, and by providing toys and dolls that reflect the world's diversity. "When kids have dolls that aren't all black or all white, they begin to see that people come in different shades of color, with different shapes of eyes," Dr. Poussaint says. "This might encourage children to ask their parents questions. Later, if they hear derogatory terms, they'll know it's not the right way to refer to people."

Seek out diversity. Parents can also bring more diversity into their family's lives by looking for culturally mixed playgroups or enrichment classes for their young children—or by involving their older kids in after-school activities or sports teams that attract people of different backgrounds. And though your choice of public school may be dictated by where you live, you can seek out a preschool program that provides a multicultural education and draws a racially mixed group of kids.

Examine your own biases. Look at the examples that you set for your kids. No parent likes to think that she is prejudiced, but small actions can sometimes send negative signals to a child. When you take your children to the park, do you tend to sit only near people of your own race? If your father-in-law tells an ethnic joke at dinner, do you smile even if it makes you uncomfortable? Do you look for opportunities to expand the racial mix of your own group of friends and acquaintances? "If you teach your kids by example that people's differences are okay, that they should be valued—that we should take joy in them—then you are giving your children a gift," says Barbara Mathias. "You are giving them a tremendous advantage when they go out into the world."

From *Parents*, July 2001, pp. 101-110. © 2001 by Gruner & Jahr USA Publishing. Reprinted by permission.

Fathers' Involvement in Programs for Young Children

Vicki P. Turbiville, Gardner T. Umbarger, and Anne C. Guthrie

Little research has been done on how fathers of young children are involved or included in educational or therapeutic settings (Turnbull 1993; Phares 1997). For many young children, one of their primary environments is a child care center. For child care settings, research and discussions on parent involvement have generally been gender neutral. The focus in these settings is on the child: a *parent* is a *parent*, without an acknowledged differentiation between mother and father. And sometimes, particularly in discussions of family-centered practices in special education, the terms *parent* and *family* actually mean *mother* (Brinker 1992).

Fathers who try to become involved with their children's educational programs often find their efforts rebuffed. They report that teachers often ask mothers to confirm information given by fathers or that their input is requested only when financial issues arise. While there is little or no research as to why fathers are not as welcome as mothers, we can speculate that their work schedules, the differences in how women and men interact, and possibly power issues play a role.

A study conducted by the Beach Center on Families and Disability at the University of Kansas in 1996–97 examined how fathers participate in their children's child care programs. Investigators surveyed four different types of programs serving young children with and without disabilities in six states (California, Georgia, Idaho, Iowa, Maryland, New Mexico) to determine how they were including fathers. These four types were NAEYC-accredited programs, Head Start programs, programs for infants and toddlers with disabilities (Part C), and programs for preschool-age children with disabilities (Part B). Fathers from each of these program models were asked to identify their priorities for participation and the strategies used to make participation easier for them. In this research, *father* was defined as any male fulfilling the father role for a child. Responses were received from biological fathers as well as stepfathers, grandfathers, and noncustodial fathers.

> **The programs that seem most successful… are those that systematically address the fathers' preferences in each and every aspect of the program from enrollment to graduation.**

Before we discuss what fathers had to say, we will discuss some of the issues that have been barriers to their participation in programs for young children.

Barriers to fathers' participation in programs for young children

Fathers in this study were not asked about the barriers to their participation; rather, they were asked what characteristics would facilitate their participation and involvement. To some extent, barriers can be identified by reversing those characteristics (discussed later in "Facilitating Fathers' Participation in Children's Programs"). Other more significant barriers to fathers' involvement in programs for young children, however, may include their work schedules (Sparling, Berger, & Biller 1992), the differing interactional styles of men and women (Tannen 1990; May 1991), and the perceived power differences between men and women.

Work schedules

Women have traditionally been the providers of care for young children, whether those children have disabilities or not (Clark-Stewart 1978; Traustadottir 1991). Fathers have traditionally been the primary breadwinners (Griswald 1993). Even in today's culture of working mothers and fathers, the mother is more likely to take time from her daily schedule to be involved in the educa-

Fathers' Role in Children's School Achievement

A 1997 U.S. Department of Education study reconfirms the important role fathers play in the school achievement of their children. This research, taken from data gathered during the 1996 census, focuses on the involvement of fathers in the school programs of children in grades 6 through 12. The study found that children from two-parent homes whose fathers participated in school activities (such as general school meetings, parent-teacher conferences, school or class events, or volunteer work at school) were more likely to receive As on assignments, participate in extracurricular activities, and enjoy school. The report, while recognizing mothers as essential to the social and emotional adjustment of the child, indicates that fathers' involvement may be more important for academic achievement (U.S. Department of Education 1997).

Children whose fathers are involved in their educational programs were reported to be less likely to ever repeat a grade or be expelled or suspended from school (U.S. Department of Education 1997). Children whose fathers are involved in their lives at school also are less likely to exhibit violent behavior in school (Smith 1995) or be involved in acts of juvenile delinquency (Elias 1996).

tional programs of the family's children (U.S. Department of Education 1997). Most generally, fathers are not available during the day to participate in the programs. In surveys to assess the use of family-centered practices in programs for infants and toddlers with disabilities, fathers consistently report less ability to meet with educational providers or teams than do mothers (Turbiville, unpublished data).

Even when schedules can be altered to facilitate the participation by fathers in programs for young children, other issues arise, including the different interactional styles of men and women.

Different interactional styles of men and women

Tannen and other mass media writers and commentators have won wide acceptance for the notion that men and women differ in the ways they talk and in their approaches to social interaction and encounters. In her book *You Just Don't Understand*, Tannen (1990) suggests that men are more individualistic and competitive, while women prefer relationship building.

Fathers seem to appreciate being asked personally to take a role and being invited to participate. They also like to know that their efforts are appreciated by the teachers and others.

Fathers often report being asked to take messages for their wives when teachers and other providers call. Some fathers are put off by this request, while others, who are as uncomfortable with the interactional style of the female educator as she is with his, are glad to take the message.

The "P" word

Power is the "ability to influence others, to be listened to, to get your way rather than having to do what others want" (Tannen 1994, 317). Men—fathers—have historically been viewed as more powerful than women. Their greater physical strength and larger body build have sometimes led to the description "fathers with fangs" (Blankenhorn 1995, 87). Blankenhorn further quotes James Barbarino: "Traditionally, men's 'work' in the family has focused on the assertion of authority and power" (p. 87). Many families today describe power in their families as shared between father and mother (Griswald 1993). However, some women, particularly those who are single parents or have experienced abusive relationships, feel anger over the physical presence of the fathers or resentment of the power that these men had in their lives.

Particularly for the women working in Head Start programs who took part in the Beach Center Study, the issue of male power was very much a part of their hesitancy to involve fathers in their programs. As part of the study, conference calls with providers were held in Head Start and other child care programs. Issues related to the power relationships between men and women were raised frequently by the various providers. Some Head Start providers were addressing the power issues directly through in-service training programs designed to increase gender sensitivity.

Most participating fathers much prefer programs that involve their wives and/or their children.

Because most child care programs have a majority of female staff members, any issues of male-female power are likely to lead to ambivalence regarding the involvement of fathers in the program.

Facilitating fathers' participation in children's programs

Today, with both parents employed, fathers are often seen dropping off or picking up their children at child care centers and preschools. Fathers in this study reported wanting to be involved in their children's programs. Research supports their involvement as a means of obtaining better outcomes for the children and the rest of the family (Frey, Fewell, & Meyer 1989).

The research reported here comes from surveys from both providers and fathers. The results suggest strategies to reduce the barriers to fathers' involvement in programs for young children. These strategies include recognizing the unique characteristics of fathers, planning programs for both mothers and fathers, and respecting the efforts to be involved made by fathers.

Fathers' Preferences

Top five activities participated in by fathers of children in NAEYC-accredited child care programs:

1. Family activities

2. Daddy and Me programs

3. Activities for both parents to learn about their child's future

4. Activities for both parents to learn about child development

5. Sporting events

Recognizing the unique characteristics of fathers

Pruett (1996), addressing one aspect of the lives of men and women, states that "mothers mother" and "fathers father." Pruett does not suggest that one way of parenting is better or more necessary than the other, but that men and women, fathers and mothers, just do things differently.

Providers traditionally have taken a female orientation to involving parents in programs for young children. This is quite understandable in that the majority of the providers and administrators at child care programs are women, and most of their interactions are with the children's mothers. With increasing role-sharing between parents (Bronstein 1988), fathers in recent years have begun to be more visible at child care and educational centers. This has prompted some centers to create programs that respond to the priorities and needs of fathers.

The study conducted by the Beach Center on Families and Disability found that fathers with children in different types of educational or care programs had different priorities and preferences for their involvement with the program. For example, fathers from Head Start programs were far more interested in employment training or classroom work with children than were other fathers. Fathers whose children had disabilities were more interested than were other fathers in accessing books and other materials about children and children's learning that they could use at home, on their own.

While some priorities for involvement by fathers whose children attended NAEYC-accredited programs (see "Fathers' Preferences") resembled those of other groups' fathers, some were different. For all groups' fathers, the highest participation was in family activities. The type of activity that NAEYC fathers next most com-

monly participated in could be called Daddy and Me programs—programs that provide opportunities for children and fathers to do things together. Fathers from other groups did not participate as often in such programs. Fifty-four percent of NAEYC program fathers indicated that they participated in Daddy and Me programs compared to 31% for Head Start, 39% for Part B programs, and 45% for Part C programs.

As indicated, 54% of NAEYC fathers participate in these programs, but another 35% of all groups of fathers indicated that they did not believe such activities were available to them. When asked what they would most like to have their children's programs offer to them, fathers again gave top billing to Daddy and Me programs. Looks like a winner!

When Beach Center staff talked with program staff about their father-involvement activities, providers many times described programs such as Donuts for Dads day or a fathers' group. Most approached the participation of fathers as one size fits all. Staff often ended their descriptions of efforts to include fathers by indicating that they do not get very large responses to them. The fathers' responses indicate strongly that one size *does not* fit all.

Providers need to talk to fathers to identify their priorities and interests and then offer program alternatives that address those priorities and interests. The programs that seem most successful in involving fathers systematically address fathers' preferences in each and every aspect of their programs, from enrollment to graduation. For instance, one program director said that they start with their intake procedures, identifying roles for fathers and for mothers in that process. They then move on to the next steps in a child's participation in their program and identify roles for both parents.

Plan programs of interest to both mothers and fathers

As part of this research, Beach Center staff asked providers in the six states to help identify programs that were doing a particularly good job of including fathers. Providers from these programs often indicated that the primary approach to including fathers was offering programs specifically for men only. Almost without exception, the first comment from providers was about the existence or absence of dad-only programs.

The fathers who responded to the Beach Center survey, however, confirmed what has been heard from fathers many times before. They indicated that they much preferred activities where their wives were also involved rather than men-only programs. Fathers want these offerings to address issues of interest to them, including responsiveness to their particular concerns and priorities, as well as those of their child's mother. This preference was reflected in low participation in father-only support groups as well as limited participation in other father-only programs.

For all groups of fathers, whether their children were enrolled in NAEYC-accredited, Head Start, Part C, or Part B programs, the highest participation was in family activities. For fathers in NAEYC programs, however, this preference was significantly stronger than it was for fathers in the other programs. One reason for this difference may be found in how family characteristics vary between the groups. Almost by definition, children who are enrolled in NAEYC-accredited programs have parents who work outside the home. With all adults in the home working, family time is extremely limited. One could speculate that because of this, fathers would be more likely to use any time they have in family activities rather than in activities for themselves only.

Fathers, particularly NAEYC fathers, also did not see having other men on staff in their child's program as making it easier for them to participate. Fathers whose children were enrolled in NAEYC programs were apparently comfortable with the frequently female-dominated culture of the child care programs. Their responses certainly blew away any idea that these fathers would come only to programs specifically offered to men. They much preferred programs that involved their wives and/or their children (Daddy and Me programs).

Providers in NAEYC-accredited programs ranked working around the school building as one of the top five ways that dads participate in their programs. They indicated that nearly two-thirds of the fathers participate in these kinds of activities. NAEYC fathers, however, did not indicate that this was one of the ways they participated. Only a third of them indicated that they helped out in their child's program in this way. Fathers in other program models, however, ranked these activities as highly effective for including fathers, demonstrating again the need to learn from the fathers in one's own individual programs what is best for them.

Respect fathers' involvement in existing programs

Providers often indicated that they needed to hire a new male staff person if they were to succeed in involving fathers in their programs. Fathers, however, indicated that this was not necessary. Providers do need to add the fathers' areas of interest, such as the child's future or information on child development and play, to their offerings.

Fathers also indicated that some "magic words" from providers would make all the difference in their choosing to participate. These are the same magic words we instill in children: *please* and *thank you*. Fathers seem to appreciate being asked personally to take a role and being invited to participate. They also like to know that their efforts are appreciated by the teacher and others.

In addition to the comments discussed previously, the fathers indicated that scheduling activities in the evening and on weekends made participation easier. This could be a bit more costly unless some flexibility is worked out in staff work schedules.

Providers want to include fathers but seem not to know the best approach to use. According to the responses to the Beach Center survey, providers will try any approach—from offering food to hiring new staff—to encourage fathers to participate, while fathers are quite specific about what makes participation easier. Drawing in fathers requires spending some time listening to fathers' priorities and openly acknowledging the contributions they make. That's a pretty easy way to improve the likelihood of fathers' involvement in programs and in the lives of their children.

And finally

We often hear that fathers are not interested in their children's educational programs. This just does not appear to be true. Eighty percent of all the fathers surveyed (85% of the NAEYC fathers) indicated some level of participation in their child's child care/educational program. We as providers must examine the steps that can be taken to make it easier and more rewarding for fathers to be involved in their children's programs.

We must rethink the definition of *involvement* (Phillips & Cabrera 1996). We simply cannot dismiss fathers as uninterested until we examine our efforts to understand their priorities and interests. We clearly cannot make assumptions about what these priorities and interests are for any individual father or group of fathers. We must open a dialogue with fathers, just as we have done with mothers, to learn what they want and need and then take steps to address those priorities.

We want all fathers to make comments like those of this father in the Beach Center survey: "All of the instructors and therapists at my daughter's early intervention program are very receptive and attentive to my needs and concerns. They welcome all suggestions and input."

References

Blankenhorn, D. 1995. *Fatherless America*. New York: Basic.

Brinker, R. 1992. Family involvement in early intervention: Accepting the unchangeable, changing the changeable, and knowing the difference. *Journal of Early Intervention* 12 (3): 307–32.

Bronstein, P. 1988. Marital and parenting roles in transition: An overview. In *Fatherhood today: Men's changing role in the family*, eds. P. Bronstein & P. Cowan, 3–10. New York: Wiley.

Clarke-Stewart, K.A. 1978. And Daddy makes three: The father's impact on mother and young child. *Child Development* 49: 466–78.

Elias, M. 1996. Teens do better when dads are more involved. *USA Today*, 22 August, D-1.

Frey, K., R. Fewell, & D. Meyer. 1989. Parental adjustment and changes in child outcome among families of young handicapped children. *Topics in Early Childhood Special Education* 8 (4): 38–57.

Griswald, R. 1993. *Fatherhood in America*. New York: Basic.

May, J. 1991. *Fathers of children with special needs: New horizons*. Bethesda, MD: Association for the Care of Children's Health.

Phares, V. 1997. Psychological adjustment, maladjustment, and father-child relationships. In *The role of the father in child development*, ed. M. Lamb, 261–83. New York: Wiley.

Phillips, D.A., & N. Cabrera, eds. 1996. *Beyond the blueprint: Directions for research on Head Start's families*. Washington, DC: National Academy Press.

Pruett, K. 1996. Child development: The facts on how fathers make a difference. *Family Resource Coalition Report* 15 (1): 8–10.

Smith, L. 1995. Guess what? Fathers matter, too. *Kansas City Star*, 26 March, H-1, H-4.

Sparling, J., R. Berger, & M. Biller. 1992. Fathers: Myth, reality, and Public Law 99–457. *Infants and Young Children* 4 (3): 9–19.

Tannen, D. 1990. *You just don't understand: Women and men in conversation*. New York: Morrow.

Tannen, D. 1994. *Talking 9 to 5*. New York: Morrow.

Traustadottir, R. 1991. Mothers who care. *Journal of Family Issues* 12: 211–28.

Turnbull, A.P. 1993. Fathers' roles in intervention programs for children at special risk: Disabled chronically ill, and children living in poverty. Paper presented at the National Research Council, National Academy of Science, Washington, D.C.

U.S. Department of Education. 1997. *Fathers' involvement in their children's schools* [Online]. Available: http://www.ed.gov/NCES/pubs98/fathrs/intro.html#intro

For further reading

Flynn, L., & P. Wilson. 1998. Partnerships with family members: What about fathers? *Young Exceptional Children* 2 (1): 21–28.

Meyer, D. 1995. *Uncommon fathers*. Bethesda, MD: Woodbine House.

Levine, J., & E. Pitt. 1995. *New expectations: Community strategies for responsible fatherhood*. New York: Families and Work Institute.

Minnesota Fathering Alliance. 1992. *Working with fathers: Methods and perspectives*. Stillwater, MN: nu ink unlimited (206 South 5th St., Stillwater, MN 55082-4917).

NAEYC. *Involving men in the lives of children*. Washington, DC: Author. Brochure.

Ortiz, R., S. Stile, & C. Brown. 1999. Early literacy activities of fathers: Reading and writing with young children. *Young Children* 54 (5): 16–18.

Turbiville, V.P., A.P. Turnbull, & H.R. Turnbull. 1995. Fathers and family-centered early intervention. *Infants and Young Children* 7 (4): 12–19.

Vicki Turbiville, Ph.D., is a project coordinator with the University Affiliated Program at the University of Kansas, Lawrence. Her work focuses on young children with disabilities and their families.

Gardner T. Umbarger III, Ph.D., is a former research associate at the Beach Center on Families and Disability at the University of Kansas, Lawrence. He is an experienced special educator.

Anne C. Guthrie, M.S.Ed., is a research assistant with the Sibling Project, School of Nursing, University of Kansas Medical School. She has worked in a variety of family support programs for persons with developmental disabilities and their families.

Children of divorce: 25 years later

A landmark new study that tracked kids from broken homes for a quarter-century finds the negative impact of divorce continues well into adulthood.

BY HARA ESTROFF MARANO

Part of me is always waiting for disaster to strike.... I live in dread that some terrible loss will change my life." That, according to psychoanalyst Judith Wallerstein, is what divorce sounds like 25 years after the fact, among those it hits hardest—the children.

Wallerstein, founder of the Center for the Family in Transition in Corte Madera, Calif., is one of the nation's leading experts on divorce. Her new book, *The Unexpected Legacy of Divorce: A 25-Year Landmark Study* (HYPERION, $24.95), contends that divorce marks offspring for life.

Her troubling, inevitably controversial study offers a close-up view of the first generation to grow into adulthood with a 50% divorce rate. Together with other recent studies that have followed large numbers of the children of divorce, it provides some answers to the question: How does divorce affect children?

Each year divorce complicates the lives of more than 1 million Americans under age 18 by creating two households and the need for two newly different relationships with their parents. But the impact can go well beyond that.

The degree of fallout and its duration depend on a number of factors. Among them:

- The nature of the marriage before the divorce.
- The nastiness and anger caused by the divorce.
- The role of divorced fathers in their children's lives.
- And, above all, the quality of parental support and control before, during and after the divorce.

Long after their parents have parted company, gone on to happier unions or attempted some other version of the good life, the children of divorce, even as adults, are still spinning from its effects, Wallerstein insists.

Karen James was 36 when she detailed to Wallerstein the long shadow cast by her parents' divorce. Like so many other children of divorce, James had embarked on a search for lasting love, yet was so deeply anxious that she was unable to trust others. A fear of abandonment kept her clinging to a string of unsuitable or troubled partners.

Twice before (in her books *Surviving the Breakup: How Children and Parents Cope With Divorce* and *Second Chances: Men, Women, and Children a Decade After Divorce*), Wallerstein had tapped into the lives of Karen James and 130 other children in San Francisco's affluent Marin County suburbs who were between ages 3 and 18 when their parents first separated. And twice before, Wallerstein has told us that divorce abruptly ends kids' childhood, filling it with loneliness and worry about their parents, and hurtling them prematurely and recklessly into adolescence.

"But it's in adulthood that children of divorce suffer the most," Wallerstein contends. Feeling totally unprepared and thoroughly pessimistic, they encounter repeated failure and heartbreak as they dive into adult relationships. With no clues to the type of person they are looking for, they enter and stick with relationships they know are doomed from the start. Even in good relationships, they expect disaster. And they go to pieces over "the mundane differences and inevitable conflicts" found in every close relationship, Wallerstein says.

By the time the children of divorce reach their 30s, she finds, only half are doing well in their personal lives. Interestingly, their work lives are unscathed.

Because only 30% of divorced fathers in her study chipped in for their kids' college educations, Wallerstein predicts a backlash by the children of divorce against their dads, now approaching their senior years. Bitter children threaten to withhold the emotional and financial aid often needed in old age as payback for fathers who

Easing the impact of divorce

Advice from America's best experts on divorce and the family:

● Recognize that divorce is not something that has to be settled only once, when the break-up occurs. Children, even adult ones, have a recurring need for information and support at life's major developmental passages.

● After divorce, children are even more in need of what they couldn't get before: a sense of their two parents collaborating on their behalf. Continuing conflict is a stress that can derail development.

● Keep your children connected to the extended family of the noncustodial parent; they need aunts and uncles and grandparents. Think of it as a social capital: The more they have, the easier life is for everyone.

● As children head into adolescence and beyond, explain generally—not in sordid detail—why your marriage broke up. Telling the kids about mistakes you made actually helps them feel hopeful.

● Step up the supervision in adolescence. Speak up—always respectfully, with explanation—if you think your children's regular friends or romantic partners are unsuitable.

did not stay connected. That could have tremendous societal repercussions. "Who," Wallerstein asks, "will take care of an older generation estranged from its children?"

Still, the portrait Wallerstein paints may be too pessimistic and her research methods flawed, others contend. Specifically, her study lacks a control group, so there's no way to know for sure whether all the problems that developed in the children of divorce stem from the divorce, from other aspects of their lives or from the normal perturbations of young adulthood.

In the short term, divorce is always troublesome for children, says Mavis Hetherington, doyenne of divorce researchers. Now professor emeritus of psychology at the University of Virginia, she has videotaped and scruti-

nized the workings of 1,400 divorced families since the early 1970s. Hetherington pinpoints a crisis period of about two years in the immediate aftermath of separation when the adults, preoccupied with their own lives, typically take their eye off parenting just when their children are reeling from loss and feeling bewildered.

In fact, divorce actually can be better for the children if there has been a great deal of conflict in the marriage, or if the household is disorganized and chaotic, say sociologists Paul R. Amato and Alan Booth of Pennsylvania State University, who followed 2,000 families for nearly two decades. They found that the kids of high-conflict families whose parents divorce wind up just as happy and do just as well as others their age who grow up with happily married parents.

It's a different story for the children of marriages that were not particularly hostile before a break-up. Typically, the husband and wife were drifting along unhappily, their sex life non-existent—but they seldom fought. Their kids didn't mind; in fact, they didn't even notice. "Divorce in a low-conflict marriage is just devastating to kids," Amato concludes. Adds William Doherty, professor of family science at the University of Minnesota, "Children are not oriented to the quality of your sex life or whether your spouse is your soul mate."

Doherty says it's "no longer clear" to him that it's fair to the children when parents leave a non-destructive marriage "to pursue your bliss or because you don't want to give children a bad model of marital intimacy."

It's not surprising that the wisest words on divorce may come from a child of divorce herself. Stephanie Staal is a 28-year-old writer who has explored the impact of marital break-up in a new book, *The Love They Lost* (Delacourt Press, $23). She interviewed 120 adult children of divorce and wound up impressed by the complexity of their reactions. Referring to the wide variation in parental support, household conflict and explanations among her subjects, she observes that "there is no typical divorce. It's the way people do it that defines its effects."

HARA ESTROFF MARANO is editor at large of *Psychology Today* and editor in chief of the upcoming publication *Infantelligence*.

UNIT 3
Care and Educational Practices

Unit Selections

Key Points to Consider

• Do you believe that there is a uniquely American cluster of characteristics that should be fostered in child care?

• Identify an authentic community need that could be met by preschoolers, with the help of elementary-age children or senior citizens.

• Find out if there have been changes over the past 5 years in the amount of time scheduled for recess for kindergarten, first, second, and third grade classes in a nearby school district.

 **Links: www.dushkin.com/online/**
These sites are annotated in the World Wide Web pages.

Canada's Schoolnet Staff Room
http://www.schoolnet.ca/home/e/

Classroom Connect
http://www.classroom.net

The Council for Exceptional Children
http://www.cec.sped.org/index.html

National Resource Center for Health and Safety in Child Care
http://nrc.uchsc.edu

Online Innovation Institute
http://oii.org

One of the things that makes teaching young children so rewarding in the United States is our understanding of quality care and educational practices. As a nation, we have many high-quality early childhood programs that are based on a rich knowledge of child development. And we are aware that appropriate practice in early childhood education depends on the teachers' own learning opportunities. As teachers grow to understand a wide range of educational practices, they are better equipped to provide effective education and care for young children. The basis for current trends in education practice is constructivism, an approach that views learning as an interactive experience. When teachers adopt elements of constructivist practice, they begin to view children as active learners. This perspective results in practice that gives priority to solving real-world problems, connecting new learning to prior experience, inquiry, and project-based work.

Our lead article counsels teachers to maintain good practice in programs for infants and toddlers. If, as a nation, we value diversity, then heavy emphasis should be placed on choice and exploration, rather than on teaching methods designed for older children. Eleanor Stokes Szanton stimulates our thinking by asking an essential question: Which is more important, teaching or learning?

"Who Cares for the Kids?" presents the findings of a landmark study of the nation's child care, focusing on the cost and quality of care. The standing and accomplishments of the 50 states reveal that the quality of child care continues to be mediocre. *Working Mother* magazine uses key factors to identify status of child care. Among the factors are accreditation, group size, and safety. One statistic that needs to increase is the number of states that have enacted universal pre-K—the state of Georgia is the only state to have taken this step.

The Reggio Emilia approach is an internationally recognized early education program that demonstrates that good things happen when children take the lead in learning. "Italian Import Creates Preschools Where Kids Shape Agenda" describes a blend of constructivist and progressive educational practices that fits well with developmentally appropriate practices in many child care centers and primary schools. The four core practices of the Reggio approach—emphasis on a stimulating environment, group projects, authentic assessment, and parental involvement—are well suited to programs whose aims are flexibility and creativity.

The time-honored method of learning in early childhood is play. Today, more than ever, the importance of play to learning needs to be reaffirmed. As preschools continue to feel the pressure for children to excel academically, teachers need reminders of the value of play. "All They Do Is Play? Play in Preschool" gives teachers basic information on the role of play centers in block, language, dramatic play, math, and science.

Service learning is a powerful method of binding learning with meaningful community experiences. For young children, this is an authentic way to learn in context, rather than by textbook. "Service Learning in Preschool: An Intergenerational Project Involving Five-Year Olds, Fifth Graders, and Senior Citizens" gives an example of a project that demonstrates that the best

learning is experiential learning. The key is for teachers to first identify connections between hands-on community projects and specific curricular goals.

Two articles in this unit focus on the need to balance children's developmental needs with achievement. The Association for Childhood Education International (ACEI) has developed a position paper underscoring the importance of "The Child-Centered Kindergarten." This professional organization continues to emphasize educating the whole child, responding to individual differences, and providing multiple opportunities for learning.

Parents are also caught in bind of escalating academics. Since they are familiar with letter grades, they expect to see their children's learning reported in that format." But what's wrong with letter grades? "'Responding to Parents' Questions About Alternate Assessment" provides help for teachers as they hold conferences with parents of primary grade children.

Unlike ACEI's child-centered position, many schools are failing to educate the whole child. With increasing pressure to spend more time on academics in preparation for testing, children are being deprived of recess and informal social interaction time. The second article calling for balance is "The Silencing of Recess Bells." As implied by the title, there are consequences of eliminating recess in primary grades and the results can be detrimental to development.

Good practice—activity that is appropriate for children's development, play that is active, and learning that is connected to real-world problems—has no shortcuts and cannot be trivialized. It takes careful thought and planning, using the latest knowledge of early childhood education, to make wise curriculum and practice choices. By working out specifics of routines and procedures, curriculum, and assessment suitable for young children, the early childhood professional strengthens skills in decision making. These are crucial tasks for a teacher interested in sound educational practice.

For America's Infants and Toddlers, Are Important Values Threatened by Our Zeal to "Teach"?

Eleanor Stokes Szanton

Editor's note: All Americans are aware of the diversity within the total U.S. population. In addition, many members of the early childhood community, and numerous other citizens, are aware that Americans do not *all* share *all* of the same values. Yet from the perspective of people living in other countries, there's a cluster of personal characteristics considered peculiarly American.

Some of us cherish all of these values, some of us dislike a few—or more than a few—of them. We may not agree on the ranking of these attributes—which attribute is more important than which. But even people who resent these values and characteristics acknowledge their existence.

In this thought-provoking article, the author discusses the values transmitted to the next generation by a majority of Americans and by many early childhood education leaders. They are reflected in NAEYC's standards of developmentally appropriate practice, which have evolved from the combined and refined input of many experts. The author points out how mainstream infant/toddler programs encourage these characteristics in children. She worries that low quality programs may interfere with the development of characteristics deemed desirable by many Americans.

We know that many readers—and even some of NAEYC's leaders—will take exception to several of the assumptions and statements in this article. Therefore we think that it will be a powerful discussion starter for staff and early childhood education students. We invite you to think as you read (we have highlighted some things you may want to think about), talk over your thoughts with others, and write to us!

Americans by and large raise their children in a very distinctive way. That is perhaps surprising neither to those who endorse it nor to those who do not approve of it. What is fascinating is seeing just how early this process begins.

From more than 40 years of observation, practice, and study of infant/toddler care and education here and abroad, I have become very aware of those common values mentioned by John Hope Franklin. But I am surprised at how little they are discussed in research and practice. Typically child development specialists speak of certain *universals of development*—attributes that growing children share the world over. On the other hand they study the impact of *group differences* in child development—what it means to grow up in one ethnic group as opposed to another, to be poor instead of rich, White instead of Black, in a rural versus an urban setting. Researchers also study *individual differences* such as temperament, ability, and resilience. But in the process they largely ignore a distinction just as important as the others—*national characteristics* that many of us believe to be a valuable source of our strength as Americans.

Even with our diversity it is important to see just how much is shared in raising our children from infancy onward—both at home and in "good" early child care. In doing so, I believe that we develop in our children a set of characteristics that are functional for life in the United States and in this new century.

Indeed, it is especially important to understand how distinctively and functionally we raise our children, because that process is now being unintentionally threatened.

Studied	Ignored	Studied	Studied
Universals of development	*National Characteristics*	Cultural and group differences	Individual differences

This article discusses how early in a child's life values held by most Americans are transmitted in good group care and education. It suggests how much more those valued competencies will be needed in this new century. And it raises a red flag about the direction of an increasing number of programs for infants and toddlers that use teaching methods designed for older children, because in doing so they may ignore the natural developmental processes of infants and toddlers and affect the future success of these children in the national culture of which they are part.

Attitudes toward diversity

The concern about understanding and honoring differences is one of the values that unite most Americans and distinguish them from people of other nations. In this era and in this country, much emphasis is placed upon those differences. This is certainly fitting. We have a highly diverse nation. And we only need look at the ethnic strife around the world and at the hate crimes and other more subtle examples of inter-ethnic hostility in our own country to believe differences are important to recognize, understand, and honor.

What is striking is to see how much American attitudes toward diversity in child care may differ from those of others. The following example serves to highlight this difference.

Not many years ago, I visited a country in Eastern Europe, observing the infant/toddler child care centers. In that country often there were three or four infant or toddler rooms in one large building, together with preschool rooms. In one room I found a child of approximately eight months lying alone on a mattress in a kind of play pen. Her eyes were open and totally listless in expression, though she did watch what was going on. No one paid any attention to her. I thought she might be unwell. All the other children were free to walk or crawl around the play area.

As we went to look at the other children's rooms, that little girl stayed in my mind. About 45 minutes later, after we had finished looking at the other groups, I asked if I could go back to the first room—the room with the listless child. When we did, I found her still lying in exactly the same position, still watching, still listless. Still no one was paying attention to her. When I asked about her, I was told, "She's Albanian." It turned out that her Albanian mother, a minority in that country, had wanted her child to be "mainstreamed" and had recently entered her in the program so that she could learn the language of the dominant culture from the beginning. The generally caring and committed staff simply did not know what to do with her. They wished her mother had decided to use one of the several Albanian child care centers that were available. They apparently planned to let her lie there as long as she "wanted to" lie alone. However, after I asked, one of the teachers picked her up and nuzzled her head in her neck. The child began to respond.

To most Americans, this is an appalling story. I do not say that this behavior—and worse—cannot happen in the United States. But it would never be held up as good practice. Demonstrating best practice and even good practice in the United States, a program would provide a primary teacher/caregiver of the same ethnic and linguistic background as the child. Failing that, the child's caregiver would have some diversity training and know something about the culture of this child, both from the family and from other sources (Lally et al. 1995; Bredekamp & Copple 1997).

There are excellent reasons for this attention to children's cultural backgrounds. In the words of one expert in infant/toddler development,

Preschoolers have formed a somewhat well-developed "working sense of self," with likes and dislikes, attitudes, and inclinations. [In contrast] infants and toddlers are in the process of forming this preliminary sense of self. Part of what infants and toddlers get from caregivers are perceptions of how people act at various times in various situations (seen as how the infant should behave), how people act toward them and others (seen as how they and others should be treated), and how emotions are expressed (seen as how they should feel). The infant uses these impressions and often incorporates them into the self she becomes. (Lally 1995, 59)

That sense of self is both an individual one and a cultural one, with cultural expectations for how people act at various times in various situations, toward them and others, and how emotions are expressed. Young children also need to build the foundations of their own language.

There is another kind of diversity that our nation honors, and that is diversity of physical and mental ability. Awareness and respect for varying abilities is reflected in good practices in our inclusive infant/toddler programs. In many countries children with special needs, especially young ones, are hidden away or kept at home as an embarrassment to family and school. Since the mid 1970s we have moved to include children with special needs in preschool programs whenever possible, both to broaden opportunities for the children themselves and to enrich the entire group (Bryant & Graham 1993; O'Brien 1997).

Individualism and independence

Good practice in early childhood care and education in the United States places a heavy emphasis on adult-child interaction. Teachers and individual children talk to each other a lot as teachers encourage joint attention and elaborate on what the child is doing, naming the activity, setting it in context, scaffolding the child's interpretation of events. Individual differences in temperament are studied and respected. Our children become used to using caregivers and teachers as resources (*Discoveries of Infancy* 1992). In the United States good practice calls for low child-teacher ratios, responsive caregiving, and an individualized approach to early childhood education (Lally et al. 1995; Bredekamp & Copple 1997).

Japan offers a good example of a contrasting approach to early childhood education. In Japan there is much more emphasis on peer groups. (I speak now not of infants and toddlers, who until recently in that country have rarely been in group care, but of children three years and older.) Children are placed in "table groups" that go through several grades together. They take on chores early in life and remind each other of their duties. The child-teacher ratio is much higher, so teachers frequently use peer pressure rather than adult-child interaction to achieve their objectives (Lewis 1995). In many non-Western societies, small children quickly become one of many in a family group, often cared for by older siblings (LeVine et al. 1996).

Clearly some things are lost in the American approach to raising young children, primarily a strong sense of belonging to a group, strong group loyalty, early responsibility for other

children. However, the difference puts in high relief what is strikingly American—the importance of individual interplay between child and adult.

Choice and exploration

Hand in hand with valuing independence and individualism goes the high value assigned to individual choice and exploration. For better or worse, the larger society in the United States puts great emphasis on independence and the ability to accomplish things on one's own. That emphasis is apparent from the earliest years of care and education (Hansen, Kaufmann, & Saifer 1996). Researchers and other observers have noticed differences between the treatment of little boys and little girls on this point, with boys being more strongly encouraged to strike out on their own (Maccoby & Jacklin 1974). Nonetheless, when compared to children in other countries, independence is fostered in toddler girls, as well.

In child care in many countries, toys are presented to toddlers to play with. They may be stored out of children's reach and brought out for them. At the same time children in these settings learn amazingly early—in American eyes—what "Do not touch" means. The concept of babyproofing is more typically American. American infants and toddlers are generally allowed to crawl and move about freely in an environment where health and safety hazards have been removed. Playpens are discouraged. In early childhood centers toddlers are free to reach toys of their own choosing, placed on low, easily accessible shelves or the floor. Children are encouraged to explore and try new things.

A visitor from one of the countries of the former Soviet Union remarked after watching the young American children choose a name for their class's new bunny, "You are really teaching democracy! We would never ask children to vote on the rab-

bit's name." Whether encouraging toddlers to select from among toys or preschoolers to make simple decisions, we raise our children to be used to, and comfortable with, making their own choices.

Initiative

Initiative is another highly functional American trait. It goes in tandem with individualism, independence, choice, and exploration.

With the glaring and tragic exceptions of those forced here in slavery and those Native Americans already here, the United States was built by people—and their descendants—who were willing to leave everything they had known and come to some place entirely different. (Even those who felt they had no choice but to flee famine, persecution, or death were different from their relatives who chose not to flee.) And many an African American family has tales of their forebears' escape and desperate survival through their wits and self-reliance.) The vast majority came to tame wilderness, build their own houses and farms and stores, form new groups and civic associations, create a new world. This frontier mentality has permeated our entire society, even down to this day.

The prominence of personal initiative in American culture was identified by Alexis de Tocqueville early on in the life of the country:

> The citizen of the United States is taught from infancy to rely upon his own exertions in order to resist the evils and the difficulties of life; he looks upon the social authority with an eye of mistrust and anxiety, and he claims its assistance only when he is unable to do without it. This habit may be traced even in the schools, where the children in their games are wont to submit to rules which they have themselves established, and to punish misdemeanors which they have themselves defined. The same spirit pervades every act of social life. (Tocqueville [1835] 1946)

In today's world this reverence for personal initiative is expressed in the attitude of Americans toward entrepreneurs who start up small businesses to organize their communities to fight an environmental problem. It is probably no accident that the United States is responsible for a very high percentage of new inventions or that the recent electronics revolution started here. Tinkering is built right in.

Not surprisingly, the high value placed on personal initiative in American culture is evident as we help our youngest children to grow and develop. In many countries children follow the lead of the teacher (e.g., teacher, getting a box of blocks down from a cupboard, says, "Suppose you build a castle. John, why don't you put that block here…"). In contrast, good practice in the United States would be to allow or encourage children to experiment with building the tower themselves—learning as much when it falls down as when it rises up. Programs for toddlers emphasize the great importance of playing with objects, of allowing children to manipulate toys in many different ways—no doubt more ways than the teacher would have thought of—and then discussing with the children or elaborating on what they are doing.

In some cultures infants and toddlers are more commonly fed with a spoon by an adult. In the United States, children more frequently are allowed and encouraged to feed themselves by manipulating bits of food with their fingers. Babies are encouraged to crawl, with less restraint than found elsewhere. Adults encourage children to learn, through practice and experience, that they can make things happen.

Floor time and the beginning of equality

Floor time, a term popularized by the infant psychiatrist Stanley Greenspan (Greenspan & Greenspan 1989), is a good characterization of the hundreds of hours parents, care-givers, and early childhood teachers spend on the floor where infants and toddlers typically play. The very act of sitting down on the same level with the crawling baby or toddling child is symbolic of a more equal relationship between adult and child. It levels the playing field. Whether an adult is sitting with feet spread apart and rolling a ball back and forth with a toddler or watching what the child is playing with and talking about it with her, that adult is giving the message, "You are as important as I am. Your interests are my interests."

Floor time is much less common outside the United States. More often adults stand or sit on chairs—or crouch or kneel. In spatial terms they are demonstrating the body language of authority. The relative absence of floor time also leaves children in other countries interacting more with *each other* than with the adults. Here again, by getting down on the floor with our children, we emphasize the value of one-on-one adult-child interaction. Floor time with infants and toddlers is the first step in education toward the deeply held American belief in equality.

Expressiveness

In many parts of the world, infants, carried everywhere by their mothers, have no need to learn to cry lustily to signal their needs. A grunt or snuffle suffices. As they get older, they may have to share a very small space with a large family. In contrast, Western children, and particularly American children, are placed in separate cribs, often in separate rooms. They learn they must use their bodies—in infancy, their voices—as a tool to make things happen. A particularly striking example of this is shown in the following research.

Japanese babies as young as two months cry much less and for a much shorter time on the whole than their American counterparts when receiving a routine immunization shot (Lewis, Ramsey, & Kawakami 1993). This difference is purely behavioral; their levels of cortisol, an indicator of internal distress, are just as high or higher than those of American children the same age. Although there may be some admixture of genetic difference here, the fact is that from the earliest months, American children have a tendency to show their reactions to an averse stimulus.

Self-expression is more highly valued throughout childhood in the United States than in other parts of the world. Here we see a higher level of activity, noisiness, and messiness permitted among infants and toddlers than elsewhere. In U.S. early childhood programs, a few squiggles on a piece of paper may be much admired; whereas, in other countries, the ability to represent a known object is much more strongly encouraged.

Parents' place in the program

In some countries I have noted that child care centers view parents virtually as contaminants. Due to a program's emphasis on cleanliness, parents may be unwelcome in the play area of an infant/toddler center. If allowed in, they must wear smocks and slippers. Children must change their home clothes for clothing provided by the center before entering the room with the other children. Parents are not encouraged to visit. There is very little discussion with them at the beginning or end of the day. The child simply leads two lives, one at home and the other at the center, with little connection between them.

In contrast, in the United States good practice calls for teamwork with parents. Especially in infant/toddler care and education, parents and staff see the need to consult constantly about events in the baby's day—feeding and diapering, degree of fussiness, amount of sleep. In addition, best practice calls for close consultation on toilet learning, discipline, sleep routines, and other issues that may cause tension between adult and child (Lally et al. 1995; Hansen & Kaufmann 1997). Again reflecting American attention to diversity, it is considered the duty of the teacher and caregiver to be familiar with the culture and expectations of the family. Where there might be strong differences between center and family on issues such as corporal punishment, best practice calls for considerable discussion and even negotiation back and forth, finding a place that honors both the expectations of families and the center's policies and philosophy.

What our children will face in this new century

We raise our children from infancy to reflect the values commonly held in our society. But what will these children need as the new century progresses? They will need to

• be always ready to try something new in a world in which the only constant is change, and a premium will be placed on creating new ideas and thinking outside the box;
• be flexible and comfortable with complicated decisions in an increasingly complex society;
• be able to get along with fellow citizens more diverse than ever in ethnicity and culture;
• be very competent with language; and if their families are immigrants, children will need to be as competent in English as in their family's language of origin;
• believe they can make things happen—that they can make a difference in their own lives and the lives of those around them;
• be comfortable speaking out, negotiating, substituting words and logic for violence in persuading others;
• have a profound sense of the importance of equal opportunity for all our citizens and of the dignity and rights of each individual; and
• be gifted parents, maintaining and strengthening the role of family in

American life, working well with services designed to help and support families.

As we know, education begins at birth. Therefore when young children start to learn about differences or express their feelings or have lots of "talk" with a caring adult down on the floor with them; when they are given a chance to move freely, play with toys of their own choosing, manipulating them in ways they choose and trying new ways; when they see their parents valued by their teachers, they are beginning the long journey of becoming adults prepared to do well in the future in the United States. They are being helped to espouse the common values of a diverse nation.

So what's the problem?

How then can there be a problem if we naturally arrange the care of young children in groups in ways that are distinctive to American culture? Why should we not simply continue what we are doing? There seem to be *two* problems.

The first is that "our own" culture includes *many* cultures within it, and not all of us agree about what quality infant/toddler child care should look like. This important problem is being discussed in many places, but is not the subject of *this* article.

Ironically, the second problem comes partly from the very realization—new to many—of the importance of the earliest years, zero to three. (The threat may also be related to the present emphasis on test scores and measurable performance in schools.) Child care programs are now seen by policymakers and the public in general not merely as babysitting for infants and toddlers while their parents work.

Early Head Start, Even Start, state level early intervention programs, and a greatly expanded number of child care programs are trying to provide meaningful learning experiences for children not yet even two years old. This is wonderful when relationships are good, the atmo-

sphere is homelike, not instructional, and the activities are age appropriate. But I also see and read curricula with lesson plans, measurable goals, and suggested teacher-led group activities to achieve them, which are being developed at a great rate. One extreme illustration of the problem that came across my desk recently was part of a center's daily schedule for its toddlers:

> 10:00 a.m.   *Math and science*
> 10:30 a.m.   *Diapering*

This distressing move toward pushing lessons on small children is not limited to early childhood programs. New parents are presently bombarded with "smart baby" products, from flash cards to videos teaching the baby to read.

Greatly magnifying this problem is the lack of staff well trained to work with the infant/toddler age group. The demand has burgeoned too fast for the supply, given the small amount of money we devote to the training and pay of our children's earliest teachers. The problem is exacerbated by the low salaries earned by teachers and caregivers of this age group, resulting in turnover rates close to 50% a year and the need to train an entirely new group of teachers.

As a result, I see too many teachers and providers from all walks of life cling to written curricula with lesson plans and lots of group activities. This can be a particular problem with teachers who have taught older children. In part they are urged on by parents, newly sensitized to the importance of stimulation in the early years, who want to know what their babies are learning.

Well-trained or experienced teachers of infants and toddlers or unusually gifted novices can answer parents in general terms. They will know what developmental tasks lie ahead of the children in their care and what kinds of play activities and experiences allow children to address them. (For infants and toddlers, of course, play *is* work.) Over a period of weeks and months, skilled providers see that their children have these experiences but at their own pace, and when they are interested in them (never "We teach colors Monday, shapes Tuesday, Mozart Wednesday"). Skilled, well-trained teachers and providers have a lot of experience in observation and consider ongoing observation essential in making available toys and tasks appropriate for children (see "Curriculum in Head Start" 2000).

Conclusion

The United States is one of the few nations that has invented itself. That invention is based not so much on the history and culture of its people—though the histories of its *peoples* is an important part of it—but rather on a set of ideas as to what people can and should become. As we have seen, this process begins very early, but it's now in danger.

It is distressing in this era of budget surplus that national policymakers argue simply about spending more on Social Security or Medicare or providing further tax relief. Is it too much to ask that they invest in adequate training and pay for those helping to raise our youngest children for life in this land in this new century?

References

Baldwin, J. 1961. The discovery of what it means to be an American. *Nobody knows my name: More notes of a native son.* New York: Dial.

Bredekamp, S., & C. Copple, eds. 1997. *Developmentally appropriate practice in early childhood programs.* Rev. ed. Washington, DC: NAEYC.

Bryant, D.M., & M.A. Graham, eds. 1993. *Implementing early intervention: From research to effective practice.* New York: Guilford.

Curriculum in Head Start. 2000. *Head Start Bulletin* 67 (March).

Discoveries of infancy: Cognitive development and learning. 1992. West Ed, Program for Infant/Toddler Caregivers (PITC). Videocassette. (Available from California Department of Education, Sacramento: 800-995-4099).

Greenspan, S., & N.T. Greenspan. 1989. *The essential partnership: How parents and children can meet the emotional challenges of infancy and childhood,* 19–62. New York: Viking Penguin.

Hansen, K.A., & R.K. Kaufmann. 1997. Families and caregivers together supporting infants and toddlers. In *Creating child-centered programs for infants and toddlers,* ed. E.S. Szanton, 135–58. Washington, DC: Children's Resources International.

Hansen, K.A., R.K. Kaufmann, & S. Saifer. 1996. *Education and the culture of democracy: Early childhood practice.* Washington, DC: Children's Resources International.

Lally, J.R. 1995. The impact of child care policies and practices on infant/toddler identity formation. *Young Children* 51 (1): 58–67.

Lally, J.R., A. Griffin, E. Fenichel, M.M. Segal, E.S. Szanton, & B. Weissbourd. 1995. *Caring for infants and toddlers in groups: Developmentally appropriate practice.* Washington, DC: ZERO TO THREE/The National Center or Infants, Toddlers and Families.

LeVine, R.A., S. Dixon, S. LeVine, A. Richman, P.H. Leiderman, C.H. Keefer, & T.B. Brazelton. 1996. *Child care and culture: Lessons from Africa.* Reprint, New York: Cambridge University Press.

Lewis, C.C. 1995. *Educating hearts and minds: Reflections on Japanese preschool and elementary education.* New York: Cambridge University Press.

Lewis, M., D.S. Ramsay, & K. Kawakami. 1993. Differences between Japanese infants and Caucasian American infants in behavioral and cortisol response to inoculation. *Child Development* 64: 1722–31.

Maccoby, E.E., & C.N. Jacklin. 1974. *The psychology of sex differences,* 303–48. Stanford, CA: Stanford University Press.

O'Brien, M. 1997. *Inclusive child care for infants and toddlers: Meeting individual and special needs.* Baltimore, MD: Brookes.

Tocqueville, A. de. [1835] 1946. *Democracy in America.* Ed. by J.P. Mayer and trans. by G. Lawrence. Reprint, New York: Knopf.

Eleanor Stokes Szanton, Ph.D., is president of Consulting for Infants and Toddlers and lecturer at Johns Hopkins School of Public Health. She was executive director of ZERO TO THREE: National Center for Infants, Toddlers and Families from 1979 to 1993 and is coauthor of Part 3 of Developmentally Appropriate Practice in Early Childhood Programs, *revised edition.*

---

10 Signs of a Great Preschool

Is your child learning or just playing? Here's what makes for an excellent early education.

What an adventure awaits your little one as he heads off to preschool—new friends, new experiences, and new kinds of fun. Though you certainly want your child to enjoy himself, he'll also be practicing important skills that will prepare him for kindergarten and beyond.

"Your 3- or 4-year-old will learn the fundamental building blocks of reading, writing, math, and science, as well as how to interact with teachers and classmates," says Barbara Willer, Ph.D., deputy executive director of the National Association for the Education of Young Children (NAEYC), in Washington, D.C. "However," she says, "the overarching goal of any preschool should be to help a child feel good about himself as a learner and to feel comfortable in a school-like setting."

Chances are you chose your child's school carefully and can rest assured that he's in good hands. However, as you look around the classroom, here's what you should see.

By Irene Daria-Wiener

1 The Right Student-Teacher Ratio

There should be one teacher for every seven to ten students and no more than 20 children per classroom, according to the NAEYC. State laws vary, however, and some permit even higher ratios. Choosing a school that follows the NAEYC guidelines will ensure that your child receives enough attention and that her teachers will get to know her as an individual.

2 Daily Circle Time

During this group meeting, children practice important social skills, such as taking turns, listening to each other, and sitting still. They'll also hone their language skills by listening to stories and singing songs. In fact, singing is very important in pre-

school. "As kids get older, they can link song words to written words, and that encourages literacy," Dr. Willer says. Songs also help children recognize rhythms and count beats, which enhances their understanding of math.

3 A Language-Rich Environment

Children should be read to every day. The classroom should have plenty of books available, as well as words posted all over the walls: signs labeling objects, weather charts, and posters describing the children's activities. Even preschoolers' artwork can be used to promote literacy; teachers should write the children's dictated descriptions ("Here is my brown dog.") on the bottom of their pictures.

4 An Art Center

This should be stocked with easels, chunky paintbrushes, and other materials, such as crayons and clay. While art—and getting messy—is certainly fun, it also allows children to express their thoughts in a way they might not yet be able to in words. In addition, art helps kids develop fine motor control and a basic understanding of science concepts, such as seeing what happens when colors are mixed and how different media create varying textures. It also gives children a sense of how things change as time passes—paint dries and clay hardens.

5 A Block Corner

Building with large blocks has been shown to help children develop crucial spatial and problem-solving skills. For example, your preschooler will learn that two of the small square blocks equal one of the longer rectangular blocks—a fundamental principle of geometry. Boys tend to gravitate to the block corner more than girls do. To help interest girls, some teachers have found it helpful to place dollhouse furniture in the block corner, because girls like to play house with the buildings that they create.

6 Rotating Chores

Besides developing a sense of responsibility and accomplishment, many chores your child will be asked to help out with in preschool foster math basics. For instance, handing out cups, paper plates, or napkins to each child at snack time introduces the key math concept of one-to-one correspondence.

7 Manipulatives

These items build the fine motor skills that are necessary for writing. In addition, puzzles strengthen spatial skills; sorting and counting buttons or beads help develop early math skills; and Peg-Boards and stringing beads require hand-eye coordination, which is also an important part of learning how to write.

8 A Water Table and a Sand Table

Not only are both of these materials fun, but children can explore so much with them—space, size, weight, force, pressure,

terrific teachers

Of course, no matter how good a school is, your child's experience there will depend on whether he has an engaging and energetic teacher. According to Barbara Willer, Ph.D., deputy executive director of the National Association for the Education of Young Children, teachers should:

• Have a bachelor's degree or a formal credential in early-childhood education. "The research is very clear that a teacher with a degree makes a big difference in the quality of the program," Dr. Willer says.
• Come over and kneel down to talk to the children at their eye level and not call to them from across the classroom.
• Greet your child by name and with a smile each morning.
• Structure the daily curriculum around the children's interests and questions and give kids freedom to choose at least some of the activities in which they participate.
• Keep parents informed of the day's activities and of any issues that their child may be having.

and volume, says Lilian Katz, Ph.D., codirector of the ERIC Clearinghouse on Elementary and Early Childhood Education at the University of Illinois at Urbana-Champaign. "Of course, 3- and 4-year-olds will

understand these concepts only on a very rudimentary level, but when they're older, they'll be able to build on their preschool experience," Dr. Katz says.

9 Physical Activity Every Day

Your child's class will probably go to the playground when the weather is nice. But the school should also have equipment (mats, climbing apparatus, tricyles, or other riding toys) and space for the kids to play actively indoors. "Three- and 4-year-olds are still developing their coordination, and need a chance to practice their basic physical skills," Dr. Katz says.

10 New Materials Introduced Frequently

Some classrooms have an official "discovery table" for displaying items such as autumn leaves or beach glass. "Bringing in new items for the children to explore leads to discussion as well as longer-term projects," Dr. Katz says. For example, an assortment of leaves may prompt a discussion of different types of trees and plants and then inspire the class to plant seeds to see how plants grow, as well as gain an appreciation for the living world around them. "Kids need the chance to wrap their mind around a topic in depth," says Dr. Katz, "and to know that there's something they can come back to and explore the next day."

From *Parents*, September 2001, pp. 191-192. © 2001 by Gruner & Jahr USA Publishing. Reprinted by permission.

WHO CARES FOR KIDS?

BY SHERYL FRAGIN

As a working mother, you know plenty about the high value of good child care. There's simply nothing as important to the quality of our lives as knowing that while we're on the job, our children are safe and happy, loved, and learning. That's why each year since 1993, *Working Mother* has presented an annual survey of what states are doing to improve and expand their child-care programs. Our landmark study of the cost and quality of care, updated this month, assesses the year's accomplishments for each of the 50 states, focusing on the creation and expansion of prekindergarten programs, safety issues, lower child-to-adult ratios, inspections, and quality of care. This year's study found little progress: The vast majority of states continue to provide care that is mediocre, at best—despite a booming economy and initial disbursements of money from the national tobacco settlement (some of which is being used to improve child-care services). This year's *Working Mother* survey found that only half of all states require training in child development for caregivers, even though research has demonstrated that taking such courses tends to make caregivers more sensitive and responsive to children's needs. The *Working Mother* survey also found that more than half of the states received a poor or mediocre ranking in terms of their ratio of children to adults.

But our research also shows that a handful of innovative states are figuring out new ways to make a real difference in children's lives. These may not be the states that spend the most money, or even those with the most stringent legal requirements; in fact, some of these states fall woefully short in those areas. What makes these innovators so important is that they are making real progress in solving problems endemic to the industry—particularly the scourge of high caregiver turnover, now running an average of 30 to 40 percent nationwide.

"Despite some problems, such as poor licensing standards, waiting lists, or inadequate health coverage, some states are really working to transform early care to ensure that all children are ready for school," says Faith Wohl, president of the Child Care Action Campaign, an advocacy group in New York City. "These states realize that delays in language and motor skills, as well as other problems, can be spotted early and fixed in high-quality child care."

No other state has been as inventive in several areas as North Carolina, which has lowered its staff turnover by 11 percent, from 42 to 31 percent. The state's ten-year-old TEACH Early Childhood Project helps finance classes, books, and transportation for caregivers studying child development and early education, bringing new professionalism to the field and making teachers feel more invested in their careers. Caregivers who complete the work receive a bonus or salary increase. A companion program, The Childcare WAGE$ Project, also rewards their commitment by offering salary bonuses based on their level of education. To date, 15 states have started their own versions of TEACH (and others are in the planning stages), while several are trying variations of the WAGE$ program.

Other encouraging news among the most innovative states: a shift in the general approach that looks at the whole range of a child's needs, rather than just spot-fixing problems. California's programs, for instance, try to address questions about the child's life outside the realm of the care center. Is the child getting a balanced diet? Does the child have transportation? Have the child's eyes been checked?

"You can't separate cognitive learning from health," says Gwen Morgan, a faculty member at Boston-based Wheelock College, which has conducted a child-care licensing study since 1986. "The brain is a physical organ. The food children eat, the sleep they get, the conditions in their family—all of it will affect their development in very long-term ways. We now know that you can't set up a narrow program that's separate from a child's family and culture and have a positive effect on the child."

All our innovators are creating strong partnerships with the business community, public schools, and churches in an effort to devise new solutions. Child care routinely ranks as one of the most pressing family needs among parents with young children, and it is likely to remain so until all states begin to think this creatively to find solutions for quality child care.

> **"CHILD CARE IS NOT JUST A PLACE TO PARK KIDS. CHILD CARE IS EDUCATION. EVERY FAMILY DESERVES A HIGH-QUALITY PROGRAM."**

"All kids need early education—and practically all families need child care," says Anne Mitchell, president of Early Childhood Policy Research, a consulting firm based in upstate New York. "Child care is not just a place to park kids. Child care is education. We have to think about child care more as we think about college; every family deserves a high-quality program, and we have to help families to get there."

KEY TO RATINGS

QUALITY
To evaluate each state, we looked at five key factors identified by researchers as crucial measures of quality care.

ACCREDITED CENTERS
Indicates how many child-care centers have been accredited by the National Association for the Education of Young Children (NAEYC), the nation's preeminent organization of early childhood educators. To gain accreditation, centers must meet standards in teacher training, adult supervision, and curriculum.

ACCREDITED FAMILY CHILD CARE (FCC)
Indicates how many family child-care providers meet standards set by the National Association for Family Child Care (NAFCC). Caregivers accredited by NAFCC must pass muster in measures of safety, health, and age-appropriate activities.

CHILD-TO-ADULT RATIOS
We report the maximum number of children one adult can care for, age by age. For comparison, experts recommend the following:

3 to 4 infants
4 to 6 toddlers
7 to 10 preschoolers

SOURCE: NAEYC.

GROUP SIZE
Studies show kids do better in smaller groups.
Good: States that meet the ideal (see NAEYC chart, below) in at least two age categories.
Poor: States that were ranked "Bad" in at least two categories.
Mediocre: All others.
None: The state does not regulate the maximum number of children in a group.

	Ideal	Good	Bad
Infants	8 or less	9 or 10	11 or more
Toddlers	12 or less	13 or 14	15 or more
Pre-K	20 or less	21 or 22	23 or more

SOURCE: WHEELOCK COLLEGE AND NAEYC.

CAREGIVER TRAINING
Trained caregivers are more responsive to children. We report the amount of preservice training required for teachers at child-care centers and for caregivers at family child-care homes—in credits (C) or hours (H). CDA is a Child Development Associate Credential. CCP is a Certified Childcare Professional Credential (similar to a CDA).
N/L: The state does not license family child-care homes.

SOURCE: WHEELOCK COLLEGE.

CAREGIVER PAY
Compensation is a predictor of quality care; low pay contributes to staff turnover. A plus sign (+) indicates that the state pays higher rates to accredited centers.

SOURCE: WHEELOCK COLLEGE.

SAFETY
ADULT SUPERVISION
Limiting the number of children one adult may care for helps to keep kids safe.
Good: States that meet the ideal in at least two age categories.
Poor: States that were ranked "Bad" in at least two categories.
Mediocre: All others.

	Ideal	Good	Bad
Infants	4 or less	5	6 or more
Toddlers	5 or less	6 to 8	9 or more
Pre-K	8 or less	9 to 11	12 or more

SOURCE: WHEELOCK COLLEGE AND CHILDREN'S FOUNDATION

SIZE AT WHICH FAMILY CHILD CARE IS REGULATED
The number indicates how many children a caregiver may take into a private home before she is required to be registered or licensed. A plus sign (+) indicates that there are exceptions: For instance, a provider may be able to take in additional children if they are related to her or if they are not receiving state subsidies. An asterisk (*) indicates that the provider is allowed to take in children from only one unrelated family before being regulated.
None: The state regulates all FCC homes.

SOURCE: CHILDREN'S FOUNDATION.

PLAYGROUND SAFETY
A plus sign (+) indicates that the state has safety requirements for playgrounds at child-care centers. Two plus signs (++) indicate that those requirements are based on the U.S. Consumer Product Safety Commission guidelines. A minus sign (–) indicates that the state has no playground safety requirements. N/A means no information available.

SOURCE: CHILDREN'S FOUNDATION.

ASBESTOS
A plus sign (+) indicates that the state requires child-care centers and FCC homes to test for asbestos, radon, lead, etc., as a condition of being licensed. Two plus signs (++) indicate that the state provides financial assistance for some or all of these tests. A minus sign (–) indicates that the state does not require any tests.

SOURCE: CHILDREN'S FOUNDATION.

CRIMINAL RECORD CHECKS
Criminal: The state requires licensed child-care centers and family child-care homes to conduct a criminal record check of employees.
Abuse: The state requires centers to check with state officials to see if employees have been found guilty of child abuse or neglect (data which sometimes, but not always, shows up on a criminal record).
Both: The state requires both a criminal record check and a child abuse and neglect check. A plus sign (+) indicates that all adults or anyone working with children must have background checks, not just the providers.

SOURCE: CHILDREN'S FOUNDATION.

INSPECTIONS
This indicates the number of unannounced inspections required by the state at child-care centers and FCC homes.
Complaint: The state requires unannounced visits only upon receiving complaints.
Rare: Such inspections occur less than once every four years.

SOURCE: CHILDREN'S FOUNDATION.

AVAILABILITY
TAX BREAKS
This indicates whether the state provides a child-care tax credit to parents.
None: No child-care tax credit.
N/T: The state has no income tax.
R: The state's child-care tax credit is refundable, making it more accessible for low-income families.
N/R: The state's tax credit is not refundable.

SOURCE: CHILDREN'S DEFENSE FUND.

R&R
Resource and referral agencies help parents find and assess child-care options. A plus sign (+) indicates that the R&R network has funding and staff. Two plus signs (++) indicate that the state significantly improved its R&R networks in the past year. A minus sign (–) indicates that the network operates with volunteer staff. A blank means there is no network at all.

SOURCE: NATIONAL ASSOCIATION OF CHILD CARE RESOURCE AND REFERRAL AGENCIES.

PUBLIC PRE-K
A plus sign (+) indicates that a state has a publicly funded pre-K program. A minus sign (–) indicates that it does not. (Georgia is the only state that has enacted universal pre-K.)

SOURCE: CHILDREN'S DEFENSE FUND.

COMMITMENT
How states improved child care since 1999.

WHO CARES FOR KIDS?

STATE	QUALITY – Accredited Centers	Accredited FCC	Ratios Infants	Toddlers	Pre-K	Group Size	Training Centers	Training FCC	Pay	SAFETY – Adult Supervision	Regulated FCC	Playground	Asbestos Centers	Asbestos FCC	Criminal Record Checks Centers	FCC	AVAILABILITY – Inspections Centers	Inspections FCC	Tax Breaks	R&R	Public Pre-K
Alabama	50	11	6	8	12	Good	0	0		Poor	None	+	-	-	Criminal+	Criminal+	1/yr	1/yr	None	-	+
Alaska	18	6	5	6	10	None	0	0		Mediocre	4+	+	-	-	Both+	Both+	Varies	1/2yr	N/T	-	+
Arizona	199	2	5	6	13	None	0	0		Mediocre	4+	+	+	-	Criminal+	Criminal+	1/yr	2/yr	None	-	+
Arkansas	58	23	6	9	12	None	0	N/L		Poor	5	+	-	-	Both+	Both+	2-4/yr	3/yr		R	+
California	572	88	4	6	12	Poor	CDA	0		Mediocre	*	+	-	-	Both+	Both+	1/yr	1/3yr	None	+	+
Colorado	149	3	5	5	10	Good	0	12H	+	Mediocre	2+	++	-	-	Both+	Both+	1/3yr	Varies	N/R	+	+
Connecti-cut	289	11	4	4	10	Good	0	0		Good	None	+	+	-	Both+	Both+	Varies	1/3yr	None	+	+
Delaware	21	11	4	7	12	None	60H	15H		Mediocre	None	+	+	-	Both	Both+	Com-plaint	1/yr	N/R	+	+
DC	50	5	4	4	8	Good	CDA	0	+	Good	None	++	+	+	Criminal+	Criminal+	1/yr	Varies	N/R	*	+
Florida	571	162	4	6	15	None	30H	3H	+	Mediocre	*	+	-	N/A	Criminal+	Criminal+	2/yr	2/yr	N/T	+	+
Georgia	170	8	6	8	15	Poor	10H	0		Poor	2	++	-	-	Criminal+	Criminal+	Varies	Rare	None	-	+
Hawaii	70	3	4	6	12	Good	CDA	0		Mediocre	2	-	-	-	Both+	Both+	Com-plaint	Varies	R	+	+
Idaho	20	2	6	6	12	None	0	N/L		Poor	6	-	-	-	Both	Criminal+	None	None	N/R	-	
Illinois	392	79	4	5	10	Poor	CDA or CCP	0		Good	3	++	N/A	+	Both+	Both+	1/yr	1/yr	None	+	+
Indiana	109	14	4	5	10	Good	0	N/L		Good	5	++	-	-	Criminal+	Both+	3/yr	Varies	None	+	+
Iowa	159	2	4	4	8	None	0	N/L		Good	6	N/A	+	-	Both+	Both+	1/yr	Rare	R	+	+
Kansas	56	4	3	5	12	Medio-cre	CDA	0		Good	None	++	-	-	Both+	Both+	1/yr	Com-plaint	N/R	+	+
Kentucky	146	7	5	6	12	Medio-cre	0	6H	+	Mediocre	3	+	-	-	Criminal+	Criminal+	1/yr	1/yr	N/R	++	+
Louisiana	54	0	6	8	14	Poor	0	N/L		Poor	6+	-	N/A	-	Criminal+	Criminal+	Varies	None	N/R	-	+
Maine	14	0	4	5	10	Poor	0	6H		Good	2	+	++	++	Criminal+	Both+	Varies	1/yr	N/R	-	+

Alabama — COMMITMENT Allocated $50 million from tobacco settlement for children, some of which will be for child care. Voters rejected a state lottery funding education, including a universal pre-K program.

Alaska — COMMITMENT Reduced state funding for child care, but increased the amount of federal money spent on child care for low-income families. Increased availability of full-day, year-round Head Start.

Arizona — COMMITMENT Invested in quality improvement for infant/toddler care, utilizing nationally recognized criteria for provider training. Changed and codified what criminal offenses bar people from working in child care.

Arkansas — COMMITMENT Increased funding for provider-training scholarships, helped local groups increase nontraditional care (odd hours, special needs, etc.), implemented new playground licensing standards.

California — COMMITMENT Increased state funding for child care by $133 million. Reduced child-care assistance for welfare-to-work families, but new budget may extend funding.

Colorado — COMMITMENT Expanded the number of pre-K slots by 250, approved $22 million in child-care tax credits, and earmarked $2.1 million for improved child care. Established a statewide Child Care Commission.

Connecticut — COMMITMENT Expanded comprehensive training program for early caregivers, added nearly 300 spaces for infants and toddlers, and implemented requirement for all children to be immunized against chicken pox.

Delaware — COMMITMENT Increased state funding for low-income children in early childhood and other child care. Developed training for infant and toddler care.

DC — COMMITMENT Invested $20 million in quality improvements on playgrounds, for caregiver training in first aid and recognizing abuse and neglect, and for expanding Head Start centers to offer full-day, year-round care.

Florida — COMMITMENT Local communities given the chance to develop child-care plans. At one point, Florida ran out of money for the working poor, leaving 42,000 children on waiting lists; state began charging parents for pre-K programs.

Georgia — COMMITMENT Increased funding for state pre-K program. Boosted income tax credits for businesses with on-site day care. Funded new training initiatives on topics like infant care and brain development.

Hawaii — COMMITMENT Made almost no improvements or advances in its weak child-care system over 1999, but did begin funding extended-day Head Start with federal block-grant money.

Idaho — COMMITMENT Raised reimbursement rates for child-care providers caring for low-income children. Allotted $25,000 to begin a TEACH program, training and credentialing child-care providers.

Illinois — COMMITMENT Created a $3 million program to improve wages and retention rate of providers. Increased regular state funding for child care by $126 million, including $10 million to expand full-day Head Start and child care.

Indiana — COMMITMENT Earmarked $82 million over two years for impoverished families. Launched pilot projects to revamp Head Start to better serve new immigrants. Piloting an apprentice program for child-care providers.

Iowa — COMMITMENT Added $5.2 million to "empowerment" program for community early childhood programs. Raised reimbursement rates for providers caring for subsidized kids and added accreditation and equipment grants.

Kansas — COMMITMENT Provided grants to hire infant/toddler specialists in each R&R agency. Implemented increased civil penalties for child-care facilities violations. Implemented Early Head Start (for birth to age 4).

Kentucky — COMMITMENT Raised reimbursement rates for licensed and certified providers of infant and toddler care, and instituted differential rates for special needs care, odd-hours care, etc. Developed 20-year plan for early childhood care.

Louisiana — COMMITMENT Will decrease child/staff ratio by one in each age category by March 2001. Expanded full-day and summer Head Start in some parts of the state. State legislature created a child-care task force.

Maine — COMMITMENT Doubled state investment to $11 million over two years (using money from the tobacco settlement), including $2 million to expand full-day, year-round Head Start. Increased odd-hours and infant care.

For an explanation of these abbreviations, see "Key to Ratings."

STATE	QUALITY Accredited		Child-to-Adult Ratios			Group Size	Training		Pay	SAFETY Adult Super-vision	Regu-lated FCC	Play-ground	Asbestos		Criminal Record Checks		AVAILABILITY Inspections		Tax Breaks	R&R	Public Pre-K
	Centers	FCC	Infants	Toddlers	Pre-K		Centers	FCC					Centers	FCC	Centers	FCC	Centers	FCC			
Maryland	98	0	3	3	10	Good	90H	9H		Good	None	-	+	-	Both	Both+	Complaint	1/2yr	N/R	+	+
Massachusetts	701	40	3	4	10	Good	3C	0		Good	None	++	+	-	Criminal+	Criminal+	1/yr	Varies	N/R	-	+
Michigan	115	17	4	4	10	None	0	0		Good	+*	++	-	-	Both	Both+	Complaint	Complaint	None	+	+
Minnesota	172	26	4	7	10	Good	CDA	6H	+	Mediocre	None	++	-	+	Both+	Both+	Varies	Varies	R	+	+
Mississippi	46	0	5	9	14	Good	0	N/L	+	Poor	5	++	-	-	Both+	Both+	2/yr	2/yr	None	-	
Missouri	77	22	4	4	10	Good	0	0	+	Good	4	++	-	-	Both+	Both+	3/yr	2/yr	None	+	+
Montana	8	4	4	4	8	None	8H	0		Good	2	+	-	+	Both+	Both+	1/yr	Rare	N/R	+	+
Nebraska	54	4	4	6	10	None	0	12H	+	Mediocre	3	+	-	++	Abuse+	Abuse+	1-2/yr	1/yr	R	-	+
Nevada	11	5	6	8	13	None	3H	3H		Poor	4	++	-	-	Both+	Both+	2/yr	2/yr	R	-	
New Hampshire	42	0	4	5	8	Poor	Some	0		Good	3	+	+	-	Both+	Both+	1/3yr	1/3yr	N/T	-	+
New Jersey	157	0	4	7	10	Poor	CCP	N/L	+	Mediocre	5	++	+	-	Abuse+	-	Varies	1/yr	None	-	+
New Mexico	58	3	6	6	12	None	0	0		Poor	4	+	-	-	Criminal+	Criminal+	Varies	1/yr	R	+	
New York	309	49	4	5	7	Good	Some	0		Good	2	-	-		Abuse+	Abuse+	Varies	Rare	R	+	+
North Carolina	148	75	5	6	15	Mediocre	0	0	+	Mediocre	2	++	-	-	Both	Criminal+	Complaint	Varies	N/R	+	+
North Dakota	5	3	4	4	7	Good	0	0		Good	5+	N/A	+	-	Abuse+	Abuse+	Varies	1/yr	None	+	-
Ohio	254	8	5	7	12	Poor	0	N/L	+	Mediocre	6+	++	-	-	Criminal+	Criminal+	1/yr	1/yr	N/R	+	+
Oklahoma	56	4	4	6	12	Good	0	0	+	Mediocre	None	++	-	-	Criminal	Both+	3/yr	3/yr	N/R	+	+
Oregon	40	2	4	4	10	Good	0	0		Good	3	+	-	-	Both+	Both+	Varies	Complaint	N/R	+	+
Pennsylvania	203	53	4	5	6	Good	0	4H		Good	3	+	-	-	Both	Both	Varies	None	None		+
Rhode Island	50	11	4	6	9	Good	BA	0		Mediocre	3	+	++	-	Both	Criminal+	2/yr	Complaint	None	*	+
South Carolina	81	0	6	6	13	None	0	0	+	Poor	None	+	+	+	Both+	Both+	Varies	None	N/R	-	+

Maryland — COMMITMENT Implemented a new child-care tax credit. Increased funding for infant/toddler-care training and funded four outreach programs for informal caregivers. Allocated funds to expand Head Start.

Massachusetts — COMMITMENT Raised maximum tax deduction for child care. Expanded off-site learning courses for providers of infant/toddler care and funded new infant/toddler spots in child-care centers.

Michigan — COMMITMENT Increased funding for state pre-K program by $5 million and earmarked funds for infant and toddler slots in child-care centers. Now offering providers $150 incentives for achieving accreditation or credentials.

Minnesota — COMMITMENT Slashed its investment in quality activities by 50 percent. Restored regulations on family child-care providers: can only care for their own children and the children of one unrelated family without being regulated.

Mississippi — COMMITMENT Added 22 full-time staff to the state licensing division for training and inspection. Implemented scholarship program at community colleges that offer child-care technology associate degrees.

Missouri — COMMITMENT Requires criminal background checks for all centers and child abuse checks for all providers paid with state or federal funds. Began expanding Early Head Start.

Montana — COMMITMENT Gave grants to five colleges to help provide CDA training and associates' degrees in early childhood development. Coursework is available statewide.

Nebraska — COMMITMENT Added tuition and transportation reimbursement for providers working with subsidized kids. Gave funding to expand the Head Start day and for infant-and child-care training and quality initiatives.

Nevada — COMMITMENT Increased funding for quality initiatives from $717,000 to $2.8 million. Established child-care apprenticeship program; gives scholarships to caregivers and bonuses to centers that allow their staff to participate.

New Hampshire — COMMITMENT Introduced graduate courses for center directors and child-care workers and a credentialing program for providers. Awarded grants to help providers expand infant and toddler capacity.

New Jersey — COMMITMENT Used $100 million in federal welfare funds to fund the child-care voucher program for low-income families. Allocated $6 million annually to fund full-day, year-round Head Start.

New Mexico — COMMITMENT Providers achieving a higher level of quality in a piloted state initiative receive additional reimbursement. Expanded Head Start funds by $1 million.

New York — COMMITMENT Increased child-care funding by 82%. Developing odd-hours care for parents who work evenings and weekends. Provided scholarships for providers seeking credentials. Added $33 million to universal pre-K funding.

North Carolina — COMMITMENT Enacted "NC Cares" initiative to offer wage supplements and health benefits to some child-care providers. Included family child-care homes in licensing system. Added $58 million to Smart Start early childhood initiative.

North Dakota — COMMITMENT Increased rates for everyone except approved relatives, whose rates were reduced in an effort to encourage them to move ahead professionally and become, at minimum, certified providers.

Ohio — COMMITMENT Passed legislation capping low-income families' child-care copayment at 10 percent of their income. Increased Head Start and public pre-K funding.

Oklahoma — COMMITMENT Doubled state pre-K program funds. Upped reimbursement for providers working with low-income families. Improved scholarship program for provider training. Allocated $2.7 million for First Start program.

Oregon — COMMITMENT Raised reimbursement rate for some trained providers. Added $1.6 million for special needs kids. Imposed new training standards for family child-care providers. Increased Head Start and pre-K funding by $2.2 million.

Pennsylvania — COMMITMENT Launched a $1.6 million CyberStart initiative to wire child-care centers. Added $9 million for quality initiatives like infant/toddler care and special needs.

Rhode Island — COMMITMENT Allocated $1.3 million to support start-ups and innovative child-care programs. Subsidized health insurance of center-based providers working with low-income kids. Set aside funds to expand odd-hours care.

South Carolina — COMMITMENT Approved $50 million for communities to enhance children's readiness for school and encourage counties to expand school-readiness programs. Added salary bonus program for providers who gain credentials.

For an explanation of these abbreviations, see "Key to Ratings."

STATE	QUALITY							SAFETY								AVAILABILITY				
	Accredited		Child-to-Adult Ratios			Group Size	Training		Pay	Adult Super-vision	Regu-lated FCC	Play-ground	Asbestos		Criminal Record Checks		Inspections		Tax Breaks	R&R	Public Pre-K
	Centers	FCC	Infants	Toddlers	Pre-K		Centers	FCC					Centers	FCC	Centers	FCC	Centers	FCC			
South Da-kota	4	0	5	5	10	Poor	0	N/L		Mediocre	12+	-	-	-	Abuse+	Abuse+	Com-plaint	1/2yr	N/T		-
COMMITMENT Increased funding for quality initiatives to $2.2. million, including provider training. Increased rates for providers working with children from birth to age 3. Helped expand Head Start full-day care.																					
Tennessee	151	6	5	7	10	Medio-cre	0	0		Mediocre	4	++	-	-	Both+	Both+	6/yr	6/yr	N/T		+
COMMITMENT New Laws require audits of certain subsidized centers, higher training stanIncreased annual unannounced inspection visits to all centers.dards for providers, and criminal background checks for new center employees.																					
Texas	401	64	4	9	17	Poor	8H	0		Poor	3	+	-	-	Both	Both+	1/yr	1/3yr	N/T	++	+
COMMITMENT Stipends of up to $1,000 approved for child-care workers. Added shaken baby syndrome training requirement for providers caring for kids under 2. Enacted preliteracy initiative with $2 million in grants.																					
Utah	20	0	4	4	12	Good	0	0	+	Good	4	++	-	-	Both+	Both+	1/yr	1-2/yr	None	+	-
COMMITMENT Now offering financial rewards for completing various levels of provider training and credentials. Allocated funds for three new Early Head Start programs and for seven Head Start/child-care partnerships.																					
Vermont	46	1	4	4	10	Good	CDA or CCP	0	+	Good	+	+	+	-	Both+	Both+	2/yr	Com-plaint	None	+	+
COMMITMENT Increased reimbursement rates by 13% and added a 15% quality bonus for accredited programs that accept subsidized families. Provided $75,000 for training and for work-ing with disabled kids.																					
Virginia	191	3	4	5	10	None	0	N/L		Good	5+	+	-	-	Both	Both+	1/yr	1/yr	N/R	-	+
COMMITMENT Added $56 million in subsidies for low-income families. Worked with child-care advocates to develop training through state community colleges for providers of care for school-age children.																					
Washing-ton	122	38	4	7	10	Good	20H	20H		Mediocre	None	+	-	-	Both+	Both+	Com-plaint	1/1.5yr	N/T	+	+
COMMITMENT Dedicated $2 million to quality enhancement. Added more than $4 million for wage supplements and training for providers. Increased training requirements for licensed child-care staff.																					
West Vir-ginia	29	2	4	4	10	None	0	0	+	Good	3+	-	N/A	-	Both+	Both+	1/yr	None	None		+
COMMITMENT Number one among states in subsidizing child care for low-income families. Offered $10,000 grant to start-up programs focusing on infant/toddler care and special needs children. Added funding for provider training.																					
Wisconsin	225	5	4	4	10	Good	Some	40H	+	Good	3+	++	-	-	Both+	Both+	1-2/yr	1/yr	None	+	+
COMMITMENT Created state-of-the-art centers in low-income neighborhoods, increased R&R funding by 25%, and slashed copayments so that no family pays more than 12% of their in-come for child care.																					
Wyoming	33	1	5	5	10	None	0	0		Mediocre	2	-	-	-	Both	Both	1/yr	Varies	N/T	+	-
COMMITMENT Allocated funds for infant/toddler training. Providers can be certified for infant care after two days of training. Implementing full-day, year-round Head Start programs.																					

For an explanation of these abbreviations, see "Key to Ratings."

Teaching Principals, Parents, and Colleagues about Developmentally Appropriate Practice

Esther H. Egley and Robert J. Egley

First teacher: What do you think of the new principal?

Second teacher: Well, I don't know much about him.

First teacher: I heard that he is a former high school principal and football coach. And I'm in shock over it. I thought it was against the law now to hire those nonelementary education types for elementary schools. Just when we thought we were on the road to developmentally appropriate classrooms, they go and hire someone who probably doesn't even know what *developmentally appropriate* means. What a nightmare!

Second teacher: What are we going to do?

First teacher: I don't know. He'll probably insist that we bring those desks back into our classrooms. And what if he believes in total silence in the classroom?

Scene one, take one, action!

The new principal enters the room.

Principal: Hello, I'm the new principal.

Teacher: So good to meet you. I'm one of the kindergarten teachers. We were just talking about you. We're so excited to have you as our new principal. We've heard wonderful things about you (*lie, lie, lie…*).

Principal: Well, your classroom sure looks… well, it looks interesting (*lie, lie, lie…*). Tell me, why do you have these tables instead of desks, and why do you have so much stuff all over the room?

Teacher: Well, you know, I try to provide a classroom that is developmentally appropriate. You know… like… well… research supports developmentally appropriate education. Yes, the research says to do this, and, anyway, this is the way I was taught to teach in college.

Cut, cut, cut...

Yes, getting a new principal who is not an early childhood educator could be an early childhood teacher's worst nightmare. It is important to remember, however, that all principals want what is best for the children and the school as a whole, but they also want to be assured that the practices being used in classrooms support learning. Therefore, teachers need to be prepared professionally at all times, but especially in situations when the administrator does not have an early childhood/elementary education background or knowledge of the field's most recent research.

In support of their practices and teaching strategies, teachers need to be prepared to share key points from current early childhood research. This means doing their homework and being informed of basic findings in the field. They can supply this information to their administrator (and others) through handouts, brochures, and posters and signs displayed in the classroom. For example, a brief synopsis of research-based teaching strategies could be formulated into a one-page flyer. Display copies in a pocket holder stapled to the wall beside the classroom door and post a sign—Take One.

By keeping in their desk several files of articles, position papers, and summaries that support the practices going on in their classrooms, teachers are ready to share information whenever it is needed. These resources are valuable persuasive tools to use with administrators, parents, teachers, media reporters, and the public at large.

When asked about research in the early childhood field, teachers can learn to speak with confidence even if there are issues with opposing views. Rather than saying, "Well, you know, there are many studies, but I can't think of any of them right now," a prepared teacher would say, "Yes, I have several copies of articles that I would be pleased to share with you concerning what research has to say about developmentally appropriate practices. Thanks for asking." Teachers need to be poised and must be ready to support their beliefs with knowledge and research.

Scene one, take two, action!

Principal: What research are you talking about? I believe in giving our children the best education we possibly can, but I want to be sure we're not just running after every new idea that comes along. So, what research are you referring to?

Teacher: I'm glad you asked, and I agree with you. We need to educate ourselves on what research says about early childhood education. These ideas are not new. They've been around for more than a hundred years and are supported now by our state department of education and many early childhood associations that I belong to such as MECA (Mississippi Early Childhood Association), SECA (Southern Early Childhood Association), and NAEYC.

As a matter of fact, our state department of education provides training for administrators on developmentally appropriate practice. Did you know about this training? Another teacher gave me this information and handout that was distributed at her school. It tells about the training and about developmentally appropriate practice. Here is a copy for you.

That's a take!

Other steps that teachers can take to help demonstrate their professionalism include the following:

1. Develop a telephone directory of professionals who use developmentally appropriate strategies in their schools. Start with a few names, then expand the list as contacts are made. Prepare a neat and readable list. Display it on a bulletin board near your work area, but be sure that others can see it. Make obvious that it is a telephone directory for a Developmentally Appropriate Network.
2. Display on the bulletin board business cards of teachers, speakers, and fellow educators whom you could call for support and assistance.
3. Keep two or more professional education journals on or near your desk to demonstrate that you are interested in best practices, high standards, current research, and educational innovations. If you don't have journals, photocopy articles to keep on your desk, your bulletin board, or the top bookshelf.
4. Place a bookcase near your desk or work area in view of adults visiting your classroom. Exhibit your practice of keeping current by having several pro-

fessional books and manuals that you value out where visitors to your classroom can peruse them.

Scene two, take one, action!

Principal: I think I understand what you're saying, and it sounds like you know what you're talking about. But I'm not sure I understand the purpose of some of the activities going on here. For example, blocks? A sand table? Looks like mostly play to me.

Teacher: Well, I don't know. The children love it. I saw another teacher do it when I was in college.

Cut, cut, cut...

Scene two, take two, action!

Principal: I think I understand what you're saying, and it sounds like you know what you're talking about. But I'm not sure I understand the purpose of some of the activities going on here. For example, blocks? A sand table? Looks like mostly play to me.

Teacher: Yes, I can see what you mean. I have had concerns at times too. But I have attended conferences and read the literature on the subject of play as learning. You are right that just because I offer these centers and place materials out for the children to use doesn't mean my objectives will be met.

But there are two things I want to share with you. My centers have been carefully chosen and with purpose. Let me show you. I have objectives for children's learning in using every center. See, displayed beside each center I have a list of the objectives so that parents and others can read for themselves and understand the purpose in the centers.

Also, I carefully plan the activities for my centers based upon the objectives I am responsible for teaching in this district and state. Let me show you how we have organized the objectives we are required to teach.

That's a take!

Teachers need to keep organized files listing the objectives required by their school districts and states. Being prepared to share this list in an instant with supervisors and parents suggests that you are focused on what you need to accomplish. Being able to demonstrate this focus assures those around you that you know what you are talking about.

As mentioned in "Scene Two, Take Two, Action," teachers need to display for children and adults the objectives for each learning center in the classroom. Having a list of broad goals of the program displayed would also be helpful. Some educators believe that labeling learning centers is misleading, causing some children to think only one activity takes place there. For communicating to visitors, it works well. Labels and displays of objectives identify hands-on areas and emphasize that they have purpose. This means of communicating to parents and administrators is useful when you, the teacher, do not have the time to stop and talk with them.

Scene three, take one, action!

Principal: OK. I hear what you're saying, but I sure don't see how it'll work. Obviously there is not enough space at this sand table for all the children to work at one time. Do you mean to tell me that you don't have all children on the same task at the same time? And, if you don't, why not?

Teacher: What a good question! Again, thanks for asking. The arrangement of my learning centers has to do with knowing that all children aren't on the same levels at the same time. All children have different interests, abilities, rates of learning, and backgrounds. By using learning centers, I am able to allow for these differences.

Principal: I think I know what you mean. In athletics and my experience as a coach, we recognize students as beginners, more skilled, and so forth, and we try to match kids to positions in a sport to which they are best suited. Is that like what you're talking about?

Teacher: Yes, exactly. Coaches don't typically call their methods developmentally appropriate, but in a way they are.

That's a wrap!

One strategy of helping the non-early childhood educator understand developmentally appropriate practice is to use that person's background as an analogy. One example of this is the administrator who was once a coach. But remember that former professional football coach Don Shula suggested, "Everyone's a coach." The coaching scenario is a perfect analogy to use in explaining developmentally appropriate practice. Believing that all of us want what is best for children and recognizing that we each bring different strengths and backgrounds to the classroom will help us learn to work in harmony. Helping administrators, supervisors, other teachers, and parents understand developmentally appropriate practice is an exercise in gaining their respect. As teachers become more professional by being prepared, knowledgeable, organized, and confident, they acquire more support and respect from many of the adults around them, even non-early childhood educators.

For further reading

Burchfield, D. W. 1996. Listen to these principals! Teaching all children: Four developmentally appropriate curricular and instructional strategies in primary-grade classrooms. *Young Children* 52 (1): 4–10.

Dunn, L., & S. Kontos. 1997. Research in Review. What have we learned about developmentally appropriate practice? *Young Children* 52 (5): 4–13.

Gratz, R. R., & P. J. Boulton. 1996. Erikson and early childhood educators: Looking at ourselves and our profession developmentally. *Young Children* 51 (5): 74–78.

Gronlund, G. 1995. Bring the DAP message to kindergarten and primary teachers. *Young Children* 50 (5): 4–13.

Hyson, M. 2000. Growing teachers for a growing profession: NAEYC revises its guidelines for early childhood professional preparation. *Young Children* 55 (3): 60–61.

Neuman, S. G., C. Copple, & S. Bredekamp. 2000. *Learning to read and write: Developmentally appropriate practices for young children.* Washington, DC: NAEYC.

Perlmutter, J. C., & L. Burrell. 1995. Learning through "play" as well as "work" in the primary grades. *Young Children* 50 (5): 14–21.

Perry, G., & M. S. Duru, eds. 2000. *Resources for developmentally appropriate practice: Recommendations from the profession.* Washington, DC: NAEYC.

Vander Wilt, J. L., & V. Monroe. 1988. Successful implementation of developmentally appropriate practice takes time and effort. *Young Children* 53 (4): 17–24.

Wardle, F. 1999. In praise of developmentally appropriate practice. *Young Children* 54 (6): 4–12.

Video Resource

Tools for teaching developmentally appropriate practice—The leading edge in early childhood education. 1998. Staff development videos, in 5–12 minute segments, provide a deeper understanding of the core content of the early childhood knowledge base. Produced by RISE. 180 min. Available from NAEYC.

Esther H. Egley, Ed.D., is a professor and head of the Department of Curriculum and Instruction at Mississippi State University. She taught kindergarten for seven years and has worked throughout the South on early childhood education initiatives.

Robert J. Egley, Ph.D., is an elementary principal in Lowndes County School District and an adjunct instructor at the Mississippi University for Women in Columbus. He previously was a football coach and strength coach at high school, college, and professional levels.

Italian import creates preschools where kids shape agenda

By Craig Savoye
Special to The Christian Science Monitor

WEBSTER GROVES, MO.

It's not unusual for a preschool class to stage an original play. But in most schools, the teacher would make the decision to produce a play, then write the show and direct it, too.

At the College School in this St. Louis suburb, things are a little different. Not only did students in this year's 4- and 5-year-old class come up with the idea to stage a play, the youngsters wrote it. They'll also be acting in it, and one of their own will direct it.

"Basically, I'm in charge of everything," explains director Ryan, interviewed on the set inside his classroom while wearing a costume consisting of a medieval collar, a cowboy vest and a camouflage hat.

Welcome to Reggio Emilia. The city in northern Italy has become a global model, and Mecca, for early childhood education. Following the devastation of World War II, townspeople decided to build preschools for their children that emphasized a new way of teaching and learning.

What came to be known as the Reggio Emilia approach soon spread beyond Italy's borders. It came to America in the early 1990s. One of the first locales to adopt it was St. Louis, where the College School and two other area schools form a Reggio cooperative.

For parents who resist the current push for more testing and a strict emphasis on basics, it's a natural alternative. According to one count by the Educational Resources Information Center at the University of Illinois, there are at least 22 schools in 15 states with fully integrated Reggio Emilia programs, plus many individual teachers who have adopted elements of the approach.

"It's spreading widely across the US in terms of people who are seeking to understand it or attempting to apply the concepts or ideas," says Brenda Fyfe, a professor of education at Webster University here and one of the leading researchers on Reggio Emilia in the United States.

Looking at children differently

Though the approach is meant to be highly dynamic, a number of elements are common to most Reggio programs: emphasis on a stimulating environment, including an atelier largely devoted to art; high level of parental involvement; two teachers per class; group projects as opposed to solitary learning; and documentation. Virtually everything is recorded in writing, on audio or video tape, or with a still camera as a way to review, share with parents, or simply imbue a child's expression with importance.

But the defining element is the image of the child it presupposes. Reggio views children as inherently curious and expressive in multiple ways. The latter capacity is known as the hundred languages of children, a metaphor for the infinite modes through which preschoolers express themselves, such as sculpture, photography and acting.

Ultimately, the normal classroom dynamic is turned on its head—instead of a reading circle and snack time at a certain hour, the approach is one of discovery, cued by the children. "You have to let the children know they have an active voice along with yours, and as soon as children realize they have a responsibility to be forming big ideas, they come up with more than we can ever explore," says Jennifer Strange, co-teacher of the 4- and 5-year-old class at the College School and a veteran of four study trips to Italy.

College School director Jan Philips recalls a group of preschoolers a few years ago becoming enamored of pirates. At first reluctant to turn high-seas scoundrels into a major subject of study, teachers eventually let the theme take root.

The classroom took on the trappings of a pirate's lair. The kids dressed up as pirates, painted pirate scenes, and dictated pirate stories. Parents even helped build the bow of a pirate ship in the school parking lot, complete with a mast and fluttering Jolly Roger—all imagined and designed by the students.

Critics complain that Reggio is too complex to implement. Indeed, it requires an enormous time commitment from teachers, since they design the curriculum as they go. The extra creativity and flexibility that's required may explain, in part, why Reggio is spreading deliberately rather than rapidly—and why it generally finds fertile ground more often in private schools.

Devlin—who taught a normal preschool curriculum for 10 years before getting involved with Reggio—thinks the approach may prevent teacher burnout. "For years, every other year, I did a dinosaur theme until it got to the point where I never wanted to see another dinosaur again," she says.

After Reggio was instituted, the students in her classes selected many themes, including dinosaurs. But they followed the themes several steps beyond checking out a library book: the kids built an enormous dinosaur in the parking lot, applying their own research, measurements and design.

Measuring the results

Because Reggio is still relatively new in the US, its long-term impact on children is difficult to gauge. Anecdotally, the College School had six National Merit Scholars last year out of a graduating eighth-grade class of 20, far ahead of the nation-wide average of less than 1 percent. But the sample is so small—and the College School's own innovative techniques begin in kindergarten after preschool Reggio ends—that trying to isolate and measure a long-term effect is difficult at best.

The positive results are not lost on parents, even as they closely monitor the effort. "It's not a cutesy kind of preschool," says Skyler Harmann, a College School parent who currently has a daughter in the Reggio program. She worries about the kids missing out on traditional preschool activities, something as simple and fun as finger painting.

Overall, however, she is convinced of Reggio's long-lasting impact. "In my 10-year-old's class, there are probably five or six kids who started in the Reggio program, and their level of thinking is just incredible. They're studying colonialism—a typical fourth-grade theme—but they even carry it over to recess. They have created out of pine cones and other items an entire colonial village. For them to synthesize all of their knowledge and use their play time to create this little village, I think is remarkable."

Creating Culturally Responsive, Inclusive Classrooms

Winifred Montgomery

Culturally responsive classrooms specifically acknowledge the presence of culturally diverse students and the need for these students to find relevant connections among themselves and with the subject matter and the tasks teachers ask them to perform.

Let's repeat that: *Culturally responsive classrooms specifically acknowledge the presence of culturally diverse students and the need for these students to find relevant connections among themselves and with the subject matter and the tasks teachers ask them to perform.* In such programs teachers recognize the differing learning styles of their students and develop instructional approaches that will accommodate these styles. In light of the value of culturally responsive instructional practices, schools and districts need to support teachers in their quest to learn about the use of these strategies (see box, "Our Increasingly Diverse Classrooms"). This article provides guidelines for creating culturally responsive, inclusive classrooms. Teachers can use these guidelines with students from culturally and linguistically diverse backgrounds in all kinds of classrooms, but particularly in inclusive settings where general and special educators work together to promote the academic, social, and behavioral skills of all students. First, teachers need to take an honest look at their own attitudes and current practice.

Many teachers are faced with limited understanding of cultures other than their own and the possibility that this limitation will negatively affect their students' ability to become successful learners.

Conduct a Self-Assessment

Many teachers are faced with limited understanding of cultures other than their own and the possibility that this limitation will negatively affect their students' ability to become successful learners. Hence, teachers must critically assess their relationships with their students and their understanding of students' cultures (Bromley, 1998; Patton, 1998). The self-assessment in Figure 1, based on the work of Bromley, 1998), is one tool teachers can use to examine their assumptions and biases in a thoughtful and potentially productive way.

Teachers need to use instructional methods that are tailored to suit the setting, the students, and the subject.

Following self-assessment, teachers need to take time to reflect on their responses (what they have learned about themselves) and make some critical decisions regarding ways to constructively embrace diversity and, thus, create learning environments that respond to the needs of their students.

Use a Range of Culturally Sensitive Instructional Methods and Materials

In addition to self-assessment, an important component of effective culturally responsive classrooms is the use of a range of instructional methods and materials (Bromley, 1998). Teachers need to use instructional methods that are tailored to suit the setting, the students, and the subject. By varying and adapting these methods and materials, teachers can increase the chances that their students will succeed. The following are effective culturally sensitive instructional methods.

Explicit, strategic instruction shows students what to do, why, how, and when.

Figure 1. Diversity Self-Assessment

- What is my definition of diversity?
- Do the children in my classroom and school come from diverse cultural backgrounds?
- What are my perceptions of students from different racial or ethnic groups? With language or dialects different from mine? With special needs?
- What are the sources of these perceptions (e.g., friends, relatives, television, movies)?
- How do I respond to my students, based on these perceptions?
- Have I experienced others making assumptions about me based on my membership in a specific group? How did I feel?
- What steps do I need to take to learn about the students from diverse backgrounds in my school and classroom?
- How often do social relationships develop among students from different racial or ethnic backgrounds in my classroom and in the school? What is the nature of these relationships?
- In what ways do I make my instructional program responsive to the needs of the diverse groups in my classroom?
- What kinds of information, skills, and resources do I need to acquire to effectively teach from a multicultural perspective?
- In what ways do I collaborate with other educators, family members, and community groups to address the needs of all my students?

Source: Adapted from Bromley (1998).

Explicit, Strategic Instruction

Explicit, strategic instruction shows students what to do, why, how, and when. An effective strategy is the think-aloud method, a procedure that takes advantage of the benefits of modeling. In a "think-aloud," the teacher reads a passage and talks through the thought processes for students. The objective is to show students how to ask themselves questions as they comprehend text.

Another important strategy is reciprocal questioning where teachers and students engage in shared reading,

discussion, and questioning (Leu & Kinzer, 1999). The primary goal of this strategy is to help students learn to ask questions of themselves about the meaning they are constructing as they read.

Many classrooms are organized around an interdisciplinary, or cross-curricular theme.

Interdisciplinary Units

Interdisciplinary units include and connect content area learning with language arts and culturally diverse literature (Cooper, 2000; Leu & Kinzer, 1999). Many effective classrooms are organized around an interdisciplinary, or cross-curricular, theme with students participating in meaningful reading, writing, listening, and speaking tasks as they explore the theme through a variety of activities and books. The topic can be drawn from children's lives and interests and sometimes from the curriculum. Teachers can help their students successfully engage in cross-curricular activities by demonstrating how to make connections across the curriculum through literature, by making explicit connections among books, and by helping them recall how previous activities and experiences relate to current studies.

Teachers can design instruction that provides just enough scaffolding, or support, for students to be able to participate in tasks that currently are beyond their reach.

Instructional Scaffolding

Instructional scaffolding involves the use of teacher demonstration and the modeling of strategies that students need to be successful with content area texts (Galda, Cullinan, & Strickland, 1997; Leu & Kinzer, 1999). In scaffolded instruction, teachers determine the difference between what students can accomplish independently and what they can accomplish with instructional support. Teachers then design instruction that provides just enough scaffolding for students to be able to participate in tasks that currently are beyond their reach. Over time, as the tasks become more under the control of the learner, the teacher can introduce more difficult tasks.

Journal Writing

Journal writing provides opportunities for students to share their personal understanding regarding a range of literature in various cultural contexts that inform, clarify, explain, or educate them about our culturally diverse society (Montgomery, in press). For example, character study journals permit students to make their own personal connections with a specific character as they read the story. Students develop their own insight into the characters and the events in the story, and they are given the independence to write what they want about the character. The teacher provides time for students to share their journal writings in small cooperative learning groups, with their teachers, with their tutor(s), or with a reading buddy.

Open-Ended Projects

Open-ended projects allow students to contribute at their varying levels of ability. Such projects work well with diverse learners because they need not start or finish at the same time. Students can explore a topic of interest drawn from their readings of culturally rich literature or a content area topic they are currently studying. They may choose to write reports or prepare oral presentations and create artwork to illustrate some of the major concepts embedded in their topic. Goforth (1998) suggests a project in which interested students make artifacts such as dolls or "story cloths" representing an ethnic or cultural group. They may also want to write stories or poems about their artifacts.

Establish a Classroom Atmosphere That Respects Individuals and Their Cultures

Teachers can enhance students' self-esteem when they construct learning environments that reflect the cultural membership in the class. This strategy goes beyond wall decoration to atmosphere: Teachers must attend to all students and try to involve them equally in all class activities. This recognition gives students a positive feeling about their worth as individuals and as productive members in their classroom. Some strategies to accomplish a positive classroom atmosphere include:

- *Current and relevant bulletin boards* that display positive and purposeful activities and events involving culturally diverse people. Include, for example, newspaper articles (local and national) reporting newsworthy events or accomplishments that involve people of color, photographs of community leaders from culturally diverse backgrounds, student-made posters depicting culturally relevant historical events, and original (student-written) stories and poems with culturally diverse themes.
- *A book corner* with a variety and range of culturally diverse literature, fiction and nonfiction (see box, "Culturally Complex Atmosphere"). The books that are chosen must also deal fairly with disabilities and special needs. The characters should be integrated naturally into the story and not depicted as anomalies or peculiarities in society (Russell, 1994).

Our Increasingly Diverse Classrooms

For many reasons, U.S. schools are serving a growing number of students from culturally and linguistically diverse backgrounds (Obiakor & Utley, 1997; Salend, 2001). In fact, the student population in the United States is growing fastest in those segments with which American education has traditionally been least successful—African Americans and Hispanics.

- *Special Education Overrepresentation.* A disproportionate number of students from culturally and linguistically diverse backgrounds are inappropriately referred to and placed in special education (Yates, 1998). Data from the Office of Civil Rights reveal that African-American and Hispanic-American students, particularly males, are overrepresented in terms of their identification in the disability categories of serious emotional disturbance and mental retardation (Oswald, Coutinho, Best, & Singh, 1999). These data also indicate that students from culturally and linguistically diverse backgrounds identified as needing special education services are more likely to be provided these services in more restrictive settings than their caucasian counterparts.
- *The Negative Effects of Tracking.* The overrepresentation of students from culturally and linguistically diverse backgrounds in special education can have a negative effect on students and their school performance because it places them in a separate and unequal track that denies them access to the general education curriculum. In addition, once placed in special education classes, these students often encounter lowered teacher expectations, a watered down curriculum, and less effective instruction that can have deleterious effects on their school performance, self-esteem, behavior, education and career goals, and motivation to achieve (Nieto, 1996). As a result, these students often do not return to general education placements and frequently leave school before graduating.
- *Need for Culturally Responsive Instruction.* Though several factors contribute to the disproportional representation of students from culturally and linguistically diverse backgrounds in special education (Artiles & Zamora-Duran, 1997), one important factor is the failure of general education teachers to use culturally responsive instructional practices that address their educational, social, and cultural needs (Smith, Finn, & Dowdy, 1993).

- *Cross-cultural literature discussion groups* in which students discuss quality fiction and nonfiction literature that authentically depicts members of diverse cultural groups. Discussion groups help all students feel pride in themselves and in their culture when they see their backgrounds valued in classroom reading and study activities. In small groups, students can read a single work of literature on their own, follow the experiences of a particular character and his or her problems, form opinions about a specific issue put forward in the text, or respond to a significant event that occurred during the character's life (Montgomery, 2000). For example, the content and characterizations in culturally diverse books such as *Amazing Grace* (Hoffman, 1991), *Local News* (Soto, 1993), *Smoky Night* (Bunting, 1994), *The Story of Ruby Bridges* (Coles, 1995) and *Black Cowboys, Wild Horses* (Lester & Pinkney, 1998) can stimulate greater interest in reading *and* in reading to learn.

- *Language arts and social studies programs* provide opportunities for students to share written and oral reports pertaining to their heritage and cultural traditions. Teachers can introduce thematic units that offer excellent opportunities for children to explore a range (in terms of readability) of different forms of literature that look intensively into a single cultural or ethnic experience (Leu & Kinzer, 1999). If learners are to be successful in understanding cultural traditions, trade books must be available in the classroom and in the school library to support these strategies.

Culturally Complex Atmosphere

Creating a *book corner* that appeals to all children can be a challenge for the teacher. The Internet has become an excellent resource for the kind of quality literature that will introduce children to other cultural contexts. Teachers will find valuable links to appropriate children's literature that will help their students appreciate and begin to understand the range of human experiences and cultural backgrounds.

- The Web site *Multicultural Resources* provides articles, reviews, and literature selections organized around specific cultural groups (http://falcon.jmu.edu/~ramseyil/multipub.html).
- An excellent Web resource for children's literature that addresses cultural differences is *The Children's Literature Web Guide* (http://www.acs.ucalgary.ca/~dkbrown/lists.html)
- *The Reading Zone of the Internet Public Library* (http://www.ipl.org/youth/lapage.html) is a central site that is useful for teachers and students.

Foster an Interactive Classroom Learning Environment

Students must have opportunities to interact with each other—to engage in shared inquiry and discovery—in their efforts to solve problems and complete tasks. The following are suggested activities for interactive engagement in the learning process:

- *Cooperative learning groups.* Cooperative groups bring students together within a variety of supportive and collaborative learning activities. The use of this kind of learning group allows all children to see the benefits of bringing together people with diverse backgrounds for problem-solving tasks. They use listening, speaking, reading, and writing together to achieve common goals and in the process become accountable since their performance affects group outcomes. They become active language users and learn to respect each other's opinions (Bromley, 1998). For example, the I-Search Strategy (Leu & Kinzer, 1999) is an interdisciplinary, student-centered inquiry process that emphasizes participation and sharing of research findings in small cooperative learning groups, as well as in whole-group settings. To implement this strategy, children choose a motivating theme; with the teacher's assistance, they formulate their own research plans; next, they follow and revise their plans as they gather information, and then they prepare papers, posters, or presentations using computer software, or they prepare oral reports.

Through the Internet, second-language learners may communicate in their native language with children from similar cultural and linguistic backgrounds.

- *Guided and informal group discussions.* Informal discussions provide opportunities for able students and less able students to collaborate in constructing meaning from text and enable them to learn from each other by sharing their reflections, opinions, interpretations, and questions. The teacher models discussion techniques and guides the students through early discussion sessions. As students develop their discussion skills and begin to feel comfortable talking about story content and their opinions, they will begin to try out ideas without worrying about being wrong or sounding as if they do not understand the story.
- *The Internet.* On the Web, children can experience exciting cultural exchanges. Keypals (see box) is the online equivalent of pen pals. It is an e-mail activity that may be particularly beneficial to second-language learners because the students are able to communicate in their native language with children from similar cultural and linguistic backgrounds. Moreover, important friendships can develop among *all* students as they find out about life in another part of the world, share useful Web sites, and

even help one another with homework (Leu & Kinzer, 1999).

Employ Ongoing and Culturally Aware Assessments

In culturally responsive classrooms, teachers employ ongoing and systematic assessment of student abilities, interests, attitudes, and social skills. This information provides a basis for instructional decision making and offers insights into what to teach and how to teach. In addition, there is an emphasis on student involvement in the assessment process. When students are permitted to participate in their assessment, they are able to reflect on their own progress and offer insights that adults may not have. Examples of culturally sensitive assessment include the following:

- *Daily observation of students' social and learning behaviors in all classroom situations.* Observations can be recorded on checklists, in notebooks, on file cards, or in any way that permits the teacher to summarize observations in a consistent and meaningful way. For example, the class roster can be used as a convenient recording form for observations. The teacher lists the names of the students in the class and then heads subsequent columns across the top of the roster to identify the project, activity, or behavior that is observed.
- *Portfolio assessment.* Student and teacher select samples of work that reveal the diverse needs and abilities of the student. Teachers, students, and family members reflect on what students have done over time, how well they are doing, and what areas need to be improved.
- *Teacher-made tests that are closely tied to the instructional program.* Special attention is given to the cognitive styles of all the students and their evolving academic skills. For example, teachers can design a test to assess students' knowledge or performance within a particular content area lesson.

Keypals

The Internet expands the appeal of pen pal activities in the classroom. A great site for Keypal contacts is: **http://www.stolaf.edu/network/iecc**

At this site, intercultural *E-Mail Classroom Connections,* teachers will find a good source for developing keypals from different countries. There are several mailing lists for teachers looking for partner classrooms. Teachers can subscribe directly from this Web page.

- *Student self-assessment.* Students can respond to questions about their learning during periodic teacher/student conferences. Portfolios can be used during these conferences. For example, students can be shown their work, discuss it with their teachers, and then assess their own progress.
- *Teacher self-evaluation.* Self-evaluation is an integral part of teaching effectiveness. The kinds of questions teachers ask themselves about their choices of teaching behaviors and strategies, the effectiveness and cultural relevance of their lessons, and their reactions and responses to the cultural diversity in their classrooms can greatly contribute to continuing growth in teaching and learning.

Collaborate with Other Professionals and Families

Collaboration and communication with culturally diverse families and with other professionals are essential elements of culturally responsive classrooms. Families are a critical component of a strong instructional program and should be regularly informed about students' progress and encouraged to participate in class and school activities whenever possible. It is also important to establish strong collaborative relationships with colleagues to develop instructional programs that broaden the learning opportunities of all students. The following are specific collaborative activities that teachers and families might use:

> ## Send newsletters to all families providing an overview of culturally responsive curriculum goals, classroom activities, and selected student-written stories and poems.

- *Consult and share ideas regularly with other teachers with whom students work.* Meet with teachers to discuss students' academic and social progress, as well as specific learning needs.
- *Communicate regularly with families.* For example, send newsletters to all families providing an overview of culturally responsive curriculum goals, classroom activities, and selected student-written stories and poems.
- *Invite families to participate in classroom cultural celebrations and to assist in planning such events.* Encourage culturally diverse families to visit the classroom to learn what occurs in the learning environment and to see how well their children are doing—academically and socially.
- *Initiate a parent volunteer tutorial program.*

- *Use culturally diverse community resources.* Invite to your classroom culturally diverse civic leaders, business leaders, artists and writers, members of the police and fire department, college professors, and academically successful high school students.

- *Attend culturally diverse community or neighborhood events.*

Final Thoughts

Of primary importance in any culturally responsive classroom is the teacher's belief that children from culturally diverse backgrounds want to learn. Second, instructional strategies and specific teaching behaviors can encourage all students to engage in learning activities that will lead to improved academic achievement. Third, the development of instructional programs that prevent failure and increase opportunities for success should be the goal of every teacher. The strategies delineated in this article can become important ways of helping all children find purpose, pride, and success in their daily efforts to learn.

Learn More About It

The following resources can help teachers evaluate the results of self-assessment:

Books

Au, K. (1993). *Literacy instruction in multicultural settings.* New York: Harcourt Brace.

Garcia, E. (1994). *Understanding and meeting the challenge of student cultural diversity.* Boston: Houghton Mifflin.

Journal Articles

Montgomery, W. (2000). Literature discussion in the elementary school classroom. *Multicultural Education, 8*(1), 33–36.

Nieto, S. (1994). Lessons from students on creating a chance to dream. *Harvard Educational Review, 64,* 392–426.

Web Sites

Cultural Diversity in the Classroom (http://education. indiana.edu/cas/tt/v212/cultural.html)

ERIC Digests on Cultural Diversity (http:// www.uncg.edu/edu/ericcass/diverse/digests/ tableoc.htm)

References

Artiles, A. J., & Zamora-Duran, G. (1997). *Reducing disproportionate representation of culturally and linguistically diverse students in special and gifted education.* Reston, VA: The Council for Exceptional Children.

Bromley, K. D. (1998). *Language art: Exploring connections.* Needham Heights, MA: Allyn & Bacon.

Bunting, E. (1994). *Smoky night.* New York: Harcourt Brace.

Coles, R. (1995). *The story of Ruby Bridges.* New York: Scholastic.

Cooper, J. D. (2000). *Literacy: Helping children construct meaning.* Boston: Houghton Mifflin.

Galda, L., Cullinan, B., & Strickland, D. S. (1997). *Language, literacy, and the child* (2nd ed.). Fort Worth, TX: Harcourt Brace.

Goforth, F. S. (1998). *Literature and the learner.* Belmont, CA: Wadsworth.

Hoffman, M. (1991). *Amazing grace.* New York: Scholastic.

Lester, J., & Pinkey, J. (1998). *Black cowboys, wild horses.* New York: Dial Books.

Leu, D. J., & Kinzer, C. K. (1999). *Effective literacy instruction, K–8* (4th ed.). Upper Saddle River, New Jersey: Merrill.

Montgomery, W. (2000). Literature discussion in the elementary school classroom: Developing cultural understanding. *Multicultural Education, 8*(1), 33–36.

Montgomery, W. (in press). Journal writing: Connecting reading and writing in mainstream educational settings. *Reading and Writing Quarterly.*

Nieto, S. (1996). *Affirming diversity* (2nd ed.). New York: Longman.

Obiakor, F. E., & Utley, C. A. (1997). Rethinking preservice preparation for teachers in the learning disabilities field: Workable multicultural strategies. *Learning Disabilities Research and Practice, 12*(2), 100–106.

Oswald, D. P., Coutinho, M. J., Best, A. M., & Singh, N. N. (1999). Ethnic representation in special education: The influence of school-related economic and demographic variables. *The Journal of Special Education, 32,* 194–206.

Patton, J. M. (1998). The disproportionate representation of African Americans in special education. *The Journal of Special Education, 32*(1), 25–31.

Russell, D. (1994). *Literature for children* (2nd ed.). New York: Longman.

Salend, S. (2001). *Creating inclusive classrooms: Effective and reflective practices* (4th ed.). Columbus, OH: Merrill/Prentice Hall.

Smith, T. E. C., Finn, D. M., & Dowdy, C. A. (1993). *Teaching students with mild disabilities.* Fort Worth: Harcourt Brace Jovanovich.

Soto, G. (1993). *Local news.* Orlando, FL: Harcourt Brace.

Yates, J. R. (1998, April). *The state of practice in the education of CLD students.* Presentation at the annual meeting of the Council for Exceptional Children, Minneapolis, MN.

Winifred Montgomery, *Associate Professor, Department of Elementary Education, State University of New York at New Paltz.*

Address correspondence to the author at Department at Elementary Education, State University of New York, 75 S. Manheim Blvd., New Paltz, NY 12561-2443 (e-mail: montgomw@matrix.newpaltz.edu).

All They Do Is Play?
Play in Preschool

BY ANGIE DORRELL, M.A.

The preschool director and parent walk into the four-year-old class and see children actively engaged. Allyson is preparing a feast with plastic foods while Katy pretends to feed a baby doll. Collin is concentrating on different colors of bear counters while Kelsey and Courtney busily rearrange the unit blocks. The parent smiles and says, "So when does the educational program begin?" The director and teacher share an understanding look as the director begins to explain.

Sound familiar? Play is extremely important to children, but this importance is not widely understood. Parents need to hear from their child's trusted teacher that building with blocks is a valuable learning experience, otherwise they come to rely on worksheets as benchmarks of their child's learning.

Why Is Play Important?

Children learn by being active participants who explore, experiment, and inquire. Vygotsky believed that during play, children are free to experiment, attempt, and try out possibilities, enabling them to reach above and beyond their usual level of abilities. Play offers children opportunities to master their environment. When children play, they are in command; they use their imagination and power of choice to determine the conditions of play. In an environment where children are allowed to discover independently, at their own pace and in their own unique way, they are more likely to become enthusiastic, inquisitive learners. The following describes the unique learning that takes place in the block, language, creativity, dramatic play, math, and science centers.

Block Center

When children place one block on top of another, they learn basic science concepts such as balance, size, and weight relations. When children make a barn for play animals, they learn to use their imagination and gain self-confidence to try their own ideas. Even clean-up time promotes learning. Important beginning math skills are learned as blocks are sorted and classified.

A good block center has:

- Carpet
- Multicultural people
- Small and large vehicles
- Shelving at child's level
- Animal sets (jungle, farm, zoo, dinosaurs)
- Complete set of wooden unit blocks (at least 340)
- Floor equipment (barn, doll house, play mats)

Additional Learning Opportunities in the Block Center

- **Social Development**: Cooperating, sharing, negotiating, developing patience, and tolerance.
- **Emotional Development**: Gaining self-confidence to try ideas, expressing feelings through role-playing, and feeling a sense of accomplishment and success.
- **Physical Development**: Strengthening fingers and hands by reaching, picking up, stacking, lifting, carrying, and fitting together, and increasing eye-hand coordination.
- **Cognitive Development**: Exploring basic science concepts of shape, size, proportions, reversibility, conservation, and gravity (blocks always fall down, not up); developing prediction and comparison skills; exploring basic math concepts such as larger than and smaller than, measuring, counting, grouping, adding, subtracting, sizing; and problem-solving skills.

- **Language Development**: Developing vocabulary about size, shape, and position.

Language and Circle Time Center

When children listen and talk about a story, they learn to love books, remember a sequence and recognize that there is a beginning, middle, and end to books and stories. When children sing as a group they learn how to participate with others, to hear and repeat rhythms, and extend their memory.

A good language and circle time center has:

- Carpet
- Chart tablet
- Puppets
- Paper and pencils
- Musical instruments
- Shelf for language materials
- Soft furniture for book reading
- Flannel board and flannel sets
- Teaching pictures or magazines
- Letter sets (sandpaper, magnetic, flannel)
- Multicultural books about a variety of topics
- Music and appropriate player (cassette, record player, etc.)
- Book shelf for books at the child's level at all times
- Language games (rhyming, opposites, spelling, bingo, lotto, matching)

Additional Learning Opportunities in the Language and Circle Time Center

- **Social Development**: Cooperating with others, working as part of a group toward a common goal, waiting for a turn, understanding, and developing a positive attitude about others.
- **Emotional Development**: Gaining independence skills and expressing ideas in different ways.
- **Physical Development**: Holding and turning pages and coordinating eye-hand movements.
- **Cognitive Development**: Increasing attention span and ability to focus, building correct concepts of objects, and forming new ideas.
- **Language Development**: Following left to right progression, learning how a book works, developing vocabulary through meaningful experiences, associating the written and spoken word, listening skills, and understanding that printed words have meaning.

Creativity and Art Center

It can be difficult to understand how the mass of lines and colors a child creates is part of the learning process. When children choose and gather paper, scissors, and crayons, they learn decision-making skills such as how to implement their ideas and how to follow through on a task. When children create with paint, they learn to mix colors and use their own ideas while exploring and discovering consequences.

A good creativity and art center has:

- Easel
- Scissors
- Paint brushes
- Washable paints
- Watercolors
- Protective clothing
- Table and child-size chairs
- Clay and playdough
- Washable ink pads and stamps
- Multicultural materials
- Paint cups or other appropriate containers
- Consumables available for daily children's choice such as: crayons, washable markers, different types of paper, collage materials (yarn, tissue, craft sticks, glue)

Additional Learning Opportunities in the Creativity and Art Center

- **Social Development**: Sharing and cooperating with others, valuing and respecting others' work, ideas, and property.
- **Emotional Development**: Expressing ideas and self freely in appropriate ways, stretching imaginations, instilling confidence in the child's vision of the world, and gaining a sense of pride.
- **Physical Development**: Strengthening muscles that will be used in writing as they grasp a crayon or mold with clay.
- **Cognitive Development**: Exploring concepts like color, size, shape, texture, and pattern helps children develop sensory abilities.
- **Language Development**: Learning new vocabulary (sticky, firm, cool, slippery, gushy).

Dramatic Play Center

When children put on dress-up clothes, they learn to express themselves and try out different roles. When children make "dinner" together they learn to cooperate, share, and make friends. A child who has a new sibling at home can express his or her feelings in a safe setting, and a child who is missing his or her Grandma can pretend to visit her.

A good dramatic play center has:

- Doll bed
- Child-size kitchen set
- Paper and pencil
- Pans, pots, cooking utensils
- Small table and chairs
- Plates, cups, silverware
- Nonbreakable mirror
- Multicultural boy and girl dolls and clothing
- Multicultural dress up clothing for boys and girls
- Multicultural food that fits in the plates and pots
- Prop box supplies including: doctor's kit, purses, shoes, hats, bags, menus, paper, pencils, etc.

Additional Learning Opportunities in the Dramatic Play Center

- **Social Development**: Learning to share, making friends, being creative, and understanding others.
- **Emotional Development**: Expressing emotions appropriately and recognizing that they are themselves regardless of how they are dressed or who they pretend to be.
- **Physical Development**: Learning life skills such as turning knobs, buttoning, and zipping.
- **Cognitive Development**: Making decisions and choices, learning problem-solving skills, and exploring new ideas from others.
- **Language Development**: Communicating effectively and appropriately with others, and incorporating print into daily activities.

Math and Manipulatives Center

To many adults, math is a difficult subject. However, if from an early age children have positive hands-on experiences, they learn math concepts in a nonthreatening way and take what they learn from one concept and apply it to the next. When children are investigating sea shells with magnifying glasses, they begin to recognize similarities and differences of objects. When children sort bear counters of different shapes and sizes, they learn to classify.

A good math and manipulatives center has:

- Stacking toys
- Dressing vests
- Counters
- Peg boards and pegs
- Puzzles and puzzle rack
- Sorting bowls or trays
- DUPLOS® (or similar type bricks)
- Lacing sets (beads, cards, etc.)
- Manipulative sets (Bristle Builders®, Flexi-blocks®, Space Links®, etc.)

Additional Learning Opportunities in the Math and Manipulatives Center

- **Social Development**: Taking turns and respecting others.
- **Emotional Development**: Feeling proud and willing to try new activities.
- **Physical Development**: Coordinating eye-hand movements, grasping, stacking, and matching.
- **Cognitive Development**: Learning about size, shape, color, and patterns, grouping, classifying, counting, weighing, measuring, time, temperature, space and volume concepts, observing and describing concrete objects, and one-to-one correspondence.
- **Language Development**: Describing objects, pronouncing new terms, and communicating questions and ideas.

Science and Sensorial Center

In order for children to understand their world, they must have opportunities to explore and question and then actively construct their own knowledge. When children pour water into containers they learn to estimate quantity. When children investigate smelling jars, they learn to use their sense of smell in new ways.

A good science and sensorial center has:

- Balance
- Magnet wands
- Sensory table or tubs
- Nonbreakable magnifying glasses
- Sand and water equipment (sand wheel, sieves, containers, scoops, measuring cups)
- Games (nature lotto, texture dominos, feely box)
- Discovery items (seashells, bird's nests, ant farm, prisms)

Additional Learning in the Science and Sensorial Center

- **Social Development**: Working beside each other at the sensory table encourages social interactions and gaining an understanding of why events happen the way they do.
- **Emotional Development**: Learning appropriate ways to relieve tension.
- **Physical Development**: Pouring and measuring develops eye-hand coordination.
- **Cognitive Development**: Observing, exploring, measuring, comparing, classifying, predicting, discovering, and learning general knowledge concepts such as round, triangular, big, and small.
- **Language Development**: Enhancing curiosity of children and recognizing similarities and differences.

Angie Dorrell, M.A., is director of curriculum for La Petite Academy, one of the nation's largest providers of early childhood education programs. She also serves as a NAEYC accreditation validator and commissioner. Most importantly, she is mother of two daughters, a toddler and preschooler.

From *Earlychildhood News*, March/April 2000, pp. 18-22. © 2000 by *Earlychildhood News*. Reprinted by permission.

Service Learning in Preschool: An Intergenerational Project Involving Five-Year-Olds, Fifth Graders, and Senior Citizens

Service Learning is a powerful form of experiential pedagogy that is gaining popularity in classrooms from preprimary settings through graduate school. It involves students in activities that explicitly and intentionally integrate community involvement with appropriate academic objectives. This article describes an intergenerational service learning project that brought together pre-schoolers, golden-agers, and at-risk elementary-aged students. *Lunch Time Book Buddies—Pass It On* included both direct service and indirect service and made valuable contributions to young children's developing literary, social-emotional, physical, and cognitive abilities.

KEY WORDS: service learning; intergenerational; emerging literacy; experiential learning; preschool.

Nancy K. Freeman[1,3] and Sherry King[2]

INTRODUCTION

Service Learning (S-L) is an increasingly popular pedagogy which explicitly connects community service with appropriate learning objectives. Well-planned S-L activities (a) meet authentic community needs, (b) are collaboratively planned by school and community representatives, (c) enhance and support students' academic development by providing opportunities for them to use newly acquired skills in real-life situations, (d) include opportunities for in-depth reflection, and (e) celebrate and acknowledge the success of participants' efforts. (Belbas, Gorak, & Shumer, 1993; Fertman, 1994).

There are three major formats for service learning: face-to-face hands-on interactions are *direct service; indirect service* projects involve students in meeting the needs of unseen others, for example collecting food for the local food bank; and *civic action* or *advocacy* projects such as letter writing (or picture drawing) campaigns, which inform policy makers as they prepare to make decisions that will affect the school or community, are a third kind of service learning. Service learning activities most often extend into the surrounding community, but it is possible, particularly when working with young children, to implement meaningful service learning projects that remain within the school's parameters.

Benefits of Service Learning Pedagogy

Service learning is appealing to teachers who embrace experiential learning because it enhances learning while engaging students in meaningful activities. Successful S-L experiences contribute to students' mastery of academic objectives, fulfill unmet community needs, and support learners' social development, sense of self-worth, and competence (Erickson & Anderson, 1997; Gomez, 1999). The potential of service learning is likely to be readily apparent to teachers of elementary-age students who could be successful collecting, delivering, and sorting donations to a local food bank or to those working in high schools where neighborhood fix-up projects might give their students an opportunity to integrate academic content into a community-based service activity. Early childhood educators working with preschoolers have been slow to recognize the promise of S-L however, perhaps because they have not identified appropriate service projects.

Once early childhood educators have become informed about S-L they are likely to readily appreciate its potential. That is because they recognize how S-L has the potential to enhance and support children's developing prosocial behaviors: caring, empathy, altruism, helping, and sharing. And those who know preschoolers well realize that they thrive on opportunities to be "helpers," and that they can effectively contribute to their community in meaningful ways that support their emerging independence and sense of self-efficacy (Patchin, 1994).

Service learning fits comfortably within the well-established theoretical framework created by Bronfenbrenner (1979) and Noddings (1992) who observe that a sustainable society relies on citizens who "have learned the sensitivities, motivations, and the skills involved in assisting and caring for other human beings" (Bronfenbrenner, 1979 p. 53). They would agree that children learn to care as they look beyond themselves, replacing a preoccupation with self and close family members with a concern for unknown individuals, the environment, and even the world of ideas (Noddings, 1992).

Serving and Learning Begin in the Early Years

Goldstein (1998) has applied these theories of caring to early childhood education, describing the characteristics of a care-based primary classroom. Her study is an extension of the work of Noddings as well as a number of researchers who have explored other dimensions of young children's prosocial abilities. Eisenberg (1992), for example, found that as early as the first 2 years of life infants and toddlers responded to others' needs when they have the opportunity to help out in authentic ways. Likewise, Zahn-Waxler, Radke-Yarrow, Wagner, and Chapman (1992) document that repeated exposures to significant adults who demonstrate caring incline preschool-aged children to be prosocial and exhibit helping, giving, and sharing behaviors.

Not unlike other learned behaviors, caring and sharing are likely to become more frequent when they are met with appropriate, specific praise or admiration (Wittmer & Honig, 1994). Making explicit the ways an act of caring has made a difference in someone else's life helps the child attribute these characteristics to him or herself and helps youngsters appreciate why acts of caring are desirable (Kitzrow, 1998). Furthermore, praise for specific prosocial behavior provides children with concrete ideas about how to sustain positive social relationships (Eisenberg, 1992).

It is worthwhile to invest in nurturing young children's developing prosocial dispositions because there is evidence that early experiences have lifelong effects on children's conceptions of how they should relate to others and to the environment. Kitzrow (1998), for one, noted that parents, caregivers, and teachers play a critical role in helping young children develop these desirable prosocial dispositions. And Honig and Wittmer (1996) and Noddings (1992) demonstrate that being engaged in caregiving activities, and receiving validation as a carer are experiences which help children clarify the dynamics of self–other relations and develop a positive sense of self. Helping children become altruistic, caring, and responsive in developmentally appropriate ways is an important responsibility shouldered by early childhood educators.

Knowledge of S-L pedagogy can help teachers see serving activities in a new light and may help them identify connections between specific curricular goals and hands-on experiential learning. It is one way to help children become compassionate and empathetic in a society where individuals too often focus on themselves and are preoccupied with materialism and conspicuous consumption (Holst, 1999). As teachers think about implementing service learning with young children it is particularly important to be realistic and sensitive to their abilities and interests. They must recognize, for example, that for their youngest students, "the community" is likely to be the toddlers in the room next door or the babies down the hall. Older groups of preschoolers, however, can extend their activities beyond the confines of their school or child care center. Then their work will look more like S-L as it is implemented with older students. Sensitivity to others' needs, knowledge of the community, a desire to develop innovative partnerships, and some creative thinking can uncover opportunities to involve young children in meaningful, worthwhile projects that meet all S-L criteria.

This paper describes a successful intergenerational S-L project that linked a class of 4- and 5-year-olds with two groups of neighbors, the community Senior Center, and fifth-graders, from a nearby elementary school. These activities were very satisfying for young children, golden-agers, and preteen participants alike. The project's success demonstrates that time and effort invested in making the links between community service and academic learning explicit is well spent, whether participants are 5, 75, or somewhere in between.

LAYING THE GROUNDWORK FOR SUCCESSFUL SERVICE LEARNING

Successful service learning projects are a unique blend of community involvement and effective teaching. Teachers need to build in time to develop collaborative relationships as well as to handle the logistics involved whenever children are preparing to venture out into the community or teachers from several classrooms coordinate their schedules so their children can work together. Following these guidelines will assure teachers' success as they implement S-L.

1. Identify *organizations* that sponsor programs where your students could perform service.
2. Identify *curriculum content* most likely to be successfully integrated into service learning.
3. Identify *funding sources* that might supply support for service learning activities.
4. Plan reflective *exercises* to help students and teachers assess the successfulness of service learning activities.
5. Plan to *acknowledge and celebrate* the project's success.

THE LUNCH TIME BOOK BUDDIES— PASS IT ON PROJECT

Lunch Time Book Buddies—Pass it On was a S-L project that included both direct and indirect service. It gave 4- and 5-year-olds the opportunity to make several visits to the community Senior Center to eat lunch and visit with their golden-aged Book Buddies. After lunch, one-on-one conversations focused on the familiar books the children's teacher had brought in her backpack. As part of each visit children and seniors signed their names in the books they had shared and children took time to draw and write in their personal journals. At the conclusion of the project fifth graders from a nearby elementary school spent an afternoon reading and playing at the Center and took the books used by the Lunch Time Book Buddies back to their school where they were distributed to children identified for being at-risk who were likely to own few books of their own.

Lunch Time Book Buddies—Pass It On, based on the theoretical framework of S-L described above, was appealing to teachers, children, and parents at this campus preschool that embraces a constructivist educational philosophy. It enhanced preschool children's cognitive, social, emotional, and physical development while enriching the lives of neighboring senior citizens and school-age children alike.

Preparing to be Book Buddies

Children prepared for their visits to the nearby Senior Center by discussing what they knew about getting along with elderly friends and relatives. Many of our students do not see their grandparents regularly, so having the opportunity to interact with healthy, active senior citizens was a valuable one. They discussed the importance of having good manners while they were eating, and observed that older friends might move slowly or may need them to talk more loudly or more carefully than usual.

Children also prepared for their first visit, and every visit, by reading and rereading the books they were preparing to take to their Book Buddies story time. It was important that Sherry King plan how these Book Buddies experiences would enhance children's literacy development. One way she did that was to make sure that they heard the stories several times. The Book Buddy books were kept in a special box so they would not get mixed up with the classroom collection and children were encouraged to ask their teachers and classroom visitors to read them regularly. One objective was that children would know some of these books "by heart" and that they would "read" them to their Book Buddy.

Throughout the Book Buddies project Sherry consistently reminded her students that they would *Pass It On*. Using books that they would eventually share with children who might not own any books of their own reminded our preschoolers of the indirect service dimension of this S-L project.

Visiting the Senior Center

Children enjoyed walking through an attractive residential neighborhood to the near-by Senior Center. Finding a destination within walking distance makes S-L projects less expensive and simplifies logistics.

Children and adults identified a reading buddy each time they visited. We did not make any attempt to assign children to particular adults, for we knew that could lead to disappointment if one or the other were not there, but it was not unusual for children and adults alike to remark how pleased they were that their special friend was there week after week, and several pairs worked together every time they were together. After locating a buddy (and sometimes two) the seniors took us to the lunchroom where they helped children navigate the buffet line and settle down to eat. Lunch time was a chance to get acquainted, renew friendships, and enjoy food and fellowship.

Before long the group moved to the activity room where two or three lunchmates headed to a quiet spot where they could enjoy the books the children had brought from their classroom. This was the most intense part of the Book Buddies program. It was interesting to see how some children easily read the books to their new-found friends; others recited their books from memory, getting most of the words right; some "read" the pictures; and still others relied on adults to read the books to them.

Not only did the children's approaches to the books vary, but so did the seniors'. Some adults expected the children to read independently and focused on word attack skills. Others took a more holistic approach, drawing children's attention to how they could "read" the pictures and make good predictions about what would happen in the story. Still others read to the children, giving them the opportunity to hear a story they enjoyed. Book Buddies usually had time to read two or three books before children were getting restless and adults' reading voices were wearing thin. On the first visits Sherry noticed that shorter books and predictable books worked better than longer ones, and made it a point to favor these titles as she planned return visits.

When a pair of Book Buddies finished reading a book both the adult and child signed their names inside the front cover. This ritual emerged spontaneously, and it was a very effective and meaningful one. As the book-reading activities were winding down each week, children drew something they remembered from the book or books they had read and also drew pictures of their visits with their Book Buddies. These artifacts are meaningful reflections that show how young children recreate memorable experiences with words and pictures.

Celebrate Reading

The Book Buddies project was frequently cause for celebration. The children basked in adults' one-on-one attention and the senior-citizen buddies demonstrated the joy and satisfaction they derived from time spent with bright-eyed, eager youngsters. Adult participants' comments indicated that they thought what they did was beneficial for the children, and we observed that they enjoyed the time together as much as the young children did. We knew we had been successful when they encouraged Sherry and her class to make return visits.

There was one particularly poignant moment when Sherry learned that one of the senior Book Buddies had died suddenly. He had been a regular participant and clearly enjoyed interacting with our young children. We were glad Sherry had a picture of him reading with his Book Buddy and she was glad to have this memento to send to his family. They expressed their appreciation for that token of appreciation, and we treasured our memories.

Celebrate Passing it On

The most obvious celebration of the success of this project took place when three fifth-graders from the neighboring elementary school came to visit the Children's Center. They took the 137 books children had collected back to their school for distribution to particularly at-risk schoolmates. Linking with this literacy project for school age children gave our S-L project an important dimension. The elementary-schoolers have become regular visitors to the Center, and when fifth-graders who have been struggling readers have the chance to read to our 5-year-olds the pleasure and motivation is palpable. It seems that we have been successful spreading the joy we find in reading and our enthusiasm for service learning pedagogy.

Learning

It is important to remember the S-L combines community service with learning. This hands-on project enhanced preschool children's cognitive, social, emotional, and physical development.

It would be natural to expect a reading project to support children's emerging literacy skills. We saw children immersed in the kinds of emotionally warm lap-reading experiences that support their growing interest in, and competence with, the written word. When children wrote their names in each book and made journal entries as part of *Lunch Time Book Buddies* another dimension had been added to the literacy learning supported by the project.

This project included many opportunities for meaningful social interactions as Book Buddies ate lunch and read together. This activity also developed students' emerging empathy, for they became increasingly sensitive to and able to anticipate and accommodate others' needs when they were visitors to the Senior Center.

Our young children faced another kind of challenge to their social and emotional development when the fifth graders came to visit their school. Then they had to think about how to welcome their guests and meet the needs of older children. Opportunities to be guests and also hosts were direct service components of this S-L project.

Walking to the Senior Center was a physical challenge for these youngsters. The sometimes-hilly terrain stretched children's stamina. Singing and marching helped them pass the time, but it was, without a doubt, a stretch for some. Many were ready for a nap when they returned after lunch—Book Buddies days were busy ones!

CONCLUSION

Interest in helping young children learn to care for others is not new, but children need the support of teachers and other committed adults in their efforts to develop a repertoire of prosocial attitudes, beliefs and behaviors. We know caring does not start sometime in the future, it can and should begin in the present as we ensure children of all ages appropriate opportunities to care for themselves, others, and the living and nonliving environment that surrounds them.

Service learning activities are particularly well suited to fill these roles. It is a pedagogy that deserves increased consideration by teachers of young children who value the prosocial behaviors that are the bedrock of our democracy.

It has been rewarding to consider the success of our efforts from a variety of perspectives. This project has demonstrated the joy that lively youngsters can bring to our neighboring Senior Center, and we are also confident our preschoolers benefited from interacting with children about twice their age. We

have no doubt that the books we have provided send a positive and valuable message about the joys of reading to the children who eventually become their proud owners.

Successful S-L activities have great potential for success, but success is no accident. Effective S-L experiences require teachers to lay the groundwork and show persistence. Extending the early childhood classroom into the community can be a time-consuming, labor-intensive, tiring, and extremely rewarding undertaking—ask the Book Buddies, they know!

REFERENCES

Belbas, B., Gorak, K., & Shumer, R. (1993). Commonly used definitions of service-learning: A discussion piece. National Service-Learning Clearinghouse. Available internet: http://www.nicsl.coled.umn.edu/who/ncsta93.htm.

Bronfenbrenner, U. (1979). *The ecology of human development: Experiments by nature and design*. Cambridge, MA: Harvard University Press.

Eisenberg, N. (1992). *The caring child*. Cambridge, MA: Harvard University Press.

Erickson, J., & Anderson, J. (eds.). (1977). *Learning with the community: Concepts and models for service-learning in teacher education*. Washington, DC: American Association for Higher Education.

Fertman, C. I. (1994). *Service learning for all students*. Bloomington, IN: Phi Delta Kappa Educational Foundation.

Goldstein, L. (1998). More than gentle smiles and warm hugs: Applying the ethic of care to early childhood education. *Journal of Research in Childhood Education, 12*(2), 244–261.

Gomez, B. (1999, March 15). *Service-Learning: Every child a citizen*. Denver, CO: Education Commission of the States Issue Paper.

Holst, C. B. (199). Buying more can give children less. *Young Children, 54*(5), 19–23.

Honig, A. S., & Wittmer, D. S. (1996). Helping children become more prosocial: Ideas for classrooms, families, schools, and communities (Part 2). *Young Children, 51*(2), 62–70.

Kitzrow, M. (1998). An overview of current psychological theory and research on altruism and prosocial behavior. In R. Bringle & D. Duffy (Eds.), *With service in mind: Concepts and models for service-learning in psychology* (pp. 19–34). Washington, DC: American Association for Higher Education.

Noddings, N. (1992). *The challenge to care in schools: An alternative approach to education*. New York: Teachers College Press.

Patchin, S. H. (1994). Community service for five-year-olds (and laughing all the way). *Young Children, 49*(2), 20–21.

Wittmer, D. S., & Honig, A. S. (1994). Encouraging positive social development in young children. *Young Children, 49*(5), 4–12.

Zahn-Waxler,, C., Radke-Yarrow, M., Wagner, E., & Chapman, M. (1992). Development of concern for others. *Developmental Psychology, 28*, 126–136.

[1]University of South Carolina, College of Education, Columbia, South Carolina.
[2]Kindergarten Teacher, University of South Carolina Children's Center, Columbia, South Carolina.
[3]Correspondence should be directed to Nancy K. Freeman, University of South Carolina, College of Education, ITE-Early Childhood, 107 Wardlaw, Columbia, South Carolina 29208; e-mail: nfreeman@gwm.sc.edu

From *Early Childhood Education Journal*, 2001, Vol. 28, No. 4, pp. 211–217. © 2001 by Kluwer Academic/Plenum Publishers. Reprinted by permission.

Parent Involvement: It's Worth the Effort

Deborah Eldridge

P*arent involvement. Parent participation. Home-school partnerships. Parent-teacher collaborations.* Just so many buzzwords? So much jargon? Or not?

Many a teacher views such terms askance. To the teacher they mean a lot of work for nothing. A lot of phone calls unreturned. A lot of notes unanswered. A lot of conferences unattended. A lot of open-house nights with a few (always the same) faces. It's discouraging!

So… what does research have to say to a teacher that is truly helpful? Just buzzwords, or not?

Why bother?

Joyce Epstein, a leader in the field of parent-teacher-school research, focuses on family involvement in the classroom and its outcomes for the child, the parent (or other adult or family member), and the teacher (in Brandt 1989; Epstein et al. 1997).

Child rewards

The benefits for young children begin with greater gains in reading for those whose parents are encouraged by the teacher to help with reading activities at home (Gillum, Schooley, & Novack 1977; Iverson, Brownlee, & Walberg 1981; Epstein 1984a, 1985; Hewison 1988). Additionally, children of parents who are involved have a more positive attitude about school, improved attendance, and show better homework habits than do children whose families are less involved (Epstein 1985, 2000; Epstein et al. 1997). Children see more similarity and less of a divide between their home and school when their parents are involved in school-related activities and they see their family values [modeled] by their teacher (Epstein 1985; Epstein et al. 1997).

Goldenberg (1989) followed nine kindergarten children who seemed headed for reading difficulties in first grade and traced the success, rather than failure, of four

of them. In each case he found that someone, either teacher or parent, had done something out of the ordinary (conferred, called, observed, or taught at home) on behalf of the child. He concluded that "the earlier in a child's school career his/her parents become involved, and that involvement is sustained, the bigger the payoff" (p. 76).

In general, then, family involvement in school rewards children in terms of achievement, attitude, and good-habit formation—and the earlier the involvement, the better.

Parent benefits

Benefits extend, as well, to the lives of parents. A parent who becomes involved in his child's schooling is likely to show positive and consistent effects on his ideas and knowledge about helping the child and on his evaluation of a teacher's merits (Epstein 1984b). Involved parents are more likely to report that they feel they should help their child at home, that they understand more about what the child is being taught, that they know more about the school program, and that they support and encourage their child's school work (Epstein 1985, 2000).

Parents involved with school in parent-related activities show increased self-confidence in parenting, more knowledge of child development, and an expanded understanding of the home as an environment for student learning (Epstein 2000). Additionally, involved parents show an increased appreciation for a teacher's merits and abilities and are more likely to view positively a teacher's interpersonal skills (Epstein 1985, 2000).

Positive teacher outcomes

Last but not least, parental involvement affects the teacher's life. A teacher who involves parents in children's learning is more likely to report a greater understanding of families' cultures, an increased appreciation for parental interest in helping their children, and a deeper respect for parents' time and abilities. Teachers who are committed to parent involvement tend to reap significant positive benefits in terms of parental perceptions of their merits through leadership in school-home communication and involvement practices (Epstein 2000).

Children of parents who are involved have a more positive attitude about school, improved attendance, and show better homework habits than do children whose families are less involved.

Essentially, involvement of a parent or other responsible family member isn't just for the child and the achievement gains that are sure to follow. Parents and teachers alike see significant and lasting effects in terms of their understanding and appreciation for each other's efforts.

So, why don't parents come to school?

If the outcomes associated with parent involvement are worth the bother, one wonders why the efforts that are made receive such dismal responses. Again, research sheds light on the issue. In an extensive project surveying more than a thousand teachers and two thousand parents in 1987, Harris and Associates found three primary barriers to home-school links: availability, awkwardness, and timing.

Parent availability

On the issue of availability, Barber (1987) reported that many parents feel like intruders on school grounds. Other researchers echoed her findings by speaking to the alienation felt by many ethnic minority families and families with low incomes (Cochran 1987; Delgado-Gaitan 1987; Menacker, Hurwitz, & Weldon 1988). Menacker, Hurwitz, and Weldon (1988), reporting on home-school relations in inner-city schools, noted that most of the adults in these families had had unsuccessful or negative school experiences themselves, which contributed to their perception of the school as unresponsive.

Parents involved with school in parent-related activities show increased self-confidence in parenting, more knowledge of child development, and an expanded understanding of the home as an environment for student learning.

Parent and teacher awkwardness

Parents' hesitancy or reluctance in communicating with schools and teachers may stem partially from their feelings of inadequacy in knowing how to help their children (Nicholson 1980; Epstein 1984a; Delgado-Gaitan 1987; Harris & Associates 1987; Goldenberg 1989). Many parents express a belief that their assistance is not needed by the schools or teachers (Barber 1987). Again and again studies report that parents hear from teachers only when there is a problem (Stallworth & Williams 1982; Cochran 1987; Harris & Associates 1987). This tendency to communicate only when there is trouble may also contribute to parents' general reluctance to approach the school uninvited.

Parents are not alone, however, in feeling some awkwardness at initiating conversations. Teachers too express a reluctance to involve families. Teacher awkwardness originates in concerns about whether they can effectively influence parents, whether parents have the necessary skills to become involved, whether it's fair to ask parents to work with their children, and whether parents really want to know more (Epstein & Becker 1982). However, Epstein (1984b) found that by having parents help at school, teachers felt more comfortable about asking parents to help their children at home.

Timing: Parent and teacher schedule conflicts

A final barrier to home-school links is a matter of timing, or the mismatch of schedules for contacts and communication between parents and educators (Harris & Associates 1987). Time constraints and conflicts in the work schedules of parents have been found to be problems in involvement efforts (Epstein & Becker 1982). Therefore, flexibility is considered a primary component of any school-based effort to involve parents (Barber 1987; Ascher 1988; Heleen 1988; Williams & Chavkin 1989).

A teacher who involves parents in children's learning is more likely to report a greater understanding of families' cultures, an increased appreciation for parental interest in helping their children, and a deeper respect for parents' time and abilities.

School resistance to full parental inclusion

Not mentioned in the Harris study is a barrier to parent involvement generated from within the schools themselves in the form of resistance to involving low-income and minority parents in school affairs (Menacker, Hurwitz, & Weldon 1988). A common misconception is that the goals of families with low incomes differ from those of middle-class schools, which leads to schools discouraging widespread parental involvement (Brandt 1989). The belief that parent involvement in school activities is a middle-class activity is misguided. In the words of Epstein,

> If schools don't work to involve parents, then parent education and family social class are very important for deciding who becomes involved. But if schools take parent involvement seriously and work to involve all parents, then social class and parent level of education decrease or disappear as important factors. (in Brandt 1989, 29)

The reasons families don't become more involved in the schools, then, stem in part from parental perceptions of school and teacher unavailability, awkwardness of communication, and missed opportunities due to conflicting schedules (Bracey 1996). Equally important, however, are the commitment and efforts of schools to involve parents or other family members and the underlying messages about whose involvement is expected and welcomed.

Yes, but what can teachers do?

Granted, it is unrealistic to expect that the task of inviting parents to participate in schools should fall on the shoulders of classroom teachers alone. Administrative support is critical, and schoolwide policies and commitment are essential elements of successful family involvement programs (Williams & Chavkin 1989).

The reasons families don't become more involved in the schools stem in part from parental perceptions of school and teacher unavailability, awkwardness of communication, and missed opportunities due to conflicting schedules.

But when widespread school commitment is slow in coming, the classroom teacher needn't feel powerless to invite parents to participate. There are some basic principles that can be extracted from the research and that, when applied, should support significant and lasting involvement efforts that benefit parents, children, and teachers alike.

Welcoming classroom climate

First and foremost, a teacher should create a classroom climate that is open and accepting of parents and is based on a partnership approach (Stallworth & Williams 1982;

Henderson 1986; Delgado-Gaitan 1987; Ascher 1988; Williams & Chavkin 1989). In this way the barriers of parental reluctance and awkwardness are lowered, and those parents who know the school to be unresponsive can begin to experience the classroom in another way.

What Can Teachers Do?

- Create a classroom climate that welcomes families.
- Use frequent, two-way, and clear communication with families.
- Tailor parent involvement to each child's learning.
- Give families explicit guidance on how to help their children learn at home.
- Offer varied times and opportunities for parental involvement.
- Be sensitive to the unique characteristics and circumstances of individual families.

Teachers might invite parents to share a strength, hobby (playing guitar and singing), or vocation (firefighting, carpentry) with the class or schedule a surprise parent reader (children know that a parent will read to them, but they don't know who) each week. Activities like these, designed on the basis of home-school partnership, validate the parents, empower them, and create in them a sense of connection with classroom goals and their effect on the lives of their children.

Good communication

Second, teacher communication with families should be frequent, two-way, and clear (Iverson, Brownlee, & Walberg 1981; Stallworth & Williams 1982; Henderson 1986; Ascher 1988; Brandt 1989; Williams & Chavkin 1989). These communications may concern a child's progress in school (Stallworth & Williams 1982; Goldenberg 1989), encourage a parent to comment on policies and contribute to decisions (Henderson 1986), or provide information about ways for parents to become involved (Stallworth & Williams 1982). At all times the communication should be clear, readable, jargon free, and in English or the family's home language whenever possible (Epstein, in Brandt 1989). Varying the form of communication through notices, handwritten notes, phone calls, tapes, videotapes, and other mediums ensures that every parent is reached at some point in some way (Epstein, in Brandt 1989).

Home-child-school link

A third consideration is that each parent's involvement should be tied to her child's learning (Becker & Epstein

1982; Stallworth & Williams 1982; Epstein 1984a; Rich 1985; Lindle 1989). Family requests to be involved are constant (Epstein 1988), and many parents express a particular desire to be involved in their children's education (Nicholson 1980; Harris & Associates 1987). Noting that a child is struggling with counting, for example, the teacher might send home a note suggesting two ways a parent can count with the child each day. Linking parents' involvement to their children's progress in ways like this strengthens ties between home and school and affects children's attitudes as well as parents' perceptions of a teacher's abilities.

Clear directions to parents

As a fourth consideration, ties to a child's school learning should include explicit instruction to parents on what to do, how to do it, and why it should be done (Becker & Epstein 1982; Stallworth & Williams 1982; Epstein 1984a; Rich 1985; Delgado-Gaitan 1987; Ascher 1988; Brandt 1989; Williams & Chavkin 1989). Research has shown that efforts to involve parents in the learning of the child at home reap the most benefits for the most people (Epstein 1984b). But most parents are reluctant to help their children because they are not sure how to do it (Nicholson 1980; Epstein 1984a).

Delgado-Gaitan (1987) notes that school-based practices are culture bound and that many parents need teachers to tell them about the basic requirements of the system and the competencies that their children are expected to acquire. In fact, while working with immigrant mothers in a large city, the author often talked with them about the school system and answered their questions about what would be expected of their children in a given grade.

Many of these mothers were completely unfamiliar with the American system of preschool and elementary school education and had no notion of what schools expected of their children or the ways in which schools achieve their goals with the children. To remedy the situation, on back-to-school night a teacher can give parents a list of five or ten competencies children will work on that year, such as number recognition, book handling, listening when someone is speaking, and suggest that parents work with their children on them at home. The teacher must explain and demonstrate what is meant, using examples from children's work or teacher practices; she cannot assume that parents share her understanding of early childhood education.

Sensitivity to parent diversity

A fifth principle involves varying the times and opportunities for parents or family members to become involved (Rich 1985; Ascher 1988; Heleen 1988; Epstein, in Brandt 1989). Families these days are diverse and ever changing. Parental involvement opportunities need to be sensitive to that diversity by reducing the number of activities that welcome only one kind of parent to participate.

Sensitivity to parent availability

Last, and related, is a sixth principle—to involve all families sensitively. This includes providing child care (for example, at an evening activity) (Ascher 1988), making equal demands on single and married parents (Epstein 1985), accommodating working parents' schedules, and responding considerately to the multiple demands made on families in today's world. Additionally, sensitivity to diversity in parental involvement means recognizing and supporting the myriad ways in which parents already interact with their children, such as talking to them about school-related activities and helping them with homework.

Teacher checklist for involving families

From these six principles, six guiding questions can be used by the teacher for self-evaluation. When planning to involve parents and families, a teacher should ask herself the following questions.

Does what I am about to do…

- welcome families as partners in their children's schooling?
- communicate clearly to everyone?
- involve each parent in his or her child's learning?
- include clear information about how and why their help is needed?
- allow for a variety of times and ways to participate?
- exclude anyone for any reason?

If the answer to all except the last question is yes, then the teacher is creating parent involvement plans that are more likely to be successful because they are based on research.

Teachers can model family involvement efforts in their own classrooms and serve as catalysts for schoolwide commitment. Despite a formerly gloomy history of parent involvement efforts, one teacher *can* make a difference in the lives of the children he teaches and in the communities in which he lives and works. Teamed with continued research efforts to advance our understanding of parent involvement, schools and teachers can transform parental involvement efforts into work that pays off.

References

Ascher, C. 1988. Improving the school-home connection for low-income, urban parents. New York: ERIC Clearinghouse on Urban Education. ERIC, ED 293973.

Barber, G.M. 1987. Increasing parental involvement in helping fourth-grade children to learn through home curriculum to improve homework habits. Ed.D. practicum, Nova University, Ft. Lauderdale, Florida. ERIC, ED 291520.

Becker, H.J., & J.L. Epstein. 1982. Parent involvement: A survey of teacher practices. *Elementary School Journal* 83: 85–102.

Bracey, G.W. 1996. SES and involvement. *Phi Delta Kappan* 78 (2): 169–70.

Brandt, R. 1989. On parents and schools: A conversation with Joyce Epstein. *Educational Leadership* 47: 24–27.

Cochran, M. 1987. The parental empowerment process: Building on family strengths. *Equity and Choice* 4: 9–23.

Delgado-Gaitan, C. 1987. Parent perception of schools' supportive environments for children. In *Success or failure? Learning and the language of minority students*, ed. H. Trueba, 131–55. Cambridge, MA: Newbury House.

Epstein, J.L. 1984a. Effects of teacher practices of parent involvement on change in student achievement in reading and math. Paper presented at the American Educational Research Association Annual Meeting in New Orleans. ERIC, ED 256863.

Epstein, J.L. 1984b. School policy and parent involvement: Research results. *Educational Horizons* 62 (2): 70–72.

Epstein, J.L. 1985. Home-school connections in schools of the future: Implications of research on parent involvement. *Peabody Journal of Education* 62 (2): 18–41.

Epstein, J.L. 1988. How do we improve programs for parent involvement? *Educational Horizons* 66 (2): 58–59.

Epstein, J.L. 2000. *School and family partnerships: Preparing educators and improving schools.* Boulder, CO: Westview.

Epstein, J.L., & H.J. Becker. 1982. Teachers' reported practice of parent involvement: Problems and possibility. *Elementary School Journal* 83 (2): 103–13.

Epstein, J.L., L. Coates, K.C. Salinas, M.G. Sanders, & B.S. Simon. 1997. *School, family, and community partnerships: Your handbook for action.* Thousand Oaks, CA: Corwin.

Gillum, R., D. Schooley, & P.D. Novack. 1977. The effects of parental involvement in three Michigan performance contraction programs. Paper by the National Institute of Education. ERIC, ED 144007.

Goldenberg, C.N. 1989. Making success a more common occurrence for children at risk for failure: Lessons from Hispanic first-graders learning to read. In *Risk makers, risk takers, risk breakers: Reducing the risks for young literacy learners*, eds. J.F. Allen & J.M. Mason, 48–79. Portsmouth, NH: Heinemann.

Harris, L., & Associates, Inc. 1987. *The American teacher 1987: Strengthening links between home and school.* New York: Metropolitan Life Survey. ERIC, ED 289841.

Heleen, O. 1988. Involving the "hard to reach" parent: A working model. *Equity and Choice* 4 (3): 60–63.

Henderson, A.T. 1986. *Beyond the bake sale: An educator's guide to working with parents.* Columbia, MD: Institute for Educational Leadership, National Committee for Citizens in Education. ERIC, ED 270508.

Hewison, J. 1988. The long-term effectiveness of parental involvement in reading: A follow-up to the Haringey reading project. *British Journal of Educational Psychology* 58: 184–90.

Iverson, B.K., G.D. Brownlee, & H.J. Walberg. 1981. Parent-teacher contacts and student learning. *Journal of Educational Research* 74: 394–96.

Lindle, J.C. 1987. What do parents want from principals and teachers? *Educational Leadership* 47 (2): 12–14.

Menacker, J., E. Hurwitz, & W. Weldon. 1988. Parent-teacher cooperation in schools serving the urban poor. *Clearing House* 62 (1): 108–12.

Nicholson, T. 1980. Why we need to talk to parents about reading. *Reading Teacher* 34 (1): 19–21.

Rich, D. 1985. Helping parents help their children learn. *Educational Leadership* 42 (7): 80.

Stallworth, J.R., & D.L. Williams. 1982. *A survey of parents regarding parent involvement in schools.* Austin, TX: Southwest Educational Development Laboratory. ERIC, ED 225682.

Williams, D.L., & N.F. Chavkin. 1989. Essential elements of strong parent involvement programs. *Educational Leadership* 47 (2): 18–20.

Deborah Eldridge, Ed.D., *is an assistant professor of reading, language arts, and literacy at Hunter College of the City University of New York. Deb was formerly the assistant director of the Intergenerational Literacy Project in Chelsea, Massachusetts.*

Applying Brain Research to Create Developmentally Appropriate Learning Environments

The validity of many developmentally appropriate practices is confirmed in the findings of brain research.

Stephen P. Rushton

The results of exciting research in the field of neuroscience may help teachers understand how the growing mind works and how the environment can facilitate learning (Sylwester 1995; Diamond & Hopson 1998). There is increasing evidence of the importance of classrooms that both support young children's development and stimulate their interest. In this vein Rushton and Larkin (2001) draw upon the findings of brain research from the last decade to amplify the recommendations of the NAEYC (Bredekamp & Copple 1997) and some tenets from constructivist educators (Caine & Caine 1997; Jensen 1998). A nonthreatening learning environment is crucial if students are to feel safe in encountering and exploring stimulating new ideas.

Thanks to the research of neuroscientists (Fitzpatrick 1995; Sylwester 1995; Diamond & Hopson 1998), cognitive psychologists (Gardner 1993; LeDoux 1996), and educators (Caine & Caine 1997; Jensen 1998), classroom teachers have important information at their disposal to help them create what Jensen calls high-activity, low-stress, brain-compatible learning environments. Many teachers with good early childhood training already apply the results of brain research by engaging children in meaningful learning experiences, encouraging cooperative learning, and supporting active learning. In fact, the validity of many developmentally appropriate practices is confirmed in the findings of brain research. Rather than offer revolutionary approaches to teaching, these findings suggest why some teaching styles and strategies may be more effective than others.

This article examines the early childhood and primary learning environments and developmentally appropriate practices in light of the findings of brain research in the mid to late 1990s.

How the brain works

As children interact with their learning environment, whether it be an open-ended learning center in the classroom or a waste-treatment center on a field trip, they assimilate large amounts of information through their senses. These sensory stimuli enter the nervous system and are relayed to the brain via the chemical and electrical firing of nerve cells' dendrites. The information is transmitted to the thalamus, a portion of the brain that acts as a sorting station to reroute the sensory input to more specialized parts of the brain for processing. The occipital lobe, located near the rear of the brain, receives and processes visual information. The temporal lobe, located in the mid-left portion of the brain, processes language, writing, hearing, and to some extent memory. The parietal lobe also processes language, along with short-term memory. Finally, the frontal lobe enables us to judge, be creative, and generally make decisions and long-term plans. All information is sent to the amygdala in the lower brain, which sorts it for emotional significance. The amygdala checks especially whether information is threatening; threats can reduce a child's ability to learn and function (Wolfe & Brandt 1998).

Effective Teacher Strategies That Optimize Learning

- Creating a positive and engaging classroom
- Building trust in a nonthreatening atmosphere
- Using creative strategies to reach all children's learning styles
- Using humor, without sarcasm
- Providing appropriate choices
- Using individualized planning
- Being well organized so that students can predict what is coming
- Behaving honestly and consistently
- Providing opportunities for student to feel empowered
- Modeling positive behaviors
- Providing opportunities for students to have ownership with their learning
- Using games
- Using rich literature and poetry
- Using plants, music, and lamps to create warm comfortable settings
- Teaching students about the brain and how it works
- Letting children know it's OK to make a mistake
- Using role-playing, simulations, story-telling
- Teaching and modeling conflict resolution

Situations That Can Hinder Learning

- Being put on the spot, not knowing the answer to a direct question, and not having the opportunity to be reflective
- Having a teacher who yells at children, causes embarrassment, uses sarcasm, accuses students of wrongdoing
- Lacking prior knowledge or being unable to connect the content to prior knowledge
- Having negative experiences with schools and teachers in the past
- Learning in a cold, unpleasant environment
- Fearing failure or the consequences of not doing well
- Experiencing poor social relationships with peers, such as being bullied
- Being tested or making oral presentations
- Losing control
- Engaging in power struggles
- Reading aloud
- Being bullied on the playground
- Experiencing peer pressure
- Having to wait to answer a question
- Being unable to meet unrealistic expectations
- Having a core belief threatened

There are billions of nerve cells in the brain. When a child is engaged in a learning experience, a number of areas of the brain are simultaneously activated. Positron emission topography (known as a PET scan) can show the different regions of the brain that are simultaneously activated when a person reads. For instance, when a child who is learning to read picks up a book, several regions of the brain start working together. As the child picks up the book, her brain's motor cortex becomes active. As she begins to look at and sound out the words, the neurons in the occipital lobe begin to fire. When the child deciphers the letters, the temporal lobe (language activation) is activated, along with the frontal lobe (reasoning skills) (Wolfe & Brandt 1998).

Teachers should aim to create a balance between meaningful experiences and optimal stimulation of the brain in their classrooms. For example, when students are engaged in cooperative learning, they are often required to work in groups of four in which they interact with each other and are

expected to create a product or result as a group. This format creates both a positive level of stress and often meaningful experiences for the children.

Research findings on how the brain functions show that high levels of stress can inhibit learning (Jensen 1998). When a child experiences stress, the amygdala stimulates the release of cortisol and other neurotransmitters, which can disrupt the learning process by inhibiting the child's reasoning abilities. Perceived fear drives us to survive, often by blocking our normal thinking abilities. When a child is belittled, or yelled at, the releasing of cortisol stops the child from thinking in a clear manner. Endorphins, such as norepinephrine, which are released when a child feels safe and secure, can help a child to relax. In addition, these hormones stimulate learning and memory and thus help focus the child's attention during the learning process.

If the amygdala perceives a threat, the body's autonomic nervous system is activated to deal with it. One byproduct of this arousal is heightened awareness mixed

with fear. When these physiological reactions take place, higher-order thinking skills involved with reasoning (frontal lobes) and language (temporal lobes) can be disrupted. Many children who experience fear in the classroom freeze up and are unable to communicate effectively. The teacher may make the situation worse by demanding that children respond to questions to which they do not know the answers. Teachers can work toward creating supportive learning environments that optimize the brain's biochemistry.

Optimal learning environment

What elements comprise a developmentally appropriate learning environment compatible with the brain's biochemistry? Such an environment provides high-involvement, low-stress activities like field trips and cooperative learning. It offers children experiences with real-life, hands-on, theme-based activities oriented to solving problems, such as children counting out play money when shopping at the store in the dramatic play center. Additionally, the environment calls into use many of children's senses and various intelligences (Gardner 1993) while they learn through social dialogue during circle time, active listening when interacting with classroom visitors, physical movement when acting out the stories they have written, as well as reading and writing. Children engage in activities that allow them—individually, in pairs, or in small cooperative groups—to make important decisions and choices about what and how they learn. It is easy to imagine the brain's synaptic networks making connections as students touch, think, discuss, eat, and interact with each other in an enriched learning environment where children have opportunities to be physically, socially, and intellectually immersed in learning.

Learning centers in the classroom

A developmentally appropriate classroom enables the connecting of learning to positive emotions, allowing students to make better, more reflective decisions and choices. Emotions are biological functions of the nervous system, and they strongly influence attention and memory. Children engaged in interesting activities at the beginning of the day will have a more positive disposition toward the day's activities as a whole. Additionally, they will retain more information when learning is associated with positive emotions. However, emotions can be a double-edged sword. A balance of emotions is needed for learning to take place. Jensen states that "a little to a moderate amount of stress is good for learning. Lasting high stress or threat, however, is disruptive. It reduces our brain's capacity for understanding and can interfere with our higher-order thinking skills" (1998, 93).

Because individual differences occur among children, not all classroom situations are going to elicit the same response from children. Extroverted children may enjoy public speaking, while introverted children may find it frightening. Some children enjoy the security of daily routine, while others enjoy opportunities for more varied activities. The box "Effective Teacher Strategies That Optimize Learning" presents techniques that influence the brain to be attentive, to absorb new information, and to store this information in long-term memory. The other box, "Situations That Can Hinder Learning," describes conditions and events that can cause a child to be less reflective, more reactive. A great deal of the child's perception of whether a situation is threatening depends upon the teacher's attitude. A potentially upsetting moment can be defused by a caring word, a gentle touch, or a smile.

The classroom environment determines, to some degree, the functioning ability of children's brains.

Learning centers provide children with the autonomy to explore their interests with positive emotions. Some students release emotional tension by playing at the sand table, petting an animal, or working with their hands-on projects. Others may begin the day by reading in a cozy beanbag chair up in the reading loft. Still others enjoy listening to music and eating a snack. Several centers located around the room allow children to participate as individuals or as members of small groups. Centers may focus on carpentry, cut-and-paste activities, science, publishing, pets, chess, reading and writing, and sand and water play.

A learning environment with a variety of centers fosters self-esteem and decision-

making ability by creating opportunities for the learner to make their own decisions and choices. Taking personal responsibility for their learning helps children learn to focus their attention. As a primary school teacher, I provided each child with a tracking sheet to help him monitor the number of times he visited the various learning centers during the week. Tracking sheets also allow the teacher to individualize the curriculum to children's specific needs. I encouraged the children to be responsible for their actions and learning during the day—to hold conversations and discussions as they interacted, played, and learned together.

Meaningful learning experiences

Because knowledge is constructed from meaningful experience, children benefit from being immersed in real-life, hands-on learning experiences that are theme based and oriented toward problem solving. Recent findings (Rushton & Larkin 2001) confirm that children learn best when provided with choices, when they find the learning experiences meaningful, and when they are actively involved in decisionmaking. Research on the brain discloses that neurons change during such experiences. As a child experiences an event for the first time, for example, new dendrites form on nerve cells. Further changes to these dendrites occur with repeated exposure to the experience. The belief is that the greater the number of dendrites and connection of dendrites to each other the greater the speed of recall and memory.

The classroom environment determines, to some degree, the functioning ability of children's brains. Neuroscientists suggest that at birth, children do not possess a fully developed brain. As Wolfe and Brandt (1998) state, "the brain that eventually takes shape is the result of interaction between the individual's genetic inheritance and everything he or she experiences" (p. 18). With this in mind it is important for early childhood and primary teachers to provide experiences that are both meaningful and relevant to the children's lives. When introducing a new theme, the teacher should create a living experience—a real-life learning experience in which the children play an active role; otherwise, the brain is not easily able to store the new information effectively.

Brain research explains why the teachings of child-centered constructivist educators like Dewey, Piaget, and Vygotsky are relevant.

For example, students may take a field trip to a landfill and subsequently make landfill models in their classroom and write about the impact and the future of landfills. Themes chosen by the children should incorporate all aspects of the learning process and integrate the classroom curriculum. Math concepts such as calculating the area of a landfill, sorting and comparing different types of garbage, or estimating and measuring the quantity of garbage that will fill the landfill are easily incorporated. If the learning that takes place in a stimulating and theme-based learning environment is meaningful and relevant to the children's lives, it stimulates their desire to learn.

Conclusion

What would John Dewey think, if he were alive today, of the numerous reports, articles, books, and scientific research relating to this hot topic, brain research? Many of the terms employed in discussing the development and learning of young children—brain-compatible learning environments, positron emission topography, dendrites, neurotransmitters, chemical and electrical synaptic impulses—did not exist in his time. Dewey believed that children learn best when interacting in a rich environment, that children construct meaning from real-life application of knowledge, and that when various senses are used simultaneously, the probability of learning is greater. Educational terminology today, such as *integrated curriculum, theme-based learning, active hands-on learning*, and *authentic teaching*, not only echoes brain research findings but also reflects many of Dewey's philosophical beliefs, thoughts, and tenets.

Research has revealed a great deal about the functioning of the brain during what has been called the *decade of the brain*. Perhaps now as we move further along in the information age, the first decade of the new millennium will become the *decade of education*, as suggested by Wolfe and Brandt (1998). Brain research is filling in gaps in our understanding of how children learn best, and it explains further why the teachings of child-centered constructivist educators like Dewey, Piaget, and Vygotsky are relevant. Hopefully, the use of developmentally appropriate practices for future generations will increase with additional understanding of how the brain works.

References

Bredekamp, S., & C. Copple, eds. 1997. *Developmentally appropriate practice in early childhood programs.* Rev. ed. Washington, DC: NAEYC.

Caine, R.N., & G. Caine. 1997. *Unleashing the power of perceptual change.* Alexandria, VA: Association for Supervision and Curriculum Development.

Diamond, M., & J. Hopson. 1998. *Magic trees of the mind: How to nurture your child's intelligence, creativity, and healthy emotions from birth through adolescence.* New York: Penguin Putman.

Fitzpatrick, S. 1995. Smart brains: Neuroscientists explain the mystery of what makes us human. *American School Board Journal.*

Gardner, H. 1993. *Multiple intelligences: The theory in practice.* New York: Basic.

Jensen, E. 1998. *Teaching with the brain in mind.* Alexandria, VA: Association for Supervision and Curriculum Development.

LeDoux, J. 1996. *The emotional brain: The mysterious underpinnings of emotional life.* New York: Simon & Schuster.

Rushton, S., & L. Larkin. 2001. Shaping the learning environment: Connecting brain research to developmentally appropriate practices. *Early Childhood Education Journal* 29 (1): 25–33.

Sylwester, R. 1995. *A celebration of neurons: An educator's guide to the human brain.* Alexandria, VA: Association for Supervision and Curriculum Development.

Wolfe, J., & R. Brandt. 1998. What we know from brain research. *Educational Leadership* 56 (3): 8–14.

Stephen P. Ruston, Ph.D., *is an assistant professor at the University of South Florida in Sarasota. Stephen is a former elementary school teacher who is interested in brain research, cooperative learning, and effective teaching.*

The Child-Centered Kindergarten**
A Position Paper

Joan Moyer

The child-centered kindergarten is not new; it has its roots in the 19th century. At that time, the kindergarten was envisioned as a "garden for children" (the literal meaning of the German word "kindergarten"), a place where children could be nurtured and allowed to grow at their own pace. While that image has changed somewhat over the years, the "roots" of sensitivity to children remain. Children's developmental needs have not changed, and so the importance of educating the whole child—recognizing his or her physical, social/emotional, and intellectual growth and development—remains. A change in the kindergarten curriculum, however, was brought about by: 1) societal pressure, 2) misunderstandings about how children learn, 3) aggressive marketing of commercial materials largely inappropriate for kindergarten-age children, 4) a shortage of teachers specifically prepared to work with young children, and 5) the reassignment of trained teachers in areas of declining enrollment.

Since its beginning more than 100 years ago as a professional organization, ACEI has emphasized the importance of the kindergarten years in a child's development. The official position of ACEI concerning kindergarten states: *The Association for Childhood Education International recognizes the importance of kindergarten education and supports high-quality kindergarten programs that provide developmentally, culturally, and linguistically appropriate experiences for children* (Moyer, Egertson, & Isenberg, 1987).

Purpose of Kindergarten

Many of the earliest kindergartens in the United States served the purpose of easing the acculturation of newly arrived immigrant children. Later, the purpose became easing the child's transition from home to the more formal aspects of the elementary school. For some children, the transition purpose continues to be important. The vast majority of children today, however, have experience at preschool and/or child care settings before they attend kindergarten. Nevertheless, many people in and out of education continue to perceive the kindergarten as the initial group experience for children (National Center on Education Statistics, 1984, p. 43)

Unfortunately, many parents and elementary educators do not view experiences in child care or other prekindergarten programs as "real learning." Spodek (1999) reported that many of the programs have shifted their emphasis from spurring kindergartners' development to highlighting specific learning goals. While programs vary in quality (as they do in elementary and secondary schools), children of any age are learning in every waking moment. Education provided for children at any level simply serves to organize their learning into more well-defined paths, governed by the philosophical orientation of program planners and the quality of the program. Although broad variations in children's abilities are evident, all children can learn. Noddings (1992) reminds teachers not to expect all children to bring similar strengths and abilities to the classroom. These variations in abilities, coupled with children's varying ethnic backgrounds and socioeconomic levels, add interest, joy, and challenge to the kindergarten program.

The work of such developmental theorists as Dewey, Piaget, and Vygotsky serves as a foundation for kindergarten practices. The theoretical background is expressed through the integrated curriculum, which also best accommodates the variations in children's understanding of the world around them. Early childhood professionals at all levels are concerned about the methods and content in the majority of kindergarten programs. Despite societal changes, kindergarten remains a place where children need a quality program in order to achieve their full potential.

Program Goals

The need for flexibility in planning programs that serve children and their families is well-documented. Parents need options so that the services they select for their children can meet family needs, as well as the needs of each child. Some parents, however, have misconceptions about the goals of the kindergarten program and, as a result, they focus on such cursory academic skills as counting and reciting the alphabet (Simmons & Brewer, 1985). Many people feel comfortable emphasizing such learning because it is easily measured. Elkind (1996) warns, however, that pushing children into academic areas too soon has a negative effect on learning, and refers to this practice as the "miseducation" of young children.

According to Katz (1985), early childhood educators need to consider children's dispositions, which she defines as "characteristic ways of responding to categories of experience across types of situations. Examples include curiosity, humor, creativity, affability, and quarrelsomeness.... Dispositions are not likely to be acquired through workbook exercises, lessons, or direct instruction" (p. 1).

Some parents, concerned over the demanding nature of the kindergarten curriculum, delay their children's kindergarten entrance. This practice has tended to institutionalize the more demanding and narrowly academic curriculum (Walsh, 1989). While 6-year-olds may be more capable of accomplishing the curricular goals, such programs try to "fit" children to the curriculum, rather than adjusting the curriculum to respond to the nature of the learner. Thus, younger children are more likely to fail.

The activity/experience-centered environment, which is essential if young children are to reach their maximum potential, provides for a far richer and more stimulating environment than one dominated by pencil-and-paper, teacher-directed tasks. A well-designed kindergarten program capitalizes on the interest some children may show in learning academic skills. At the same time, it does not have that same expectation for *all* children; nor does it use up precious time to inculcate skills and knowledge for which children have no immediate use or real understanding. Learning to learn should be the emphasis in the early years (Bloom, 1981).

Program Content

Kindergarten programs must be related to the needs and capacities of the children enrolled in them. In spite of major sociological and technological changes, developmental rates have not accelerated, nor are children more intelligent than they used to be (Elkind, 1986). Only the variety and intensity of early experiences have changed. Most kindergarten children are only 5 years old, and they have the basic needs of this age group, whether or not they have attended preschool or know how to read (Webster, 1984). Young children still need supportive environments, rich in direct experiences that are meaningful to them (Nebraska State Department of Education, 1984). A high-quality kindergarten program provides a strong foundation upon which children can build the skills, knowledge, and attitudes toward schooling necessary for lifelong learning.

Program Implementation

An effective, individually and culturally developmentally appropriate kindergarten program:

- Recognizes and accepts individual differences in children's growth patterns and rates by setting realistic curriculum goals that are appropriate to their developmental levels.

- Educates the whole child—with attention to his or her physical, social/emotional, and intellectual developmental needs and interests.

- Responds to the needs of children as developing, thinking individuals by focusing on the process of learning rather than on disparate skills, content, and products.

- Provides multiple opportunities for learning with concrete, manipulative materials that: 1) are relevant to children's experiential background; and 2) keep them actively engaged in learning and discovering through use of all the senses, leading to more input upon which thought is constructed.

- Provides a variety of activities and materials by incorporating: 1) learning activities that encourage active participation through "hands-on" activity, communication, and dialogue; 2) large blocks of time to pursue interests; 3) time to ask questions and receive answers that develop concepts and ideas for use at varying levels of difficulty and complexity; and 4) time to *reflect upon* and abstract information when encountering viewpoints that are different from one's peers.

- Views play as fundamental to children's learning, growth, and development, enabling them to develop and clarify concepts, roles, and ideas by testing and evaluating them through the use of open-ended materials and role-enactment. Play further enables children to develop fine and gross motor skills, to learn to share with others, to learn to see others' points of view, and to be in control of their thoughts and feelings.

- Provides many opportunities for the use of multicultural and nonsexist experiences, materials, and equipment that enhance children's acceptance of self and others; these experiences
enable children to accept differences and similarities among people, including those who are challenged in some way.

- Embraces the teaching of all content areas, especially when they are presented as integrated experiences that develop and extend concepts, strengthen skills, and provide a solid foundation for learning in language, literacy, math, science, social studies, health, art, and music and movement.

- Allows children to make choices and decisions within the limits of the materials provided, resulting in increased independence, attention, joy in learning, and the feelings of success necessary for growth and development.

- Utilizes appropriate assessment procedures, such as observation techniques and portfolios, to measure learning for all kindergarten children.

Play Is Essential

The pressure for academic achievement, coupled with the mistaken idea that today's children have outgrown the need to play, have led to increased emphasis on "basic skills" in kindergarten. The principal source of development in the early years is play (Vygotsky, 1976); in fact, Catron and Allen (1999) state that the optimal development of young children is made possible through play. When viewed as a learning process, play becomes a vehicle for intellectual growth, and it continues to be the most vital avenue of learning for kindergartners. In contrast, research indicates that academic gains from non-play approaches are not lasting (Schweinhart & Weikert, 1996). Play involves not only use of materials and equipment, but also words and ideas that promote literacy and develop thinking skills, Consequently, in addition to the three R's, play also promotes problem-solving, critical thinking, concept formation, and creativity skills. Social and emotional development also are enhanced through play. Play fosters holistic learning (Isenberg & Jalongo, 1997). "Children integrate everything they know in all domains when they play" (Almy, 2000, p. 10). The classic words of Lawrence Frank (1964) remain as meaningful as ever today:

> A conception of play that recognizes the significance of autonomous, self-directed learning and active exploration and manipulation of the actual world gives a promising approach to the wholesome development of children.... It is a way to translate into the education of children our long-cherished, enduring goal values, a belief in the worth of the individual personalities, and a genuine respect for the dignity and integrity of the child. (p. 73)

Suransky (1983) warns that "eroding the play life of early childhood has severe implications for the children we attempt to 'school' in later years" (p. 29). Froebel believed that in free play children reveal their future minds (cited in Bruce, 1993). It is important to emphasize that critics of the current practice of emphasizing academic work over free play are not advocating an environment that makes fewer demands on children. Almy, Monighan, Scales, and Van Hoorn (1984) state, "Teachers who, drawing on recent research and their own classroom research, justify an important place for play in the early childhood curriculum will not lose sight of their responsibility as instructors.... Teachers have responsibility... for providing the play opportunities in which children can consolidate and make personally meaningful the experiences they have had" (p. 22).

Kindergarten teachers agree with researchers and experts who contend that child-centered activities that provide cognitive challenges, and also facilitate the development of autonomy and social skills, are essential for young children (Spidell Rusher, McGrevin, & Lambiotte, 1992). Wardle (1999, p. 7) writes "... as we [have] seen many of our public funded early childhood programs become downward extensions of public schools, we need to advocate for the children's right to play."

Appropriate Physical Environment

Kindergarten children are active, curious learners who need adequate space, a variety of materials, and large blocks of time in which to try out their ideas. Attention to the arrangement of physical facilities is an integral part of their educational experience. How teachers arrange kindergarten classrooms affects children's interests, level of interaction and involvement, initiative development, skill development, and overall attitude toward schooling and learning. A classroom arrangement that supports learning gives attention to the organization and use of space, the arrangement of materials, and the role of both adults and children in the learning environment.

How space is organized and used influences how comfortable children feel and how they work, contributing to a challenging and satisfactory learning environment. Because children's activity patterns change as they gain new skills and mature, and because spatial organization influences other behaviors, the physical facilities must be flexible enough to change to accommodate the children.

Similarly, the arrangement of learning materials determines their level and use. How well materials are arranged also affects the ideas and connections children can make with the materials.

Although children and teachers occupy the same physical space, their perceptions and use of that space are not the same. Kindergarten teachers must arrange the space from the *kindergartner's* point of view and perspective. In order to build a sense of community, kindergarten classrooms should reflect the children, individually and as a group, as well as the teacher.

The following environmental principles address spatial organization, use of materials, and the role of adults in the kindergarten:

- Rooms should be arranged to accommodate individual, small group, and large group activities.
- Interest areas should be clearly defined; differ in size, shape, and location; and attend to traffic patterns while permitting continuity of activity and reducing distractibility. All spaces should be clearly visible to the teacher.
- Rooms should be arranged to facilitate the activity and movements of children at work by attending to available paths for their use and minimizing the amount of interference.
- Learning materials should be arranged and displayed so that they are inviting to children and suggest multiple possibilities for use; they should be clearly visible and accessible, enabling children to return and replace materials as easily as they can get them. Clear, well-organized materials facilitate children's ability to use and explore them.
- Materials should be changed and combined to increase levels of complexity, thus helping children become more self-directed and increasing their level of involvement.
- Children perceive space they can see, reach, and touch. Teachers can support, stimulate, and maintain children's involvement in learning by providing a variety of raw materials for exploration, tools for manipulation, containers for storage and displays, adequate work spaces, inviting displays at eye level, and appropriate sources of information within the children's reach.

Textbooks and Materials

Considerable discussion in the educational and popular media has focused on the quality of textbooks used in schools. The concerns of early childhood educators, however, appear to have been overlooked in this discussion. Many kindergarten teachers are expected to use commercial texts that present information and activities that are developmentally inappropriate. These materials also may be culturally inappropriate. Many "how to" books for teachers are simply collections of reproducible worksheets that result in a pencil/paper curriculum. Such practices do not reflect what we know about how young children learn. Today's kindergarten programs must reflect developmentally appropriate practices that promote active learning, and should match goals and content to the child's level of understanding (Isenberg & Jalongo, 2000).

The introduction of technology into kindergarten classrooms, while promising (and becoming more common), still requires the teacher to determine appropriate uses of that technology. "Used appropriately, technology can enhance children's cognitive and social abilities" (National Association for the Education for Young Children, 1996, p. 12). Elkind (1996) cautions: "The danger is that the young child's proficiency with the computer may tempt us to ignore what we know about cognitive development.... If we rate a child's intellectual competence by his or her performance on a computer, then we will have lost what we have been working so hard to attain—a broad appreciation of developmentally appropriate practice" (p. 23).

Teachers for Kindergartens

Aside from parents, teachers frequently are the most significant adults in young children's lives. Therefore, quality kindergarten programs must be staffed by caring teachers who have faith in every child's potential to achieve and succeed.

Assigning primary and upper elementary teachers to the kindergarten is a questionable practice—indeed, it is cause for great concern. Many of these teachers have limited understanding of appropriate programs for 5-year-olds, and so they operate under the false assumption that young children learn in the same way that older children do (Association for Childhood Education International et al., 1986). Consequently, they use a "watered-down" primary curriculum, replete with workbooks, textbooks, and one-dimensional tasks that can be readily evaluated.

ACEI advocates developmentally appropriate kindergartens staffed with early childhood teachers who:

- Are knowledgeable in child development, committed to children, and able to plan a curriculum that will promote the full development of each child—enabling teachers to have a profound influence on children's lives.
- Listen thoughtfully to children, extend children's language about ideas and feelings, ask questions that encourage insights and highlight contradictions, and promote and value creative, divergent responses from all children.
- Regularly assess children's interests, needs, and skill levels—enabling them to plan continuous, flexible, and realistic activities for each child.
- Design learning environments that provide for successful daily experiences by matching activities to each child's

developmental level, and by using positive interactions, encouragement, and praise for children's efforts.

- Promote a positive self-image by helping children succeed in a variety of activities and experiences, and by providing techniques to help children establish their own limits. Children's self-esteem affects what they do, say, and think.
- Utilize a variety of instructional approaches, including individual, small group, large group, role-enactment activities, and activity centers—all suited to kindergartners' wide range of ability, interests, and needs.
- Provide varied experiences about which kindergarten children can communicate by: 1) encouraging them to use their own experiences as a basis for developing language activities through individual and small group interactions with peers and adults; 2) arranging for periodic change of materials, equipment, and activities in the environment; and 3) providing experiences for children to use their senses as they interact with people and materials.

Such teachers provide effective interaction with children, as well as encouragement, support, and guidance.

Program Support

Parental involvement is essential if they are to understand the purpose of kindergarten education, assist in achieving kindergarten goals and reinforce those lessons in the home setting. Parents who are unable to participate directly in the classroom can contribute in myriad other ways (Barbour & Barbour, 2000; Isenberg & Jalongo, 1997). Parents can show their support for their children's learning by volunteering in the classroom, exchanging information with teachers, acting as chaperones on field trips, helping with homework, reading to children, discussing the school day with the kindergarten child, informing teachers about home situations that may affect the child's behavior at school, and paying attention to materials sent home. Parents must advocate for child-centered kindergarten programs for their children, in part by informing administrators and school boards of their eagerness to support these programs. Teachers, administrators, and parents must work together as advocates for child-centered kindergarten programs.

Central administrators, supervisors, and building principals who oversee the kindergarten program also must be educated about the developmental needs of kindergarten children and the unique needs of the kindergarten program. As Spidell Rusher, McGrevin, and Lambiotte (1992) state, "Communication among teachers, principals, policymakers, experts in childhood education, and parents is vital" (p. 294). With this knowledge, they can provide the administrative support essential to the success of the kindergarten program, value its uniqueness, and interpret it to the community professionally and with integrity. Elkind (1986) cautions that "the risks of miseducating children are both short- and long-term. In each case, the potential psychological risks of early intervention far outweigh any potential educational gain" (p. 634).

ACEI advocates child-centered kindergarten programs that encourage active experiential learning, are developmentally appropriate, increase independence, and promote joy in learning—staffed by teachers who are professionally prepared to work with young children.

As Lewis (2000) writes, "Perhaps what is needed are super programs that provide balance, giving every child a chance to succeed and to play" (p. 564).

**An earlier version of this paper was published in *Childhood Education* (April 1987), 63(4), pp. 235–242.

References and Other Readings

Almy, M. (2000). What wisdom should we take with us as we enter the new century? *Young Children, 55*(1), 6–10.

Almy, M., Monighan, P., Scales, B., & Van Hoorn, J. (1984). Recent research on play: The teacher's perspective. In L. Katz (Ed.), *Current topics in early childhood education, V* (pp. 1–22). Norwood, NJ: Ablex.

Association for Childhood Education International et al. (1986). Literacy development and pre-first grade: A joint statement of concerns about present practices in pre-first reading instruction and recommendations for improvement. *Childhood Education, 63,* 110–111.

Ballenger, M. (1983). Reading in the kindergarten: Comment. *Childhood Education, 59,* 186–187.

Barbour, C., & Barbour, N. H. (2000). *Families, schools and communities: Building partnerships for educating children.* Upper Saddle River, NJ: Prentice-Hall.

Bloom, B. (1981). *All our children learning.* New York: McGraw-Hill.

Border, G., & Berkley, M. (1992). Educational play: Meeting everyone's needs in mainstreamed classrooms. *Childhood Education, 69,* 38–42.

Bredekamp, S., & Copple, C. (Eds.). (1997). *Developmentally appropriate practice in early childhood programs* (Rev. ed.). Washington, DC: National Association for the Education of Young Children.

Bruce, T. (1993). The role of play in children's lives. *Childhood Education, 69,* 237–238.

Catron, C., & Allen, J. (1999). *Early childhood curriculum.* Upper Saddle River, NJ: Merrill/Prentice-Hall.

Christie, J., & Enz, B. (1993). Providing resources for play. *Childhood Education, 69,* 291–292.

Elkind, D. (1986). *Miseducation: Preschoolers at risk.* New York: Knopf.

Elkind, D. (1996). Young children and technology: A cautionary note. *Young Children, 51,* 22–23.

Frank, L. K. (1964). The role of play in child development. *Childhood Education, 41,* 70–73.

Frost, J., Wortham, S., & Reifel, S. (2000). *Play and child development.* Upper Saddle River, NJ: Merrill/Prentice-Hall.

Isenberg, J., & Jalongo, M. (Eds.). (1997). *Major trends and issues in early childhood education: Challenges, controversies, and insights.* New York: Teachers College Press.

Isenberg, J., & Jalongo, M. (2000). *Creative expression and play in early childhood* (3rd ed.). Upper Saddle River, NJ: Merrill/Prentice-Hall.

Isenberg, J., & Quisenberry, N. L. (1988). Play: A necessity for all children. *Childhood Education, 64,* 138–145.

Katz, L. (1985). Dispositions in early childhood education. *ERIC/EECE Bulletin, 18*(2), 1–3.

Lewis, A. (2000). 'Playing' with equity and early education. *Phi Delta Kappan, 81*(8), 563–564.

Moyer, J., Egertson, H., & Isenberg, J. (1987). The child-centered kindergarten. Position paper of the Association for Childhood Education International. *Childhood Education, 63,* 235–242.

National Association for the Education of Young Children. (1996). Position statement: Technology and young children—ages three through eight. *Young Children, 51*(6), 11–16.

National Center on Education Statistics. (1984). *Digest of education statistics, 1983–84.* Washington, DC: U.S. Government Printing Office.

Nebraska Center on Education Statistics. (1984). *Position statement on kindergarten,* 1–8. Lincoln, NE: Author.

Noddings, N. (1992). *The challenge to care in schools: An alternative approach to education.* New York: Teachers College Press.

Okagaki, L., & Sternberg, R. (1994). Perspectives on kindergarten. *Childhood Education, 71,* 14–19.

Schweinhart, R., & Weikert, D. (1996). *Lasting differences: The High/Scope preschool curriculum comparison study through age 23. Monographs of the High/Scope Educational Research Foundation, No. 12.* Ypsilanti, MI: High/Scope Press.

Simmons, B., & Brewer, J. (1985). When parents of kindergartners ask "why?" *Childhood Education, 61,* 177–184.

Spidell Rusher, A., McGrevin, C., & Lambiotte, J. (1992). Belief systems of early childhood teachers and their principals regarding early childhood education. *Early Childhood Research Journal, 7,* 277–296.

Spodek, B. (1999). The kindergarten. In K. Pachiorek & J. Munro (Eds.), *Sources: Notable selections in early childhood education* (2nd ed.) (pp. 101–111). Guilford, CT: McGraw-Hill.

Stone, S. (1995–96). Integrating play into the curriculum. *Childhood Education, 72,* 104–107.

Suransky, V. (1983). The preschooling of childhood. *Educational Leadership, 40*(6), 27–29.

Swick, K. (1993). *Strengthening parents and families during the early childhood years.* Champaign, IL: Stipes Publishing Company.

Vygotsky, L. (1976). Play and its role in the mental development of the child. In J. Bruner (Ed.), *Play: Its role in development and evolution.* New York: Basic Books.

Walsh, D. (1989). Changes in kindergarten: Why here? Why now? *Early Childhood Research Quarterly, 4,* 377–391.

Wardle, F. (1999). Play as curriculum. *Early Childhood News,* March/April, pp. 6–9.

Wassermann, S. (1992). Serious play in the classroom: How messing around can win you the Nobel Prize. *Childhood Education, 68,* 133–139.

Webster, N. (1984). The 5's and 6's go to school: Revisited. *Childhood Education, 60,* 325–329.

Wing, L. (1995). Play is not the work of the child: Young children's perceptions of work and play. *Early Childhood Research Quarterly, 10*(2), 223–248.

Joan Moyer is Professor, College of Education, Arizona State University, Tempe.

ORDEAL WITH A NO. 2 PENCIL

Standardized tests have become a grueling rite of passage for students in most states—and they are more important than ever. How you can help your children do their best.

BY DANIEL MCGINN

A few mornings each year, the Torres family goes through a special ritual. Guadalupe, the 33-year-old mother of seven, cooks pancakes to give her kids energy for the big day. The kids are nervous, and Mom calms them down. "I get nervous, too, so I count to 10," Guadalupe says. "And we pray." They're asking God for a special kind of wisdom—the kind that helps children pass the Iowa Basic Skills Test. In Chicago, where the Torreses live, students in third, sixth and eighth grades must pass the exam or repeat the grade. Jennifer, 15, has felt the mix of emotions that accompanies failure. "I didn't know what to do," she says. "I was pretty mad at myself. I was pretty sad." While repeating eighth grade, she says, "I felt bad because I was practically the oldest one in my class." Eventually Jennifer passed; today she's a high-school freshman.

Standardized tests like the Iowa have long been part of the rhythms of school days. But in most states, those fill-in-the-bubble rites of passage are taking on new importance. After two decades of debate about the quality of schools, educational reform is now all the rage, and new tests are a key feature. Unlike old-style tests, which were used to assign kids to higher- or lower-level classes, the new tests are what experts call "high stakes" exams. Students who fail face real penalties, like staying back or being barred from graduating. School scores are being spotlighted, too. The result is that test scores have never played a bigger part in the way our children are taught. So parents who take an active role in their children's education should be ready to deal with their scores.

For many families, this will be no big deal. Lots of kids excel on these tests. For those lucky ones, the exams are a chance to bond with a No. 2 pencil, and then life moves on. But not everyone is so fortunate. Some otherwise strong students fare poorly on standardized exams, due to nervousness or time pressure. Even solid test takers can be tripped up by these new exams, many of which are more difficult than past tests; sometimes, they test children on material they've never been taught. In many states, the majority of students fail at least one section of the exam. Although schools are working to boost test scores, it's mostly up to parents to deal with the emotional punch that low scores deliver, and to ensure they don't turn a kid off from learning altogether. Parents will also have to decide whether to seek remedial help, whether it's done at home, in school-sponsored programs or through an outside tutor.

Experts offer simple advice for parents whose kids bring home a low exam score. First, relax. Anyone can have an off day; a single test score doesn't signal big deficiencies in your child. Next, don't be too quick to tell a young child his scores. At many schools, kids trade scores like Pokémon cards, but if a child fails, it's better if his friends don't know. Instead of showing your child his scores, provide directional feedback. Let him know he did better in math than reading, say, or needs extra work on long division. "Kids are inclined to believe that tests are written by God—that there's something objective and smart about them," says John Katzman, chief executive of

WHAT TO ASK

- Find out if there are practice tests available for your state. Experts worry about parents "teaching to the test" at home. But in states that put heavy weight on testing, parents need to know how to drill their children.
- Ask how difficult the next test is going to be. As the process evolves, some tests turn out to be harder than earlier ones. That's one reason that good students sometimes fail.
- Make sure the school doesn't give test scores directly to children. Try to keep your child from learning the exact result. Instead, provide general feedback on areas that need improvement—and areas in which the child was successful. If your child fails part or all of a test, don't panic. The most useful thing you can do about it is to play a more active, everyday role in your child's education.

the Princeton Review Corp., which primarily helps students prepare for SAT tests. Schools are already making a big deal out of these tests; being discreet with your child's results can keep them from taking on a life of their own.

What can parents do to help kids boost scores? The most basic advice is to simply take as active a role as possible in their education. Read their homework. Know what they're studying, and when that big history project is due. "Study with kids, give them pop quizzes," says Dr. Richard Bavaria, vice president at Sylvan Learning Systems. The next step: learn as much as you can about the test itself. "Just because there's a test given and a child scores at the 25th percentile doesn't mean the child isn't able," says testing expert W. James Popham. "You have to understand what the test is measuring." Some questions test skills, like "spatial capacity," which are largely inherited. Others may be culturally biased. Popham, author of "Testing! Testing! What Every Parent Should Know About School Tests," says parents who educate themselves about their school's testing regimen and don't like what they find should work to get bad tests out of their schools.

No matter how objectionable tests are, in many states kids won't graduate until they pass them. As a result, schools are bearing down to help them pass. In many districts, students now spend long hours doing drills, work sheets and practice tests to boost scores. Those lessons often continue after class ends. Since 1997, nearly three quarters of Chicago's 489 public elementary schools have offered the Lighthouse Program, an after-school skill-building clinic. At Rachel Carson Elementary School on the city's Southwest Side, Susan Bohman guides her eighth-grade pupils through a complicated maze of geometric concepts. Behind her on the wall is a poster listing

tips for taking the Iowa. Elizabeth Zargoza, who was promoted from third grade to fourth grade in January after passing the test on her third attempt, credits the Lighthouse tutors, who work with at-risk pupils like her in groups of three or fewer.

Down the hall, Rosa Alvarez holds up colorful flash cards as her Lighthouse third graders tackle today's lesson on compound words. There are 18 faces gazing up from a large, gray throw rug; together they shout "toothbrush... bathroom" in unison before writing the words in their notebooks. Later Alvarez will guide the students through dry runs of the Iowas. She hands out practice answer sheets, plays a little calm-down music—Mozart is the favorite—then instructs them to close their eyes, clear their minds and maybe stretch a little bit. The students will take practice tests several times before May, when they take the real thing. A key goal, she says, is for them to become familiar with taking tests under time constraints. That pressure threw eighth-grader Luis Garcia for a loop when he took the test last time. "There were a lot of passages and long stories for the time it gave us," he says. The after-school study has helped. "You get more attention from the teacher," he says. He takes the test for a third time this May.

The private sector is rushing to lend a hand, too. SmarterKids.com, a highly rated online retailer of educational toys, is testing a system where parents can input a child's test scores and receive customized recommendations of products that will shore up weak spots. Marta Anders, 42, of Cornwall on Hudson, N.Y., is making use of the site. Anders knows a lot about standardized tests, since she teaches SAT prep courses at a nearby high school. Her own child, Elizabeth, is a home-schooled second grader, but under New York state law she'll have to pass a proficiency exam in fourth and eighth grades. They've been using games like Draw-Write-Now and Fun Thinkers Match Game to help her build the skills she'll need. Anders supplements those lessons with simple test-taking skills, like using the process of elimination on multiple-choice questions. With Elizabeth, as well as her high-school students, Anders reinforces the message that test scores are imperfect indicators of academic performance. "There is no correlation between those numbers and what you will achieve down the road," she says. But Elizabeth will be ready. "The test is two years away, but I'm not worried," says Anders. "We'll do what we have to do."

Tutoring companies are entering the grade-school test-prep business as well. These companies—led by SCORE! Educational Centers and its online affiliate, eSCORE.com (SCORE! is copublisher of this guide and, like NEWSWEEK, is owned by The Washington Post Company), Sylvan Learning Systems, Huntington Learning Centers and the Princeton Review—have become fixtures in many communities as parents turn to outside professionals for remediation and enrichment because they worry that schools aren't doing the job. These firms make some people uneasy because they feed on parents' insecurities and because their prices are out of reach for many families. Now, for better or worse, they're beginning to help kids prep for state assessment tests. "It's good news for students who have access to the ace-the-[test]-products," editorialized The Boston Globe last fall. But it also "raises the issue that haunts college admissions tests: Prep classes may give some students an edge," if they can afford it.

IN MANY DISTRICTS, STUDENTS SPEND LONG HOURS DOING DRILLS, WORK SHEETS AND PRACTICE TESTS TO BOOST SCORES. LESSONS OFTEN CONTINUE AFTER SCHOOL.

Sometimes entire schools are enrolled in these programs, paid by tax dollars, reducing worries over fairness. Thomas Simes, a fourth grader in Sacramento, Calif., used to vomit and suffer migraines when he took tests. But this year, his class spends 45 minutes, four times a week, working on test-taking strategies with a teacher trained in methods by Kaplan, SCORE's parent company. Thomas says it's fun—especially history, where they've written essays and studied California's mission churches. Looking ahead, he's confident about his next state test. "I think I'm going to do well because of all the testing skills we've been doing," he says. Michelle Simes, his mom, says his practice scores have improved, and he seems more confident. "I've noticed a difference in him personally," she says. The biggest plus: no more vomiting on test days.

Parents willing to work intensively with their kids to boost scores can also utilize free—or nearly free—resources. States are sharing more information about their tests. Some place old copies of tests on Web sites. Kaplan publishes inexpensive, easy-to-understand test-prep guides covering exams in Massachusetts, Texas, Florida and New York; similar products from other publishers should soon be available.

Experts like Popham, a retired UCLA professor, are leery about parents' "teaching to the test" by prepping in this manner, since it ignores what children are really learning by focusing on the end instead of the means. For parents who are forced by state laws to focus on test scores, he says, drilling kids with practice tests closely aligned to the real exams is the key. "The closer the match, the better the preparation, the bigger the payoff." But as schools become increasingly test-driven, parents can also do a service by counter-programming, experts say. "Don't forget arts, sports, extracurricular activities— all of these things help children learn," says Sylvan's Bavaria. As testing intensifies, parents need to keep things in perspective.

With SARAH DOWNEY *in Chicago,*
RENA KIRSCH *in Boston and* JOAN
RAYMOND *in Cleveland*

"But What's Wrong With Letter Grades?"

Responding to Parents' Questions About Alternative Assessment

Linda Doutt Culbertson
and Mary Renck Jalongo

Imagine attending a parent/teacher conference, this time as a parent without any professional training in the field of education. You have just been presented with a folder of information that documents your child's progress. This portfolio includes notes about daily achievement, checklists showing areas of strength, child-selected work samples, and even artwork and interest inventories that show that the school recognizes talents beyond academics. Your child enjoys coming to school and you have seen steady improvement in his or her reading and math capabilities; in fact, your child is blossoming not only in schoolwork, but also in everyday situations.

While you understand that the portfolio folder shows your child's academic growth for this term, nagging questions about the process of student evaluation remain. You wonder, "What is wrong with a simple letter grade? I had them in school and so did my parents. Why make a sudden change in the way my child is evaluated? Can you convince me that portfolios are superior to report cards?"

Parents are the most significant influence in a child's life (Gelfer, 1991), and they expect and deserve answers to questions about alternative assessment. This article attempts to answer some of parents' most common questions, including:

- Why is there a need for change?
- Just what is alternative assessment?
- How can parents recognize an alternative assessment?
- What contributions can alternative assessment make to a comprehensive evaluation plan?

Why Is There a Need for Change?

We all have experienced the pounding hearts and churning stomachs when we realize that the exam in front of us does not cover the material we studied. A feeling of powerlessness overcomes us, and we wish we were anywhere else but sitting in that chair taking that test. Thoughts such as "Why didn't I study something else?" and "Will I fail?" triumph over the more important questions of "What do I know?" and "How can I improve?" The feeling of panic that results can last for a day or for a lifetime, as when people say, "I always 'freeze up' on tests."

"What is wrong with a simple letter grade? I had them in school and so did my parents. Why make a sudden change in the way my child is evaluated? Can you convince me that portfolios are superior to report cards?"

Unfortunately, the practice of testing specific material at one particular point in time is a common practice in many American classrooms. Our children are now experiencing the same feelings of powerlessness that we experienced as students when confronted by the pressures of testing. Schools' testing procedures often serve to both label and demoralize children by separating them into groups. Those who obtain high test scores are likely to be placed into the "academic" group and will receive the best teachers and the best learning opportunities; those who do not score as well often are left with drill-and-practice exercises, presumably to compensate for their deficiencies (Goodwin, 1997).

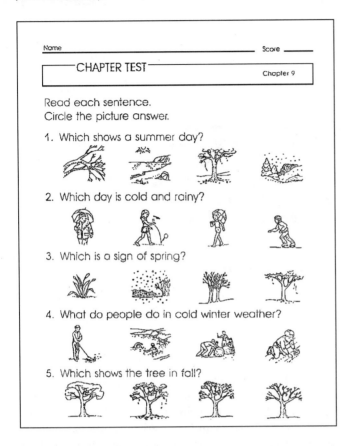

Traditional test used to assess seasonal changes © Silver, Burdett & Ginn.
Figure 1

Because technology has expanded the amount of information available, we can no longer base education on a factory model of learning in which knowledge is poured into children, who memorize it for tests and forget it shortly thereafter. Fairness to children demands that we teach them the skills necessary to think and to make decisions about the knowledge that is available to them. Traditional testing offers no opportunity for a child to stop and say, "But wait! This test doesn't show what I can do! I didn't understand the question you were asking, but when you word it differently, I know the answer. Give me a chance to explain… then you'll see!" It is no longer reasonable to provide advantages only to those who are good test takers; we must base students' evaluations on the quality of their work and not merely on their ability to recall information for a test.

Just What Is Alternative Assessment?

What if you were asked to rate a loved one on a scale of 1 to 10? Perhaps you would use all kinds of information (e.g., emotional strength, physical appearance, social skills) to arrive at the final number. Now imagine that only the number itself is reported to your loved one. Would you feel comfortable sharing the number without any explanation?

In the same manner, it makes more sense for teachers to determine what children know and can do based upon experiences that can be explained and expanded upon, rather than on multiple-choice, true/false, or other traditional forms of testing that offer no opportunities for explanation. Alternative assessment is based upon the performance of a task that the child is likely to encounter outside the classroom (Hamayan, 1995); therefore, it provides for a more natural and less stressful way of evaluating students than traditional testing does. It makes more sense, for example, to evaluate students on their ability to make correct change by setting up a classroom store than by having them complete a worksheet of addition and subtraction problems. Too often, the abilities demanded on a simple task like basic computation do not "translate" well to a practical situation. If you go to a fast food restaurant, for example, you will see that the cash register is set up with icons of the food items and that the cash register distributes the correct change. This way of making change came about mainly because while employees could pass a simple math test, they still did not know how to handle money. Clearly, it is possible to master "the basics," yet still be unable to function well on the job.

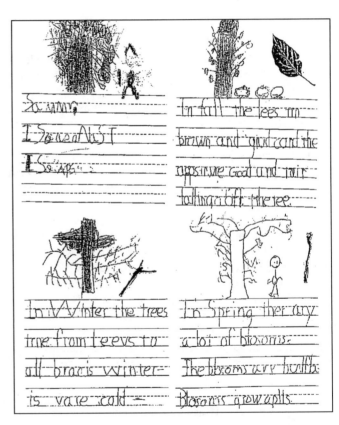

Alternative assessment used to evaluate knowledge of seasonal changes. "Summer. I saw a nest. I saw apples. In Fall the leaves turn brown and gold and the apples are very good and they're falling off the tree. In Winter the trees turn from leaves to all branches. Winter is very cold. In Spring there are a lot of blossoms. The blossoms are very beautiful. Blossoms grow apples."
Figure 2

Informal methods of assessment are an integral part of daily life. We evaluate waiters and waitresses on performance—their efficiency in taking our order and delivering our food. It would mean very little to us that they might get a good grade on a multiple-choice "Server's Examination." In the same manner, we evaluate our accountants based upon the amount of money they save us at tax time, and our children's teachers based upon how well our children respond to their instruction. In fact, a national survey (conducted by the Carnegie Foundation for the Advancement of Teaching) found that parents' number one criterion for evaluating teachers was the teacher's ability to motivate their child to learn (Boyer, 1995), an ability that would be extremely difficult to measure on a test. Thus, basing evaluation on real-world evidence and actual job performance makes learning more relevant.

Figure 1 shows a traditional science examination given to assess 1st-graders' knowledge of seasonal changes. Figure 2 provides an alternative assessment in which children made seasonal visits to an apple tree and then recorded their observations. Although the alternative assessment measures the same information as the traditional test does, it provides a much more meaningful, easily remembered way to learn about seasonal changes. Traditional and alternative methods of assessment are not necessarily in opposition to one another; rather, the alternative methods are ways of providing a more complete picture of children's knowledge, understanding, and ability to apply what has been learned.

How Can I Recognize an Alternative Assessment?

Alternative assessment operates on the assumption that students should be evaluated according to criteria that are important for the performance of a given task (Wiggins, 1989). The measures used should give teachers and parents a clear picture of what the child can or cannot do in order to help the child in a given area. Many parents are accustomed to seeing their children arrive home from school each day with a backpack full of worksheets and papers. They assume by the amount of paperwork that their child is learning certain skills. The notion of equating a large amount of paperwork with learning, however, is a false one; children are learning all of the time even without direct instruction. In fact, they learn best if they are actively involved in the process (Newmann & Wehlage, 1995). Ironically, the same adults who speak despairingly of becoming "paper pushers" at work are often the first to demand that children begin doing this as soon as possible in school. Outside the classroom, the opposite assumption is made. When teaching children to use inline skates, play a musical instrument, or build a model airplane, we expect learning to occur when children are actively involved in firsthand experiences.

The specific form of alternative assessment will depend upon the subject area, the students being instructed, and an individual teacher's preference. The following examples provide insight into the most common types of alternative assessment (Darling-Hammond, Ancess, & Falk, 1995). They can be used to help

parents recognize the many different ways that a child's effort, growth, and academic achievement are being recognized and documented.

> **FIRST QUARTER SKILL CHECKLIST**
> **FIRST GRADE**
>
> **Language Arts:**
>
> Identifies capital letters _____
> Identifies lower case letters _____
> Identifies initial consonant sounds _____
> Identifies final consonant sounds _____
> Recognizes vowels (a, e, i, o, u) _____
> Recognizes basic sight words (to current level) _____
> Uses temporary spelling to express ideas _____
> Uses spaces between words in writing _____
>
> **Math:**
>
> Forms sets using objects and numerals _____
> Writes numerals correctly from 1-10 _____
> Can count aloud to . . . _____
> Recognizes numbers to . . . _____
> Can complete and identify basic patterns _____
> Can combine sets to form a new number _____
>
> *A check in the box indicates mastery to grade level expectancy.*
>
> Parent Signature: _____ Date _____
> Teacher Signature: _____ Date _____

A checklist used for first grade.
Figure 3

Teacher Observation. Imagine calling your mechanic after your car has broken down on the freeway. After explaining how the car performed, you ask the mechanic to diagnose the problem over the telephone; your mechanic, however, insists upon actually *seeing* the car before making any kind of assessment. Although observing the car is not the only way to determine what is wrong, it certainly helps the mechanic make a more accurate assessment of the problem.

Teachers likewise use observation to become more informed about children. It allows teachers to get to know students as individuals, with talents and abilities uniquely their own (Wortham, 1995). Observation is a way for teachers to familiarize themselves not only with the academic aspects of a child's development, but also with social, emotional, physical, and cultural influences on learning. Many circumstances—both in and out of school—influence learners, and observation paints a clearer picture than testing ever can.

Checklists. Think about your last visit to a physician's office. Did the receptionist ask you to fill out a checklist so that the doctor would know about your family history and prior illnesses? If you checked "yes" for an illness, you were probably asked to provide further information. The doctor could then refer to the checklist during your visit to make sure that all pertinent questions had been asked and that no possible factor had been overlooked. The checklist provided an easily accessible and consistent manner in which to record your medical history, and it gave the doctor concrete information with which to work.

For the classroom teacher, checklists provide a way to make sure that all areas of a child's education have been evaluated. Checklists are designed and based upon a particular grade level's curriculum, and they provide a framework for assessment that can be used to communicate a child's progress to parents (Wortham, 1995). By providing specific details concerning a child's performance, the checklist in Figure 3 provides parents with more information than a letter grade does. Brief comments also can be recorded on the checklist for elaboration.

Projects and Exhibitions. Think about the displays and exhibits that are used to advertise new products at a home show, grocery store, or shopping mall. Posters, videos, and photographs—along with actual samples—invite passersby to take a closer look. The displays provide succinct information about each product.

In the school setting, projects and exhibitions are types of alternative assessment that can furnish concrete evidence of a child's most significant accomplishments. Book reports, creative writing, computations, photographs, videotapes, audiotapes, and other media are highly motivating, because these methods allow students to demonstrate and document understanding. They also enable children to share their successes as learners in a tangible way with peers and family members. Because projects and exhibitions provide a tangible measurement of learning, children can learn to take pride in their accomplishments and strive for excellence.

Portfolios. Did your parents proudly keep a folder stuffed with your papers, photographs, drawings, and so forth from kindergarten through 12th grade? Perhaps you still own some of these items or have since reviewed them with your child. Collections of documents like these are worth a second look because they chronicle a child's developmental changes and new skills.

Unlike the folders kept by parents, classroom portfolios are organized, purposeful collections of student work that help to tell the story of a student's efforts, progress, or achievement in a given area. Portfolios provide an alternative to drill worksheets, standardized tests, and other measures that reflect skills development rather than developmental progress (Graves & Sunstein, 1992). Portfolios can represent all areas of the curriculum and may include papers, checklists, summaries, or other items that adequately demonstrate a student's performance. Portfolios offer a wonderful opportunity for students, parents, and teachers to not only see test scores, but also actually experience a child's growth. Figure 4 shows a sample letter sent home to parents to explain a child's portfolio.

When Does Alternative Assessment Occur?

In the workplace, you may have had a supervisor observe and assess your performance over a long period of time, perhaps for an entire year. Even if (or because) we know such evaluations are coming, our nervousness may impair our ability to perform. As adults, we appreciate it when the quality of our work is judged fairly, and in the right context. Most of us also prefer to have continuous feedback from supervisors rather than have everything depend upon one brief sample of behavior that may not be representative of our overall performance.

Dear Mom or Dad,

This is my portfolio. It is a collection of my best work in different subjects in school. My portfolio is so special because my teacher did not choose the pieces of work for it . . . I DID! Sometimes with your help, I picked out the pieces that I felt good about.

I have included some of my journal wirting from September of this year so that you can see my improvement. You will see that I have learned how to express my ideas much better and use lots more periods, capital letters, and other punctuation marks in the right places.

You will also see some of my best work in math, reading, art, and other subjects. There is even a book I've written! Please be sure to notice my improvement throughout the year. I've been working so hard. What a change you'll see!

I have met with my teacher to talk about why I chose what I did for my portfolio. I know you will see how I have grown this year by looking at it. I am very proud of my work and hope that you are too!

Love from your child,

_____

A letter sent to parents describing their child's portfolio.
Figure 4

One of the greatest strengths of alternative assessment is its ability to allow the teacher to see the child as a whole person and not purely as a learner of basic skills. Instead of assessing children at one time on a given measure, alternative assessment allows the teacher to evaluate children's work on various projects as they proceed. The teacher is able to gain a comprehensive view of student progress from many sources and can collect varied work samples to gain an understanding of how students think about and learn new skills (Campbell, 1997).

Many children, just like adults, grow apprehensive, become demoralized, or give up entirely when given only one "high stakes" chance to prove themselves. Alternative assessment is based upon the premise that students grow and change continuously, and that measurement of their knowledge, abilities, and skills is seriously limited by a one-shot approach to testing (Isenberg & Jalongo, 1997).

How Does Alternative Assessment Contribute to Children's Learning?

1. Alternative assessment makes sense to students.
Would you be happy if you were given one test to determine your salary, benefits, and promotion opportunities for the upcoming year? Furthermore, would such a procedure make sense to you? Being judged by our performance is much more meaningful than being judged by a contrived measure that is unrelated to our daily lives. This concept makes sense to children as well.

Alternative assessment invites students to think about what they have learned, and it gives children the opportunity to make connections from classroom experiences to the outside world (Gardner, 1993). When learning is personally relevant, children can continuously monitor their progress and assess their own learning (Glazer, 1992). Because alternative assessment makes sense to students, they have a much better understanding of what is expected of them and, therefore, have a much better chance of meeting those expectations (Earl & LeMahieu, 1996).

2. Alternative assessment fosters responsibility in students.
Students can develop responsibility for their own learning by having opportunities to choose work for portfolios, discuss their observations, and determine where they need help. Whereas multiple-choice tests promote competition among students, alternative assessment promotes skill in self- and peer evaluation. Students develop responsibility and independence by learning to help, share, cooperate, and care about others (Osin & Lesgold, 1996).

Alternative assessment allows children to make choices, and it gives them responsibility for living with those choices within a classroom setting where the teacher is a guide and facilitator. Before students are placed in real-life decision-making situations, alternative assessment provides them with plenty of practice in making decisions within classroom walls. Students become problem-solvers in a non-threatening atmosphere that encourages them to learn from their mistakes.

3. Alternative assessment emphasizes the process, rather than the product, of learning.
By focusing on the entire learning process, rather than on one small product (e.g., a test at the "end" of learning), alternative assessment helps children to realize that what they do each day in school is part of an important and ongoing process. By focusing on intense, concentrated involvement in an activity (Osin & Lesgold, 1996), students gain more information than they would from a single evaluation product or test. Rather than memorizing facts for a test that will soon be forgotten, children build upon their knowledge and are encouraged to evaluate their own growth. This meaningful process helps to create an environment in which learning is remembered. Alternative assessment provides opportunities for the process of work to be challenging, pleasurable, and rewarding (Osin & Lesgold, 1996).

4. Alternative assessment motivates children to continue learning.
If each of us were assigned the task of constructing a birdhouse, we would probably approach it in very different ways. Some would prefer to work with a group; others would work better alone. Some would be able to create an original from materials found at home, while others would buy a kit and follow the directions to the letter. Most of us would want to find out which structures attract which birds and study examples of birdhouses before beginning our task. Having choices motivates us much more than being told, "Your birdhouse must look exactly like the other 25 in your neighborhood, and you must complete it at exactly the same time and in the same sequence as everyone else." By the same token, students either can be motivated by having choices in reaching high standards, or they can be defeated by being forced to do things exactly as others in their class are doing. Alternative assessment allows for student selection of learning opportunities, based upon the assumption that having an interest in something will be motivation to learn more about it. Teachers and parents can work together with the child to choose projects that are "natural challenges," and that lead to real accomplishments (Osin & Lesgold, 1996). Alternative assessment motivates children by giving them a voice in their own education (Schneider, 1996).

Conclusion

No parent wants his or her child to fail in the school system. Although looking at a letter grade on a report card or a percentage score from a traditional test is familiar, based on our own experiences as children, it does little to help us form accurate, detailed perceptions about a child's strengths or academic needs (Newman & Smolen, 1993). Alternative assessment can provide us with information about daily progress and insight into the process of learning. It also encourages children to become lifelong learners, rather than memorizers and forgetters of information. The major purposes of any assessment practices in schools should be to help children really understand what they are learning, enable them to concentrate and investigate ideas in depth, and encourage them to produce high-quality work that will be useful to them, not just in school but also throughout their lives (Newmann & Wehlage, 1995). Although changes in assessment practices may be disconcerting at first, adults who really care about children and their learning will need to concentrate more on children's futures than on their distant pasts, if they are to improve education for all students.

References

Boyer, E. L. (1995). *The basic school: A community for learning.* Princeton, NJ: The Carnegie Foundation for the Advancement of Teaching.

Campbell, L. (1997). Variations on a theme: How teachers interpret MI theory. *Educational Leadership, 55*(1), 14–19.

Darling-Hammond, L., Ancess, J., & Falk, B. (1995). *Authentic assessment in action: Studies of schools and students at work.* New York: Teachers College Press.

Earl, L. M., & LeMahieu, P. C. (1996). Rethinking assessment and accountability. In A. Hargreaves (Ed.), 1997 ASCD Yearbook: *Rethinking educational change with heart and mind* (pp. 149–168). Alexandria, VA: Association for Supervision and Curriculum Development.

Gardner, H. (1993). *Frames of mind: The theory of multiple intelligences.* New York: Basic Books.

Gelfer, J. I. (1991). Teacher-parent partnerships: Enhancing communications. *Childhood Education, 67,* 164–167.

Glazer, S. J. (1992). Assessment in classrooms: Reality and fantasy. *Teaching K-8, 22*(8), 62–64.

Goodwin, A. L. (1997). *Assessment for equity and inclusion: Embracing all our children.* New York: Routledge.

Graves, D. H., & Sunstein, B. S. (1992). *Portfolio portraits.* Portsmouth, NH: Heinemann.

Hamayan, E. V. (1995). Approaches to alternative assessment. *Annual Review of Applied Linguistics, 15,* 212–226.

Isenberg, J. P., & Jalongo, M. R. (1997). *Creative expression and play in early childhood* (2nd ed.). Upper Saddle River, NJ: Merrill/Prentice Hall.

Newman, C., & Smolen, L. (1993). Portfolio assessment in our schools: Implementation, advantages, and concerns. *MidWestern Educational Researcher, 6*(1), 28–32.

Newmann, F. M., & Wehlage, G. G. (1995). *Successful school restructuring: A report to the public and educators.* Madison, WI: University of Wisconsin-Madison, Wisconsin Center for Educational Research, Center on Organization and Restructuring of Schools.

Osin, L., & Lesgold, A. (1996). A proposal for the re-engineering of the educational system. In F. B. Murray & J. Raths (Eds.), *Review of education research: Winter 1996* (pp. 621–656). Washington, DC: American Educational Research Association.

Schneider, E. (1996). Giving students a voice in the classroom. *Educational Leadership, 54*(1), 22–26.

Science test masters grade 1. (1987). Morristown, NJ: Silver, Burdett & Ginn.

Wiggins, G. (1989). A true test: Toward more authentic assessment. *Phi Delta Kappan,* 703–713.

Wortham, S. C. (1995). *Measurement and evaluation in early childhood education.* Englewood Cliffs, NJ: Prentice Hall.

Linda Doutt Culbertson is Teacher, Edinboro Elementary School, Edinboro, Pennsylvania. Mary Renck Jalongo is Professor, Indiana University of Pennsylvania, Indiana, Pennsylvania, and Editor, Early Childhood Education Journal.

From *Childhood Education,* Spring 1999, pp. 130-135. Reprinted by permission of Linda Doutt Culbertson and Mary Renck Jalongo, and the Association for Childhood Education International, 17904 Georgia Avenue, Suite 215, Olney, MD. © 1999 by ACEI.

The Silencing of Recess Bells

Judith Kieff

In approximately 40 percent of American elementary and middle schools, recess or break time bells have been silenced. Recent policies severely limit or eliminate children's opportunities to engage in self-chosen activities such as free play, unstructured and vigorous physical exercise, and informal social interactions during the school day (Alexander, 1999). This growing trend toward restricting children's freedom to interact and play in relatively unsupervised settings is also affecting the United Kingdom and Australia (Blatchford, 1996). Policymakers cite issues related to the use of time in schools and to playground safety as reasons for curtailing such activity. Unfortunately, informal and unstructured break time, commonly called "recess" in American elementary schools, often is eliminated because many teachers, parents, and policymakers underestimate both the immediate benefits of recess as a partner to quality instruction, and the cumulative and deferred benefits of play for children's learning and development.

There is both theoretical and empirical evidence that allowing time for recess or playground activities can yield immediate and long-term benefits for children of all ages, throughout their school careers (Bar-bour, 1996; Blatchford, 1996; Dempster, 1988; Johnson, 1996; Pellegrini & Bjorklund, 1996; Pellegrini & Davis, 1993; Pellegrini, Huberty, & Jones, 1995; Pellegrini & Smith, 1993). Therefore, it is important to re-examine those issues related to time and safety while developing policies that are sensitive to the nature of child development and learning. Pairing recess with quality instruction provides an essential feature of the school day that promotes learning across domains.

Issues Related to Time

In this age of accountability and test-driven instruction, "time-on-task" has become a common battle cry of administrators. Indeed, the time-on-task literature (see Brophy & Good, 1974, for a summary) clearly shows that achievement is directly related to the amount of time spent on a related task. Increasing time in the classroom by eliminating recess may, at first glance, appear to be a sound policy that could lead to improved student achievement. Pellegrini and Bjorklund (1996) state that assuming "a positive correspondent between increased work time and increased student learning... is not the same as stating that more intense, break-free hours of instruction will enhance learning" (p. 5).

Children learn more effectively when their efforts are distributed over time rather than concentrated into longer periods (Ebinghaus, 1964; Hunter, 1929). This phenomenon is known as "task spacing" or "distributed effort" (see Dempster, 1988, for a review). Pellegrini and Bjorklund (1996) point out that "the positive effects of distributed effort have specifically addressed the ways in which children learn numerous school-like tasks, such as native and foreign language vocabulary, recall from text, and math facts" (p. 8). Therefore, when recess or break time is paired with quality instruction, the spacing of these activities generally provides an immediate, positive effect on learning.

Further evidence supporting recess as a partner to quality instruction is found in the work of Pellegrini and his colleagues (Pellegrini & Davis, 1993; Pellegrini et al., 1995). These researchers examined how using recess to separate cognitively demanding tasks affected elementary children's ability to pay attention. The results showed that children paid the most attention when their efforts were spaced apart; the effects are even greater for cognitively immature children (see Pellegrini & Bjorklund, 1996, for a summary).

Pellegrini (1991) explains that recess fulfills children's need for novelty.

> Children need recess because they are temporarily bored with their immediate classroom environment. When they go outdoors for recess they seek novelty by interacting with different peers in different situations. But, when the novelty of the recess environment begins to wane, they again need to change. At this point, the classroom becomes a novelty and children actually pay closer attention. (p. 40)

Therefore, it is not a good idea to eliminate recess as a way to increase time-on-task. Indeed, what may at first seem a logical and easy strategy aimed at increasing student achievement can actually backfire. Without consistent breaks, children become restless, fidgety, and unfocused. Since breaks between cognitive tasks support learning, and time is an issue in schools because of the mass of material that must be covered, it is important that break time be structured to maximize potential learning. Instead of silencing the recess bell, administrators should make every effort to provide high-quality recess experiences for children.

The Cumulative and Deferred Benefits of Play

High-quality recess experiences are those in which children of all ages have a high degree of choice in their activities. Primary-age children will most likely engage in vigorous outdoor play such as climbing, running, jumping rope, skipping, and bouncing and catching balls, either alone or with one or two favored pals. Older students will most likely engage in cooperatives games and other activities of a highly social nature. Recess may be the only time during the school day that children can interact with others on their own terms. The playful aspects of recess activities, which include choice, spontaneity, social interaction, creative use of time, and problem solving, provide children not only opportunities to learn, but also a rich context that fosters development across all areas of development. Play gives children a chance to learn, consolidate, and practice skills necessary for further growth and learning (Bateson, 1976; Piaget, 1962; Vygotsky, 1978). Play is valuable for children primarily as a medium for development and learning (Bergen, 1998); therefore, its effects are both cumulative and deferred. Most children regard recess as fun and look forward to it. Yet recess not only provides a break, it also adds to the overall quality of a child's school experience.

Issues Related to safety

Many policymakers point to concerns about safety when justifying the elimination of recess. Unfortunately, many school playgrounds have fallen into disrepair over the years, posing safety hazards. School budgets are tight, often leaving little funding to replace play equipment. Teachers and administrators may even cancel recess because of some children's behavior. If schools can offer safe playground environments that promote positive interactions, however, children can reap the immediate benefits of recess for learning and the long-term benefits for their general development.

Steps can be taken to develop playground rules and routines that support social development, encourage physical development, and provide a needed break in academic instruction. Consistent supervision is one key aspect to effective recess. Having interesting activities is another. Teachers or paraprofessionals may need special training to supervise playground activities effectively. Parents, community members, senior citizens, or high school or college students can serve as playground volunteers, not to supervise but to teach and engage children in games, help children resolve conflicts, and help them organize their own play.

Conclusion

At first glance, eliminating recess may seem like a logical and expedient decision, one that adds time to the instructional day. Such a decision is not based on empirical evidence, however. High-quality recess experiences have immediate and deferred positive effects on children's learning and development. Administrators, teachers, and parents should work together to create environments that promote quality recess experiences for students in elementary and middle schools. Let the recess bells ring again, along with the laughter of children on the playground.

References

Alexander, K. K. (1999). Playtime is canceled. *Parents, November*, 114–118.

Barbour, A. C. (1996). Physical competence and peer relationships in 2nd graders: Qualitative case studies from recess play. *Journal of Research in Childhood Education, 11*(1), 35–46.

Bateson, P. P. G. (1976). Rules and reciprocity in behavioral development. In P. P. G. Bateson & R. A. Hinde (Eds.), *Growing points in ethology* (pp. 401–421). London: Cambridge University Press.

Bergen, D. (Ed.). (1998). *Readings from… Play as a medium for learning and development*. Olney, MD: Association for Childhood Education International.

Blatchford, P. (1996). "We did more then": Changes in pupils' perceptions of breaktime (recess) from 7–16 years. *Journal of Research in Childhood Education, 11*(1), 14–24.

Brophy, J., & Good, T. (1974). *Teacher-student relationships*. New York: Holt, Reinhart & Winston.

Dempster, F. N. (1988). The spacing effect. *The American Psychologist, 43*, 627–634.

Ebinghaus, H. (1964). *Memory*. New York: Teachers College Press. (original work published in 1885)

Hunter, W. (1929). Learning III: Experimental studies of learning. In C. Murchison (Ed.), *The foundation of ex-*

perimental psychology (pp. 564–627). Worcester, MA: Clark University Press.

Johnson, J. E. (1996). Playtime revisited: Growing is not necessarily for noses only. *Journal of Research in Childhood Education, 11*(1), 82–88.

Pellegrini, A. D. (1991). Outdoor recess: Is it really necessary? *Principal, 70*(5), 40.

Pellegrini, A. D., & Bjorklund, D. F. (1996). The place of recess in school: Issues in the role of recess in children's education and development, an introduction to the theme issue. *Journal of Research in Childhood Education, 11*(1), 5–13.

Pellegrini, A. D., & Davis, P. (1993). Confinement effects on the playground and classroom behavior. *British Journal of Educational Psychology, 63*, 88–95.

Pellegrini, A. D., Huberty, P. D., & Jones, I. (1995). The effect of play deprivation on children's recess and classroom behaviors. *American Educational Research Journal, 32*, 845–862.

Pellegrini, A. D., & Smith, P. K. (1993). School recess: Implications for education and development. *Review of Educational Research, 63*, 51–67.

Piaget, J. (1962). *Play, dreams, and imitation.* New York: Norton.

Vygotsky, L. S. (1978). *Mind in society.* Cambridge, MA: Harvard University Press.

Judith Kieff is Associate Professor, Early Childhood Education, University of New Orleans, New Orleans, Louisiana.

UNIT 4

Guiding and Supporting Young Children

Unit Selections

Key Points to Consider

• In order to work effectively with a child who has been traumatized, what qualities does a teacher need to display?

• What is your perspective on using tangible reinforcers, such as prizes, in preschool?

• From your observations in an early childhood classroom, describe a conflict situation in which the teacher used positive intervention.

• Make a list of personal characteristics teachers need in order to foster the emotional well-being of children.

 **Links: www.dushkin.com/online/**
These sites are annotated in the World Wide Web pages.

Child Welfare League of America (CWLA)
http://www.cwla.org
National Network for Family Resiliency
http://www.nnfr.org

Early childhood teaching is all about problem-solving. Just as children work to solve problems, so do teachers. Every day, teachers make decisions about how to guide children socially and emotionally. In attempting to determine what could be causing a child's emotional distress, teachers must take into account a myriad of factors. They consider physical, social, environmental, and emotional factors, in addition to the surface behavior of a child. Whether it is an individual child's behavior or interpersonal relationships, the pressing problem involves complex issues that require careful reflection and analysis. Even the most mature teachers spend many hours thinking and talking about the best ways to guide young children's behavior: What should I do about the child who is out of bounds? What do I say to parents who want their child punished? Should intrinsic motivation be taught to every child or are tangible reinforcers appropriate for some? How do I guide a child who has experienced trauma and now acts out violently?

Helping children cope with stress can be a struggle for teachers in these times of upheaval and trauma. Today's children—and their teachers—are learning that terrorism is a fact of life. With acts of violence occurring randomly across the nation, teachers must be more alert than ever to the effects of stress on young children. These are times that call for teachers to demonstrate good coping skills and then teach children how to cope. In some circumstances, children affected by trauma may begin showing symptoms of severe emotional disorder. Teachers need to be prepared to help these children. In "Children and Post Traumatic Stress Disorder: What Classroom Teachers Should Know," the author defines the symptoms to look for and provides a set of strategies for helping children.

As children with special needs are included in early childhood programs, some instruction and discipline methods may change. The authors of "Reinforcement in Developmentally Appropriate Early Childhood Classrooms" link two approaches that are typically considered incompatible. They believe that behavioral strategies using positive reinforcement or tangible reinforcers can be used appropriately with young children. A set of guidelines for using reinforcers is particularly helpful in understanding how reinforcers can be used effectively without violating principles of developmentally appropriate practice.

Successful interactions among children depend greatly on the support, encouragement, and guidance from adults, according to Linda Wolfson-Steinberg, author of "'Teacher! He Hit Me!'" "'She Pushed Me!'"—Where Does It Start? How Can It Stop?" Sometimes teachers need to reevaluate conflicts for under-the-surface dynamics. It is not always the usual provocateur at fault—some incidents require looking at the group from a different perspective. Other incidents will require positive intervention, which enlarges the circle of support to include parents and consultants. Teachers should be willing to look beyond the surface conflict so that children will experience fairness and learn self-control.

The teacher's role in the emotional development of preschoolers is important to consider in determining strategies of guidance and discipline. The teacher-child relationship is foundational for emotional well-being and teaching social competence. The better teachers are at reading children's emotional cues and responding strategically, the better children will understand emotions and relate to others. "Promoting the Emotional Development of Preschoolers" outlines specific strategies for building children's socioemotional development.

Working to gain an understanding of the child in the context of family and culture is a harder task than applying a single set of discipline techniques. Instead of one solitary model of discipline applied strictly, a broad range of techniques is more appropriate. An eclectic approach allows teachers to look at children individually, assessing not only the child but the impact of family cultures as well. It is well worth the effort, for understanding is what ensures appropriate, effective guidance.

Children and Post Traumatic Stress Disorder: What Classroom Teachers Should Know

Susan J. Grosse

Post traumatic stress disorder: development of characteristic symptoms following exposure to an extreme traumatic stressor involving direct personal experience of an event that involves actual or threatened death or serious injury, or other threat to one's physical integrity; or witnessing an event that involves death, injury, or a threat to the physical integrity of another person; or learning about unexpected or violent death, serious harm, or threat of death or injury experienced by a family member or other close associate (APA, 1996).

School children may be exposed to trauma in their personal lives or, increasingly, at school. Classroom teachers can help prepare children to cope with trauma by understanding the nature of trauma, teaching children skills for responding to an emergency, and learning how to mitigate the after-effects of trauma.

PTSD Related Trauma

By the very unexpected nature of trauma, one can never totally prepare for it. And because each individual responds differently to emotional upset, it is impossible to predict trauma after-effects. Under certain circumstances, trauma can induce Post Traumatic Stress Disorder (PTSD). Unrecognized/untreated PTSD can have a lifelong negative impact on the affected individual. Teachers, who spend up to eight hours each day with the children in their charge, can influence the outcome of a child's response to trauma stress by creating an environ-

ment in which PTSD is less likely to develop to the point of life impact.

Not all emotionally upsetting experiences will cause PTSD. Trauma sufficient to induce PTSD has specific characteristics and circumstances, including situations

- perceived as life-threatening,
- outside the scope of a child's life experiences,
- not daily, ordinary, normal events,
- during which the child experiences a complete loss of control of the outcome, and
- when death is observed.

Disasters, violence, and accidents are just some of the experiences that can lead to PTSD. Preparing children for trauma involves giving them skills and knowledge to survive the experience and emerge with as little potential as possible for developing PTSD.

Skills to Survive Traumatic Experiences

Survival skills for traumatic experiences are essentially emergency action plans. Carrying out emergency action plans not only helps a child retain some personal control, but increases the potential for a healthy outcome. Children **must** know how to:

- Follow directions in any emergency (i.e., stay in their classroom during a lock down)
- Get help in any type of emergency (i.e., dial 911 or call a neighbor)

- Mitigate specific emergencies (i.e., take shelter during a tornado)
- Report the circumstances (i.e., tell an adult if a stranger approaches them or touches them)
- Say "no" and mean it (i.e., firmly shouting "no, don't touch me")

Implementing survival skills requires knowing right and wrong. Children must know or be able to recognize:

- Appropriate vs. inappropriate touching (i.e., shoulder vs. genitals)
- Appropriate vs. inappropriate information sharing (i.e., who is at home at what times)
- Presence of appropriate vs. inappropriate people (i.e., the teacher on playground duty vs. a prowling stranger)

Skills to Mitigate PTSD

While there is no predictability in who will develop PTSD, it is possible to take steps to prepare children ahead of time and by doing so, lessen the PTSD potential. Children need to be taught lessons about trauma. Learning about people who have experienced trauma and gone on to live healthy lives gives children role models and hope for their own future.

During a traumatic experience, children will survive better if they have a structure to follow and can maintain some sense of control. Learning the survival skills will aid in maintaining this control. Children need accurate and specific information about their immediate safety, about what has happened and about what will happen to them next (James, 1989). Knowledge helps them control their thoughts and feelings.

Following a trauma, debriefing is critical. Children will vary concerning their willingness and readiness to talk about their experiences. Some will play out the event, while others may be more comfortable writing or drawing about the event. What is important is the opportunity to communicate. There are different avenues for the child to communicate, including online discussion forums for children (Sleek, 1998).

A child's initial debriefing should be child-centered and nonjudgmental. The adult should recognize that each child did his or her best, no matter what the outcome, and refrain from offering advice. Adults should recognize that no two children will have the same thoughts, feelings, or opinions. All expressions about the trauma are acceptable.

Following a trauma, it is also important to help a child reestablish control. Reviewing survival skills and drills and planning for "next time" reestablishes strength. Allowing a child to make choices reestablishes their governance over their own lives.

Identifying PTSD

Everyone reacts to trauma. What differentiates normal reaction from PTSD is the timing of the reaction, its intensity, and the duration of the reaction. Trauma includes emotional as well as physical experiences and injury. Even second-hand exposure to violence can be traumatic. For this reason, all children and adolescents exposed to violence or disaster, even if only through graphic media reports, should be watched for signs of emotional distress (National Institute of Mental Health, 2000).

Symptoms lasting more than one month post trauma may indicate a problem. Specific symptoms to look for include:

- Re-experiencing the event (flash-backs),
- Avoidance of reminders of the event,
- Increased sleep disturbances, and
- Continual thought pattern interruptions focusing on the event.

In children, symptoms may vary with age. Separation anxiety, clinging behavior, or reluctance to return to school may

be evident, as may behavior disturbances or problems with concentration. Children may have self doubts, evidenced by comments about body confusion, self-worth, and a desire for withdrawal. As there is no clear demarcation between adolescence and adulthood, adult PTSD symptoms may also evidence themselves in adolescents. These may include recurrent distressing thoughts, sleep disturbances, flashbacks, restricted range of affect, detachment, psychogenic amnesia, increased arousal and hypersensitivity, and increased irritability and outbursts of rage.

Helping the Child

Making the diagnosis of PTSD requires evaluation by a trained mental health professional. However, regular classroom teachers have a major role in the identification and referral process. Children often express themselves through play. Because the teacher sees the child for many hours of the day including play time, the teacher may be the first to suspect all is not well. Where the traumatic event is known, caregivers can watch for PTSD symptoms. However, traumatic events can involve secrets. Sexual abuse, for example, may take place privately. Sensitive teachers should monitor all children for changes in behavior that may signal a traumatic experience or a flashback to a prior traumatic experience.

Teachers can help a child suspected of post traumatic stress disorder by:

- Gently discouraging reliance on avoidance; letting the child know it is all right to discuss the incident;
- Talking understandingly with the child about their feelings;
- Understanding that children react differently according to age—young children tend to cling, adolescents withdraw;
- Encouraging a return to normal activities;
- Helping restore the child's sense of control of his or her life; and
- Seeking professional help.

Professional assistance is most important since PTSD can have a lifelong impact on a child. Symptoms can lie dormant for decades and resurface many years later during exposure to a similar circumstance. It is only by recognition and treatment of PTSD that trauma vic-

tims can hope to move past the impact of the trauma and lead healthy lives. Thus, referral to trained mental health professionals is critical. The school psychologist is a vital resource, and guidance counselors can be an important link in the mental health resource chain.

Although professional assistance is ultimately essential in cases of PTSD, classroom teachers must deal with the immediate daily impact. Becoming an informed teacher is the first step in helping traumatized children avoid the life long consequences of PTSD.

References

American Psychiatric Association. (1996). *Diagnostic and statistical manual of mental disorders IV*. Washington, DC. American Psychiatric Association.

James, B. (1989). *Treating traumatized children: new insights and creative interventions*. Lexington, MA: D. C. Health

National Institute of Mental Health (2000). *Helping children and adolescents cope with violence and disasters*. Washington, DC: NIMH. Available online at http://www.nimh.nih.gov/publicat/violence.cfm

Sleek, S. (1998). After the storm, children play out fears. *APA Monitor, 29*(6). Available online at http://www.apa.org/monitor/jun98/child.html.

Resources Available from ERIC

These resources have been abstracted and are in the ERIC database. Journal articles (EJ) should be available at most research libraries; most documents (ED) are available in microfiche collections at more than 900 locations. Documents can also be ordered through the ERIC Document Reproduction Service (800-443-ERIC).

Demaree, M. A. (1995). Creating safe environments for children with post-traumatic stress disorder. *Dimensions of Early Childhood, 23*(3), 31–33, 40. EJ 501997.

Demaree, M. A. (1994). *Responding to violence in their lives: Creating nurturing environments for children with post-traumatic stress disorder* (conference paper). ED378708.

Dennis, B. L. (1994). *Chronic violence: A silent actor in the classroom*. ED376386.

Karcher, D. R. (1994). *Post-traumatic stress disorder in children as a result of violence: A review of current literature* (doctoral research paper). ED379822.

Motta, R. W. (1994). Identification of characteristics and causes of childhood post-traumatic stress disorder. *Psychology in the Schools, 31*(1), 49–56. EJ480780

Richards, T., & Bates, C. (1997). Recognizing post-traumatic stress in children. *Journal of School Health, 67*(10,) 441–443. EJ561961.

Other Resources

American Academy of Child and Adolescent Psychiatry, 3615 Wisconsin Avenue, NW, Washington, DC, 20016-3007, 202-966-7300, http://www.aacap.org

American Psychiatric Association, 1400 K Street, NW, Washington, DC 20005, 202-682-6000; http://www.psych.org

American Psychological Association, 750 First Street, NE, Washington, DC 20002, 202-336-5500, http://www.apa.org

Anxiety Disorders Association of America (ADAA), 11900 Parklawn Drive, Suite 100, Rockville, MD 20852, 301-231-9350; http://www.adaa.org

Disaster Stuff for Kids, http://www.jmu.edu/psychologydept/4kids.htm

Federal Emergency Management Agency http://www.fema.gov/kids

International Society for Traumatic Stress Studies (ISTSS), 60 Revere Drive, Suite 500, Northbrook, IL 60062, http://www.istss.org

National Center for Kids Overcoming Crisis, (includes *Healing Magazine* online) 1-800-8KID-123, http://www.kidspeace.org/facts

National Center for PTSD, 215 N. Main Street, White River Junction, VT 05009; 802-296-5132; http://www.ncptsd.org/

National Center for Post-Traumatic Stress Disorder of the Department of Veterans Affairs http://www.ncptsd.org/

National Institute for Mental Health (NIMH) 6001 Executive Boulevard, Rm 8184, MSC 9663, Bethesda, MD 20892-9663; 301-4513, Hotline 1-88-88-ANXIETY, http://www.nimh.nih.gov

This digest is co-produced with the ERIC Clearinghouse on Counseling and Student Services.

From *ERIC Clearinghouse on Teaching and Teacher Education,* September 2001, pp. 1, 2. © 2001 by ERIC Clearinghouse on Teaching and Teacher Education, Digest #EDO-SP-2001-1. Reprinted by permission.

Reinforcement in Developmentally Appropriate Early Childhood Classrooms

As greater numbers of children with disabilities participate in early childhood programs, teachers are faced with the challenge of expanding their repertoire of teaching and guidance practices to accommodate the needs of children with diverse abilities and needs.

Tashawna K. Duncan, Kristen M. Kemple, and Tina M. Smith

*E*ach day from 10:30 to 11:00, the children in Mrs. Kitchens's 1st-grade classroom are expected to sit silently in their desks and copy words from the chalkboard into their notebooks. Children who finish early are required to remain silently in their seats. After five minutes has passed, Mrs. Kitchens assesses whether every child in the class has been behaving according to the rules. If they have been, she makes a check mark on the chalkboard and announces, "Good! There's a check." If even one child has violated the rules, she announces "no check." At the end of the week, if 20 or more checks have accrued on the board, the whole group is awarded an extra-long Friday recess period. This longed-for reward is rarely achieved, however.

Five-year-old Rodney has recently joined Mr. Romero's kindergarten class. On his first day in his new class, Rodney punched a classmate and usurped the tricycle the other boy was riding. On Rodney's second day in the class, he shoved a child off a swing and dumped another out of her chair at the snack table. In an effort to deal with Rodney's problematic behavior, Mr. Romero is taking a number of steps, including making sure that Rodney knows the classroom rules and routines, helping Rodney learn language and skills to resolve conflicts, exploring ways to make Rodney feel welcome and a special part of the class, and arranging for a consultation with a special education specialist to see if support services would

be appropriate. Mr. Romero is concerned for the emotional and physical safety of the other children, and he believes that Rodney will have a hard time making friends if his reputation as an aggressor is allowed to solidify. He feels the need to act fast. Deciding that a system of reinforcement, along with other strategies, may help Rodney control his aggressive behavior, Mr. Romero implements a token reinforcement system. Rodney earns a ticket, accompanied by praise, for each 30-minute period during which he does not behave aggressively. At the end of the day, Rodney can trade a specified number of earned tickets for his choice of small toys.

The above examples illustrate two teachers' efforts to use the behavioral strategy of reinforcement—with varying degrees of appropriateness. In Mrs. Kitchens's class, reinforcement is being used as a means to get children to sit still and be quiet in the context of a developmentally inappropriate lesson. In an effort to keep children "on task," Mrs. Kitchens substitutes a control tactic for a meaningful and engaging curriculum. Mr. Romero, on the other hand, is making efforts to identify and address the reasons for Rodney's behavior. Furthermore, he believes that Rodney's behavior is so detrimental to himself and to the other children that additional measures must be used to achieve quick results and restore a sense of psychological safety in the classroom community. Mr. Romero utilizes a variety of strategies in the hopes of creating lasting change in Rodney's behavior.

Inclusion of Children With Special Needs

The trend toward including children with disabilities in early childhood education settings is growing (Wolery & Wilbers, 1994). As greater numbers of children with disabilities participate in early childhood programs, teachers are faced with the challenge of expanding their repertoire of teaching and guidance practices to accommodate the needs of children with diverse abilities and needs. To this end, teachers responsible for the care and education of diverse groups of young children are encouraged to examine their beliefs about their role in promoting children's development and learning, and to explore their understanding of developmentally appropriate practices as outlined by the National Association for the Education of Young Children (NAEYC) (Bredekamp & Copple, 1997).

Historically, early childhood special education has had stronger roots in behavioral psychology and applied behavior analysis than has early childhood education.

Recent federal legislation requires that children be educated in the "least restrictive environment." This means that, to the maximum extent possible, the setting in which children with special needs are educated should be the same as that in which typically developing children are educated, and that specialized services should be provided within the regular classroom (Thomas & Russo, 1995).

Early Childhood Education and Early Childhood Special Education

Most early childhood teachers have little or no training in early childhood special education. Historically, differences have existed between teachers who work with young children with disabilities and teachers who work with typically developing children, including different educational preparation, separate professional organiza-

tions, and reliance on different bodies of research (Wolery & Wilbers, 1994). As both groups of children are increasingly cared for and educated in the same programs, early childhood educators and early childhood special educators are called upon to work in collaboration to ensure that children receive individually appropriate education. This collaborative effort requires that all teachers have familiarity with and respect for the philosophy and practices of both disciplines.

Historically, early childhood special education has had stronger roots in behavioral psychology and applied behavior analysis than has early childhood education. As Wolery and Bredekamp (1994) noted, developmentally appropriate practices (DAP) (as outlined by NAEYC) have their roots primarily in maturational and constructivist perspectives. While current early childhood special education practices also tend to be rooted in constructivist perspectives, the additional influence of cultural transmission perspectives (including behaviorist models of learning) is evident. Given their diverse origins, it should not be surprising that the two disciplines would advocate, on occasion, different practices (Wolery & Bredekamp, 1994). This potential tension is exemplified in an editor's note found in the recent NAEYC publication *Including Children With Special Needs in Early Childhood Programs* (Wolery & Wilbers, 1994). Carol Copple (the series' editor) stated,

> Certainly early childhood educators are well aware of the limits of behaviorism as the sole approach to children's learning and are wary of overreliance on rewards as a motivational technique. From this vantage point, some readers may have a negative first response to some of the techniques described in this chapter. Although we must be aware of the limitations and pitfalls of such methods, I urge readers to keep an open mind about them.… They are not for every situation, but when used appropriately, they often succeed where other methods fail. (Wolery & Wilbers, 1994, p. 119)

The current authors hope that readers will be open to considering the judicious use of methods of reinforcement described in this article. When included as part of a total developmentally appropriate program and used after careful assessment of individual needs, these methods can be important tools for implementing *individually* appropriate practice.

Developmentally Appropriate Practice

In 1987, NAEYC published *Developmentally Appropriate Practice in Early Childhood Programs Serving Children From Birth to Age 8* (Bredekamp, 1987), which was revised and published in 1997 as *Developmentally Appropriate Practice in*

Figure 1

DAP Guidelines:
Developmentally Appropriate Practice for 3- Through 5-Year-Olds: Motivation and Guidance*

Appropriate Practices

Teachers draw on children's curiosity and desire to make sense of their world to motivate them to become involved in interesting learning activities. Teachers use verbal encouragement in ways that are genuine and related to an actual task or behavior, and acknowledge children's work with specific comments like, "I see you drew your older sister bigger than your brother."

In cases of children with special needs, such as those identified on an Individualized Education Plan, those resulting from environmental stress, such as violence, or when a child's aggressive behavior continually threatens others, teachers may develop an individualized behavioral plan based on observation of possible environmental "triggers" and/or other factors associated with the behavior. *This plan includes motivation and intervention strategies that assist and support the child to develop self-control and appropriate social behaviors.* (italics added)

Inappropriate Practices

A preponderance of experiences are either uninteresting and unchallenging, or so difficult and frustrating so as to diminish children's intrinsic motivation to learn. *To obtain children's participation, teachers typically rely on extrinsic rewards (stickers, privileges, etc.) or threats of punishment.* (italics added) Children with special needs or behavioral problems are isolated or punished for failure to meet group expectations rather than being provided with learning experiences at a reasonable level of difficulty.

Teachers constantly and indiscriminately use praise ("What a pretty picture"; "That's nice") so that it becomes meaningless and useless in motivating children. (italics added)

*Guidelines for 6-to 8-year-olds are virtually identical. See Bredekamp & Copple, 1997.

Early Childhood Programs (Bredekamp & Copple, 1997). Many have argued that DAP (see Figure 1) provides an appropriate educational context for the inclusion of young children with disabilities, assuming that the interpretations of DAP guidelines leave room for adaptations and extensions to meet the child's specific needs (Bredekamp, 1993; Carta, 1995; Carta, Atwater, Schwartz, & McConnell, 1993; Carta, Schwartz, Atwater, & McConnell, 1991; Wolery & Bredekamp, 1994; Wolery, Strain, & Bailey, 1992; Wolery, Werts, & Holcombe-Ligon, 1994). For some young children, this may mean the use of behavioral strategies, such as planned programs of systematic reinforcement. In fact, the current DAP guidelines do not identify reinforcement systems as inappropriate practice. Some early childhood educators, however, view many forms of reinforcement as completely unacceptable. If inclusion is to succeed, it may be necessary for teachers to consider using such strategies for particular children in particular circumstances.

While reinforcement through use of stickers, privileges, and praise is *not* identified as developmentally *inappropriate* practice, it does become inappropriate when used in exclusion of other means of promoting children's engagement and motivation, and when used indiscrimi-

nately (for the wrong children, and/or in the wrong situations). Children's active engagement is a guiding principle in both DAP and early childhood special education (Carta et al., 1993). As Carta et al. (1993) have pointed out, however, many young children with disabilities are less likely to engage spontaneously with materials in their environments (Peck, 1985; Weiner & Weiner, 1974). The teacher's active encouragement is needed to help such children become actively involved in learning opportunities. A principal goal of early intervention is to facilitate young children's active engagement with materials, activities, and the social environment through systematic instruction (Wolery et al., 1992). Such instruction may include use of reinforcement as incentives.

Behavioral Strategies in Early Childhood Education

Behavioral theory holds that behaviors acquired and displayed by young children can be attributed almost exclusively to their environment. Several behavioral strategies are employed by early childhood teachers to facilitate children's learning, including the use of praise and external rewards. However, practitioners often fail to identify these strategies in their repertoire and dismiss, out of hand, their use in the classroom. Misunderstandings may exist concerning the appropriate use and potential effectiveness of these strategies for young children. As a result, they are not always well accepted in the early childhood community (Henderick, 1998; Rodd, 1996; see also Strain et al., 1992).

A review of contemporary literature suggests that behavioral strategies are appropriate for creating and maintaining an environment conducive to growth and development (e.g., Peters, Neisworth, & Yawkey, 1985; Schloss & Smith, 1998). Research has demonstrated that behavioral strategies are successful in school settings with various diverse populations, including those with young children (Kazdin, 1994). Furthermore, while many such "best practices" are unrecognized by early childhood professionals, they are grounded in behavioral theory (Strain et al., 1992).

The Use of Positive Reinforcement

Positive reinforcement is perhaps the strategy most palatable to educators who are concerned about the misuse of behavioral strategies. A particular behavior is said to be positively reinforced when the behavior is followed by the presentation of a reward (e.g., praise, stickers) that results in increased frequency of the particular behavior (Schloss & Smith, 1998). For example, Stella has been reluctant to wash her hands before lunch. Mrs. Johnson be-gins consistently praising Stella when she washes her hands by saying, "Now your hands are nice and clean and ready for lunch!" Stella becomes more likely to wash her hands without protest. In this case, we can say that Stella's handwashing behavior has been positively reinforced.

Most frequently, positive reinforcement strategies are used to teach, maintain, or strengthen a variety of behaviors (Zirpoli, 1995). Although some early childhood teachers may be reluctant to endorse the use of reinforcement, they often unknowingly employ reinforcement strategies every day in their classroom (Henderick, 1998; Wolery, 1994).

Types of Reinforcers

Reinforcers frequently used by teachers generally fall within one of three categories: social, activity, or tangible (see Table 1). These three categories can be viewed along a continuum ranging from least to most intrusive. Social reinforcers are the least intrusive, in that they mimic the natural consequences of positive, prosocial behavior. At the other end of the continuum are tangible reinforcers. Tangible reinforcers involve the introduction of rewards that ordinarily may not be part of the routine. In selecting a reinforcer, the goal is to select the least intrusive reinforcer that is likely to be effective. If reinforcers other than social ones are necessary, teachers should develop a plan to move gradually toward social reinforcers. The following sections describe each category of reinforcers and how they can be used effectively within the context of developmentally appropriate practice.

Table 1

Examples of Social, Activity, and Tangible Reinforcers in the Early Childhood setting

Social	Activity	Tangible
Praise	Extra playground time	Stickers
Smile	A special recording or tape	Prizes
Hugs	A party	Trinkets
Pat on back	Tablewasher or other desirable privilege	Tokens
Light squeeze on shoulder	Playing with an intriguing new toy	

Intangible - Tangible

Social reinforcers. Teachers employ social reinforcers when they use interpersonal interactions to reinforce behaviors (Schloss & Smith, 1998). Some commonly used social reinforcers include positive nonverbal behaviors (e.g., smiling) and praise (Alberto & Troutman, 1990; Sulzer-Azaroff & Mayer, 1991). Because they are convenient, practical, and can be highly effective, social reinforcers are the most widely accepted and frequently used type of reinforcer in the early childhood classroom (Sulzer-Azaroff & Mayer, 1991). One means of effectively reinforcing a child's behavior via social reinforcement is by using a "positive personal message" (Gordon, 1974; Kostelnik, Stein, Whiren, & Soderman, 1998). For example, Ms. Tarrant says, "Sally, you put the caps back on the markers. I'm pleased. Now the markers won't get dried up. They'll be fresh and ready when someone else wants to use them." This positive personal message reminds Sally of the rule (put the caps on the markers) at a time when Sally has clear and immediate proof that she is able to follow the rule. The personal message pinpoints a specific desirable behavior, and lets the child know why the behavior is appropriate. When used appropriately, social reinforcers have been shown to enhance children's self-esteem (Sulzer-Azaroff & Mayer, 1991). When used in tandem with less natural (e.g., tangible) reinforcers, social reinforcers have been shown to enhance the power of those less natural reinforcers (Sulzer-Azaroff & Mayer, 1991).

Many early childhood teachers have concerns about the use of tangible reinforcers and believe that they cannot be used appropriately in the early childhood classroom.

Of the various types of social reinforcers, praise is used most frequently and deliberately by teachers (Alberto & Troutman, 1990). In recent years, several articles have been published on the topic of praise (Hitz & Driscoll, 1988; Marshall, 1995; Van der Wilt, 1996). While praise has the potential to enhance children's self-esteem, research has demonstrated that certain kinds of praise may actually lower children's self-confidence, inhibit achievement, and make children reliant on external (as opposed to internal) controls (Kamii, 1984; Stringer & Hurt, 1981, as cited in Hitz & Driscoll, 1988). These authors have drawn distinctions between "effective praise" (sometimes called "encouragement") and "ineffective praise." Effective praise is consistent with commonly held goals of early childhood education: promoting children's positive

self-concept, autonomy, self-reliance, and motivation for learning (Hitz & Driscoll, 1988).

Effective praise is specific. Instead of saying, "Justin, what a lovely job you did cleaning up the blocks," Mrs. Constanz says, "Justin, you put each block in its place on the shelf." In this case, Mrs. Constanz leaves judgment about the *quality* of the effort to the child. By pinpointing specific aspects of the child's behavior or product (rather than using vague, general praise), Mrs. Constanz communicates that she has paid attention to, and is genuinely interested in, what the child has done (Hitz & Driscoll, 1988).

Effective praise generally is delivered privately. Public uses of praise, such as, "I like the way Carlos is sitting so quietly," have a variety of disadvantages. Such statements are typically intended to manipulate children into following another child's example. In the example, the message was, "Carlos is doing a better job of sitting than are the rest of you." With time, young children may come to resent this management, and resent a child who is the frequent recipient of such public praise (Chandler, 1981; Gordon, 1974). As an alternative, the teacher could whisper the statement quietly to Carlos, and/or say to the other children, "Think about what you need to do to be ready to listen." As individual children comply, the teacher may quickly acknowledge each child, "Caitlin is ready, Tyler is ready; thank you, Nicholas, Lakeesha, and Ali…" (Marshall, 1995).

Another characteristic of effective praise is that it emphasizes improvement of process, rather than the finished product. As Daryl passes out individual placemats to his classmates, he states their names. Mrs. Thompson says, "Daryl, you are learning more names. You remembered Tom and Peg today." She could have said, "Daryl, you are a great rememberer," but she chose not to, because Daryl knows that he did not remember everyone's name, and tomorrow he may forget some that he knew today. In this example, Mrs. Thompson's praise is specific and is focused on the individual child's improvement.

Activity reinforcers. Teachers employ activity reinforcers when they use access to a pleasurable activity as a reinforcer (Sulzer-Azaroff & Mayer, 1991). Some commonly used and effective activity reinforcers include doing a special project, being a classroom helper, and having extra free-choice time (Sulzer-Azaroff & Mayer, 1991). When using activity reinforcers, teachers create a schedule in which an enjoyable activity follows the behavior they are trying to change or modify (Sulzer-Azaroff & Mayer, 1991). Teachers often use such activity reinforcers unknowingly. Following social reinforcers, activity reinforcers are the most frequently used (Alberto & Troutman, 1990), probably because teachers view them as more convenient and less intrusive than tangible reinforcers (Sulzer-Azaroff & Mayer, 1991). When used appropriately, activity reinforcers can modify a wide variety of be-

---

Figure 2

Guidelines for Using Reinforcers

Reinforcers are unique to an individual. There are no universal reinforcers. What one child finds reinforcing another child may not. Therefore, teachers must consider each child's interests when selecting appropriate reinforcers.

Reinforcers must be perceived by children as being worth the time and energy it takes to achieve them. In other words, the reinforcer must be more desirable to the child than the behavior the teacher is attempting to modify.

Teacher expectations must be clear to the children. Children must clearly understand what specific behaviors are expected of them and know what is required of them to earn the reinforcer.

Reinforcers must be awarded immediately after the desired behavior. If reinforcers are not awarded immediately, they will not be effective.

Use more natural reinforcers whenever possible. Teachers should first consider the least intrusive reinforcer to modify children's behavior. For example, consider social reinforcers before tangible reinforcers.

Use reinforcers less frequently when children begin to exhibit the desired behavior. Later, after the targeted behavior is modified, teachers can phase out the use of reinforcement.

---

haviors. The following examples illustrate the appropriate use of activity reinforcers.

> *In Miss Annie's class, a brief playground period is scheduled to follow center clean-up time. Miss Annie reminds the children that the sooner they have the centers cleaned up, the sooner they will be able to enjoy the playground. It appears that the playground time is reinforcing children's quick clean-up behavior: They consistently get the job done with little dawdling.*

> *As part of a total plan to reduce Christopher's habit of using his cupped hands to toss water out of the water table, Mrs. Jackson has told Christopher that each day he plays without throwing water out of the table, he may be table washer after snack time (which Christopher delights in doing). This strategy was implemented following efforts to help Christopher develop appropriate behavior through demonstrations and by redirecting him with water toys chosen specifically to match his interests.*

Tangible reinforcers. Teachers sometimes employ tangible reinforcers, such as stickers and prizes, to strengthen and modify behavior in the early childhood classroom. Tangible reinforcers are most often used to modify and maintain the behavior of children with severe behavior problems (Vaughn, Bos, & Schumm, 1997).

Stacey, who has mild mental retardation, is a member of Miss Hamrick's preschool class. She rarely participates during free-choice activities. Miss Hamrick has tried a variety of strategies to increase Stacey's engagement, including using effective praise, making sure a range of activity options are developmentally appropriate for Stacey, modeling appropriate behaviors, and implementing prompting strategies. None of these strategies appear to work. Aware of Stacey's love of the TV show "Barney," Miss Hamrick decides to award Barney stickers to Stacey when she actively participates. Stacey begins to participate more often in classroom activities.

One major advantage of tangible reinforcers is that they almost always guarantee quick behavioral change (Alberto & Troutman, 1990), even when other strategies (including other types of reinforcers) fail. Although the use of tangible reinforcers can be very effective, their use in early childhood classrooms has been highly controversial. Many early childhood teachers have concerns about the use of tangible reinforcers and believe that they cannot be used appropriately in the early childhood classroom. Such reinforcers often are intrusive, and their effective use requires large amounts of teacher time and commitment.

Given these disadvantages, when using tangible reinforcers teachers should gradually move toward using more intangible, less intrusive reinforcers (Henderick, 1998). Teachers can accomplish this goal by accompanying all tangible reinforcers with social reinforcers (e.g., praise). Later, as children begin to exhibit the desired behavior consistently, the teacher may begin to taper off the use of tangible reinforcers while maintaining the use of social reinforcers. Eventually, the teacher will no longer need to award tangible reinforcers after the desired behavior occurs. In time, the teacher also should be able to fade out the use of social reinforcers, and the children will begin to assume control over their own behaviors.

References

Alberto, P. A., & Troutman, A.C. (1990). *Applied behavior analysis for teachers* (3rd ed.). Columbus, OH: Merrill.

Bredekamp, S. (1987). *Developmentally appropriate practice in early childhood programs serving children from birth through age eight.* Washington, DC: National Association for the Education of Young Children.

Bredekamp, S. (1993). The relationship between early childhood education and early childhood special education: Healthy marriage or family feud? *Topics in Early Childhood Special Education, 13*(3), 258–273.

Bredekamp, S., & Copple, C. (1997). *Developmentally appropriate practice in early childhood programs* (Rev. ed.). Washington, DC: National Association for the Education of Young Children.

Carta, J. (1995). Developmentally appropriate practice: A critical analysis as applied to young children with disabilities. *Focus on Exceptional Children, 27*(8), 1–14.

Carta, J. J., Atwater, J. B., Schwartz, I. S., & McConnell, S. R. (1993). Developmentally appropriate practices and early childhood special education: A reaction to Johnson & McChesney Johnson. *Topics in Special Education, 13,* 243–254.

Carta, J. J., Schwartz, I. S., Atwater, J. B., & McConnell, S. R. (1991). Developmentally appropriate practice: Appraising its usefulness for young children with disabilities. *Topics in Early Childhood Special Education, 11*(1), 1–20

Chandler, T. A. (1981). What's wrong with success and praise? *Arithmetic Teacher, 29*(4), 10–12.

Gordon, T. (1974). *Teacher effectiveness training.* New York: Wyden.

Henderick, J. (1998). *Total learning: Development curriculum for the young child.* Columbus, OH: Merrill.

Hitz, R., & Driscoll, A. (1988). Praise or encouragement? *Young Children, 43*(5), 6–13.

Kamii, C. (1984). The aim of education envisioned by Piaget. *Phi Delta Kappan, 65*(6), 410–415.

Kazdin, A. E. (1994). *Behavior modification in applied settings* (5th ed.). Pacific Grove, CA: Brooks/Cole.

Kostelnik, M. J., Stein, L. C., Whiren, A. P., & Soderman, A. K. (1998). *Guiding children's social development* (2nd ed.). New York: Delmar.

Marshall, H. H. (1995). Beyond "I like the way…" *Young Children, 50*(2), 26–28.

Peters, D., Neisworth, J. T., & Yawkey, T. D. (1985). *Early childhood education: From theory to practice.* Monterey, CA: Brooks/Cole.

Rodd, J. (1996). *Understanding young children's behavior: A guide for early childhood professionals.* New York: Teachers College Press.

Schloss, P. J., & Smith, M. A. (1998). *Applied behavior analyses in the classroom* (Rev. ed.). Boston: Allyn and Bacon.

Strain, P. S., McConnell, S. R., Carta, J. J., Fowler, S. A., Neisworth, J. T., & Wolery, M. (1992). Behaviorism in early intervention. *Topics in Early Childhood Special Education, 12*(1), 121–141.

Sulzer-Azaroff, B., & Mayer, G. R. (1991). *Behavior analysis for lasting change.* New York: Harcourt Brace.

Thomas, S. B., & Russo, C. J. (1995). *Special education law: Issues and implications for the 90's.* Topeka, KS: National Organization on Legal Problems of Education.

Van der Wilt, J. (1996). Beyond stickers and popcorn parties. *Dimensions of Early Childhood, 24*(1), 17–20.

Vaughn, S., Bos, C. S., & Schumm, J. S. (1997). *Teaching mainstreamed, diverse, and at-risk students in the general education classroom.* Boston: Allyn and Bacon.

Wolery, M. (1994). *Including children with special needs in early childhood programs.* Washington, DC: National Association for the Education of Young Children.

Wolery, M., & Bredekamp, S. (1994). Developmentally appropriate practices and young children with disabilities: Contextual issues in the discussion. *Journal of Early Intervention, 18,* 331–341.

Wolery, M., Strain, P. S., & Bailey, D. (1992). Reaching potentials of children with special needs. In S. Bredekamp & T. Rosegrant (Eds.), *Reaching potentials: Appropriate curriculum and assessment for young children. Vol. 1* (pp. 92–111). Washington, DC: National Association for the Education of Young Children.

Wolery, M., Werts, M. G., & Holcombe-Ligon, A. (1994). Current practices with young children who have disabilities: Issues in placement, assessment and instruction. *Focus on Exceptional Children, 26*(6), 1–12.

Wolery, M., & Wilbers, J. S. (1994). Introduction to the inclusion of young children with special needs in early childhood programs. In M. Wolery & J. S. Wilbers (Eds.), *Including children with special needs in early childhood programs* (pp. 1–22). Washington, DC: National Association for the Education of Young Children.

Zirpoli, T. J. (1995). *Understanding and affecting the behavior of young children.* Englewood Cliffs, NJ: Merrill.

Tashawna K. Duncan is a doctoral candidate, Department of Educational Psychology; Kristen M. Kemple is Associate Professor, School of Teaching and Learning; and Tina M. Smith is Assistant Professor, Department of Educational Psychology, University of Florida, Gainesville.

From *Childhood Education,* Summer 2000, pp. 194-199. Reprinted by permission of Tashawna K. Duncan, Kristen M. Kemple, Tina M. Smith and the Association for Childhood Education International. © 2000 by ACEI.

Use the Environment to Prevent Discipline Problems and Support Learning

Nancy Ratcliff

Good teachers are familiar with many ways to address discipline problems in the classroom. When young children exhibit aggressive behaviors, we look for the possible reasons and help children learn appropriate behaviors using behavioral techniques, positive reinforcement, and other supportive strategies.

An organized and well-thought-out classroom and the structure of activities, the daily schedule, routines, and transitions can help prevent discipline problems.

We realize that in some situations there are no easy answers or quick solutions to discipline problems. But two important areas are often overlooked: the physical and programmatic environments. An organized and well-thought-out classroom and the structure of activities, the daily schedule, routines, and transitions can help prevent discipline problems.

Here are eight points that may be familiar to experienced teachers but are worth reviewing from time to time. For quick reference and ongoing assessment,

teachers can use the "Checklist for Supporting Positive Behaviors."

The physical environment

1. Design clearly defined activity areas and pathways that minimize crowding.

Research shows that placing young children in relatively small areas may increase aggressive behavior (McGrew 1972). More accidental physical encounters—head bumping and fingers getting stepped on—occur in crowded areas, and children's play and/or creations can be interrupted or accidentally destroyed. Young children often don't see a difference between accidental and intentional actions and respond with aggression (Gump 1975).

Establishing clearly defined learning areas and pathways is relatively easy. Shelving units are the most practical solution—solid barriers and great storage. Stacked milk crates, even sturdy cardboard boxes, also work.

2. Provide adequate space for each interest area.

Consider the nature of the activities that take place in each area. If crowded, the block, dramatic play, and art areas tend to create a higher number of aggressive behaviors. A minimum 10-by-12-square-foot area is best for those areas. In classrooms that do not accommodate areas of this size, teachers need to determine the number of children who can safely work in each area at one time. They should discuss with the children the reasons for any limits; children are more likely to follow rules when they understand the rationale and help set them.

3. Monitor potential problem areas.

Teachers of young children understand the importance of proper supervision throughout the day, yet they can't be everywhere every minute of the day. One effective strategy is to identify the classroom areas in which aggressive behavior occurs most frequently and then carefully monitor those areas during playtime. The block, dramatic play, and woodworking centers typically produce more numerous and intense instances of

Checklist for Supporting Positive Behaviors

Strategy	Yes/No	Notes
Physical environment		
1. Design clearly defined areas		
Interest areas		
Group meeting time		
Pathways		
2. Provide adequate space for interest areas		
Set limits of number of children using area		
Discuss rules with children		
3. Monitor potential problem areas		
Blocks		
Dramatic play		
Sand/water play		
Woodworking		
Other		
4. Maintain relaxed, calm, interesting environment		
Engaging activities every day		
Images/words at eye level		
Materials on low, open shelves		
Neatly organized items		
Labeled shelves and containers		
Programmatic environment		
5. Assess structure of activities		
Open-ended activities		
Balance between unstructured/structured activities		
6. Follow age-appropriate schedule		
Alternate active and quiet times		
Group times short		
Group times spread throughout the day		
Children's cues used to assess group time limits		
Adequate choice time		
7. Establish routines		
Consistent yet flexible		
No wait times		
Posted schedule with pictures and words		
8. Plan transitions		
Use consistent signal for end of choice time		
Allow 5 or more minutes for ending activities/cleanup		
Give verbal warning to all children		
Plan and use transitions every day		

aggressive behavior, probably because of the high levels of interaction within these areas (Shapiro 1975; Rubin 1977; Quay, Weaver, & Neal 1986). Positioning an adult within close proximity of these areas ensures quick response, and many situations can be diffused. While intervening, teachers can help children learn to express feelings, solve problems, and resolve conflicts through positive, peaceful means. Once children have had many opportunities to practice these skills, the close proximity of an adult can prevent aggressive behaviors from occurring at all.

4. Maintain a relaxed, calm, and interesting environment.

The physical arrangement of the classroom helps set a tone that states this is a place where children are welcomed and valued. Children are more likely to be helpful and cooperative if they are relaxed and engaged in interesting activities (Eisenberg & Mussen 1989). The classroom should be inviting and attractive. Children's work—words and images—are at their eye level. Materials are easily accessible, organized neatly on low, open shelves, encouraging children to explore all the interest areas. Labels clearly showing where items belong encourage children to replace materials with minimal adult supervision and decrease conflicts during cleanup time.

The progammatic environment

Once the physical aspects of the environment are addressed, teachers must assess the *programmatic environment*. They should look at the structure of activities, the daily schedule, classroom routines, and transitions.

5. Assess the structure of activities offered throughout the day.

The level of structure within a program can contribute to aggressive behaviors in the classroom. Highly structured programs provide limited opportunities for children to develop self-control, engage in cooperative behavior, or make informed decisions. To promote positive social skills, programs must give children opportunities to engage in many open-ended activities. However, teachers must be aware that, while these activities promote social interaction and prosocial behaviors, they may also create higher levels of assertiveness and aggressive behavior (Huston-Stein, Friedrich-Cofer, & Susman 1977). Teachers must be prepared to effectively deal with conflicts. A program designed with a balance of unstructured and structured activities, in which problem-solving strategies are used to address conflicts, provides the opportunities children need to develop self-control and self-discipline.

6. Follow a schedule appropriate for the age group.

Some young children can easily become overstimulated or bored, which contributes to the potential for aggressive behavior. Teachers should carefully assess the daily schedule to determine if it allows for alternating periods of active and quiet time. Group times should be relatively short and interspersed throughout the day. Teachers can assess the time limit for group times by picking up on clues provided by the children. When children become distracted or "antsy," it is time to wrap up the activity. A beginning point is 10 to 15 minutes for most children ages three to five. The time can be increased as children demonstrate their ability to focus for longer periods of time.

Another important scheduling aspect is planning for choice time. Substantial periods of time, a *minimum* of one hour, should be set aside for children to engage in activities of their own choosing, exploring and learning about their environment (Slaby et al. 1995; Bredekamp & Copple 1997).

7. Establish classroom routines.

An appropriate daily schedule, with consistent routines and well-planned transitions that eliminate wait time, helps create a positive classroom climate. A schedule that is consistent, yet flexible enough to meet the needs and interests of the children, can help reduce aggressive behavior. A visual representation of the schedule—with pictures and words depicting the activities and times—should be displayed and referred to. Teachers can easily make references to the schedule throughout the day. For example, at the conclusion of storytime, the teacher may point to the appropriate picture on the schedule and ask children what activity happens next.

8. Plan transitions to signal the end to activities.

Although a visual representation of the schedule helps children know the sequence of daily activities, most young children are unable to understand the amount of time allocated for an activity. Therefore, teachers should provide a signal that activities are about to end. This signal gives children the opportunity to end one activity and to prepare for another. For example, "We have time to sing one more song before getting ready to go outside." "It is almost time for lunch. We have time for two more people to share." "Before we start planning for activity time, we need to take the lunch count."

A warning is especially important before the end of choice times so children can complete or store their projects, put away toys and materials, and prepare to move to the next activity in a calm manner. It also demonstrates to the children the teacher's respect for their work and the need to plan ahead (Slaby et al. 1995).

Warning cues and styles vary from teacher to teacher. Good teachers know their children: how much time they need for cleanup and for getting centered before moving on to the next activity. A minimum of five minutes is recommended—more if necessary.

The most effective closing technique is walking around the room, interacting with each child or group of children and reminding them that only five minutes remain for the activity. A timer or musical signal reinforces the message. Sometimes it helps if teachers ask children to acknowledge the fact they have heard the warning and understand that the end of playtime is near. It is also a good idea to be flexible when possible, allowing a child to complete a thoroughly engaging activity while the rest of the group moves on.

Carefully assessing the physical and programmatic environment and taking preventative measures can help alleviate some aggressive behaviors in the classroom. Time, consistency, and the presence of caring adults are the critical components necessary for helping young children develop self-discipline.

References

Bredekamp, S., & C. Copple, eds. 1997. *Developmentally appropriate practice in early childhood programs.* Rev. ed. Washington, DC: NAEYC.

Eisenberg, N., & P.H. Mussen. 1989. *The roots of prosocial behavior in children.* New York: Cambridge University Press.

Gump, P.V. 1975. Ecological psychology and children. In *Review of child development research*, vol. 5, ed. E. M. Hetherington, 75–126. Chicago: University of Chicago Press.

Huston-Stein, A.C., L. Friedrich-Cofer, E. J. Susman. 1977. The relationship of classroom structure to social behavior, imaginative play, and self-regulation of economically disadvantaged children. *Child Development* 48: 908–16.

McGrew, W.C. 1972. Aspects of social development in nursery school children with emphasis on introduction to the group. In *Ethnological studies of child behavior*, ed. N.B. Hones, 129–56, New York: Cambridge University Press.

Quay, L.C., J. H. Weaver, & J. H. Neal, 1986. The effects of play materials on positive and negative social behaviors in preschool boys and girls. *Child Study Journal* 16 (1): 67–76.

Rubin, K.H. 1977. The social and cognitive value of toys and activities. *Canadian Journal of Behavioral Sciences* 9: 382–85.

Shapiro, S. 1975. Some classroom ABC's: Research takes a closer look. *Elementary School Journal* 75: 436–41.

Slaby, R.G., W.C. Roedell, D, Arezzo, & K. Hendrix. 1995. *Early violence prevention: Tools for teachers of young children.* Washington, DC: NAEYC.

Nancy Ratcliff, Ph.D., *is an assistant professor of early childhood education at the University of South Florida in Tampa. Her research focuses on early childhood teacher licensure and preservice teacher portfolio assessment. Nancy taught in public school for 12 years before entering the teacher education field.*

"Teacher! He Hit Me!" "She Pushed Me!"
—Where Does It Start? How Can It Stop?

Linda Wolfson-Steinberg

Every teacher, every year, has a group of children that usually includes one or more challenging kids—children who create trouble or find it. If we're lucky, there are only one or two per classroom. There are also some children who are easy, cooperative, friendly.

In this article, I suggest looking at the group dynamics in the classroom so that every child has a better chance at interacting successfully. Success for children means that we too have a greater possibility of maintaining our professional equilibrium and pride.

The causes of conflict

My experience one year fit a pattern that I had been noticing for at least six years of my teaching. Increasingly I was finding a need to look differently at the group dynamics. While searching for what was motivating the troublemaker, I simultaneously began to look more carefully at the so-called good kids to learn if they were playing any part in provoking trouble in subtle or manipulative ways. I found that the causes of conflict often began in surprising places.

My use of terms such as *good kid* and *troublemaker* and the like does not in any way imply judgment about a child. In fact, a belief in the inherent goodness of every single child underlies observations, interactions, and interventions in every caring classroom regardless of the children's ages. *Good* and *bad* are also used as emotionally illustrative terms by adults and children when describing others (Katz & McClellan 1997). Unfortunately they then are meant to convey stereotypical comments and perceptions.

Strong self-esteem depends on more than having the ability to cooperate and behave. Although labels are grossly inadequate, children do want to see themselves as good kids, worthy of affection, attention, and recognition. Additionally, issues of status among peers, and social competence, affect self-esteem and so too does the relationship between teacher and student, including both tone and content. The bottom line is that children need to feel good about themselves.

Successful peer interactions and supportive encouragement and guidance from adults contribute significantly to self-esteem throughout children's school life. It is within our power as teachers to facilitate safe and fair conflict management, increased cooperative behavior, and, therefore, good feelings about the self. It is that end toward which this article focuses.

An example in the classroom

One year I had a four-year-old boy in class who was struggling in all areas. Socially he was clumsy and often rejected by his peers. Some parents had already tried to have him removed from school for aggressive behavior. Classmates blamed him for a multiplicity of broken rules. This picture had been evident for more than two years in our nursery school.

Billy was not a particularly attractive child, and classmates sometimes made fun of his appearance. His large- and small-motor skills were both weak, and participation in large-group activities such as music, story, and circle time was quite erratic.

The home situation for Billy was filled with a variety of significant challenges, including some serious health problems his parents faced.

He was the oldest of three boys quite close in age. Additionally, Billy's grandmother (who usually brought him and picked him up each day) frequently said inappropriate things within his hearing, such as "OK, where is the nudge?" or "What did he do wrong today?"

The picture was one of a child who had a rough time at almost everything and everywhere in his young life. His dysfunctional behavior reflected his familial and social disadvantages (Katz & McClellan 1997). Yet Billy had a wonderful imagination, and every day he tried again and again to get into the Little Boys Club in the room. He also was more than willing to play with the girls when they allowed him in. His speech was distinct; his language was vivid and clear.

By the third month of school, Billy had clearly demonstrated progress and brought himself over to sit in the group without loudly distracting its activity (which he had done for the first months). His social interactions too were increasingly peppered with sincere, positive interchanges.

I could really feel for Billy and had been focusing my attention on making sure that he didn't hurt anyone or disrupt the class. Now seemed an appropriate time during which connections could be made and friendships begun. In the first weeks of school, Billy was almost a full-time job by himself. Nonethe-

less, I honestly liked him (although he drove me absolutely wild sometimes). The change was dramatic.

After Billy had been responding well to the classroom environment, the crisis came. The pattern of his progress had been steady, and I was confident in assessing real growth in his ego strength and social abilities. Yet one day it all seemed to have blown away. When I returned from taking a child to the bathroom, I learned that Billy had hit Jason on the head with a stone from our nature table.

Cute, talented, and relatively popular, Jason was the older of two brothers. Both his parents were active, productive participants in the school. His dad was a firefighter. Jason had status in his own right but also because of his family. The other children thought it impressive to have a firefighter parent. Jason's parents felt that because of what they did for the school, certain extra attention should be paid to all of their queries.

Look twice before you assume that the class "bad boy" did it. Careful observation may well reveal other provocateurs and subtle instigators.

Later that week after the first incident with Billy, Jason came crying to me that Billy had punched him in the eye (like the first incident, this one also occurred out of eyesight). I knew something was wrong. The details Jason was reporting seemed incomplete. Billy had not hurt anyone even slightly since mid-October, and now it was January.

I needed, I thought, to seriously reevaluate what was happening in class. (A separate and crucial topic itself is addressing the boys themselves.) But what was it that I had *not* been seeing and understanding? Obviously a *big* problem lay in the dynamics of expressed conflict between these boys. Either I was

wrong in my assessment of Billy's growth, or he was regressing for a reason that I had to uncover. *I had to look at the entire group from a different perspective.*

When the puzzle remains, what then?

Many of us in early childhood face scenarios similar to that of Billy and Jason. One child, more often a boy, gets into fights with classmates and does not easily cooperate with teachers. A good kid, girl or boy, becomes the victim, with teachers rarely actually seeing what's going on when the injury occurs.

More often than not, we throw up our hands and repeat, as we have again and again, "School has to be safe for everyone. I won't let people hurt you and you *cannot* hurt anyone else. What you did is dangerous. Hurting people is *not* OK. You have to use your words." This response, or some variation on the theme, has all the firm but nurturing elements. But sometimes it just doesn't work. The victim continues to get hurt by the same aggressor. If to the best of your ability you can eliminate regression as the cause of this conflict, and if you trust your initial assessment, then you have to keep looking for the answer.

When the puzzle remains, a new teacher strategy is needed. If your Billy has made any progress and shown growth in ego strength, then something else is probably happening. With my Billy, I felt I needed to look at the entire class group with new eyes, particularly to observe closely the recurrent victim. I must as, "What is Jason doing just before Billy slugs him?" When there are multiple victims, we need to listen in and see what is going on before our Billy hits. What triggers his frustration or anger?

Seeing the other factors

Jason's parents were very upset about their little boy being victimized by a perceived bully. I couldn't blame them. I spoke to the school ed-

ucational consultant because of the severity of what had occurred. With her knowledge and support, I agreed to watch Billy closely over the next days to get him back on track. Then, however, after rehashing with the consultant and my director what had been happening, it made sense to focus my attention on Jason too.

My instinct told me that Jason was contributing substantially to the missing piece of the picture. I knew that in watching him, his safety would be intact and I could collect more information. Including our educational consultant turned out to be a critical move. Whatever I might discover would carry the added weight of another objective, professional person. Jason's parents also would hear about the situation from the consultant's perspective.

An interesting dynamic came to light and made the picture clearer. Jason often played intentionally out of direct line of vision. As I took notes describing moments in class, examples began to accumulate. Repeatedly, Jason looked over to check if anyone could see him.

In one instance Jason teased another child by rough play and pushed the boy's head into the sand. The playmate was quiet and did not tell Jason to stop or ask for help from the adults. Instead, the playmate took action against Jason; only he got

caught pushing Jason's face into the ground. However, my assistant had seen the chain of events and told me that Jason was the first aggressor.

A second instance occurred as the children were walking down the steps to the gym. Jason shoved Billy into the wall. In the past Billy would have just hauled off and slugged him or called him something very inflammatory. But I was right there, and I told Jason immediately and firmly, "Don't shove Billy. You are not allowed to hurt anyone." Given the history of this situation and the fact that we were on our way to a specialty class, there was no time to allow the boys to work it out with each other, as we normally would do in class.

On another day, when Billy was absent, Jason raced to capture a seat that Sam had gotten to and sat in it first. After I said that Sam was there first, Jason sat sulking in the corner. Sam, who was normally quiet about any difficulties arising with peers, spoke up, saying, "Jason pinched me."

Early the next day, one mother noticed Jason sitting with her son Mark behind the easels. Jason was hitting him. When my assistant went over, Mark didn't even blame Jason. He just said, "No, it's OK, he can have it."

Incredible! In the space of one week, I'd documented four instances in which Jason had surreptitiously

hurt another child. And he primarily had chosen children who would not tell on him. Billy also wouldn't tell, but his pattern was to react physically—aggressively—then *he* was the one to get in trouble.

Approaches to resolution

Resolving these conflicts required an approach on three different levels: communication with Billy, Jason, and Jason's parents. First, the child with weak or fragile impulse control needs constant reminders (verbal and actual) that the teacher will listen to his position but under no circumstance tolerate physical aggression.

Billy needed to hear the message that I care for him and know he is a good boy. Supporting his self-esteem was an important piece of the puzzle. He also needed to know that when he is angry or frustrated he cannot hurt anyone and that if there is trouble his own words can't fix, he needs to ask an adult for help—and *will get immediate assistance.*

Second, the good or easy child needs to hear and experience the clear message that she too must respect every single child. For the more cooperative and popular child whose self-image is strong, our responsibility as teachers is slightly different. These children need guidance and modeling in not taking ad-

---

Resolving conflicts involves

- reminding a child with weak impulse control to talk, not hit, and that you will listen;
- ensuring that the "good child" respects other children and is accountable for his actions too; and
- working in a gentle, caring, yet honest way with an aggressive child's parents, rather than alienating them, so as to become partners with them in guiding the child.

---

vantage of their power. They cannot stretch or break the rules simply because another child is more likely to strike out. Teachers need to watch and notice what every child is doing, not just the ones who say bad words or use their hands aggressively.

For Jason, consequences exist for both provocative *and* aggressive behavior. He needed to know that I care for him too and that *he* is a good boy. But Jason must understand he cannot manipulate or provoke another child into getting in trouble without bearing the consequences of his own actions. He needed proof that he too was answerable to rules of fair play.

Jason also needed practice in using his words to try to resolve difficulties. He must ask a teacher for help when talking doesn't work. If someone bothers Jason and won't stop when asked, then Jason should turn to the teacher next. If a more impulsive classmate does not cooperate, this does not give Jason

permission to pinch or push or use mean words to get a reaction or express his annoyance.

Third, dealing with parents is perhaps the most difficult part of a situation and needs a delicate, caring, yet honest approach. Facing parents is frequently a complex political and professional situation. I definitely could not have related to Jason's parents without system support. They legitimately needed to hear that the safety of their child was secure.

I had to find a way to communicate about their child's provocative and aggressive behaviors without alienating them. This took multiple conversations between the director of our program and Jason's mother, the educational consultant and his mother, and finally with me. One week later life in class had smoothed down, and the aggression had all but disappeared.

Positive intervention

The system that worked was one that began with my classroom observations and then informing my director about what was happening. Because of the dramatic nature of the injury, the director and I conferred with the educational consultant about what I was seeing before I called the parents. The consultant helped me put into objective language what I saw as happening. We discussed how best to approach the parents, based on their needs. In Jason's situation, the consultant met and spoke with his mother before I called.

I called Jason's home to inform his family that a minor injury had occurred. (Thankfully the rock had not drawn blood.) I assured Jason's mother that her son was OK and

asked for a time later that day in which we could meet and talk at length. Although not minimizing the safety factor for her son, my message to Jason's mother was that the situation was complex.

When we spoke, I said how critical safety is for every child in school and that I had documented several incidents in which her son had hurt other children. I asked her if anything was going on at home that might be causing stress. Then I requested that she support my message to her son that if his words don't work, he should ask for help. (This aspect of the problem solving, not fully addressed here, deserves attention as well.)

Conclusion

None of this positive resolution can happen if teachers stop at the point of their frustration with a naughty child. We must look beyond the surface ripples to uncover the source or sources of a child's disruption. The critical message that children need to experience is one of fairness toward everyone.

Reference
Katz, L.G., & D.E. McClellan. 1997. *Fostering children's social competence: The teacher's role.* Washington, DC: NAEYC.

For further reading
Boutte, G.S., D.L. Keepler, V.S. Tyler, & B.Z. Terry. 1992. Effective techniques for involving "difficult" parents. *Young Children* 47 (3): 19–22.

Buzzelli, C.A. 1992. Research in Review. Young children's moral understanding: Learning about right and wrong. *Young Children* 47 (6): 47–53.

Clewett, A.S. 1988. Guidance and discipline: Teaching young children appropriate behavior. *Young Children* 43 (4): 26–31.

Cohen, D.H., V. Stern, & N. Balaban. 1997. *Observation and recording the behavior of young children*. New York: Teachers College Press.

Dowrick, P. 1986. Disturbed children. In *Social survival for children*. New York: Brunner/Mazel.

Eaton, M. 1997. Positive discipline: Fostering the self-esteem of young children. *Young Children* 52 (6): 43–46.

Elias, M.J., J.E. Zins, R.P. Reissberg, K.S. Frey, M.T. Greenberg, N.M. Haynes, R. Kessler, M.E. Schwab-Stone, & T.P. Schreiber. 1997. Developing social and emotion skills in classrooms. In *Promoting social and emotional learning*. Alexandria, VA: Association for Supervision and Curriculum Development.

Furman, R.A. 1995. Helping children cope with stress and deal with feelings. *Young Children* 50 (2): 33–41.

Gartrell, D. 1995. Misbehavior or mistaken behavior? *Young Children* 50 (5): 27–34.

Greenberg, P. 1987. Ideas That Work with Young Children. Good discipline is, in large part, the result of a fantastic curriculum! *Young Children* 42 (3): 49–51.

Greenberg, P. 1987. Ideas That Work with Young Children. Child choice—Another way to individualize—Another form of preventive discipline. *Young Children* 43 (1): 48–54.

Greenberg, P. 1988. Ideas That Work with Young Children. Avoiding "me against you" discipline. *Young Children* 44 (1): 24–29.

Greenberg, P. 1988. Ideas That Work with Young Children: Laughing all the way. *Young Children* 43 (2): 39–41.

Honig, A.S. 1989. *Love and learn: Discipline for young children*. Washington, DC: NAEYC. Brochure.

Kaiser, B., & J. Rasminsky. 1999. *Meeting the challenge: Effective strategies for challenging behaviours in early childhood environments*. Ottawa, ONT: Canadian Child Care Federation. (Available through NAEYC.)

Kemple, K. 1992. Understanding and facilitating preschool children's peer acceptance. *ERIC Digest* EDO–PS–92–5. Champaign-Urbana, IL: ERIC Clearinghouse on Elementary and Early Childhood Education.

Killinger, J. 1980. The loneliness of children. In *The cruelty of peers*. New York: Vanguard.

Levin, D.E. 1994. *Teaching young children in violent times*. Philadelphia: New Society.

Lightfoot, S.L. 1978. *Worlds apart: Relationships between families and schools*. New York: Basic Books.

Marion, M. 1997. Research in Review. Guiding young children's understanding and management of anger. *Young Children* 52 (7): 62–67.

NAEYC. 1986. *Helping children learn self-control*. Washington, DC: Author. Brochure.

Oden, S. 1980. A child's social isolation: Origins, prevention, intervention. In *Teaching social skills to children*, eds. G. Cartledge & J. Fellows Milburn. Elmsford, NY: Pergamon.

Reinsberg, J. 1999. Understanding young children's behavior. *Young Children* 54 (4): 54–57.

Sandall, S., & M. Ostrosky, eds. 1999. Practical ideas for addressing challenging behaviors. Reston, VA: Council for Exceptional Children/Division for Early Childhood. (Available through NAEYC.)

Sapon-Shevin, M. 1980. Teaching cooperation in early childhood settings. In *Teaching social skills to children*, eds. G. Cartledge & J. Fellows Milburn. Elmsford, NY: Pergamon.

Schreiber, M.E. 1999. Time-outs for toddlers: Is our goal punishment or education? *Young Children* 54 (4): 22–25.

Stone, J.G. 1978. *A guide to discipline*. Rev. ed. Washington, DC: NAEYC.

Wolf, J.S., & T.M. Stephens. 1989. Parent/teacher conferences: Finding common grounds. *Educational Leadership* 47 (2).

Linda Wolfson-Steinberg, M.S., is an adjunct lecturer in education and psychology at Kendall College in Evanston, Illinois. She has taught in early childhood settings for 15 years, developed student assessment tools as well as school-community newsletters, and done presentations at professional training seminars. Photos © The Growth Program.

Promoting the Emotional Development of Preschoolers

This paper looks at evidence pertaining to the emotional development of preschoolers. The issues talked about include a synopsis of emotional expression, emotional understanding, the regulation of emotions, and their developmental significance. Furthermore, the role of the caregiver–child relationship as indicated by the security of attachment is provided. It is argued that caregivers influence the emotional development of children as they model, coach, and contingently respond to children. The implications of emotional development and the quality of the caregiver–child relationship for teachers as they pertain to affective displays, negotiation skills, affect regulation, and expectancies of children are discussed. Finally, some strategies for enhancing emotional development are suggested.

KEY WORDS: caregiver–child relationship, emotional development; attachment; social competence.

Godwin S. Ashiabi[1,2]

INTRODUCTION

Both theoretical and empirical essays point to the role of poorly functioning caregiver–child relationships in the development of later socioemotional difficulties of children (Robinson, Emde, & Korfmacher, 1997). For emotional development to take place, relationships with caregivers and peers are necessary because they provide differing experiences and serve disparate functions. Caregiver–child relationships provide children with comfort, protection, and security during the early years, and basic social skills emerge within them (Hartup, 1989; Sroufe, 1997).

Relationships with peers, on the other hand, are contexts in which children elaborate on the skills acquired in the caregiver–child relationship with individuals who are more or less similar to themselves and master the complexities of cooperation and competition (Hartup, 1989). In essence, the caregiver–child relationship is a training ground for emotional skills, as the skills acquired in it are transferred into relationships with peers.

The foregoing shows that emotional development is linked with advances in social development, because emotions are not only expressed in a social context but also within the matrix of caregiving relationships (Sroufe, 1997). Thus, we see that a child's ability to deal effectively with his or her social world emerges largely from experience in close relationships (Hartup, 1989).

My goal is to show how the caregiver–child relationship influences the emotional development of preschoolers. Toward that goal, this paper is organized into four sections. The first section reports some evidence pertaining to emotional development, such as, the expression of emotions, understanding of emotions, and regulation of emotions. In the second section, the role of the caregiver–child relationship in emotional development is examined. In the third section, the implications of findings relating to emotional development and the role of the caregiver–child relationship for teachers are examined. In the final section, some strategies for promoting emotional development of preschoolers are suggested.

YOUNG CHILDREN'S EMOTIONAL DEVELOPMENT

We can think of an emotion as an organized reaction to an event that is relevant to the needs, goals, and interests of the individual and is characterized by physiological, experiential, and overt behavioral change (Robinson *et al.*, 1997; Sroufe, 1997). From this perspective, a child's emotions serve two functions: motivational and communicative. As a motivator, emotions determine the behavior of a child. For example, a child approaches a novel phenomenon if it is not interpreted as threatening; however, avoidance results if the interpretation is associated with a threat. Children use the communicative function of emotions to let others respond to their distress or needs, such as an infant's cries or smiles (Robinson *et al.*, 1997).

Although the child brings a particular set of abilities to his or her emotional life, other persons play a role in the development of emotional competence; that is, inborn differences and early care interact to create the early adaptation of the child (Vaughn *et al.*, 1992).

Emotional Expression

The ability of children to appropriately express their emotions is paramount for social interactions. A child's social competence is judged by the type, frequency, and duration of the emotion expressed. If a child consistently displays anger over long periods, this means that potential social partners will be discouraged from further interaction with the child. The reason being that the experience and expression of emotion affect a child's behavior, which in turn provides information to potential social partners about whether to engage the child or to retreat from further interaction with the child (Denham, 1998).

Empirical evidence shows that children are responsive to others, are aware of the perspectives of others, and display altruistic behaviors (Mussen & Eisenberg, 1977). By age 2, on the condition that they are emotionally secure and have had experience with emotions (Strayer, 1980), children are able to (a) broadly interpret others' emotional states, (b) experience these feeling states in response to others' predicaments, and (c) attempt to alleviate discomfort in others (Eisenberg et al., 1990; Zahn-Waxler & Radke-Yarrow, 1990).

By age 3, the context and identities of social partners become determinants of the type of emotion expressed. Additionally, children are able to alternate modes and intensity of expressiveness as the situation demands (Malatesta, Culver, Tesman, & Shepard, 1989; Zeaman & Garber, 1996). Children also learn to employ display rules (i.e., culturally appropriate ways of expressing emotions) to substitute, mask, minimize, or maximize their emotional expressiveness in accordance with certain situations and for self-preservation purposes (Ekman & Friesman, 1975). For example, a child will maximize affective displays by crying to gain adults' attention and response.

The Understanding of Emotions

It is important that children understand the emotions of their play partners because it enables them to perceive the communicative function of the emotions they or another person is feeling. The understanding of emotions serves a survival function, for example, in the face of danger, the fear that is aroused is a signal to the child to seek the comfort, security, and protection of a caregiver. Subjectivity and meaning are important elements in understanding of emotions because they explain why one emotion, rather than another, is aroused in similar situations and they explain individual differences in emotional expressiveness (Sroufe, 1997).

The understanding of causal factors in emotional situations improves over the preschool period. Children begin to use the contextual information in their everyday experiences to understand the basic emotions—fear, anger, sadness, and happiness—and why they occur (Dunn & Hughes, 1998). They are also able to talk about their feelings as they understand the causal complexities of emotions. Through their own experiences and increased social sensitivity, children develop the ability to (a) assess the emotions of others when contextual cues are less salient, (b) recognize different emotional experiences,

(c) regulate emotion, and (d) experience more than one emotion simultaneously (Denham, 1998).

Children need to experience moderate levels of a variety of emotions in order to construct social scripts about emotions, because they first reflect on and make judgments about their own emotions, and then generalize these judgments to others' feelings (Smiley & Huttenlocher, 1989). It is important to allow children to experience emotions, to encourage positive emotion, and assist them in managing negative emotions in socially acceptable ways (Denham, 1998).

Emotional Regulation

An important part of emotional competence is the regulation of emotion. Both negative and positive emotions can exceed a child's resources. When this happens, the child's behavior, thought, or both may become disorganized. If the emotional experience is arousing, caregivers typically soothe; alternatively, a child can appear passive and withdrawn, in such situations caregivers typically try to stimulate the child and encourage play (Robinson et al., 1997).

Children's ability to manage the emotional arousal that accompanies social interactions is fundamental for their growing ability to interact with and form relationships with others (Saarni, 1990). In that sense, the way children express their emotions is related to the evaluations of their social competence by people in their social world. Thus, in the process of learning to get along with agemates the child is constrained toward regulating emotional expressiveness (Denham, 1998).

Emotional regulation takes the form of a transfer of responsibility from caregiver to dyad to the child (Sroufe, 1989). At first caregivers have almost total responsibility for keeping arousal tolerable. In time, the child plays an active role in the regulation process, responding to caregivers, and ultimately, instigating regulatory assistance through deliberate efforts, such as, crying and running to a caregiver when they get hurt. The caregiver in a sense trains the child in tension management (Denham, 1998; Sroufe, 1989, 1997).

THE CAREGIVER–CHILD RELATIONSHIP

The issue explored in this section is how the caregiver–child relationship affects the emotional development of children and their need to form social and emotional relationships with others (Ainsworth, 1973; Bowlby, 1969).

The quality of the caregiver–child relationship has been conceptualized in terms of an attachment relationship that hypothesizes that (a) differing quality of care leads to differences in expectations of children regarding the dependability and responsiveness of the caregiver, and (b) these differences in expectations have an impact on children's later expression of emotion, the understanding of emotion and later regulation of emotion (Sroufe, 1997).

The quality of caregiver–child relationship also influences the strategies and behavior patterns of children in interactions with their caregivers. The child who has a secure relationship with the caregiver initiates positive interaction, and responds positively to initiations by the caregiver. On the other hand, the child who has an insecure relationship with the caregiver displays various strategies that include ignoring caregiver's behavior and initiations, heightening expression of negative emotions in order to ensure that the caregiver remains close, or acts in a hostile manner toward the caregiver (Cassidy, 1994; Main & Cassidy, 1988).

Caregiver–Child Relationship and Emotional Development

The caregiver–child relationship influences emotional development and the need to form social and emotional relationships with others (Ainsworth, 1973; Bowlby, 1969), as caregivers model, coach, and respond to or do not respond to the distress signals and needs of children (Halberstadt, 1991). These processes also influence emotional development of children through the distortions that occur in emotional expressiveness, emotional understanding, and emotional regulation (Sroufe, 1997).

Modeling and Emotional Development. Children's expressiveness reflects their caregivers' total emotional expressiveness (Cummings & Cummings, 1988). For example, caregivers who often exhibit anger are more likely to have children who show anger, because through modeling, caregivers give children information about the nature of emotions, their expressions, and how to cope with their own emotions and those of others (Saarni, 1987). By modeling various emotions, caregivers, implicitly teach children those emotions that are acceptable, those emotions that are appropriate for specific types of situations, and the common behaviors associated with their expression. Modeling by caregivers also provides an overall affective environment to which the child is exposed (Denham, 1998).

Coaching and Emotional Development. Caregivers encourage children's exploration and understanding of emotions directly by verbally communicating with them the experiential meaning of emotions (Saarni, 1987). Caregivers who talk about emotions and foster this ability in children enable them to express optimal patterns of emotions, and to separate impulse and behavior (Denham, 1998). Caregivers also use direct commands and instructions about emotions as the guiding and socializing language in their discourse about emotions. Additionally, caregivers contribute by managing the information given to the child about potentially emotional events (Denham, 1998).

Contingent Responding and Emotional Development. The emotional and behavioral reactions of caregivers to children's emotions help children in differentiating among emotions. These reactions can be important ways for letting children know what behaviors are appropriate when they feel different ways, and what events merit emotion expression at all (Denham, 1998). Caregivers can be rewarding or punitive in their responses to the emotions of children. Affectively balanced, integrated emotional development is promoted when caregivers assist the child in maintaining a positive affect and tolerate the child's negative affect as valid and worthy of regard

and concern. This helps children to cope with powerful emotions (Denham, 1998). On the other hand, caregivers who are punitive ignore or deny children's emotional experience and fail to use emotional moments as a chance to get closer to the child or to help the child learn lessons in emotional competence (Goleman, 1995).

IMPLICATIONS FOR TEACHERS: EMOTIONAL DEVELOPMENT AND THE CAREGIVER–CHILD RELATIONSHIP

What does the evidence on the emotional development of children mean for teachers? First, it helps teachers understand that children are emotionally sophisticated; that is, they can be empathic and show concern for others, which is contrary to the Piagetian view of the egocentric nature of children. Second, it means that teachers can be able to identify children who are not developing the emotional skills necessary for positive social interaction with peers, as per their inability to express and regulate their emotions in social interactions with peers. Third, it means that teachers can and should talk to children about emotional issues.

Knowledge of caregiver–child relationships helps teachers understand that the quality of the caregiver–child relationship influences children's affective displays, negotiation skills, affect regulation, and the transfer of expectancies. It helps teachers understand that children who have a secure relationship with their caregivers tend to be compromised as they may inhibit their affect, falsely display an affect that does not match how they feel, or they may exaggerate their affective displays (Crittenden, 1992).

In terms of their negotiation skills, children who have a secure relationship with their caregivers will tend to use open and direct negotiation to exchange information; whereas children with an insecure relationship may refuse to negotiate in order to avoid rejection, or for those who are not afraid of rejection, they may use coercive behaviors (Crittenden, 1992).

In terms of their negotiation skills, children who have a secure relationship with their caregivers will tend to use open and direct negotiation to exchange information; whereas children with an insecure relationship may refuse to negotiate in order to avoid rejection, or for those who are not afraid of rejection, they may use coercive behaviors (Crittenden, 1992).

We know that children with secure relationships are able to regulate their feelings (i.e., both internal feeling states and affective displays) by seeking and obtaining help from caregivers. However, children with insecure relationships will attempt to regulate their feelings through their own efforts, given that past experiences have taught them that their caregivers will not help them to resolve uncomfortable feelings of anxiety or anger (Crittenden, 1992).

How are the expectancies created in the caregiver–child relationship transferred into other relationships? This question stresses the influence of the child's expectations of others that cause the child to approach potential social partners with relational biases. For example, a child may have an image of others that includes not trusting them to be available and responsive to his or her needs. Thus, all other relationships which the child enters into are approached with a negative expectation and it is as though the child is seeking confirmation of that expectation. If social partners behave in ways consistent with the negative expectations of the child, then it is more likely that the child would behave in a manner that will be construed as socially incompetent. However, if social partners do not feed into the negative expectations of the child, then the expectations of the child are challenged by a different source of information (i.e., some caregivers are available and responsive) and may result in the child seeking resolution by trying to assimilate the new information into his or her thoughts about relationships with others. This new information, once assimilated, forms the basis of a new notion of relationships pertaining to that specific individual. It is like the child stores memories of various relationships and acts the role when he or she is in a specific social situation.

For teachers this means that they have to be available and responsive to the needs of all the children in their classrooms. When they respond in a consistent manner, they help children develop alternative views of the world and relationships. By being dependable and responsive, they teach children that emotional experiences need not be overwhelming and that they can be controlled. In time, the children are able to regulate their emotions with little or no help.

SOME STRATEGIES FOR PROMOTING THE SOCIOEMOTIONAL DEVELOPMENT OF CHILDREN

Other individuals, apart from the primary caregiver, can influence a child's emotional development. A teacher can develop a relationship with a child that is positive and supportive of the growth of emotional competence. During interactions with children, teachers have to be open to the transactions taking place, because as developmental changes occur, there will be changes in their relationships with children; however, the affective basis for these relationships continues to involve a desire for proximity in times of stress and feelings of trust (Hartup, 1989).

Some of the strategies teachers can use to promote the emotional development are (a) acknowledgement time, (b) feelings time, (c) affection activities, (d) emotional management techniques, and (e) social problem-solving.

Acknowledgment Time. Teachers can set some time aside regularly to help children express their feelings. This time of emotional expressiveness, involves talking about and handling emotions. This time allows children to show their appreciation and regard for others whom they may perceive as really nice to them. It also encourages the building of relationships as children express their affection for each other.

Feelings Time. This involves webbing of ideas about the primary emotions. The goals are to let children talk about (a) the causes of their emotions, (b) what they do when they experience those emotions, (c) how they think they can make those feelings go away, and (d) what they think another child might do. By helping children to attach labels to their feelings, it helps them understand each other's feelings and how each feeling state influences thinking. When children realize the connection between the feeling and thinking, they understand that the way they feel will to a greater extent determine what they do.

Affection Activities. A teacher can do any number of activities so children can show their affection toward others. A teacher can invite children to sit down and then ask one of them to pick a numbered card; with the number card indicative of the number of children the child may shake hands with, or give a hug, or give a kiss on the cheek. The goal is to teach children how to learn to be friends and appropriately express their emotions (Twardosz, Nordquist, Simon, & Botkin, 1983).

Emotional Management Techniques. The goal of this strategy is to teach children self-regulatory and monitoring skills when they are emotionally overwhelmed by negative emotions. Teachers can create a space in a corner—if it is available (Denham, 1998). This corner is a retreat where children who may be experiencing strong emotions can go to calm down. What the teacher should also bear in mind is to try to calm down the child: the goal is not to use the corner as a punishment or timeout because the teacher's actions during this time are important.

Social Problem-Solving Approach. The goal is to help children think through and resolve interpersonal problems effectively. It involves an empathic component in which children come to realize the effects of their actions upon others. The conflict children experience can be used to teach them about emotions. Conflict means that children must learn to communicate, negotiate, compromise, and interact (Camras, 1980). Two approaches could be used. The first involves using puppets and role play to teach children how to resolve interpersonal problems without resorting to aggression. The second approach is to allow children to attempt to resolve conflicts on their own whenever a disagreement arises. However, the goal is to let the children come to tell the teacher how they resolved the conflict so the teacher can use the occasion to offer some feedback to the children and promote positive peer interaction (Killen & Turiel, 1991).

CONCLUSION

Because of their verbal limitations, emotions become important social signals for children. Educators need to recognize the importance of emotional competence for socially competent behavior in young children and find means to cultivate it. Additionally, we need to realize when and how young children are at risk for delay, and learn to recognize disturbances in expected milestones of emotional competence (Denham, 1998).

Children's emotional development has long-term implications for their adaptation in the preschool and school settings and in peer relationships. Early emotional dysregulation is a frequent precursor to behavior problems of early and middle childhood (Cicchetti, Ganiban, & Barnett, 1991). Children who understand emotions and how those feelings are expressed, are able to empathize with other children who may be in distress; they are also able to communicate how they feel.

Children who are emotionally competent are frequently regarded by peers as better play partners and more fun to be with; they may be able to strategically use their expressiveness to obtain social goals; they are at an advantage when responding appropriately to others' emotions during play; and they may be better liked (Walden & Field, 1990).

In summary, caregivers contribute to children's emotional development by reading the child's cues accurately and responding sensitively. The consistent and appropriate responsiveness of caregivers then tutors the children in how to regulate their emotions (Robinson *et al.*, 1997), which in turn contributes to emotionally competent behaviors throughout life.

REFERENCES

Ainsworth, M. D. S. (1973). The development of infant-mother attachment. In B. M. Caldwell & H. N. Ricciuti (Eds.), *Review of child development research* (Vol. 3., pp. 1–94). Chicago, IL: University of Chicago Press.

Bowlby, J. (1969). *Attachment and loss. Vol 1: Attachment.* New York: Basic.

Camras, L. A. (1980). Children's understanding of facial expressions used during conflict encounters. *Child Development, 51,* 879–885.

Cassidy, J. (1994). Emotion regulation: Influences of attachment relationships. In N. Fox (Ed.), The development of emotion regulation. *Monographs of the Society for Research in Child Development, 59* (2–3, Serial No. 240), 228–249.

Cicchetti, D., Ganiban, J., & Barnett, D. (1991). Contributions from the study of high-risk populations to understanding the development of emotion regulation. In J. Garber & K. A. Dodge (Eds.), *The development of emotion regulation and dysregulation* (pp. 15–48). Cambridge, UK: Cambridge University Press.

Crittenden, P. M. (1992). Quality of attachment in the preschool years. *Development and Psychopathology, 4,* 209–241.

Cummings, E. M., & Cummings, J. L. (1988). A process-oriented approach to children's coping with adult's angry behavior. *Developmental Review, 8,* 296–321.

Denham, S. S. (1998). *Emotional development in young children.* New York: Guilford.

Dunn, J., & Hughes, C. (1998). Young children's understanding of emotions within close relationships. *Cognition and Emotion, 12,* 171–190.

Eisenberg, N., Fabes, R. A., Miller, P. A., Shell, R., Shea, C., & May-Plumlee, T. (1990). Preschoolers' vicarious emotional responding and their situational and dispositional prosocial behavior. *Merrill-Palmer Quarterly, 36,* 507–528.

Ekman, P., & Friesen, W. V. (1975). *Unmasking the face.* Englewood Cliffs, NJ: Prentice-Hall.

Goleman, D. (1995). *Emotional Intelligence.* New York: Bantam Books.

Halberstadt, A. G. (1991). Socialization of expressiveness: Family influences in particular and a model in general. In R. S. Feldman & S.

Rime (Eds.), *Fundamentals of emotional expressiveness* (pp. 106–162). Cambridge, UK: Cambridge University Press.

Hartup, W. W. (1989). Social relationship and their developmental significance. *American Psychologist, 44,* 120–126.

Killen, M., & Turiel, E. (1991). Conflict resolution in preschool social interactions. *Early Education and Development, 2*(3), 240–255.

Main, M., & Cassidy, J. (1988). Categories of response to reunion with the parent at age 6: Predictable from infant attachment classifications and stable over a 1-month period. *Developmental Psychology, 24,* 415–426.

Malatesta, C. Z., Culver, C., Tesman, J. R., & Shepard, B. (1989). The development of emotional expression during the first two years of life. *Monographs of the Society for Research in Child Development, 54* (1–2, Serial No. 219).

Mussen, P., & Eisenberg, N. (1977). *Roots of caring, sharing, and helping: The development of prosocial behavior in children.* San Francisco: Freeman.

Robinson, J. L., Emde, R. N., & Korfmacher, J. (1997). Integrating an emotional regulation perspective in a program of prenatal and early childhood visitation. *Journal of Community Psychology, 25,* 59–75.

Saarni, C. (1987). Cultural rules and emotional experience: A commentary on Miller and Sperry's study. *Merrill-Palmer Quarterly, 33,* 535–540.

Saarni, C. (1990). Emotional competence. In R. A. Thompson (Ed.), *Nebraska Symposium on Motivation: Vol. 36. Socioemotional development* (pp. 115–161). Lincoln: University of Nebraska Press.

Smiley, P., & Huttenlocher, J. (1989). Young children's acquisitions of emotion concepts. In P. Harris & C. Saarni (Eds.), *Children's understanding of emotion* (pp. 27–79). Cambridge, UK: Cambridge University Press.

Sroufe, L. A. (1989). Pathways to adaptation and maladaptation: Psychopathology as developmental deviation. In D. Cicchetti (Ed.), *Rochester Symposium on Developmental Psychopathology: Vol. 1* (pp. 13–24). Hillsdale, NJ: Erlbaum.

Sroufe, L. A. (1997). *Emotional development: The organization of emotional life in the early years.* Cambridge, UK: Cambridge University Press.

Strayer, J. (1980). A naturalistic study of empathic behaviors and their relation to affective states and perspective-taking skills in preschool children. *Child Development, 51,* 815–822.

Twardosz, S., Nordquist, V. M., Simon, R., & Botkin, D. (1983). The effect of group affection activities on the interaction of socially isolated children. *Analysis and Intervention in Developmental Disabilities, 3,* 311–338.

Vaughn, B., Stevenson-Hinde, J., Waters, E., Kutsaftis, A., Lefever, G., Shouldice, A., Trudel, M., & Belsky, J. (1992). Attachment security and temperament in infancy and early childhood: Some conceptual clarifications. *Developmental Psychology, 28, 463–473.*

Walden, T. A., & Field, T. (1990). Preschool children's social competence and production of discrimination of affective expressions. *British Journal of Developmental Psychology, 8,* 65–76.

Zahn-Waxler, C., & Radke-Yarrow, M. (1990). The origins of empathic concern. *Motivation and Emotion, 14,* 107–130.

Zeaman, J., & Garber, J. (1996). Display rules for anger, sadness, and pain: It depends on who is watching. *Child Development, 67,* 957–973.

Department of Child and Family Studies, University of Tennessee, Knoxville.

Correspondence should be directed to Godwin S. Ashiabi, 1021-1611 Laurel Avenue, Knoxville, Tennessee 37916-2052.

From *Early Childhood Education Journal,* 2001, Vol. 28, No. 2, pp. 79-84. © 2001 by Kluwer Academic/Plenum Publishers. Reprinted by permission.

UNIT 5
Curricular Issues

Unit Selections

Key Points to Consider

- What are the benefits of the visual arts in the curriculum?

- How can blocks play an integral part in the learning curriculum?

- Are learning centers effective ways for children to learn?

- What information should teachers be sending to parents about their child's early literacy experiences?

- How can parents best be kept informed about the learning experiences their child has encountered in school?

- What is the appropriate use of technology and computers during the early childhood years?

- How can science and math learning activities allow for hands-on learning?

 **Links: www.dushkin.com/online/**
These sites are annotated in the World Wide Web pages.

Association for Childhood Education International (ACEI)
http://www.udel.edu/bateman/acei/
California Reading Initiative
http://www.sdcoe.k12.ca.us/score/promising/prreading/prreadin.html
Early Childhood Education Online
http://www.ume.maine.edu/ECEOL-L/
International Reading Association
http://www.reading.org
Kathy Schrock's Guide for Educators
http://www.discoveryschool.com/schrockguide/
Phi Delta Kappa
http://www.pdkintl.org
Reggio Emilia
http://ericps.ed.uiuc.edu/eece/reggio.html
Teachers Helping Teachers
http://www.pacificnet.net/~mandel/
Tech Learning
http://www.techlearning.com

Parents and administrators are beginning to value more the contributions of creativity to the total learning experience of students. "Integrating the Visual Arts—Building Young Children's Knowledge, Skills, and Confidence" draws our attention to the benefits of the arts in a curriculum for young children. Early childhood educators are adamant about the importance of the arts as an integral part of the learning experience. We must continue to provide appropriate experiences to enhance all areas of creativity.

We can learn so much about our current practices with young children by examining our roots. One of the key components of a good learning environment over the years has been the availability of a variety of blocks. Now, more than ever, it is important for teachers to provide an ample supply of blocks in the classroom. Math, creativity, science, social development, and problem solving are all enhanced through blocks. Karen Hewitt provides a historical examination of the use of blocks in early childhood classrooms in "Blocks as a Tool for Learning: Historical and Contemporary Perspectives." Blocks are quite possibly the best play material for young children.

Marie Sloane provides many suggestions for enhancing learning centers in "Make the Most of Learning Centers." The suggestions she offers will encourage a teacher who is not sure about how to develop appropriate learning centers in his or her classroom to give it a try. The children, when given the opportunity, will provide additional suggestions of activities and will continue to contribute to the learning experiences.

One responsibility of teachers that is often neglected is documenting and communicating the learning that is going on in the classroom. Teachers get so involved in the day-to-day teaching, that they often forget to keep track of what the children are doing and to provide ways for families and administrators to become familiar with the learning opportunities in the classroom. In "Using Documentation Panels to Communicate With Families," the reader can find ideas for educating families about their child's learning. We have a responsibility to keep parents informed, especially since young children cannot provide detailed verbal descriptions of their learning experiences. Actual photographs, drawings, and conversation about works in progress draw the parents into the curriculum.

oung children are eager to delve into curriculum that is compelling. Activities that will allow them to investigate, dig deep, and roll up their sleeves and get involved are the types of learning experiences that send the message, "learning is fun, and I can be successful." What they often are presented with is watered down, teacher directed, and lacking in true discovery. When we rob children of contributing to the learning process by providing all of the neatly cut papers for them to glue, or worksheets for them to complete, we take away their desire to explore and investigate. When their learning is served to them on a platter, they never learn that they can gather information by themselves. Become a facilitator for learning instead of a dispenser of information. A number of the articles in unit 5 provide opportunities for the reader to reflect on the authentic learning experiences that are available for children. How can they investigate, explore, and create while studying a particular area of interest? Make children work for their learning.

This unit is full of articles addressing different curriculum areas. Ten recommendations for appropriate use of technology are included in "Children and Computer Technology: Analysis and Recommendations." Also included are three articles that address different curriculum areas, but with a similar message. Active child involvement leads to enhanced learning. Suggestions for project based activities in mathematics, literacy, and science are included. Again, the theme runs deep. Hands-on = Minds on!

Integrating the Visual Arts—
Building Young Children's Knowledge, Skills, and Confidence

Jill Englebright Fox and Deborah Diffily

Art and appreciation of art constitute a general capacity or talent of man, and should be cared for early.... A universal and comprehensive plan of human education must, therefore, necessarily consider at an early period singing, drawing, painting, and modeling; it will... treat them as serious objects of the school. Its intention will not be to make each pupil an artist..., but to secure each human being full and all-sided development, to enable him to see man in the universality and all-sided energy of his nature, and, particularly to enable him to understand and appreciate the products of true art. (Froebel, 1826/trans. 1974, pp. 227–228)

Froebel viewed the arts as a necessary part of the early childhood curriculum, not for the purpose of developing child prodigies, but with the intention of facilitating each child's "all-sided" development (1826/trans. 1974). Almost two centuries after Froebel, the focus of quality early childhood programs is still on developing the whole child. Professionals recognize the importance of nurturing all developmental domains and attempt to provide learning experiences that encourage socioemotional, psychomotor, and cognitive development.

Why Art Is Important

All of the arts—music, drama, dance, and visual art—can play an important role in early childhood education. The visual arts are explored in this article as a means to develop skills and abilities across the curriculum and as an end to nurture young children's aesthetic development.

Art Benefits Socioemotional Development

The benefits of art for children's socioemotional development are frequently cited by advocates for the arts in education. Choosing the topic and media for an art experience may introduce children to decision making, and is a significant step in their developing autonomy. Art production enhances children's perceptions of themselves by providing opportunities for expression of thoughts and feelings (Klein, 1991; Sautter, 1994).

When children work on their art in small groups, they negotiate the use of materials, take turns, and provide appropriate feedback to others—important social skills in any setting (Sautter, 1994). Hearing thoughtful feedback from peers also contributes to self-esteem as children improve their artistic perceptions and techniques.

Seefeldt (1993) stated that art production is emotionally satisfying for children because they have control over materials and objects. Research on the development of the human brain suggests a close connection between learning and emotions (Caine & Caine, 1994; Healy, 1994). Knowledge and understanding are influenced and organized by the individual's emotional response to the topic. Thus, the emotional satisfaction engendered by children's engagement with creative materials may well serve as the means through which they come to know and understand the concepts being explored.

Art Strengthens Psychomotor Development

Young children engaged in art production are developing control of their large and small muscles (Koster, 1997). Drawing or painting at an easel or on large paper allows children to use large arm movements, building strength and coordination. Cutting with scissors, modeling with clay, and drawing or painting requires the use of smaller muscle groups in fingers, hands, and wrists. As muscle strength increases, so does control over many tools that are used in other artwork and writing.

Children engaged in making art also refine their eye-hand coordination (Koster, 1997). As they add details to their work, consider placement of objects, and make pieces fit together, children learn to coordinate hand and finger movements with what they see before them. Coordinating these movements develops dexterity for many activities and influences the ability to form letters and to space words as children begin to write formally.

Art Encourages Cognitive Development

Very young children enjoy the sensory properties of art production: feeling a crayon move across the paper or seeing a splotch of color grow. Kamii and DeVries (1993) suggested that the primary value of art for young children is in their construction of physical knowledge. Through the exploration of art materials, children build a knowledge of the physical properties of objects in their environment.

As children move out of exploration and into symbolic representation in their artwork, it becomes evident that drawing has specific benefits for cognitive development. Drawing

- helps children form mental representations and fosters more freedom of thought (Lansing, 1981)
- is an avenue for conducting research, enabling children to consolidate learning from many different activities (Thompson, 1995)
- encourages flexibility in children's thinking, gives them a concrete way to express what they have learned, and sets the stage for using words to represent objects and actions in formal writing
- is interrelated with writing (Koster, 1997), a relationship essential for emergent writers as they experiment with recording their ideas on paper

Art explorations also support higher-level thinking skills such as decision making, evaluation, and problem solving. Klein (1991) defined four decisions that preschool children make during the artistic process. First, children choose what they will portray in their artwork. Next, they determine the media, spatial arrangement, and perspective they will use. Children then decide at what pace to proceed, and finally, choose the criteria by which they will evaluate their work. This selection of evaluation criteria is a gradual process. Children learn to evaluate their work with standards based on what they like, along with messages from their culture about what is pleasing and beautiful (Feeney & Moravcik, 1987).

The arts play an key role, both in life and in the curriculum, in developing and maintaining the brain's problem-solving capacities (Sylwester, 1995). In seeking solutions to challenges children encounter while creating three-dimensional objects or portraying different visual perspectives, for example, children's problem-solving abilities are stimulated through "pleasant and metaphoric activities" (p. 53).

Although not reflected in many standard measures of cognitive development, higher-level thinking skills are integral to Gardner's definition of intelligence as "the ability to solve problems or fashion products that are of consequence in a particular cultural setting or community" (Gardner & Walters, 1993, p. 15).

Gardner (1985, 1993) suggested that it is the responsibility of schools, particularly for young children, to provide opportunities for exploration and development in each of eight intelligences (see sidebar). He indicated that art can be a part of each of the eight intelligences, as individuals engage in an artistic use of language, bodily movement, or musical interpretation.

Both art appreciation and creative production are important for the development of intelligence:

> Particularly at younger ages (below, say, 10), production activities ought to be central in any art form. Children learn best when they are actively involved in their subject matter; they want to have the opportunity to work directly with materials and media; and in the arts, these strengths and inclinations almost always translate into the making of something. (Gardner, 1993, p. 141)

Gardner identified eight intelligences in his theory of multiple intelligences (Gardner, 1985, 1993; Checkley, 1997)

- logical-mathematical
- linguistic
- interpersonal
- intrapersonal
- bodily kinesthetic
- musical
- naturalist
- spatial

Make Curriculum Connections

Schirrmacher (1986) cautioned, however, that art activities should not be valued simply because of benefits in other areas of learning. Children's art has value in and of itself. The focus for early childhood art programs should be to engage children in their own creative experiences, not craft or other look-alike projects.

Creation and Appreciation

Active engagement is the central idea in the National Standards for Arts Education (Consortium of National Arts Education Associations, 1994), which were developed to define what all children should know and be able to do in the arts. The standards for kindergarten through fourth grade encourage teachers to make curriculum connections between visual art and other content areas in ways that are meaningful to children.

Components of an integrated art program for young children

- Access to a classroom art center in which children choose the topic and media for their work
- Aesthetic display of children's artwork in a classroom museum for which the children serve as curators and docents
- Exposure to masterpiece art through field experiences, artists-in-residence, and reproductions in the classroom
- Adults who model art appreciation and develop an aesthetically appealing classroom
- Use of illustrations in children's literature to provide an introduction to art as an expression of ideas
- Art activities at home to involve families

Although creation is seen as the "heart of instruction," the standards also emphasize the need for art appreciation as a component in the early childhood art curriculum. Rather than requiring children to identify specific artists and their works, the standards emphasize the importance of helping children to understand that the discipline of art has its own history and specific relationships to different cultures.

Integrating Art Into the Curriculum

As the national standards (Consortium of National Arts Education Associations, 1994) indicate, art appreciation and production are essential components of early childhood curricula if programs are to meet the needs of the whole child. "The years of early childhood represent a golden period in artistic development—one that may rapidly fade and therefore one that teachers and parents are challenged to maintain and flourish" (Gardner, 1980, p. 99).

The challenge for teachers is to design a program that includes art appreciation and creation; is tailored to children's abilities, backgrounds, and interests; and can be integrated across all content areas. Objectives for young children might include:

- constructing an understanding of art as a means to communicate curriculum concepts and personal feelings
- viewing themselves as artists capable of self-expression in their work
- demonstrating an enjoyment of art appreciation and creation as evidenced by their independent choice of art activities

In integrating an art program into the curriculum, teachers look for ways to use art to support

children's learning in all areas. Components of an integrated art program for young children include:

1. access to a classroom art center in which children choose the topic and media for their work
2. aesthetic display of children's artwork in a classroom museum for which the children serve as curators and docents
3. exposure to masterpiece art through field experiences, artists-in-residence, and reproductions in the classroom
4. adults who model art appreciation and develop an aesthetically appealing classroom
5. use of illustrations in children's literature to provide an introduction to art as an expression of ideas
6. art activities at home to involve families

Art in Action: One Early Childhood Classroom

This description of a kindergarten classroom for 5- and 6-year-old children illustrates how art components are integrated throughout the curriculum. The same principles basically apply to classrooms for children across a much wider age span, from about 2 and into adolescence.

Access to an Art Center

Easy access to a variety of art materials and people who encourage exploration of those materials is essential to the creative process. Equally important is the children's freedom to select their topics and to stay with an activity until they determine it is finished (Edwards & Nabors, 1993). Open-ended materials, including paints, crayons, markers, pastels, pencils, scissors, glue, clay, and paper, were placed on shelves for independent access by the children. The teacher typically introduced each new medium, although occasionally she simply offered new materials and observed the children's exploration. She supported children in making independent choices and setting timelines for completion of their work.

Remarkably different types of art were produced each week. Children worked in the art center as often as they wished and produced as many or as few creations as they chose. If a child opted to create repeated rainbow pictures, this decision was supported in the same way as that of the child who used several different media to create complex works. The support this approach provided for children's creativity was evidence in the wide variety and originality of the work produced.

Classroom Museum

Displaying children's work highlights their efforts not only for classroom visitors, but also for the children themselves and for their peers. As Klein (1991) stated, when children see their work displayed, "they recognize it as uniquely their own, thus preserving the relationship between the child as artist and the product" (p. 87).

In this program, a bulletin board near the art center was designated as the art museum. Shelves were placed under the bulletin board to allow the display of sculpture and other three-dimensional creations. Following the model of local museums, a label for each creation was dictated by the child, including the title, artist's name, medium, and year of creation. The child also selected the color mats for drawings and paintings and the location for the display. In a class meeting, students decided that each child could have one piece displayed at a time, and that they could change it once a week.

The classroom art museum helped children to identify themselves as artists and quickly became a focal point during tours that student-docents gave to visitors.

Two easels are moved to the playground to encourage children to continue their exploration of spring during outside play. As Matthew works, Devin, a first grader from another classroom comes to watch.
Devin: "What is that?"
Matthew: "I'm painting. Spring stuff, like Monet."
Devin: "I'm an artist, too. We paint in our classroom."
Matthew: "If you're an artist, you hang your stuff up in a museum. Do you have a museum?"
Devin: "Yeah, I've been to a museum before, lots of times. I even went to museum school. I'm an artist because I went to museum school."
Matthew: "But you have to hang your stuff up in a museum. Did you hang your stuff up?"

Exposure to Masterpiece Art

Throughout the year, masterpiece art was an integral part of the children's learning experiences in many content areas. Reproductions were displayed prominently throughout the classroom. Prints of cityscapes were hung in the block center to stimulate more complex constructions. Spring landscapes were exhibited in the science center beside the children's sketches and photographs of trees in the neighborhood. A photograph of Rodin's *The Thinker* (see Warash & Saab, 1999) was used as the sign labeling the location for group meetings in the classroom. Other masterpiece prints were used to indicate gender on the restroom doors and the focus of each learning center.

Children were also exposed to original masterpiece art. Three well-known museums are located in the vicinity of the school, and field trips were frequent. Each visit prompted changes in the students' art production. After one visit to view a display of pre-Columbia sculpture, two girls began working with clay daily, reproducing the squared human shapes they had seen. Many children in the class followed their lead and, for a 3-week period, clay was the medium of choice.

Following a trip to a William Johnson exhibit, children began mixing brown, black, white, red, and yellow paints, attempting to replicate skin tones for portraits.

Mario shows his painting to Takesha and she responds, "Boy, you made that man's hands way too big."
Mario looks back at his painting, and says, "So did William Johnson. I'm painting just like him. It makes my men look like super heroes."

Masterpiece art was also used in integrated learning activities. As children learned to discuss and describe story characters, portraits were hung in the reading center to stimulate these discussions. The children chose their favorites and dictated their thoughts about the character portrayed.

Benefits of a kindergarten arts-integrated curriculum

- Children developed a significant body of knowledge about art.
- Children came to view themselves as artists capable of expressing ideas through their work.
- Children tried new art techniques and developed their skills.
- Children responded to each other's artwork with comments about originality and style.
- Parents were impressed with the body of knowledge their children developed, but were more impressed with the children's confidence.
- Children asked to visit museums on weekends as often as they asked to go to the zoo or the park.
- Children developed abilities and skills that applied in many other areas of the curriculum.
- Children developed appreciation for the art of other peoples and cultures.

When students learned to recognize dialogue, they worked in small groups, dictating conversations between two portraits after reading The Gentleman and the Kitchen Maid (Stanley, 1994). Here is one example of a conversation between El Greco's Giacomo Bosio and Van Gogh's Mrs. Augustine Roulin as dictated by the children. The children have named the two characters portrayed Grandma and Grandpa.

Grandma: "Why do you look so sad?"
Grandpa: "My feet hurt. Why do you look so happy?"
Grandma: "Our grandchildren are coming to visit. I'm going to bake cookies."

Grandpa: "Bake some peanut butter ones. That's their favorite."
Grandma: "But you hate peanut butter."
Grandpa: "I'll eat it anyways. It's only important what they like."

At other times, children were asked to sort through masterpiece postcards to find works of art portraying a topic the class was studying: the five senses, mammals, or storms. Masterpiece art was used as a learning material in the classroom, in much the same way as math manipulatives or children's books.

Adult Models of Art Appreciation

In order to foster a sense of aesthetic awareness in young children, adults must "reflect on the role of beauty in their own lives, become aware of it, and share it with children" (Feeney & Moravcik, 1987, p. 11). Adults call children's attention to aesthetic elements in the environment by discussing them, and encouraging children to give opinions and make comparisons. Although children's initial responses may be limited, adult consideration will gradually encourage critical thinking and more elaboration.

Children do have an aesthetic sense that can be cultivated. Very often, environments for children, their classrooms, bedrooms and playrooms, are cluttered and decorated with cute commercial products. Removing cartoon characters from walls and bulletin boards and replacing them with "aesthetically pleasing artwork, wall hangings, tapestry, posters, stained glass panels, or prints" (Schirrmacher, 1998, p. 181) is a first step in cultivating children's aesthetic sense.

Feeney and Moravcik (1987) reported that "young children tend to respond most favorably to art with bright and contrasting colors, familiar objects, simple composition, and unambiguous spatial relations" (p. 9). As children get older they tend to prefer realism and complexity in art. Children's art preferences should be acknowledged in environments created specifically for them.

Many features of the kindergarten classroom discussed here were reminiscent of a living room rather than a classroom. The group meeting area was defined by two couches and a wing-backed chair. Table lamps in the reading and listening centers offered soft lighting. Textured wall hangings, pottery, masterpiece prints, and live plants added to the aesthetics of the room. Periodically, the teacher changed these items, explaining to the children why she found the new items pleasing or interesting. She also invited children to express their opinions about the objects and encouraged them to bring appealing items from home.

> On occasion children would arrive at school bringing live plants, pottery, or prints from home. As Jonathan shared an original watercolor painting by his aunt, he announced, "I bringed this to make our classroom prettier!"

Children's Books

Children's trade books can be used to support visual art in the curriculum in three main ways.

1. Children's literature may be used to help children understand the value of visual art as a means of self-expression. Young children can understand that artists convey an idea in a drawing or painting in much the same way that authors use words to write a story.
2. Books with high-quality illustrations can be used to introduce artistic styles and media.
3. When the discussion that follows a picture-book reading focuses on the illustrations as well as the text, children are encouraged to extend their artwork by adding illustrations to other familiar stories or to tell their own stories and then illustrate them.

Quality children's literature was as much a part of this classroom as masterpiece art. Just as the class had discussions about elements of stories and poetry, the children identified the illustrator's choice of medium and technique, talked about connections between text and illustrations, and used illustrations as a strategy to decode meaning.

> One day when the teacher started to read a new book to the class, Quentin volunteered, "I know this is a Tomie DePaola book 'cause he always makes a heart on the cover."

Art at Home

The teacher, who knows the importance of involving families in the classroom, kept parents informed of class activities through weekly letters. She encouraged families to participate in museum trips and planned several weekend excursions to museums so families could share these experiences. The teacher was careful to explain how art production and appreciation were integrated into curriculum areas, particularly reading and writing. In helping parents understand that art was integral to children's learning experiences, they became supportive, rather than skeptical, of the emphasis on art in the classroom.

The teacher also encouraged children to continue their creative activities at home by providing artists' knapsacks for the children to check out. Each knapsack featured a different medium, such as paint and paper or modeling clay. The knapsack resource was introduced to parents at the beginning of the school year. Explicit directions were not given in each knapsack, to encourage the same creative use of materials at home as in the classroom.

Children were also able to take home favorite classroom puzzles, games, and art reproductions to share with their families. These at-home activities stimulated children to talk about classroom experiences at home and encouraged parent participation in their learning.

Values of Arts Integration for Children

Several benefits of this arts-integrated program were observed. First, children developed a significant body of knowledge about art. They were able to recognize works of many well-known artists and discuss the elements which made those artists unique. Parents frequently reported that their children recognized and discussed artists or pieces of art outside of the classroom.

Angela's mother shared with the teacher a conversation she had with her daughter at a local restaurant. Angela was staring at the tiled ceiling as she ate. Her mother asked her to sit more like a lady, and Angela said, "But, Mom, look! Doesn't this remind you of Michelangelo? You know he did some of his best work on the ceiling!"

Children's growing knowledge was particularly evident during museum field trips. During early visits, the children's participation in tours focused on their like or dislike of objects portrayed in paintings or sculptures. As the year progressed, however, the nature of children's participation changed. During later field trips, children independently identified particular works or artists, discussed the media used, and described elements of various artistic styles. Time that children spent viewing each piece of artwork also increased as they became more intent on looking at details and talking about what they saw.

The children had studied Matisse and his use of patterns during a math unit. During a museum visit, Jordan and Malika spent several minutes examining Matisse's L'Asie. Jordan points out to the docent, "There are three different patterns in this painting: patterns in the wall paper, patterns in the beads, and patterns in the lady's skirt."

A second outcome of this program was evident in the way children came to view themselves as artists capable of expressing ideas through their work. Having recognized that adult artists express ideas through different media and styles, the children became comfortable with using new materials and experimenting in their work. Throughout the year, the art center remained the center of choice as children tried new art techniques and developed their skills.

A change was also noticed in the ways that children responded to each other's artwork. Although their responses initially focused on the amount of realism portrayed, later comments began to include originality and style.

As Marques was adding colored pencil and black marker to the water color of a flower garden he had done yesterday, Katherine passed by the art center and commented: "Ooh, you're better than Monet—he just used paints for his gardens!"

At the beginning of the year, many families were skeptical about including art in the curriculum to such an extent. They expressed concern that the basics would not be prepared for later grades. As the year went by, they were impressed with the body of knowledge their children developed, but were more impressed with the children's confidence. They described their pleasure when children asked to visit museums on weekends as often as they asked to go to the zoo or the park.

With regular exchanges of information with the teacher and by observing their children's learning, changing attitudes, and growing confidence, families became convinced that integration of art into the curriculum was worthwhile.

Through the learning experiences described here, and many more, children developed abilities and skills that applied in many other areas of the curriculum. At the same time, children developed appreciation for the art of other peoples and cultures, and the confidence to express their own thoughts and feelings through art. This integration of visual art into early childhood curriculum contributed to the "all-sided development" of the children. All of the arts—music, drama, dance, and visual art—are a significant component of every early childhood curriculum.

References

Boyer, E. (1992). *Ready to learn: A mandate for the nation.* Princeton, NJ: The Carnegie Foundation for the Advancement of Teaching.

Caine, R. N., & Caine, G. (1994). *Making connections: Teaching the human brain.* Menlo Park, CA: Innovative Learning Publications.

Checkley, K. (1997). The first seven… and the eighth. *Educational Leadership, 55*(1), 8–13.

Consortium of National Arts Education Associations. (1994). *National standards for arts education.* Reston, VA: Music Educators National Conference.

Edwards, L. C., & Nabors, M. L. (1993). The creative arts process: What it is and what it is not. *Dimensions, 48*(3), 77–81.

Feeney, S., & Moravcik, E. (1987). A thing of beauty: Aesthetic development in young children. *Young Children, 42*(6), 7–15.

Froebel, F. (1974). *The education of man* (W. N. Hailmann, Trans.). Clifton, NJ: A. M. Kelley. (Original work published 1826)

Gardner, H. (1980). *Artful scribbles: The significance of children's drawings.* New York: Basic.

Gardner, H. (1985). *Frames of mind: The theory of multiple intelligences.* New York: Basic.

Gardner, H. (1993). *Multiple intelligences: The theory in practice.* New York: Basic.

Gardner, H., & Walters, J. (1993). A rounded version. In H. Gardner, *Multiple intelligences: The theory in practice* (pp. 13–34). New York: Basic.

Healy, J. M. (1994). *Your child's growing mind: A guide to learning and brain development from birth to adolescence.* New York: Doubleday.

Kamii, C., & DeVries, R. (1993). *Physical-knowledge in preschool education.* New York: Teachers College Press.

Klein, B. (1991). The hidden dimensions of art. In J. D. Quisenberry, E. A. Eddowes, & S. L. Robinson (Eds.). *Readings from Childhood Education* (pp. 84–89). Olney, MD: Association for Childhood Education International.

Koster, J. B. (1997). Growing artists: *Teaching art to young children.* Albany, NY: Delmar.

Lansing, K. M. (1981). The effect of drawing on the development of mental representations. *Studies in art education, 22*(3), 15–23.

Sautter, R. C. (1994). An arts education reform strategy. *Phi Delta Kappan, 75*(6), 433–440.

Schirrmacher, R. (1986). Talking with young children about their art. *Young Children, 41*(5), 3–7.

Schirrmacher, R. (1998). *Art and creative development for young children* (3rd ed.). Albany, NY: Delmar.

Seefeldt, C. (1993). *Social studies for the preschool-primary child* (4th ed.). New York: Merrill.

Stanley, D. (1994). *The gentleman and the kitchen maid*. New York: Dial.

Sylwester, R. (1995). *A celebration of neurons: An educator's guide to the human brain*. Alexandria, VA: Association for Supervision and Curriculum Development.

Thompson, C. M. (1995). Transforming curriculum in the visual arts. In S. Bredekamp & T. Rosegrant (Eds.), *Reaching potentials: Transforming early childhood curriculum and assessment, Vol. II* (pp. 81–98). Washington, DC: National Association for the Education of Young Children.

Warash, B. G., & Saab, J. F. (1999, Winter). Exploring the visual arts with young children. *Dimensions of Early Childhood, 27*(1), 11–15.

Jill Englebright Fox, Ph.D., is Assistant Professor, Early Childhood Education, Virginia Commonwealth University, Richmond.

Deborah Diffily, PH.D., is Assistant Professor, Early Childhood Education, Texas Wesleyan University, Forth Worth.

From *Dimensions of Early Childhood,* Winter 2001, pp. 3-10. © 2001 by Southern Early Childhood Association. Reprinted by permission.

Blocks As a Tool for Learning: Historical and Contemporary Perspectives

Karen Hewitt

Children have always built, testing their theories about the physical and social world. They stack units, knock them down, enclose spaces, bridge gaps, and repeat and refine ideas—often without the intervention of adults or the introduction of commercial materials.

The natural world provides abundant building material: heavy stones to pile, sticky burdock to connect, green twigs to tie and weave. And children are quick to pick up discarded construction and commerical materials such as wood pieces or boxes. Purchased building blocks and construction sets afford days of open-ended play and learning.

That children's impulse to construct is inherent and connected to learning is an old idea. It can be found in the writings of Plato (429–347 B.c.), Comenius (1592–1670), and Pestalozzi (1746–1827), as well as in the work of modern thinkers such as Jean Piaget (1896–1980).

COURTESY OF THE AUTHOR
Ivory Soap advertisement, early 20th century

The importance of play as a recognized mode of learning for young children is clearly reflected in the history of blocks and construction toys. As educators, we should appreciate the central historical and contemporary role of these toys in early childhood education.

COURTESY OF THE AUTHOR
Trade card, late 19th century

Whether blocks were advertised for home use or found their way into the classroom as an educational device, they have always been linked to learning. In *Some Thoughts Concerning Education*, English philosopher John Locke (1693) went against the prevailing trend in childrearing and placed the carrot before the stick: "The chief art is to make all that [children] have to do, sport and play too.... Learning anything they should be taught, might be made as much a recreation to their play, as their play is to their learning."

153

Toys now began to be considered influential in a positive way—not as sinful pastimes or baubles, but as a necessity. Locke described what was to become one of the most popular educational block sets—the alphabet blocks—extolling the merits of sweetened learning.

In mid- to late nineteenth century, a small group of European and U.S. manufacturers began producing building toys, often as a sideline to their main woodworking or printing business. The blocks for the commercial market were characterized by three distinct ideas linking learning and play. The first centers on the building unit as a surface for displaying symbols—letters, words, narratives. The second addresses the pure activity of building—constructing with simple, abstract forms. The third focuses on the transmission of a cultural heritage—building a model of an important architectural structure and, through this process, learning architectural styles.

Although the categories often overlap in one block type, it is important to look at each one to understand the pedagogical implications and to consider the discrepancy between what adults want children to do or think they are doing and what children actually do.

Literacy and blocks

The tradition of cladding the surface of blocks with symbols and narratives burgeoned in the mid-nineteenth century and continues today, blending learning and amusement with a mix of symbol, fantasy, and vibrant color. S.L. Hill, one of the first manufacturers of spelling and alphabet blocks, patented his spelling blocks in 1858. Some were thin tablets, which emphasized symbol over structure, while others were cubes, more conducive to building. Hill sold thousands of these sets, and other companies, such as Westcott and Bliss, followed his lead.

COURTESY OF SCHECTER ME SUN LEE, NEW YORK

Wide-Awake Alphabet Blocks, Charles M. Crandall Co., Montrose, Penn., ca. 1870s

Charles Crandall, a manufacturer of furniture and croquet sets, and Jesse Crandall, his brother, produced two unique building toys that resulted from the manufacturing process rather than a priori design. Charles, so the story goes, observed his children building with the thin cutoff pieces of wood used in the manufacture of finger-joint boxes for his croquet sets. Inspired by his children's complex constructions, he began to manufacture his alphabet and construction blocks in 1867, adapting the finger-joint design. In 1881 Jesse Crandall, looking for an efficient way to pack the blocks, began producing nested blocks, a perfect marriage of efficient design and an understanding of children's developmental needs.

COURTESY OF ROBERT HULL FLEMING MUSEUM, BURLINGTON, VT.

Alphabet Blocks and Building Blocks, S.L. Hill Co., Williamsburg, N.Y., ca. 1860

Literacy, in addition to knowing the letters of the alphabet, also meant a familiarity with stories, especially biblical ones. The biblical theme was common to a number of toys in the early and mid-nineteenth century, following the tradition of the popular Noah's Ark.

The design of the Cob House Blocks, produced by the McLoughlin Brothers in 1885, clearly placed the act of building on a par with word construction and the narrative possibilities of storytelling. Adults presumed—or at least hoped—that alphabet and story blocks would lead their children to an understanding of symbol systems, enticing them to learn their *ABCs*, arrange numerals in sequence, read simple words, and follow a narrative order.

For 200 years now, letters and numbers have been neatly painted, stamped, or chromolithographed and silk-screened on blocks, yet children continue to think spatially, piling these blocks, making towers and towns, and often blissfully ignoring the attempt of their elders to inject a dose of literacy.

Blocks as pure form

Playing with forms in space is an activity that has always been valued by artists, architects, and mathematicians as well as young children. These building sets contain unadorned wood forms with a serious intent. Although some sets come with plans or are packaged in a box whose cover indicates some possible building ideas, constructing seems to be the prime focus.

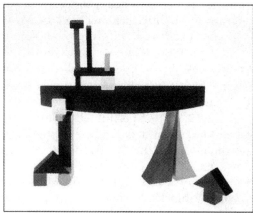

COURTESY OF COLLECTION CENTRE CANADIEN
D'ARCHITECTURE/CANADIAN CENTRE FOR
ARCHITECTURE, MONTREAL

Bauspiel blocks, Alma Siedhoff-Busher, designer (1923); Kurt Naef, Zeiningen, Switzerland, ca. 1980

The Embossing Company produced numerous sets of plain building blocks, some with the added feature of holes that turned them into construction sets. Dandonah, The Fairy Palace, a German block set based on the architectural designs of Bruno Taut, reflects the modernist interest in form for form's sake. Bauspiel was designed by Alma Siedhoff-Busher in Weimar, Germany, where the Bauhaus marriage of art and industry influenced the world of architecture, design, and education after World War I. These blocks, and the theory behind them, parallel the pedagogy and aesthetics of many of the blocks designed by educators for school use and for the home.

A further extension of the use of pure form is the building sets designed for children to make their own repeatable forms. The child as a constructive worker, learning to be a useful part of the great industrial world, is implicit in these building sets. Also implicit is a strong gender bias, so often portrayed on the covers and advertisements of building toys, sometimes subtly, other times as blatant as The Boy Contractor—"Practical Construction for Boys."

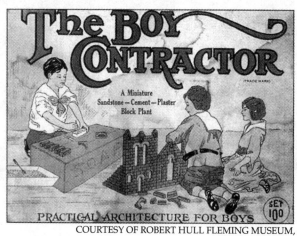

COURTESY OF ROBERT HULL FLEMING MUSEUM,
BURLINGTON, VT.

The Boy Contractor, Cruver Manufacturing Co., Chicago, 1919

Blocks as transmitters of culture: Rebuilding architectural history

The idea that children could be taught a range of building types and architectural styles and highlights of architectural history was a dominant focus of blocks designed by the European and American toy market. F. Ad Richter and Company produced thousands of building sets using blocks made of artificial sandstone and linseed oil. Perfectly proportioned and colored in muted tones of red, gray, and blue, these sets were compactly packaged (a lesson in spatial organization) and were accompanied by plan books and scale drawings of real and imagined buildings. They were a great success.

COURTESY OF THE AUTHOR

Anchor Blocks instruction sheet, F. Ad Richter and Co., Germany and New York, 1899

Many block sets depicted buildings from "exotic" countries. The Peking Palace (1870), a fanciful set of German wood blocks with architecture decorations lithographed on paper, encouraged children to rearrange the building into a variety of forms, thus inventing their own versions of a palace.

Sets of village blocks were also common. Some sets contained simple block forms that represented specific buildings, allowing children to create arrangements of nineteenth-century town plans. Other village sets had components that could be combined like a three-dimensional puzzle to build a church or other familiar architectural structure. Although children most likely built many other wildly imaginative structures, at least their parents were reassured that they were being both constructive and religious—a winning combination for learning in the 1880s.

New building toys emerging in the early twentieth century encouraged children to represent more modern architectural forms. For example, the Bilt E-Z The Boy Builder construction set paralleled the curtain wall of the new modern skyscraper. Building toys were declared a necessity for every home. Newspapers and magazines

155

and, later, television advertised an abundant variety of educational building blocks, and parents purchased them in ever-increasing quantity.

Learning materials in the classroom

During the late nineteenth century when the McLoughlin Brothers were pumping out their charming nested blocks, children faced primary classrooms devoid of visual stimulation and, certainly, of objects of play. Although some nineteenth-century rural schoolteachers used the natural environment as part of their lessons—picking flowers, making baskets from reeds, collecting birds' nests—most teachers stuck to the slate board and seat work.

But a revolution in the education of very young children was brewing, a revolution that emphasized the importance of building/construction materials in the learning process. This began with Friedrich Froebel (who was certainly influenced by Johann Pestalozzi's hands-on learning approach), followed by Maria Montessori, Caroline Pratt, and Patty Smith Hill, and continued into the 1950s with George Cuisenaire and into today with computers and Seymour Papert. Although many theorists study the play behavior of children, only a few go on to design play/learning material and to write passionately about its use.

COURTESY OF ROBERT HULL FLEMING MUSEUM, BURLINGTON, VT.

Froebel Gifts 5 and 6, Milton Bradley Co., Springfield, Mass., 1869

The materials designed by Froebel, Montessori, and Pratt were austere and monochromatic, emphasizing the structural relationships between the units. In contrast, the alphabet and picture blocks manufactured by Jesse Crandall, S. L. Hill, and R. Bliss were decorated with colorful images, following Locke's idea of mixing pleasure with learning.

If Froebel (1782–1852) is the father of kindergarten, then perhaps his Gifts and Occupations are the mother of manipulatives. Before Froebel, geometric blocks/toys were used as simple building materials or as drawing models. Froebel's series of Gifts and Occupations were designed as part of a systematic method for children to learn through play.

Based on the construction and transformation of forms, the materials were presented in a strictly determined sequence. Children began with solid shapes—the sphere, the cylinder, and the cube—moved to the flat plane and the line, and finally returned to three-dimensional construction with points and lines using peas or waxed pellets and sticks. Children would build three basic forms with the blocks: "forms of life" (representing objects from the world—houses, furniture, trees), "forms of knowledge" (giving physical substance to abstract ideas—number and geometry); and "forms of beauty" (creating imaginative designs, mainly based on symmetry, for aesthetic appreciation).

Although Froebel's work ([1826] 1887) was based on highly abstract ideas, symbolized by blocks and other three-dimensional materials, the fact that children were given physical objects to play with as the basis for learning revolutionized early childhood education.

The kindergarten movement, which started in Germany in the 1840s, quickly spread to the United States through the efforts of educators who had observed the Froebelian kindergartens in action. Milton Bradley, an enterprising lithographer, began in 1869 to manufacture the Gifts and Occupations for the American school market.

But by the 1890s the Froebelian materials and methods were under attack by kindergarten reformers. They criticized the formal, sequential use of the gifts, the lack of what they considered self-determined purpose in the child's play, the small size of the items, and the emphasis on sedentary activities.

Cooperative building with Patty Smith Hill blocks, ca. 1930

In 1905 Patty Smith Hill, a faculty member of Teachers College/Columbia University, questioned the lack of free play and proceeded to make modifications to the blocks.

Recognition of the child's need for large-motor activity and the child as a social being led to the design of larger blocks.

The Hill Blocks, first manufactured by the Schoenhut Company in Philadelphia, continued to be made in modified form into the 1950s. They consisted of a series of blocks, square pillars, and metal rods that secured the pieces. Because of their size and weight, the blocks necessitated the involvement and cooperation of several children to construct a building.

It is clear why John Dewey was in sympathy with the work of Patty Smith Hill: "The [Hill] kindergarten, as a laboratory of democratic citizenship, was in keeping with Dewey's pragmatic policy of expanding the school's social responsibility" (Weber 1979, 31). Children worked together as "a miniature community, an embryonic society" (Dewey 1899, 41) as they explored and represented the world they knew—their home, their neighborhood, and the larger community.

In 1913 Caroline Pratt, an educator who had received woodworking training in Sweden, developed unit system blocks for her experimental classroom at Harley House and at the City and Country School that she helped found in New York City. She designed "do-withs," wood figures of family and community workers, to accompany the unit blocks. Pratt's designs, and her pioneering work on the use of blocks ([1948] 1990) as a social, intellectual, and aesthetic learning tool, still resonate today.

Harriet Johnson, in her *Children in the Nursery School* ([1928] 1972), documented the block work of children 14 months to three years old at The Nursery School, a project of the Bureau of Educational Experiments, organized in New York City in 1917 by Harriet Johnson, Caroline Pratt, and Lucy Sprague Mitchell. The City and Country School and Bank Street School for Children still carry on this strong block-building tradition.) This classic book presents a richly detailed discussion of children using blocks in a natural setting.

At the Casa dei Bambini in Italy, Maria Montessori (1870–1952) originated a series of blocks called "didactic materials" based on the systematic training of the senses as a way for children to understand the world. She observed that children between the ages of two and six go through a period in which they are interested in the placement of objects.

Montessori's sensorial materials, used on small mats, were designed to isolate a specific attribute such as height, length, width, depth, or color. For example, the Pink Tower builds up incrementally from large to small. The resulting structure is taken down and rebuilt over and over again until the child tires of the process.

In *Spontaneous Activity in Education*, Montessori wrote, "Our sensorial material, in fact, analyses and represents the attributes of things: dimensions, forms, colors, smoothness or roughness of surface, weight, temperature, flavor, noise, and sounds. It is the qualities of the object, not the objects themselves, which are important,

COURTESY OF ROBERT HULL FLEMING MUSEUM, BURLINGTON, VT.

Pink Tower, Maria Montessori, designer (ca. 1908); Nienhuis Montessori USA, Mountain View, Calif., 1985

although these qualities, isolated one from the other, are themselves represented by objects" ([1917] 1971, 203).

The materials designed by Montessori were precisely crafted and either painted with a single color or left natural. With little alteration, they are still being made for Montessori classrooms today.

COURTESY OF GUMMY LUMP (WWW.GUMMYLUMP.COM)

Unit Blocks

The blocks of Hill, Pratt, and Montessori were based in great part on the observation and knowledge of children's natural interests. Children's interaction with open-ended materials has been observed and studied by several developmental psychologists, beginning with G. Stanley Hall in the 1890s, by Arnold Gesell at the Yale Clinic in the 1930s, in clinical settings, and by Piaget with his own children. Teachers, informed by these studies and the work of early progressive educators, rallied together and tried to influence the selection of classroom materials and to change the prevailing methods of pedagogy.

Unit blocks can be found today in most preschools, nursery schools, and some kindergartens. More infrequently they are found in the early grades, where they are usually in the guise of math manipulatives; the floor blocks, literally and figuratively, have been elevated to the table, assuming an academic aura.

This math emphasis began in the late 1950s as a reaction to the former Soviet Union's launch of Sputnik, with the U.S. government declaring that schools needed to improve the teaching of math and science. The initiative led to the development of a wide variety of manipulatives and supporting educational guides, derived in part from the work of Froebel, Montessori, and Pratt—for example, Cuisenaire Rods, the Stern Apparatus, Dienes Logiblocs, Unifix Cubes, and the Lowenfeld Poleidoblocs.

The richness of block building was funneled into one specific area of knowledge: mathematical thinking. "The variety of shapes and sizes in Poleidoblocs G and A enables children through construction and experiment to discover the basic structure of mathematics. The range of shapes gives wide opportunities for discovering and establishing equivalencies in length, height, area, and volume, making tangible, and therefore real, what children have so far learned only symbolically (Educational Supply Association 1971, 28). But the originators of the new manipulatives also encouraged free play and exploration.

Electronic blocks

Computers, though seemingly not blocklike at all, have entered the block market. Gryphon Bricks, a CD-Rom developed in 1996 by Gryphon Software Company, is one of several software programs that allow children to "construct" on the computer.

Advertisements and articles extol the advantages of virtual computer blocks over physical blocks for the classroom teacher since they are "neat," "convenient," and "easy to manage"—not a convincing pedagogical argument. Although the computer has vast possibilities as a "manipulative," it is not a substitute for building in three dimensions.

The most complex and far-reaching work combining blocks and computers is occurring at the MIT Media Laboratory. Over the last 10 years, researchers there have developed a group of digital manipulatives (for example, LEGO MindStorms programmable bricks).

> We believe that these new manipulatives can combine the best of the physical and the digital worlds, drawing on children's passions and intuitions about physical objects, but extending

those objects to allow new types of explorations. In this way, digital manipulatives are starkly different from traditional use of computers in education, which tend to draw children away from the physical-world interactions. (Resnick et al. 2000, 2)

MindStorms is aimed at children beyond preschool, but the underlying idea is common to all block building: "Learners are particularly likely to make new ideas when they are actively engaged in making some type of external artifact—be it a robot, a poem, a sandcastle, or a computer program—which they can reflect upon and share with others" (Kafai & Resnick 1996, 1).

Educators, developmental psychologists, designers, and manufacturers have helped develop and promote the educational value of blocks and open-ended play. Yet, except as math manipulatives, blocks are still rarely seen in classrooms beyond kindergarten. Even in many early childhood classrooms today, their full potential as learning tools is not considered.

The destructive/deconstructive activity characteristic of block play, an integral part of this activity, makes some adults uncomfortable. However, as in all learning, we cannot understand until we take apart, examine, and rebuild. Children need an environment with open-ended materials and teachers who understand, encourage, build on, and even participate in this basic and complex mode of learning. This means having enough

- classroom space devoted to block play;
- time set aside for serious and ongoing play with blocks;
- focus on block work as evidenced by teachers' interaction with children through observation, documentation, revisiting structures, and sometimes participating in the play process; and
- time for teachers to share observations with colleagues and understand how children's block play connects with the development of literacy, physical knowledge, and mathematical thinking.

Blocks have been with us for a long time—and the activity of building even longer. The rich potential of blocks as a learning tool for young children to invent and represent ideas is still a challenge for teachers today.

References

Dewey, J. 1899. *The school and society*. Reprinted in *Dewey on education,* ed. M.S. Dworkin (New York: Teachers College Press, 1959). Out of print.

Educational Supply Association. 1971. *Educational Supply Association Limited*. Harlow, Essex, UK: Author.

Froebel, F. [1826] 1887. *The education of man*. Trans. WN. Hailmann. New York: Appleton.

Johnson, H. [1928] 1972. *Children in the nursery*. New York: Bank Street College of Education.

Kafai, Y, & M. Resnick, eds. 1996. *Constructionism in practice. Designing, thinking, and learning in a digital world.* Mahwah, NJ: Erlbaum.

Locke, J. 1693. *Some thoughts concerning education.* Text available online at www.socsci.kun.nl/ped/whp/histeduc/locke/index.html. See sections 63, 74.

Montessori, M. [1917] 1971. *Spontaneous activity in education.* Trans. F. Simmonds. Cambridge, MA: Robert Bentley.

Pratt, C. [1948] 1990. *I learn from children.* New York: Harper & Row, Perennial.

Resnick, M., M. Eisenberg, R. Berg, D. Mikhak, & D. Willow. 2000. Manuscript. Learning with digital manipulatives: New frameworks to help elementary-school students explore "advanced" mathematical and scientific concepts. Available online at www.media.mit.edu/papers/mres/digital-manip/.

Weber, E. 1979. Play materials in the curriculum of early childhood. In *Educational toys in America. 1800 to the present*, eds. K. Hewitt & L. Roomet. Burlington, VT: Robert Hull Fleming Museum.

For further reading

Exhibition catalogs from the Canadian Centre for Architecture, Montreal, Quebec:
Building in boxes. Architectural toys from the CCA. 1990.
Potential architecture: Construction toys from the CCA collection. 1991.
Toys that teach. 1992.
Toys in the modernist tradition. 1993.
Dream houses, toy homes. 1995. Toy town. 1998.
Toy town. 1998

Brosterman, N. 1997. *Inventing kindergarten. Nineteenth century children.* New York: Abrams.

Cartwright, S. 1988. Play can be the building blocks of learning. *Young Children* 43 (5): 44–47.

Cartwright, S. 1990. Learning with large blocks. *Young Children* 45 (3): 38–41.

Cartwright, S. 1995. Block play: Experiences in cooperative learning and living. *Child Care Information Exchange* (May): 30–41.

Charney, R., M.K. Clayton, & C. Wood. 1990. *Bringing blocks back to the classroom.* Greenfield, MA: Northeast Foundation for Children.

Clements, D. 1999. Young children and technology. In *Dialogue on early childhood science, mathematics, and technology education.* Washington, DC: American Association for the Advancement of Science. Available online at www.project2o6l.org/newsinfo/earlychild/experience/clements.htm.

Cuffaro, H.K. 1986. The development of block building. In *Building block art*, ed. P.H. Sperr. Philadelphia: Please Touch Museum.

Cuffaro, H.K. 1995. Block building: Opportunities for learning. *Child Care Information Exchange* (May): 36–38.

Cuffaro, H.K. 1995. *Experimenting with the world: John Dewey and the early childhood classroom.* New York: Teachers College Press.

Forman, G.E. 1982. A search for the origins of equivalence concepts through microanalysis of block-play. In *Action and thought. From sensorimotor schemes to symbolic operations*, ed. G.E. Forman. New York: Academic.

Guanella, F. 1934. Blockbuilding activities of young children. *Archives of Psychology* 174: 1–92.

Gura, P., ed. 1992. *Exploring learning. Young children and block play.* New York: Paul Chapman.

Hewitt, K. 1998. The building toy/the toy building: Symbol, structure, and style. In *Toying with architecture: The building toy in the arena of play.* Katonah, NY: Katonah Museum of Art.

Hirsch, E.S., ed. 1996. *The block book.* 3d ed. Washington, DC: NAEYC.

Papert, S. [1980] 1999. *MindStorms: Children, computers, and powerful ideas.* 2d ed. New York: Basic.

Reifel, S. 1984. Block construction: Children's developmental landmarks in representation of space. *Young Children* 40 (1): 61–67.

Reifel, S., & P.M. Greenfield. 1982. Structural development in symbolic medium: The representational use of block construction. In *Action and thought: From sensorimotor schemes to symbolic operations*, ed. G.E. Forman. New York: Academic.

Reifel, S., & J. Yeatman. 1991. Action, talk, and thought in the block corner: Developmental trends. In *Play and the social context of development in early care and education*, eds. B. Scales, M. Almy, A. Nicolopoulou, & S. Ervin-Tripp. New York: Teachers College Press.

Stritzel, K. 1995. Block play is for ALL children. *Child Care Information Exchange* (May): 42–47.

Make the Most of Learning Centers

Wondering how to start to use learning centers or to revitalize the ones you have? Here are many practical ideas to create centers that are valuable settings for children's learning.

Marie W. Sloane

Imagine an active, center-based early childhood classroom. Children in the block area are building a doctor's office and discussing what they need. Several seated nearby debate how to write "class doctor." A small group of children in the science center are examining different types of insects, trying to identify the mysterious-looking bug they found on the playground. In the art and construction area, children paint, draw, and build marvelous creations with "beautiful junk." Over in the math center, three children play a counting game. Two more in the library pour over an *I Spy* book, looking for the items a teacher read to them. The teachers circulate around the classroom, asking questions, showing children new things, and celebrating interesting discoveries. The room is filled with the hum of busy children, actively engaged in learning.

Similar classroom scenes are found in many preschool classrooms. They do not, however, simply happen. Teachers who use learning centers plan, think through, and create developmentally and culturally appropriate learning environments (Bredekamp & Copple, 1997). They work hard to help children make productive use of their time.

Why Learning Centers?

Children learn by doing. They actively construct knowledge by interacting with the world around them (Dewey, 1916). What they understand and believe changes as they integrate new experiences with previous knowledge (Piaget & Inhelder, 1971). As they encounter situations that challenge their ideas, or extend their understandings, they learn (Gardner, 1991; Vygotsky, 1978). Far from being passive blank slates, children's natural desire to find out everything they can leads them to constantly seek out new and interesting experiences.

Centers in early childhood classrooms provide ideal environments for active learning. Open-ended in nature, they support activities that challenge children as well as expose them to concepts appropriate for their ages and abilities (Patton & Mercer, 1996). The variety of materials found in centers contributes to learning from many different cultural perspectives. Centers set the stage for meaningful hands-on exploration, experimentation, and practice. In order to realize the exciting potential centers offer, teachers see themselves as facilitators of learning.

Teachers Can Facilitate Learning

One way to describe teachers' roles is to specify where their teaching strategies fall on a continuum of directiveness (see Figure 1). Different teaching behaviors are seen in all areas, from the least directive actions of observing and acknowledging students, through facilitating and supporting learning, to the highly directive actions of demonstrating and directing activities (Bredekamp & Rosegrant, 1992).

In order to create a challenging and engaging environment, teachers' efforts primarily fall in the middle of the continuum: facilitating and supporting learning. Teachers and children are actively involved in what takes place in the classroom. Both have responsibility for initiating ideas and making decisions. Children are constantly challenged to learn.

Centers in early childhood classrooms provide ideal environments for teachers to facilitate learning (see Figure 2). These are a few of the teaching strategies that support active learning:

- Provide open-ended materials
- Organize centers to encourage independent activity
- Introduce materials and how to use any tools
- Brainstorm ideas
- Extend children's learning

Provide open-ended materials

Centers are not simply places where everyone goes to carry out the same assignment. They need to contain enough variety for the children to engage in many different activities. A teacher's first step to facilitate active learning is to find a variety of open-ended materials (Patton & Mercer, 1996). Open-ended materials are those that

Figure 1. Continuum of teacher roles (derived from Bredekamp and Rosegrant, 1992, p. 39)

Least directive...Most directive
Observe, acknowledge, facilitate, support, demonstrate, direct

Examples:

Observe who children play with regularly and document this information.

Acknowledge children's accomplishments: "Martha, look at all the different parts you added to your block structure!"

Facilitate a new child entering a group playing at the sand table by offering the child a sifter.

Support a child's interest in birds by getting guide books from the library.

Demonstrate how to clean paint brushes.

Direct children's activities: "No, Adam, you may not hit Jordan. You need to use your words instead!"

Figure 2. Ideas for learning centers

- Writing
- Graphic arts (drawing, painting, clay)
- Math
- Science
- Construction (boxes, tubes, containers)
- Blocks and building
- Pretend play
- Computer
- Sensory (sand, water, wood shavings)
- Library/listening
- Fine arts (music, dance, drama)
- Woodworking
- Sewing
- Outdoor

children can use in many different ways, and that support learning from initial explorations to mastery levels.

When collecting materials, think about the potential they provide for both the teacher and children to be active participants in learning. With teddy bear counters, for example, children can count, sort, make patterns, create designs, add, subtract, use them for markers in board games, and act out their favorite stories about bears. Along with a magnifying glass in a science center, include tools children can use to measure, draw, feel, closely observe, compare, and experiment with natural and manufactured items. Start with basics and expand as children's interests and skills change throughout the year.

Organize for independence

Centers are best organized in a way that not only promotes order and ease of clean up, but also supports sorting, classification, and independent activity (Eliason & Jenkins, 1994). See Figure 3 for an example of room arrangement.

Children should be able to select activities that match their own ideas and interests (Dodge & Colker, 1996). Some centers might include one or two items that students need assistance to operate (e.g., a sewing machine in the sewing center), but materials should generally be organized so that children can work independently.

Place materials on low shelves where children can reach them. To keep things organized, use clear, sturdy containers that children can take with them around the room. Label both these bins and the spots on the shelves where they belong with words and/or pictures to promote early reading skills.

Group common materials within each center. In the writing center, different types of paper could be stored near each other, as could the various animals, people, and furniture in the building area. This practice helps children

learn to organize and classify, and facilitates independent work. Good organization makes it easier to involve everyone in clean up!

Introduce centers

After collecting and organizing materials, it is time to teach children how to use any new tools or techniques. Dive right in with several new centers, or introduce them one or two at a time, whatever is right for the group. If children are going to make the most out of the available resources, they need to know how to proceed as independently and safely as possible.

Very young children may still be learning how to effectively handle even basic tools such as scissors. Observe children and then decide how much direct instruction to give, either to individuals or the entire group, to introduce new centers and materials. Demonstrate basic correct and safe use, and remember to focus on the process, rather than giving directions about how to make something particular. In a woodworking center, for example, children would learn recommended techniques for using hammers and nails, rather than how to build a bird house.

Ask children to help generate their own rules to set the tone for their actions. This empowers children and helps them feel invested in taking care of the materials and each other much more than if the teacher imposes all of the rules (DeVries & Zan, 1995). Together, think through what will keep the materials in good condition and everyone safe. If children come up with a list of negative rules (Don't break the crayons) help them rephrase rules in a more positive way (Handle crayons gently). Write down their rules and post them in the learning center (see Figure 4).

Brainstorm ideas

A second way to engage children right from the start is to ask children to suggest center themes, materials, and activities. Being part of this process also empowers children and gives them a sense of ownership of what hap-

Figure 3. An example of a room arrangement with learning centers

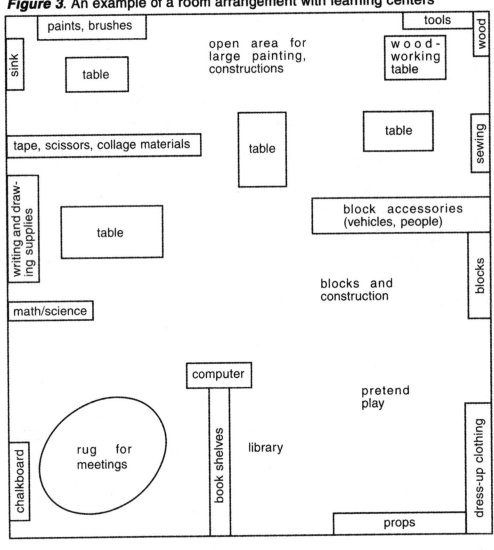

pens in their classroom. Something as simple as a collection of cardboard tubes of varying sizes can lead to creative ideas about what children could do with them: binoculars, castle towers, chutes for cars to go through, log cabins, kaleidoscopes. Children are inspired by hearing so many ideas, and often build on each others' suggestions, trying ideas out in their own ways.

Occasionally, write down children's brainstorming ideas and post them. Refer to these lists when a child is looking for suggestions of what to do, or after someone has completed an activity from the list that she wants to share with the rest of the class. Explain brainstorming to families, so they can see how their children are learning by pursuing their own ideas and interests.

Centers Engage Children, Families, and Teachers

During center time it is natural for children to be active learners, as they choose their own activities and interact

with the materials and each other. Children who are simply turned loose will certainly make interesting discoveries. The best learning usually takes place, however, when the teacher is just as actively involved, acting as the children's facilitator and guide (Brooks & Brooks, 1993).

> ## Share ideas enthusiastically and connect them with children's interests.

Teachers can support meaningful learning during center time by extending children's activities (Dodge & Colker, 1996). Observe children and think through what each is ready to learn. Then decide how to incorporate new knowledge and skills into the context of what a child is already able to do. Ask yourself: What would add more depth, encourage this child to try something new, or incorporate an academic skill into an activity?

Figure 4. Children's rules for their woodworking center

In the woodworking center we:
- Handle the tools safely.
- Wear goggles.
- Ask for a turn with the tools.
- Put tools away when we are done.
- Label our creations with our names.
- Ask teachers for help when we are not sure what to do.

Have fun!

Although children need not follow every suggestion, encourage them to try something more than they would have on their own. Give several ideas, and let children choose which one(s) to pursue. Share ideas enthusiastically and connect them with children's interests. For example, if Stacy is lining up rabbits and bears along the top of a block structure, her teacher has several options to extend her activity. A teacher could

- encourage Stacy to make a pattern with the rabbits and bears

- wonder aloud how many there are and help Stacy count them

- ask Stacy if there are more rabbits or bears and help her figure it out

- find out if there is a story Stacy would like to tell about the rabbits and bears

- see whether Stacy would like to dictate her story and read her creation to the rest of the class

To choose between all of these possibilities, consider what the teacher knows about Stacy. What might she be ready to learn next? What might she find fun or interesting? Suggest an idea or two and let Stacy decide what to do next.

Teachers who routinely extend children's activities become excited by all of the opportunities for learning they see around them. Children even think of ways to extend activities themselves! What started out as a few children playing cats and dogs in the dramatic play center can become a story that they act out in front of the class or their families. What began as a simple block structure can become a model of a castle complete with authentic details taken from books or pictures of castles. Adding a child's name and several words or sentences of description to a picture she painted exposes her to writing and adds to what she was able to do on her own.

Extending activities combines the children's ideas and interests with the teacher's knowledge of new concepts that they are ready to grasp or skills they could practice. Both the teacher and the children are highly engaged in learning.

Be sure to document these exciting classroom developments, too. Share the good news with children's families! Talk with families about centers during informal conversations and describe them in a newsletter. Post signs that explain "In the Block Center children learn..." around the classroom. When a child works hard and accomplishes something new, point it out.

Take pictures of interesting events as children build, figure out, or create. Post photos for children, families, and visitors to see. Add brief captions about what the children said, did, and what they learned. Put photos in a class album or portfolio for them to revisit at a later time. Children love to remember their accomplishments and talk about "when we learned about..." Take credit, along with the children, for all the wonderful things they are learning!

References

Bredekamp, S., & Copple, C. (Eds.). (1997). *Developmentally appropriate practice in early childhood programs* (Rev. ed.). Washington, DC: National Association for the Education of Young Children.

Bredekamp, S., & Rosegrant, T. (Eds.). (1992). *Reaching potentials: Appropriate curriculum and assessment for young children.* Washington, DC: National Association for the Education of Young Children.

Brooks, J., & Brooks, M. (1993). *In search of understanding: The case for constructivist classrooms.* Alexandria, VA: Association for Supervision and Curriculum Development.

DeVries, R., & Zan, B. (1995). Creating a constructivist classroom atmosphere. *Young Children, 51*(1), 4–13.

Dewey, J. (1916). *Democracy and education: An introduction to the philosophy of education.* New York: Macmillan.

Dodge, D., & Colker, L. (1996). *The creative curriculum for early childhood.* Washington, DC: Teaching Strategies.

Eliason, C., & Jenkins, L. (1994). *A practical guide to early childhood curriculum.* New York: Macmillan.

Gardner, H. (1991). *The unschooled mind: How children think and how schools should teach.* New York: Basic Books.

Patton, M., & Mercer, J. (1996). "Hey where's the toys?" Play and literacy in 1st grade. *Childhood Education, 73*(1), 10–16.

Piaget, J., & Inhelder, B. (1971). *Psychology of the child.* New York: Basic Books.

Vygotsky, L. (1978). *Mind in society: The development of psychological processes.* Cambridge, MA: Harvard University Press.

Marie W. Sloane, M.S.T., is Assistant Director, The Little Ones Nursery School, and an Educational Consultant, in Lincolnshire, Illinois.

Reprinted with permission from *Dimensions of Early Childhood,* Winter 2000, pp. 16-20. © 2000 by the Southern Early Childhood Association, 8500 W. Markham Street, Suite 105, Little Rock, AR, 72205; 800/305-7322.

Using Documentation Panels To Communicate With Families

Teachers have always faced the challenges of developing communication between the home and the school, as well as of conveying their understanding about how children learn.

Judith Brown-DuPaul, Tracy Keyes, and Laura Segatti

Upon arriving at her son's classroom one afternoon, a mother noticed several other parents and children clustered around a table. The table contained a large, three-sided board filled with photographs, simple text, and some children's artwork. As the mother approached the group, she heard excitement in the voices of the children: "Oh look! That's when we tried to rub all the trees with crayons." "See, I'm in the picture where we put all the tree parts into piles on trays." Finally, her son saw her and pulled her toward the large board. He said, "Look, Mom! The teacher finished the big board on all the stuff we did with trees!"

The large board that caused all of the excitement in the classroom is called a documentation panel. Such panels showcase class photographs and children's artwork and dictation, which are linked with educational captions, information from books and journals, and curriculum webs. Traditionally, many early childhood programs have used bulletin boards to display art projects and class photographs for parents to enjoy. One of the main differences between such displays and documentation panels is that the panels are a communicative tool (Tarini, 1997).

When teachers pair these materials with clear captions about the knowledge children are constructing, parents begin to develop an understanding of how children learn. For example, by linking art samples to captions describing color mixing, problem-solving, and creativity, teachers can help parents to understand the benefits of a hands-on, open ended curriculum. The panel mentioned in the above vignette showed how, through many child-initiated and planned experiences, the class had been studying trees. The [panel], Science for Young Children, show[ed] the documentation panel teachers created to share with families some of the activities and learning

that had occurred during this tree project. The panel emphasized that learning occurs during everyday learning experiences, such as rubbing a tree with crayons and classifying all of the parts of trees.

Benefits of Documentation Panels

Teachers have always faced the challenges of developing communication between the home and the school, as well as of conveying their understanding about how children learn. Documentation panels are a unique way to highlight classroom learning; teachers can use them to communicate with families about a myriad of concepts and issues. The panels can effectively document learning in classrooms with students of all ages, from infancy through elementary school.

The web in Figure 1 details some common foci for panels. While many teachers choose to create panels about certain curriculum areas or projects, the specific topics will vary depending on the age of the children, that particular class's interests, parental questions or concerns, and the message that the teacher wants to communicate.

Teachers traditionally have communicated their educational philosophies to families through parent workshops or newsletters. These methods have their drawbacks, however. The barriers that limit attendance at parent meetings have been well-chronicled (Foster, 1994; Kieff & Wellhousen, 2000). Newsletters may be discarded or not read thoroughly; and those that are only written in English distance parents for whom English is not their home language (National Association for the Education of Young Children, 1996).

Documentation panels, because of their interactive format, and because they draw parents into the classroom,

Construction of Documentation Panels

Make a decision on what you want to communicate

Projects or themes
Special events
Specific curriculum areas
Learning environments
Skill acquisition
Child development

Collected materials for the panel

Children's actual work or photocopies
Observation notes/anecdotal records
Information and quotes from books and journals
Curriculum webs
Quotes and dictation from children and teachers
Photographs
   —various sizes (enlarge or shrink on a photocopier)
   —color, or black-and-white

Select the best items that represent the idea or theme of your panel

Write an educational caption for each piece
Use a type size large enough to be read from a distance

Layout of panel

Determine where the panel will be displayed (on a table or wall?)
Select type of panel: poster board (best for wall) or three-sided board

Title the panel
Select a strong image as the focal point on the panel
Aesthetics are important
   —Matte work and photographs
   —Use colored paper to support, not detract from, the images
   —Less is best; too many items will distract the viewer
   —Remember that people tend to look at things from left to right and top to bottom
Use the following Guiding Questions to check for changes:
   —Does the panel convey your intended message?
   —How many different kinds of documentation do you see?
   —What can you add now?
Will this panel entice children and families to view it?
Ask someone to give you feedback on the layout before attaching pieces to the panel
Attach the items to the panel with glue or double-sided tape

Display

Place the panel in a location where families and children may easily view it, such as the entryway into the classroom or near children's cubbies.

(Adapted from *Spreading the News* by Carter and Curtis, 1996)

Table 1

are much more effective than newsletters. Parents are particularly attracted by the visual appeal of the panels, as well as of children's photographs and work samples. Furthermore, as the vignette from the beginning of the article illustrated, children will often prompt parents to look at the panels. Together, the adult and the child may discuss an art experience, classroom project, or field trip that is highlighted on the panel (Saltz, 1997).

Families who linger in the center reap additional benefits. They have the opportunity to observe teacher-child interactions, ask the teacher questions, offer feedback about curriculum or development, and meet other families. Family-school partnerships are strengthened when families are encouraged to spend more time in the classroom and offered more information about their children's education (McBridge, 1999). Hence, viewing the panels in the classroom opens and supports homeschool communication more readily than does reading a newsletter at home.

Some researchers hypothesize that parents become more involved as their awareness of classroom learning grows (Carter & Curtis, 1996; Katz, 1994). After viewing panels, parents may feel more comfortable volunteering or offering suggestions for future projects. Family members also may choose to extend some of the learning experiences or projects at home. This "search for common ground" between the home and school environment may lead to more successful family involvement programs (Coleman & Wallinga, 2000, p. 209).

Using Panels To Convey Educational Philosophy

Because information must be conveyed succinctly, documentation panels help teachers to clarify their understanding of how children learn. Carter and Curtis (1996) emphasize that "collecting stories of children's activities and broadcasting them through documentation displays offers a method and a motivation to pay closer attention to the value of children's play" (p. 17). This reflection should influence teachers' planning and help them to articulate their philosophy to families. This process is especially important in those circumstances when parents question the value of play or of emergent curriculum (Breign-Allen & Dillon, 1997) and, consequently, pressure teachers for tangible evidence of children's learning, such as dittos or worksheets. Documentation panels provide evidence that children are engaged in active learning.

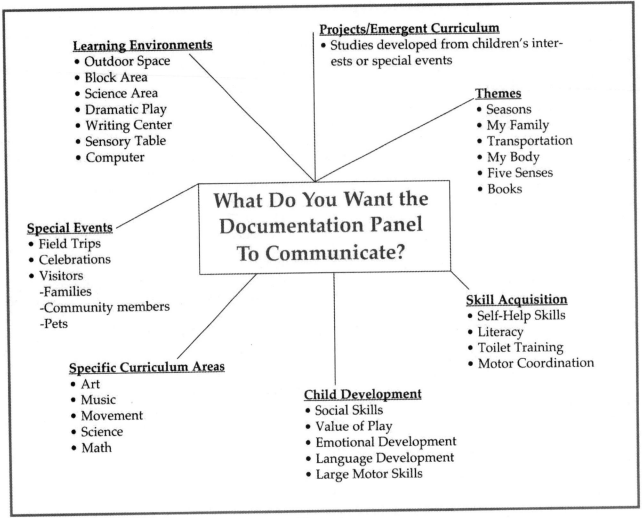

Figure 1

When parents see the panels, they may stop asking, "How could she be here for four hours and 'do nothing'?" or "All he ever does is play… when are you going to teach him something?"

Integrating Visual and Written Knowledge

Documentation panels educate parents through two distinct modes of information. One is visual knowledge, such as photographs of children building with blocks; the other is a written explanation. An example of written knowledge is a caption that describes the benefits of block play ("It stimulates children's creativity, teaches them cooperative problem-solving methods, and helps them learn about gravity, physics, classification, and shapes"). By exploring these concepts in more than one way, parents may develop a better understanding of the teacher's preferred teaching philosophy.

Photographs and visual aids are especially meaningful in centers with multilingual populations. Captions could be printed in more than one language, to provide a way for everyone to participate in their children's learning experiences.

Constructing Documentation Panels

Some guidance is in order to ensure that the documentation panels are educational and are not simply attractive bulletin boards (see Table 1 for ideas.) Initially, teachers need to decide what—through photographs, work samples, observation notes, and children's dictation—they hope to communicate to parents. Supporting information, such as curriculum webs or quotes from academic sources, can then be integrated with descriptive captions.

Paying attention to aesthetics will give the panel a professional, attractive appearance. The colors and materials need to catch the viewer's eye, yet should not detract from the purpose of the panel. Some consideration also should be given to achieving a balance of children's artwork, photographs, and text. See Carter and Curtis (1996) for specific recommendations on designing panels. As culminating step, teachers need to take time to ask themselves guiding questions (see Table 1) to ensure that the documentation panels are as engaging and instructional as they are attractive.

Displaying Documentation Panels

These family education tools can be used in numerous ways. Panels may be posters mounted on walls, or they may be three-sided, free-standing boards used alone or with three-dimensional objects (Helm, Beneke, & Sternheimer, 1988a, 1988b). In some centers, panels are displayed for extended periods of time. Panels dealing with developmental issues provide an ongoing source of information for families. Panels can help prospective families or parents who are new to the center learn more about its philosophy. Some panels may be displayed for shorter time periods, or may be added to throughout the year.

To maximize exposure, centers often display panels in high traffic areas near the cubbies or in the hallways. When home visits are an option, teachers may bring small portable boards with them to foster home-school communication.

Panels provide a professional centerpiece for a parent meeting, and offer information for any family members who could not attend an event or workshop. Hand-outs may help teachers highlight key points from the panels.

Conclusion

A documentation panel is an innovative way to "document with our pens and camera the learning process of our children and adults" (Carter & Curtis, 1996, p. 8). The panels provide an opportunity for parents to become more fully aware of what occurs in their child's learning environment. For staff, creating the panels becomes part of the documentation of children's learning, a process that may lead to more activities that are attuned to each child's interests and skill levels. Finally, the panels promote parent-teacher partnerships by providing a springboard for discussion of best practices, projects or themes, classroom experiences, curriculum, and child development.

References

Breig-Allen, C., & Dillon, J. U. (1997). Implementing the process of change in a public school setting. In J. Hendrick (Ed.), *First steps toward teaching the Reggio way* (pp. 126–40). Columbus, OH: Merrill.

Carter, M., & Curtis, D. (1996). *Spreading the news*. St.Paul, MN: Red Leaf Press.

Coleman, M., & Wallinga, C. (2000). Connecting families and classrooms using family involvement webs. *Childhood Education, 76*, 209–214.

Foster, S. (1994). Successful parent meetings. *Young Children, 50*, 78–80.

Helm, J. H., Beneke, S., & Steinheimer, K. (1998a). *Windows on learning: Documenting young children's work*. New York: Teachers College Press.

Helm, J. H., Beneke, S., & Steinheimer, K. (1998b). *Teacher materials for documenting young children's work: Windows on learning*. New York: Teachers College Press.

Katz, L. (1994). Images from the world: Study seminar on the experience of the municipal infant-toddler centers and preprimary schools of Reggio Emilia, Italy. In L. Katz & B. Cesarone (Eds.), *Reflections on the Reggio Emilia approach* (pp. 7–19). Urbana, IL: ERIC/EECE.

Kieff, J., & Wellhousen, K. (2000). Planning family involvement in early childhood programs. *Young Children, 55*, 18–25.

McBride, S. (1999). Research in review: Family-centered practices. *Young Children, 54*, 62–68.

National Association for the Education of Young Children. (1996). NAEYC Position Statement: Responding to linguistic and cultural diversity—Recommendations for effective early childhood education. *Young Children, 51*, 4–12.

Saltz, R. (1997). The Reggio Emilia influence at the University of Michigan-Dearborn Child Development Center: Challenges and change. In J. Hendrick (Ed.), *First steps toward teaching the Reggio way* (pp. 167–180). Columbus, OH: Merrill.

Tarini, E. (1997). Reflections on a year in Reggio Emilia: Key concepts in rethinking and learning the Reggio way. In J. Hendrick (Ed.), *First steps toward teaching the Reggio way* (pp. 56–69). Columbus, OH: Merrill.

Judith Brown-DuPaul is Adjunct Faculty, Teacher Education Programs, Lehigh-Carbon Community College, Schnecksville, Pennsylvania. Tracy Keyes is Assistant Professor, Elementary Education, Kutztown University, Kutztown, Pennsylvania, Laura Segatti is Assistant Professor, Teacher Education Programs, Lehigh-Carbon Community College.

Correspondence regarding this article should be addressed to Judith Brown-DuPaul, Teacher Education Programs, Lehigh-Carbon Community College, 4525 Education Park Drive, Schnecksville, PA 18078-2598.

From *Childhood Education,* Summer 2001, pp. 209-213 with permission of the authors, Judith Brown-DuPaul, Tracy Keyes and Laura Segatti. © 2001 by the Association for Childhood Education International.

Children and Computer Technology: Analysis and Recommendations

"Across the world there is a passionate love affair between children and computers... And more than wanting [computer technology], they seem to know that in a deep way it already belongs to them. They know they can master it more easily and more naturally than their parents. They know they are the computer generation."

—Seymour Papert, *The Connected Family*, 1996

Feeding children's passion for computers, billions of dollars in both public and private funds are being spent to give children access in school, at home, and in the community. Nearly every school is now equipped with computers,[1] and over two-thirds of our nation's children have access at home.[2] But is computer technology improving children's lives? This journal issue examines how children are affected by the emerging world of computers. It explores how computer use is affecting children's development physically, intellectually, socially, and psychologically; whether computers are increasing or decreasing the disparities between rich and poor; and whether computers are being used effectively to enhance classroom instruction....

The Importance of Access

Computer technology has transformed society in profound ways. For better or worse, the increasing pervasiveness of computer technology is a reality no one can ignore. Computers are fast becoming integrated into nearly every aspect of daily living—from school to work, to banking and shopping, to paying taxes and even voting. They provide access to a wide range of information without a trip to the library. They convey personal messages in place of the post office or telephone. And they compete with newspapers, radio, and television in providing entertainment and news of the day.

Computer technology also has a profound effect on our economy. Not only are computers changing the way goods and services are manufactured, distributed, and purchased, but they are also changing the skills workers need to be productive and earn a living. Almost every job today requires at least some knowledge of computers, and for an increasing number of jobs, productivity is directly related to an individual's level of computer expertise.[3] As the economy moves increasingly to computer-based work, the changes are bringing a societal transformation as significant as the Industrial Revolution. Just as society was transformed when families migrated from an agrarian way of life to work in factories 200 years ago, in the "Digital Age," computer technology is transforming society by enabling many people to work anytime, anywhere, freed from a workplace anchored in time and space.[4]

Political participation is also changing because of computer technology. The Internet is increasingly the primary access point for disseminating information about government policies, programs, and services. E-mail lists and chat rooms have become popular vehicles for forming political coalitions at the national, state, and local levels. In 1999, more than 23 million individual taxpayers (about 19%) filed their returns via the Internet, and the number is expected to double by 2006.[5] And in what many see as the wave of the future, the nation's first legally binding public election using the Internet took place in March 2000, when 42% of those voting in Arizona's Democratic Party presidential primary cast their ballots online.[6]

The public generally agrees that for children to participate socially, economically, and politically in this new and different world, they must acquire a certain level of comfort and competence in using computers. National polls indicate widespread support for providing children with access to computers to enable them to learn adequate computer skills and improve their education.[7] In surveys, most parents and children report that they view computers and the Internet as a positive force in their lives, despite concerns about exposure to inappropriate commercial, sexual, and violent content.[8] Most parents believe that the Internet can help children with their homework and allow them to discover fascinating, useful things, and that children without access are disadvantaged compared to those with access.[9] According to Chen's commentary in this journal issue, in the minds of many parents and policymakers, "equality of digital opportunity" is fast becoming synonymous with "equality of educational opportunity."

As a result, growing numbers of parents are providing their children with access to computers at home.[2,10,11] Among households with children ages 2 to 17, home computer ownership jumped from 48% in 1996 to 70% in 2000, while connections to the Internet catapulted from 15% to 52% over the same 5-year period.[2] This rapid diffusion of technology is quite phenomenal—the spread of Internet access has been described as nine times faster than that of radio, four times faster than the personal computer, and three times faster than television.[12]

In addition, Congress has made it a national priority to provide all our nation's children with access to computers at school. Declaring that the use of technology can help students meet high standards of learning, and that such use is essential to develop and maintain a technologically literate citizenry and an internationally competitive workforce, in 1994 Congress enacted the Goals 2000: Educate America Act and the Improving America's Schools Act and created several programs to help elementary and secondary schools acquire and use technology to improve the delivery of educational services.[13] Largely as a result of these programs, between 1994 and 1999, the percentage of public elementary and secondary schools with computers connected to the Internet increased from 35% to 95%.[1]

Children are spending an increasing amount of time with computers at school and at home, yet surprisingly little systematic research has examined the effects of computer use on children. Nevertheless, as detailed throughout the remainder of this article, the limited data available, combined with the rich body of literature on child development, learning, and children's use of other media, suggest certain general observations. First, children's healthy development requires involvement in a variety of physical and social activities. The time children spend in front of screens of any type should not take up a disproportionate amount of their day. Second, parents, teachers, and other adults who work with children need guidance and support in their efforts to ensure that all children learn to use computers effectively and responsibly. More "high-quality" digital content and models of exemplary technology-supported practices are needed—uses of computers to educate and inspire, not just entertain. And third, evidence suggests that use of computers can improve learning among children under certain circumstances, but these circumstances may be more limited than parents and policymakers realize. Much remains to be accomplished if we are to ensure that our nation's chil-

dren not only acquire the necessary skills to use computers effectively as a tool in their daily lives, but also benefit from technology's potential to enrich their learning both inside and outside the classroom.

The Risks and Benefits of Use

Excessive, unmonitored use of computers, especially when combined with use of other screen technologies, such as television, can place children at risk for harmful effects on their physical, social, and psychological development. Children need physical activity, social interaction, and the love and guidance of caring adults to be healthy, happy, and productive.[14] Too much time in front of a screen can deprive children of time for organized sports and other social activities that are beneficial to child development.[15] In addition, children may be exposed to violent, sexual, or commercial content beyond their years, with long-term negative effects.[16] To ensure healthy and appropriate use of computers both at school and at home, children's computer time must be limited and their exposure to different types of content must be supervised.

Limits on Extent of Exposure Needed

At present, excessive use of computers among children, especially younger children, is not typical. National survey data gathered in spring 2000 indicate that children ages 2 to 17 spent about 34 minutes per day, on average, using computers at home, with use increasing with age.[17] (Preschoolers ages 2 to 5 averaged 27 minutes per day, school-age children ages 6 to 11 averaged 49 minutes per day, and teens ages 12 to 17 averaged 63 minutes per day.) Available data on computer use at school suggest that exposure in the early primary grades, at least, is relatively modest. A spring 1999 survey of 26 elementary schools in the heart of Silicon Valley, where computer use might be expected to be high, found that although 70% of teachers in kindergarten through third grade had their students do some work on computers, the students' computer time averaged less than 10 minutes per day.[18] These data suggest that younger children in particular are not currently using computers for excessive amounts of time.

Usage is on the rise, however, and some children—especially older teenage boys—have reported spending 4 hours a day or more using their home computers.[19] In addition, it appears that time spent using home computers does not displace much, if any, time spent watching television; instead, access to home computers appears to increase the amount of children's overall "screen time."[20] Survey data gathered in spring 2000 indicate that when children between the ages of 2 and 17 have access to computers and video games as well as television, they spend, on average, about 5 hours a day in front of some type of screen, over an hour more than children without such access.[21]

Children who spend an excessive amount of time in front of computers and other screens are likely to be displacing activities required for healthy development and increasing their risk of obesity. In addition, children' increased computer time could expose them to harmful impacts on their eyes, backs, and wrists.[22] Although the number of studies documenting the relationship between children's computer use and such harmful effects is limited, such studies, taken together with findings on the effects of other media on children and findings on the effects of computer use on adults, suggest that the risks of excessive computer use can be significant.

For example, although little systematic research documents the relationship between children's computer use and obesity, evidence does show that obesity in children is linked to excessive time in front of a television screen—defined as five or more hours a day.[23] The sedentary time spent in front of a computer screen likely poses a similar risk.

Also, some researchers have issued warnings about the risk of repetitive strain injuries from use of computers at workstations not well designed for children, and possible harmful effects on children's vision from staring too long at a computer screen.[24] Most of the evidence concerning these physical risks is inferred from studies of adult use of computers in the workplace. For example, the Occupational Safety and Health Administration (OSHA) within the U.S. Department of Labor has reported that each year, 230,000 workers suffer injury from over-exertion or repetitive motion, such as that caused by excessive computer use.[25] Citing the potential risks from, among other things, "using a keyboard again and again," in November 1999, OSHA proposed new ergonomics requirements to reduce injuries among workers caused by excessive computer use. Excessive use of computers by children could put them at risk for similar injuries. More child-focused studies are needed to determine how much computer use is too much for children of different ages and how to intersperse breaks and provide ergonomic supports to minimize risk.

Excessive computer use may also affect children's social development. By the age of about seven years, a child's interactions with family, peers, school, community networks, and media all play an important role in the development of interpersonal skills and social competence.[26] Computers are not part of that mix, and concerns have been raised that children who form "electronic friendships" instead of human friendships might be hindered in developing interpersonal skills.[27] Such concerns are heightened by reports that among children ages 8 to 16, some 20% have computers—and 11% have Internet access—in their bedrooms,[28] which suggests that a sizable number of children may use computers in social isolation. Indeed, some research has documented negative social effects from time spent on computers. For example, one in-depth analysis of the effects of Internet use among a group of 93 families found that, during their first year

with access, teens who spent more time online experienced greater declines in social involvement and increases in their feelings of loneliness and depression.[29] Similarly, in the school setting, although group use of computers is more common, concerns have been raised about the possibility that computers may be used to replace, rather than augment, child-to-child and child-to-teacher relationships.[22]

To minimize the increased risk of obesity, as well as several other harmful effects of extensive media exposure, the American Academy of Pediatrics advises parents to limit children's time spent with computers, video games, and other media to perhaps no more than one to two hours a day, and to emphasize alternative activities such as imaginative play and sports.[30]

Supervision of Activities and Content Quality Needed

In addition to the extent of time, the types of activities children engage in while using computers can also affect their intellectual, social, and psychological well-being. The allure of computers stems from the fact that they can be used for a wide range of purposes. Although 1998 census data indicated children were still using computers primarily to play games and to run stand-alone software,[31] their use of the Internet is increasing rapidly.[17] As of 2000, an estimated 21 million children and teens were accessing the Internet from home.[32] And once online, a child can choose to engage in activities across a wide range of possibilities. When games were the principal option, boys spent much more time with computers than girls did.[33,20] Now that the array of nongame applications has widened, girls report use of home computers as often, and with as much confidence, as boys do.[34] Children of both genders surf the Web for music and photos of movie stars, use e-mail to exchange messages with friends, and especially among teens, use the Internet to visit multiuser domains (MUDs) and chat rooms.

Not surprisingly, the effects of computer use vary significantly by the type of activity and the quality of content. The experiences of children playing violent computer games are quite different from those playing educational games; the experiences of children visiting information, nonprofit Web sites are quite different from those logging on to sites sponsored by media conglomerates and toy companies; and the experiences of children exchanging e-mails with friends and family are quite different from those communicating with strangers in MUDs and chat rooms....

Playing Games

Playing games has long been the most common computer activity for children, especially younger boys. But computer games vary widely in terms of content and potential effects. Some, such as SimCity,[35] have been shown to have considerable educational value. Others, however, such as Duke Nukem and Doom, expose children to extreme violence, possibly disposing them to subsequent aggressive behavior.[20]

As reported in the article by Subrahmanyam and colleagues in this journal issue, some studies suggest that moderate use of computers to play games has no significant impact on children's friendships and family relationships, and can even enhance certain visual intelligence skills, such as the ability to read and visualize images in three-dimensional space, and to track multiple images simultaneously. Such skills, Subrahmanyam and colleagues contend, can serve as an important building block to computer literacy, and may be especially useful in the fields of science and technology. However, Healy questions these claims in her commentary in this journal issue, noting that there is little, if any, evidence that the visual-spatial skills fostered by computer games contribute in any meaningful way to the academic skills needed for math and science.

In addition, however, just as research has documented that watching violent films and television programming can lead to increased hostility and aggression in children,[36] some research also suggests an association between playing violent computer games and increased aggression.[37] Although the causal direction of the association is unclear, the critical variable linked to subsequent aggressive behavior appears to be the child's preference for playing such games. According to Subrahmanyam and colleagues, the amount of aggression and violence has increased in each generation of computer games, and parents are often unaware of the extent of the violence, even though many of the most popular games have violent themes.[33,38] A 1998 content analysis of popular video games found that nearly 80% had aggression or violence as an objective.[39] In September 2000, the Federal Trade Commission reported that violent computer games rated "mature" (for adults only) were being marketed aggressively to children under age 17.[40] We agree with the commission that sanctions should be imposed for such marketing violations, and that parental understanding of the ratings should be increased by including the reasons for the rating in all advertising and product packaging....

RECOMMENDATIONS

More public and private research dollars should be allocated to assessing the effects of extended computer use and exposure to various types of computer content on children's physical, intellectual, social, and psychological development....

Parents, teachers, and other adults working with children should limit the amount of time children spend using computers and supervise the content children are exposed to, including games, software, and the Web....

Public, private, and nonprofit groups concerned with the role of computer technology in society should support and encourage the dialogue that has been initiated among researchers, software and Internet companies, and government agencies to create new incentives for developing high-quality content for children....

Schools and community organizations should provide media literacy training for teachers, parents, other adults who work with children, and children themselves to strengthen their critical understanding of the motives underlying much of the software and content found on the Web and to empower children to make good choices about their computer use....

State and local education agencies should refine and adopt age-appropriate guidelines for children's computer fluency. Such guidelines should be disseminated to all elementary and secondary teachers and incorporated into pre-service and in-service technology training sessions....

The U.S. Department of Commerce should work with industry to expand opportunities for low-income families to acquire home computers and Internet access....

Public and private funders should support efforts by libraries and community centers to include components, within their technology programs focused specifically on children and to provide staff with training in the skills and types of exposure appropriate for children of different ages....

The U.S. Department of Education should assist the poorest schools in applying for E-rate discounts and encourage all schools to offer a broad range of technology-related experiences to their students, preferably connected to the curriculum in ways that have been shown to be appropriate and effective....

When acquiring new hardware and software, schools should consider options that incorporate universal design features to facilitate access to computers for all students, including those with special needs....

More public and private research dollars should be allocated to assessing the effectiveness of technology-supported practices in the classroom across various subjects and grade levels and to disseminating the results to state and local education agencies and teachers....

Conclusions

Computer technology is rapidly transforming society. Although the task may seem daunting, we can take several steps to help ensure that children use computers in ways that improve their lives now and in the future.

First, we can ensure that children acquire the necessary skills to navigate the digital world effectively and responsibly. Parents, teachers, and other adults who work with children can teach children to make good choices about the time they spend with computers, to be savvy digital consumers, and to seek out software and online content that educates and inspires, not merely entertains. With our guidance and enthusiasm, children can use the computer to learn about other people and parts of the world, for example, as well as to play video games. If use of higher-quality content increases, industry can be challenged more effectively to meet the demand.

Second, we can ensure that children have opportunities to use computer technology more actively to create, to design, to invent, and to collaborate with children in other classrooms and communities. These are types of activities that empower children to play active roles in the emerging digital world, not merely to navigate through it. With the assistance of highly trained mentors, children can learn to use computers to create finger paintings, or to design and build bird feeders, for example, as well as to surf the Web for the lyrics of hit songs.

Third, we can help reduce disparities between rich and poor by working to narrow the gap in computer access between children who live in low-income neighborhoods compared with those in high-income neighborhoods. Initiatives that help low-income families to afford home computers and that support technology programs in public libraries and community centers can play an important part in equalizing access. As the primary access point for most low-income children, however, schools must play the critical role. To promote "equality of digital opportunity" we can ensure that schools in low-income neighborhoods are well equipped with up-to-date hardware, high-quality software, and well-trained teachers so that children learn the skills they will need to live and work in the twenty-first century.

Finally, to harness the potential of computer technology to enhance children's learning, we can explore ways to use technology effectively in the classroom, ways that add value to traditional curricula and reach students who fail to respond to traditional approaches. Although computers may not be the panacea envisioned by some, certain uses of technology have been demonstrated to benefit students by making learning more interesting and engaging and by providing new approaches to learning complex concepts and critical thinking. We should identify the technology-supported practices that show the most promise for enhancing learning and support efforts to integrate these practices into the classroom.

Computer technology is only a tool—whether it serves to improve children's lives depends on how it is used. By taking these steps today, we can help empower all children to use the tool effectively, responsibly, and creatively to shape the digital world of tomorrow.

Margie K. Shields, M.P.A.

Richard E. Behrman, M.D.

Notes

1. National Center for Education Statistics. *Internet access in public schools and classrooms: 1994–99*. Stats in Brief. Washington, DC: U.S. Department of Education, Office of Educational Research and Improvement, February 2000.

2. Woodward E. H. IV, and Gridina, N. *Media in the home 2000: The fifth annual survey of parents and children*. Philadelphia: Annenberg Public Policy Center, University of Pennsylvania, 2000, p. 11.

3. Committee on Information Technology Literacy and Computer Science and Telecommunications Board, Commission on Physical Sciences, Mathematics, and Applications, National Research Council. *Being fluent with information technology*. Washington, DC: National Academy Press, 1999, pp. 6–14.

4. Nie, N. H. and Erbring, L. *Internet and society: A preliminary report*. Stanford, CA: Stanford Institute for the Quantitative Study of Society, February 17, 2000.

5. Internal Revenue Service. Projections of returns to be filed in calendar years 2000–2006. Table 1. In *Statistics of Income Bulletin*, Winter 1999/2000. IRS Publication 1136, rev. February 2000.

6. Ain, S. In brief: Election.com calls test in Arizona a success. *Sunday Long Island Weekly Desk*. March 19, 2000; see also Ladd, D. Casting your vote on the Internet: Yea or nay. *Interactive Week from ZDWire*. July 3, 2000.

7. Trotter, A. Question of effectiveness. *Education Week: Technology counts '98*, October 8, 1998. 18: 6–9.

8. National School Boards Foundation. *Safe and smart: Research and guidelines for children's use of the Internet*. Alexandria, VA: NSBF, March 28, 2000.

9. Turow, J. *The Internet and the family: The view from parents, the view from the press*. Philadelphia: Annenberg Public Policy Center. University of Pennsylvania, May 1999, pp. 14, 25.

10. Roberts, D. F., Eoehr, U. G., Rideout, V. J., and Brodie, M. *Kids and media @ the new millennium*. Menlo Park, CA: Henry J. Kaiser Family Foundation, 1999.

11. National Telecommunications and Information Administration. *Falling through the Net: Defining the digital divide*. Washington, DC: U.S. Department of Commerce, July 1999.

12. Chaney, H. The U.S. "digital divide" is not even a virtual reality. *Bridge News*. March 12, 2000.

13. Coley, R. J., Cradler, J. and Engel, P. E. *Computers and classrooms: The status of technology in U.S. schools*. Princeton, NJ: Educational Testing Service, Policy Information Center, 1996, p. 8; and Public Law 103-382, Improving America's Schools of 1994. October 20, 1994, Title III, Technology for Education, Part A, Technology for Education of All Students, Sections 3111 and 3112.

14. See, for example, Benson, P. L. *All kids are our kids: What communities must do to raise caring and responsible children and adolescents*. San Francisco: Jossey-Bass, 1997, pp. 32–33; Steinhauser, P. D. *The primary needs of children: A blueprint for effective health promotion at the community level*. Working paper for the Promotion/Prevention Task Force, Sparrow Lake Alliance, prepared October 1995; see also Pipher, M. *The shelter of each other: Rebuilding our families*. New York: Grosset/Putnam Books, 1996.

15. American Academy of Pediatrics. Fitness, activity, and sports participation in the preschool child. *Pediatrics* (December 1992) 90: 1002–04.

16. American Academy of Pediatrics. Media education. *Pediatrics* (August 1999) 104: 341–43

17. See note no. 2, Woodward and Gridina, p. 19.

18. Special analyses from survey database described in Penuel, B., Golan, S., Means, B., et al. *Silicon Valley Challenge 2000: Year 4 report*. Menlo Park, CA: SRI International, 2000.

19. For example, a survey conducted by America Online in February 1997 found that among the 290 respondents, 20% of boys ages 6 to 19 reported using the Internet 29 hours or more per week.

20. See the article by Subrahmanyam and colleagues in this journal issue for further discussion of this topic.

21. See note no. 2, Woodward and Gridina, p. 24.

22. Alliance for Childhood. *Fool's gold: A critical look at children and computers.* College Park, MD: Alliance for Childhood, September 12, 2000.

23. See, for example, Gortmaker, S. L., Must, A., Sobol, A. M., et al. Television viewing as a cause of increasing obesity among children in the United States, 1986–1990. *Archives of Pediatrics and Adolescent Medicine* (April 1996) 150: 356–62.

24. Mendels, P. School computers may harm posture. *New York Times.* January 17, 1999, at 16; see also Harris, C., and Straker, L. Survey of physical ergonomics issues associated with school children's use of laptop computers. *International Journal of Industrial Ergonomics* (2000) 26: 337–46; Palmer, S. Does computer use put children's vision at risk? *Journal of Research and Development in Education* (Winter 1993) 26: 59–65.

25. Occupational Safety and Health Administration. *Women and ergonomics.* Washington, DC: U.S. Department of Labor, OSHA, March 2000.

26. Griffiths, M. D. Friendship and social development in children and adolescents: The impact of electronic technology. *Educational and Child Psychology* (1997) 14: 25–37.

27. Colwell, J., Grady, C., Rhaiti, S. Computer games, self esteem, and gratification of needs in adolescents. *Journal of Community and Applied Social Psychology* (1995) 5: 195–206.

28. See note no. 2, Woodward and Gridina, p. 3.

29. Kraut, R., Patterson, M., Lundmark, V., et al. Internet paradox: A social technology that reduces social involvement and psychological well-being? *American Psychologist* (1998) 53: 1017–31.

30. See note no. 16, AAP. The Academy had earlier advised that television viewing should be limited to no more than one to two hours per day. See American Academy of Pediatrics. Children, adolescents, and television. *Pediatrics* (October 1995) 96: 786–87.

31. Based on original analysis of Census data included in the article by Becker in this journal issue.

32. *eCME News.* Electronic Newsletter of the CME. September 8, 2000. Available online at http://www.cme.org/publications/ecme/vol1_no1.html.

33. Funk, J. Reevaluating the impact of video games. *Clinical Pediatrics* (1993) 2: 86–89.

34. Gallup Organization, in conjunction with CNN, *USA Today*, and the National Science Foundation. *U.S. teens and technology*. 1997. Some gender disparities continue to exist, however. See National Center for Education Statistics. *Trends in educational equity of girls and women.* Washington, DC: U.S. Department of Education, Office of Educational Research and Improvement, March 2000; see also American Association of University Women. *Tech-savvy: Educating girls in the new computer age.* Washington, DC: AAUW, 2000.

35. See the article by Roschelle and colleagues in this journal issue.

36. Zillmann, D., and Weaver, J. Psychoticism in the effect of prolonged exposure to gratuitous media violence on the acceptance of violence as a preferred means of conflict resolution. *Personality and Individual Differences* (May 1997) 22: 613–27; see also Zillman, D., and Weaver, J. Effects of prolonged exposure to gratuitous media violence on provoked and unprovoked hostile behavior. *Journal of Applied Social Psychology* (1999) 29: 145–65.

37. Fling, S., Smith, L., Rodriquez, T., et al. Videogames, aggression, and self-esteem: A survey. *Social Behavior and Personality* (1992) 20: 39–45.

38. Oldberg, C. Children and violent video games: A warning. *New York Times.* December 15, 1998, at A16.

39. Dietz, T. L. An examination of violence and gender role portrayals in video games: Implications for gender socialization and aggressive behavior. *Sex Roles* (1998) 38: 425–42.

40. Federal Trade Commission. *Marketing violent entertainment to children: A review of self-regulation and industry practices in the motion picture, music recording and electronic game industries.* Washington, DC: Federal Trade Commission, September 2000.

Special thanks to Barbara Means and to Elise Cappella for their insightful comments and support throughout the development of this analysis.

Children Are Born Mathematicians:
Promoting the Construction of Early Mathematical Concepts in Children under Five

Eugene Geist

Children are mathematicians from the day they are born. They are constructing knowledge constantly as they interact mentally, physically, and socially with their environment and with other people. Young children may not be able to add or subtract, but their relationships with people and their interactions with a stimulating environment set the stage for the development of mathematical concepts (Sinclair et al. 1989). There is even some evidence that the ability to comprehend some mathematical concepts may be innate (Starkey & Cooper 1980; Wynn 1995; Koechlin, Dehaene, & Mehler 1997).

Innate ability to acquire mathematics

Perhaps, just as Chomsky (1999) has shown strong evidence for an innate *language acquisition device* that provides humans with a framework for learning language, there is a *mathematics acquisition device* that provides a framework for mathematical concepts. If such a mathematics acquisition device were present, we would expect children to naturally acquire mathematical concepts without direct teaching, to follow a standard sequence of gradual development, and most important, to show evidence of construction of mathematical concepts from a very early age. With careful examination of infants, toddlers, and preschoolers, one can see evidence for all of these criteria.

Emergent mathematical understanding

Perhaps it is time to begin looking at the construction of mathematical concepts the same way we look at literacy development—as emergent. The idea that literacy learning begins the day that children are born is widely accepted in the early childhood field. Children learn language by listening and by eventually speaking and writing. This language learning is aided by an innate language acquisition device that acts as a foundation for grammatical development and language learning (Chomsky 1999). Reading to infants, toddlers, and preschoolers is known to be an early positive step toward literacy success because it promotes and supports learning to read and write by immersing children in language and giving them an opportunity to interact with it (Ferreiro & Teberosky 1982).

> It is time to begin looking at the construction of mathematical concepts the same way we look at literacy development— as emergent.

Mathematical learning can be viewed in a similar way. Children begin to construct the foundations for future mathematical concepts during the first few months of life.

Before children can add or even count, they must construct ideas about mathematics that cannot be directly taught. Ideas that will support formal mathematics later in life include order and sequence, seriation, and classification.

The seemingly simple idea that a number represents a specific quantity actually involves a complex relationship that children must construct. Quantification is the basis for formal mathematics, and it is a synthesis of order (the basic understanding that objects are counted in a specific sequence and each object is counted only once). Seriation is the ability to place an object or group of objects in a logical series based on a property of the object or objects. Classification is the ability to group like objects in sets by a specific characteristic. This synthesis takes place by children interacting with objects and putting them in many different types of relationships.

A child constructing math concepts

An example of a child not yet capable of this synthesis, but beginning the process of constructing math understanding, is the three-year-old with whom I shared the following interactions. The girl's parents had asked her to say her numbers for me and she correctly counted to 20 with no errors. I then pulled out 20 pennies that I had in my pocket. I asked her if she could figure out a way to make sure we both got the same number of pennies. She looked at the pile of pennies, split the pile down the middle, slid a handful over to me, and took the rest. My pile contained 12 pennies and hers contained 8. I asked her how she knew we had the same amount, and she attempted to count the pennies in front of me by pointing at the pile saying, "One, two, three, four, five, six, seven." However, she did not have an understanding of the importance of order, and therefore counted some pennies twice and missed some completely. I then asked her to count her pennies, and she counted 10. When I again asked her if we both had the same amount, she made another quick visual inventory and replied "yes."

I then lined up eight pennies in a row and asked her to make a row with as many pennies as I had laid out. She took the rest of the pennies (12) and made a row below mine. I again asked her if there were the same number of pennies in each row. She counted her row and replied, "Yes. See—one, two, three, four, five, six, seven, eight, nine, ten." I asked her to count mine, and she came up with eight. I asked her again if they had the same number, and she again replied "yes."

This child was not yet able to coordinate order, classification, and seriation and therefore could not compare the penny quantities. Children as young as two may be able to count to 10 or even 20, but if they do not link their counting to quantification it is no different from memorizing their ABCs or a list of names like Bob, Joe, and Sara.

Because she did not understand that the numbers she recited each represented a specific quantity, this child could not perceive a numerical relationship between the two sets of objects.

This three-year-old used visual cues to estimate the sameness and difference of the sets instead of using number. Her logic and problem-solving ability were still perceptually bound. However, as she continually interacted with the objects and with other children and adults, she would come to realize the limits of her method and begin to construct new ways of reaching a solution. This type of confusion, or what Piaget called *disequilibrium* (Piaget & Inhelder [1964] 1969), is what leads a child to make further constructions and to strengthen her understanding of mathematical concepts.

The development of more complex understanding

Eight months later I had an opportunity to interact with this girl again. We repeated the game with the pennies. This time when I asked her to divide the pennies, she used a one-to-one correspondence method. She gave me a penny and then one to herself until all the pennies were distributed. When I asked her how she knew we had the same number, she counted each penny only once and in a specific order to get the correct answer.

I collected all the pennies in one pile, then showed the girl one more penny and added it to the pile. I asked her if she saw what I had done, and she said, "Yes, you added one more penny!" I then asked her to figure out a way to divide the pennies and make sure we both got the same number. She used the same method of one-to-one correspondence she had used previously. I asked her if we had the same number of pennies and she replied "yes." When I asked her to count them, and it turned out that I had one more penny, she was quite perplexed. She could not figure out how that had happened.

The child had made significant progress in her understanding of basic mathematical concepts. Her method of dividing the pennies was no longer visual. She used number concepts to solve her problem. However, her understanding of quantification was still weak and broke down when strongly challenged. Again, we see the disequilibrium that will lead the child to search for better ways of solving a problem. Through the process the child will construct new mathematical understanding.

Even very young children construct math knowledge

Children even younger than three years of age can use their developing understanding of order, seriation, and classification and their natural problem-solving ability. I observed an 18-month-old child playing in a large pit filled with different-colored balls. The child dropped one ball, then a second ball, and then a third ball over the side of the pit. The child then went to the opposite side of the pit and dropped two balls. He returned to the first side, reexamined the grouping of balls, then moved again to the second side and dropped another ball over the side to make the second grouping a set of three.

This may seem unimpressive by adult standards, but for an 18-month-old child, the coordination and comparison of threes on opposite sides of a structure is evidence of making a mathematical relationship. It is not yet a numerical relationship because the child is using visual perception to make the judgment of same or different. However, the coordination of dropping three balls each time is evidence of an understanding of more and less and basic equality. The child may not be developmentally ready for counting and quantification, but this simple task shows that children as young as 18 months can understand some rudimentary mathematical relationships.

Teachers of infants and toddlers need to be aware of these actions and abilities and help provide activities to encourage construction of mathematical concepts. Activities that provide children with concrete experiences manipulating objects and interacting with other children and adults, such as distributing snacks or sorting items by color or size, promote this type of construction.

Promoting emergent math

Although these basic mathematical concepts cannot and should not be directly taught, educators of young children need to emphasize and encourage children's interaction with their environment as a means of promoting and encouraging emergent math concepts. Children's logical and mathematical thinking develops by being exercised and stimulated. Teachers who encourage children to put objects into all kinds of relationships are promoting children's emergent understanding of mathematics.

Before children can add or even count, they must construct ideas about mathematics that cannot be directly taught.

Making sure that children from birth through age four have a stimulating environment and opportunities to explore many different kinds of relationships can support their emerging understanding of mathematics. Teachers in infant, toddler, and preschool programs can do a number of things, like offering objects to compare, using rhythm activities and music, modeling mathematical behavior, and incorporating math into everyday activities to facilitate the emergent mathematical learning within every child. The basic framework for math cannot be directly taught but can be easily promoted in the classroom.

Birth to two

Infants and toddlers explore their environments using their senses. Piaget and Inhelder ([1964] 1969) called this time the sensorimotor stage because children explore and learn about their environments through motor activity and by touching, seeing, tasting, and hearing. It may not seem that any mathematical construction is going on during this time. However, children begin to perceive relationships between and among objects as they begin to construct ways to classify, seriate, compare, and order objects. Classification begins with a child's ability to match objects and evolves into a system of organizing objects into groups with similar characteristics. Classification is an important foundation for future mathematical concepts such as comparing sets of numbers and quantification.

Rhythm and music. Rhythm and music activities and materials are excellent for promoting emergent mathematics. Using bongo drums with infants and toddlers can help children experience mathematics. Teacher and child take turns repeating each other's beats; the teacher beats the drum twice, and the child beats the drum twice. If the child takes the lead, the teacher echoes the child's playing. This helps support the child's understanding of a one-to-one correspondence. It also demonstrates a matching relationship, which helps refine the child's ability to classify.

Using synthesizers with automatic beat generators is another good way to promote math through music. Let children play notes on the keyboard along with the generated beat. These synthesizers come with headphones so children can play whatever they feel like and not bother other children in the classroom.

I observed one teacher encouraging her children to organize a marching band using the musical instruments and items in the room. The children decided how to march. One child even insisted that he say "one, two, one, two" as they marched. The children for the most part coordinated their beat as they marched through the hall of the center, outside, and back to their room with one child saying "one, two" the whole time to keep them all together.

Using numbers, counting, and quantification in everyday activities. Even children under the age of two can be exposed to math during everyday tasks and activities such as snack time or circle time. Any opportunity to count should be taken advantage of to help the children understand one-to-one correspondence of quantity. Teachers should count and use math whenever possible and even ask children questions about simple mathematical relationships. This type of interaction helps children to recognize the importance of numbers and promotes construction of emergent mathematics. Even children of this age can understand the concept of more. Asking chil-

Music

Call and response using beats on bongo drums
Marching to music
Playing a xylophone (relation of size to tone)
Clapping
Playing music on a synthesizer along with a beat generator
Creating their own music

Shapes

Sorting attribute blocks
Playing with different-colored blocks, balls, and other items
Building with blocks
Completing puzzles
Using manipulatives

Everyday activities

Snack time

Distributing snack
Counting the number of people at the table
Estimating

Circle time

Voting
Making time relationships (e.g., "Did we get into our circle slower or faster than yesterday?")
Calendar activities

Playground

Counting (e.g., the number of times a child rides the tricycle around the course)
Measuring (e.g., "How high do you think you can build your sand structure?")

Feeding classroom pets

Measuring amounts of food
Exploring "more" and "less" relationships

Project approach

Using math to solve problems
Using counting to solve disputes
Using math to explain and demonstrate an idea
Using math to plan

dren to compare groups of objects or quantities encourages the development of *more, less,* and *the same* concept.

Although children in this group have not yet constructed an understanding of number, this is no reason not to use math around them. Just as reading to infants and toddlers helps them develop literacy skills, using math around children helps them construct number concepts.

Blocks and shapes. Children who are surrounded with interesting objects are naturally led to make relation-

ships between those objects. Determining whether objects are the same or different, matching, and classifying all require a child to focus on a certain quality of the object in order to make the comparison. The more frequently children make comparisons, the more complex their comparisons become. The simple act of adding an increasing variety of colored balls or blocks to the child's choices can facilitate more and more complex mathematical relationships. These activities support the concepts of seriation and classification.

Shapes can be used to show matching relationships. In infant and toddler rooms there should be an abundance of different-shaped blocks and tiles for children to match and compare. Because their mathematical development is still in its early stages, infants and toddlers naturally look for exact matches. This is the level of classification that they can handle. Infants and toddlers cannot see something as the same and different at the same time.

I observed a teacher working with a 12-month-old. They were examining a group of blue and yellow triangle blocks. The child gave a yellow triangle to the teacher and then picked up another yellow triangle and gave it to the teacher. The teacher then picked up a blue triangle and showed it to the child. The child grasped it and threw it back in the pile, found another yellow triangle and gave it to the teacher. To the child, the yellow and blue triangles are not matches because they are different colors.

Construction using cardboard boxes can also help children make relationships. In my experience, infants and toddlers love to play with cardboard boxes. Boxes of all sizes can be made available for the children to stack and arrange to make structures. Larger boxes can have doors or holes in them for the children to crawl in and out. These boxes can be put together in a variety of ways, and each combination or sequence is another relationship that the child has made. In the process of arranging the boxes, children have discussions and social interactions that also promote the making of new social relationships.

As children develop their matching and classifying skills, they will be able to see more complex relationships. But to construct these concepts, children need time and interaction with objects and other people. Even if children are "prewired" for math, they still have to construct the concepts piece by piece. Children slowly construct formal mathematics understanding step by step, over the infant, toddler, and preschool years. This is why it is so vitally important to offer children as young as a few months old opportunities to match, classify, and compare.

Three- and four-year-olds

As children begin to move out of their sensorimotor stage of development and into what Piaget and Inhelder ([1964] 1969) called the preoperational stage, the big change is that children are able to think representationally and begin to acquire a certain degree of abstract thinking. Due to these abilities, children can think about objects that are not right in front of them, and they can begin to make connections between current and previous experiences. Children of this age can make much more complex relationships between objects. This is important for emerging mathematical concepts because it is during this time that the mental structures allowing a child to understand quantity are constructed.

The concepts of seriation, classification, and order take on a new dimension as children begin to understand more abstract relationships. Three- and four-year-olds can make comparisons to objects that are not present or events that took place in the past. This allows children to synthesize order, seriation, and classification to construct abstract mental structures that will support quantification and formal mathematics.

Children begin to make mental mathematical relationships that build on and refine the idea of *more* into "one more" or "two more." This refinement eventually leads to the child's being able to understand that three is one more than two and two more than one. This is the core idea behind quantification.

Manipulatives. An easy way to promote math to three- and four-year-olds is simply to ask children to use mathematical concepts in their activities. If a child is using blocks, a teacher can ask, "How many blocks do you have?" or "How many more do you need?" Children are willing and even excited to count objects and make mathematical relationships if the teacher encourages them.

A four-year-old child was making a chain out of different-colored plastic links. I asked him how long he was trying to make the chain. He did not respond, so I tried a more direct question, "How many links do you have so far?" He put on the next link and then proceeded to count each link. There were eight. After he put on another link, I asked again, "How many do you have now?" He went back to the beginning and counted each link again and got an answer of nine. When he again added a link, I asked him a more leading question: "You had nine and you put one more on. How many do you have now?" Again the child counted all the links until he got the answer of 10. After that I did not have to ask him again. Each time he put on a new link, he would count all the links. He eventually made a chain with 27 links.

After 15 links this child's counting became erratic. Sometimes he counted carefully and got the correct answer, and other times he missed some links in his counting. For example, after correctly counting 26 and adding one more, the boy counted again and missed a few. After completing the counting he triumphantly announced, "Fifteen!" The fact that he now had fewer than before did not seem to trouble him. Although he made mistakes and showed an incomplete understanding of number concepts, he was getting closer to using mathematics in a conventional manner. His actions were like those of children who move from drawing squiggles to writing words in the process of learning to write conventionally.

Everyday activities. Just as with the infants and toddlers, everyday activities such as snack and circle times can be used with three- and four-year-olds to promote the use of math. Dividing up snack, counting plates, and other activities can be assigned to children. They then have to use their own mathematical problem-solving ability to figure out the best way to perform the tasks. A child who is assigned to put out the plates for his table of five may do it by going to the stack of plates, getting one plate and placing it in front of one child, then going back to the plates to get another plate for the next child, and so on until everyone has a plate. Eventually the child will realize that he can count the children, then go to the plates, count out five plates, and distribute them accordingly. Allowing the child to use her own method of solving a problem such as this allows emergent understanding of math to develop in a child-centered developmental pattern.

Everyday activities such as snack and circle times can be used to promote the use of math.

Assigning two children to figure out how to solve an everyday problem as described above promotes problem solving even more. The children can discuss, plan, and even debate the best way to solve the problem. This give-and-take will push both children to construct new ways of seeing the problem (Kamii & Lewis 1990; Kamii 1991). In an argument, the children must clearly communicate their ideas to another person and at the same time evaluate the other person's ideas. In the process, both children examine and perhaps modify their own ideas.

Whenever a decision needs to be made in which children can have input, voting allows the teacher to use math in an integrated way. Not only does it offer an opportunity to count, but to compare numbers as well. Children can be asked to vote on which book to read first. The teacher asks the children to vote for one book. As the teacher counts the hands, she encourages the children to count with her. If the vote is six to five, the teacher can ask the children which book has won.

The project approach

The project approach to early childhood education allows children to explore their world and construct knowledge through genuine interaction with their environment. Lilian Katz (1989) states that young children should have activities that engage their minds fully in the quest for knowledge, understanding, and skill. When engaging in the project approach, children are not just gathering knowledge from a worksheet, structured activity, or teacher but are actively making decisions about not only what to learn, but also how and where to learn it. Through this method, children construct problem-solving techniques, research methods, and questioning strategies.

When children work on projects, a number of opportunities arise for them to use math. In a recent project on construction and transportation, children had an opportunity to use measurement to help them build a truck. They measured how long, tall, and wide they wanted it and then transferred their numbers to the cardboard they were using to make their truck. Their measurements were not accurate, and they did not really understand the concept of using a measuring tape. Still, these activities were at the beginning on the continuum of math learning, just as writing scribbles is a beginning step in literacy learning.

Questioning strategies, activities, and simple games offer a great opportunity for teachers to help children construct basic mathematical concepts.

The children also learned about blueprints, and when they made their own the teacher asked them how many windows they wanted in their house, how many bathrooms, and how many rooms in total. They discussed the layout of the house, which rooms would have windows, and how the rooms were located in the house. The children had to plan, count, use number, and measure to complete the activity.

Conclusion

There are many easy things that teachers can do to encourage the emerging mathematician in every child. Questioning strategies, activities, and simple games offer a great opportunity for teachers to help children construct basic mathematical concepts. An active, stimulating environment and a teacher who is willing to see the child's ability to construct mathematical concepts are invaluable to a child's construction of mathematics.

If we are to view the development of mathematics as emergent, we must understand that construction of mathematical concepts begins the day a child is born. Children construct the basic concepts of mathematics such as quantification, seriation, order, and classification without much interference or direct teaching from adults. The understanding of these concepts is not something that *can* be taught to children; they must construct it for themselves. The role of the teacher is to facilitate learning by offering infants, toddlers, and preschoolers opportunities and materials to promote their construction of mathematical thinking.

References

Chomsky, N. 1999. On the nature, use, and acquisition of language. In *Handbook of child language acquisition*, eds. W.C. Ritchie & T.K. Bhatia, 33–54. San Diego, CA: Academic Press. (Note: This reprinted chapter originally appeared in 1987, Special Issue [11] *Sophia Linguistica*.)

Ferreiro, E., & A. Teberosky. 1982. *Literacy before schooling*. Exeter, NH: Heinemann.

Katz, L.G. 1989. *Engaging children's minds: The project approach*. Norwood, NJ: Ablex.

Kamii, C., & B.A. Lewis. 1990. Research into practice. Constructivist learning and teaching. *Arithmetic teacher* 38 (1): 34–35.

Kamii, C., & others. 1991. Reform in primary mathematics education: A constructivist view. *Educational Horizons* 70 (1): 19–26.

Koechlin, E., S. Dehaene, & J. Mehler. 1997. Numerical transformations in five-month-old human infants. *Mathematical Cognition* 3 (2): 89–104.

Piaget, J., & B. Inhelder. [1964] 1969. *The early growth of logic in the child: Classification and seriation*. New York: Norton.

Sinclair, H., M. Stambak, I. Lezine, & S. Rayna. 1989. *Infants and objects: The creativity of cognitive development*. San Diego, CA: Academic Press.

Starkey, P., & R.G. Cooper, Jr. 1980. Perception of numbers by human infants. *Science* 210 (4473): 1033–35.

Wynn, K. 1995. Origins of numerical knowledge. *Mathematical Cognition* 1 (1): 35–60.

Eugene Geist, Ph.D., is an assistant professor of child and family studies at Ohio University in Athens. His research is focused on understanding how young children develop mathematical concepts and discovering the best ways to facilitate construction of mathematical knowledge in the early childhood years.

Playing With Literacy in Preschool Classrooms

Play-based literacy offers a much-needed reasonable response
to the increasing expectations placed on young children
(and their teachers) for literacy achievement.

Laura Klenk

In the professional literature on emergent literacy, substantial reports support the literacy-enhanced play center as a context in which young children may experiment with emergent writing (Neuman & Roskos, 1990; Schrader, 1989; Vukelich, 1991) and emergent reading and storytelling (Galda, 1984; Martinez, 1993; Martinez, Cheyney, & Teale, 1991; Morrow, 1989). Preschoolers observed by Neuman and Roskos (1990) developed three types of discourse, or talk, about literacy in their print-rich play centers. These children named literacy-related objects, negotiated the meaning of print, and assisted each other in using print to achieve desired outcomes in their play. Children with access to literacy supplies also experiment with writing in their play (Isenberg & Jacob, 1983; Morrow, 1990; Moss, 1986; Schrader, 1989; Vukelich, 1990), and they learn to identify context-specific environmental print in their play centers (Neuman & Roskos, 1990; Vukelich, 1994).

Play-based literacy offers a much needed reasonable response to the increasing expectations placed on young children (and their teachers) for literacy achievement. While these experiences do not hinge on formal instruction, they are authentic and purposeful. In one study of kindergartners playing in their class grocery store (Klenk, in review), the children were observed writing grocery lists, producing orders for depleted stock, and making boldly lettered signs for the shelves. One youngster in the class assumed the role of the store manager, hiring people

and working on a makeshift computer. One day, this "manager" caught an alleged shoplifter in the store and called for help from the police. A third child, a boy identified as developmentally delayed and who resisted every opportunity for writing, was occupied at another play center when he heard the call for help. He became so incensed at the alleged crime that he immediately began writing out a "shoplifting ticket," a laborious process for him. This incident reveals the earnest spirit with which children enter dramatic play and the intense effort it inspires.

In addition to providing rich, authentic opportunities in which to acquire print-related skills, play-based literacy affords teachers a rich context for assessment. Observations of children engaged in play-based learning are often more valuable than those conducted under stressful or unreliable circumstances meant to document student learning, such as standardized tests. As children play with storybooks, dramatizing the plots or orally reenacting a text, teachers can note their comprehension and their use of storybook (or written) language (Sulzby, 1985). Written artifacts can be used to monitor children's understanding of print direction, as well as their emerging understanding of spelling and other written conventions (Temple, Nathan, Temple, & Burris, 1993). All of these observations can become useful entries in a child's school portfolio, as they show authentic use of print and the development of new understandings over time.

Despite the well-documented value of play-based literacy, many preschool teachers are not familiar with developmentally appropriate strategies for enhancing play centers with print. Two such teachers, Cheryl and Cynthia, enrolled in the author's graduate course on literacy acquisition and instruction. These experienced preschool teachers understood the importance of reading storybooks to their young students, and both kept supplies of inviting books available to their students; neither of them, however, had considered just how much the children might learn if their play centers were stocked with a diversity of print material.

During the course of the semester, Cheryl and Cynthia observed their students and reflected on their daily routines. Both saw opportunities to enhance literacy engagement in their classrooms. Cheryl became intrigued with the notion of emergent writing; Cynthia wanted to foster more engagement with storybooks in her classroom as she introduced her students to multicultural literature. In this article, the two teachers share the thoughts and ideas they had as they planned and carried out their semester projects for the graduate course. The children they describe are all identified by pseudonyms.

Cheryl: Until this year, the terms "emergent literacy" and "emergent writing" were completely unfamiliar to me. Since its opening in 1970, the preschool in which I teach has been developmentally appropriate in many ways. There is an emphasis on stories and songs, movement, process-oriented art projects, and encouragement of play. Before last year, however, the only children's writing one might see in the room was their names on papers. Pencils, markers, and paper were generally available only at art time, or by request. Last year, I gathered a box of supplies, including paper of various sizes, stamp pads and stamps, markers, crayons, pencils, and pens, and made it available at least once a week to each class of 3's and 4's. The box always drew several children at a time, and I did notice some writing along with drawing. I viewed it as an "art box," however, and was not particularly looking for writing. More may have occurred than I noticed.

Through my attendance at professional conferences and from my graduate coursework, I began to gather information about placing writing and drawing materials in preschool classrooms. I decided to add open shelves stocked with writing materials, along with envelopes, stickers, old greeting cards, scissors and glue, and individual pocket folders for each child. Although I still did not see 3- and 4-year-olds as "writers," I was eager to explore my role as a facilitator or "modeler" of literacy.

Cynthia: In the past years, I had fallen into the trap of teaching a somewhat "Hallmark curriculum," revolving around holidays, primarily Christian holidays, and how they are celebrated. As I acquired a sensitivity to other cultures, I wanted the children in my program to do the same. At the same time, I became familiar with the process of reading acquisition from an emergent literacy perspective, and I wondered how I could increase the time the 4- and 5-year-old children in my class spent reading books. In my classroom, books were displayed near the circle area, and were available for the children to read after completing art activities, or while waiting for a friend to finish an activity. To encourage children to read at home, we also started a classroom lending library. Several children took advantage of this service regularly, and they even wanted to sign their names on the library list posted outside the classroom door. To encourage even more children to borrow books, I organized a class library in a loft above the housekeeping area, near the book display. It was a cozy setting, furnished with large pillows and a beanbag chair, several books, stuffed animals, and dolls. Because of space limitations, only two children were allowed to be in the library at any time. Unfortunately, I noticed that the children did not frequently visit this classroom library.

During the first two months of school, only 4 of the 19 children in this class used the loft area for reading—the same children who checked out books from the lending library. Very little social interaction took place in the loft, and the children initiated only a few instances of reading-like behavior (such as reading to a toy). On several occasions, at a child's request, my student teacher or I entered the area to read a story. I began to realize that the library in the loft was being used more as a private sanctuary for the children. I understand and recognize the need for young children, especially those in full-day school situations, to find a place to be alone. Nevertheless, I seemed to have missed the mark in trying to create a specific purpose for the loft area. This realization became even more clear to me after the children were exposed to the new library center.

The Beginning Steps

As Cheryl and Cynthia pursued this reflective, self-evaluative process, both became intrigued by researchers whose work addressed their questions and described routines and activities that seemed appropriate for their purposes. In this section, Cheryl and Cynthia describe the initial steps they took to create change in their respective classrooms, as well as some of the sources of information that guided their efforts.

Cheryl: In order to investigate the effects of my acting as a facilitator during play, I wanted to set up at least two sociodramatic play centers. Schrader's (1989) report was especially helpful because it diagrammed and described very simple settings. I decided to enhance the housekeeping center by adding note pads and pencils, Post-it notes, and play money. I also decided to set up a very basic veterinary hospital for the 4-year-olds. Using the piano bench (pulled out perpendicular to the piano) and the closed piano cover, I set out a variety of medical supplies.

These included two small surgical shirts (scrubs), adhesive and gauze, toy medical implements, note pads and pencils, and empty prescription medicine containers.

Cynthia: I knew that I wanted the children's story re-enactments to be spontaneous and creative rather than teacher-directed, so I decided to create a new library and listening center for this project. This "literacy center" was quite different from the library in the loft. I selected a variety of multicultural books, many of which came with an audiotape or record. I added a tape recorder and a record player that the children could operate independently as they followed along with the books. I also gathered brightly colored dress-up clothes, a variety of cloth and stick puppets, a flannel board with story pieces, and a box of musical instruments. To accommodate and encourage the participation of more children, I moved the rocking boat into an open space in front of the new center. Finally, in keeping with the multicultural theme, I added posters of children and adults from a variety of ethnic backgrounds.

Implementation

Cheryl and Cynthia were ready to introduce their young students to these new play-based literacy activities. The children responded enthusiastically in both classes, incorporating their own particular background experiences into new play routines. As they describe the children's engagement in these new play areas—some of whom had been reluctant players up to this point—Cheryl and Cynthia also note the changes in their own participation.

Cheryl: On the first day of my intervention with the 3-year-olds, I entered the housekeeping area armed with notepads, pencils, and a grocery store ad. I sat at the table, opened the ad, and asked, "I need to make a grocery list. What do I need to buy today?" I pointed to words and pictures in the ad, began to name them aloud, and wrote them down. Within seconds, several children had gathered around to watch. As soon as I put down my pencil, they began to make their own lists. I asked the children to read their lists back to me. After I looked in a cookbook for a recipe, Rebecca wrote directions for the chicken noodle soup she was cooking. I used the play telephone to order a pizza, and later Melissa wrote a phone message. All of the writing produced by the children resembled scribble-like forms, but it was all done very seriously and most of the children participated at least briefly.

The next day, I added Post-it^{TM} notes to the writing supplies and reenacted this scene with my class of 4-year-olds. I received curious looks from the children—this was new behavior on my part. Ricky asked, "What are you doing?" I continued making my list. Within minutes, a "writing explosion" began. Interestingly, while the 3-year-old girls had been more interested in writing the day before, the 4-year-old boys now took over the housekeeping area. Many of the children began writing grocery lists. Nicholas

wrote "The store is empty" on a Post-it note and stuck it on a play food stand—which then became a store. Several children wrote prices on food containers. Ricky, a child who preferred outdoor activities and who seldom engaged in imaginative play, was delighted by the Post-its, which he had never used. He made dollar signs on the notes and stuck them on the food stand. He also wrote, "Food, food, food. You love food." Three boys stopped playing with action figures and joined the play. Yellow notes appeared everywhere, and I observed some great symbolic play. I remained available to comment positively on children's writing, to ask them to read what they had written, and to show interest in what they were doing.

The following week, I set up the veterinary center. Anxious to see what type of play and writing would develop, I situated myself at a table with a stuffed dog, telephone, note pad, and paper. Ricky questioned me, "What are you doing with that dog?" Once again, this was new behavior from me—and they noticed. I dialed the phone, spoke to the "vet," and wrote down an appointment time. Immediately, two boys hurried over to say, "I'll be the doctor, I'll be the doctor! Where's the animal hospital?" I took my dog to the piano bench and they came along. I explained that my dog had not been eating and I was worried that he might be sick. The boys immediately began an examination. Then they discovered the gauze and tape. "Is this real?" they asked. A "cut" was noticed and bandaged. I asked for a bill, and for written instructions on how to care for my dog at home. I received a note reminding me to "come back next week." Suddenly, several more animals were in need of medical attention. I stepped back to observe. The children took turns wearing the surgical shirts; several wrote out prescriptions and instructions for the dog's care. The children did not write as much as they had in the housekeeping center, although they did a lot of bandaging.

To maintain interest, I introduced something new into the veterinary center each day, such as a clipboard with paper and a receipt book, which also served as a checkbook and a prescription pad. The day I brought Band-Aids^{TM}, a large number of animals suddenly needed prompt attention. Carla, the doctor on duty at that point, pulled a chair over to the examining table and became busy, quietly writing. Suddenly, the table was crowded with animals. Taking her job seriously, and frustrated with this rush of activity, Carla called out, "Mrs. B., there's too many people needing help!" I suggested she ask them to make an appointment or form a line. She insisted her clients get into a line, which they did. Carla then efficiently examined their pets, writing notes and prescriptions. Meanwhile, I enjoyed listening to the "doctor's" running commentary:

"What do you have here? He gots a ear infection... Next! He has a sore throat... Next!... You know what's the problem? He has growing

Table 1

WRITING SAMPLES PRODUCED IN THE SOCIODRAMATIC PLAY CENTERS IN CHERYL'S CLASS

Writing Strategy (Form)	*Translation of the Writing/Level of Development*
1. One word, copied from environmental print. The 'S' is reversed. "CLOSED"	Sign posted at grocery store: "The store is closed". *Conventional (copied)*
2. Four lines of random letter and number strings. "no 52 n n n 01 2n"	"Grocery list (unspecified items) *Prephonemic*
3. One uppercase letter and number. "M40"	"Food price: "Oatmeal—Forty dollars." *Early phonemic—one salient consonant (M) represents one word*
4. String of random letters using elements of the child's name (Hannah). "hADADQANhoNoOQA"	"Grocery list: chicken and bread *Prephonemic*
5. One 8 1/2" x 11" sheet filled with three lines of tall, bold scribble, wavy, and cursive-like letters.	Veterinary Center: "This is how doctors write." *Prephonemic*
6. Name elements mixed with psuedo-letters, written across several lines. P p b OL L L I 0 0 0	Veterinary Center: "This baby horse is sick, so make sure you come on Wednesday to pick it up." *Prephonemic*
7. Ten lines of cursive-like scribble.	Grocery list: "bread, cereal, milk, candy corn, hot dogs, rolls" *Prephonemic*
8. Short story written with five lines of wavy and cursive-like scribble.	"I like my toys so much I love them. I don't want to give them away. I love them so much, I don't like to tease them (or) they'll get upset." *Prephonemic*
9. List of names of family members written as correctly spelled words; the same list in scribble writing. Bryan MOM DAD Keith LOAKT (Dana)	Family names and family dog's name. *Conventional (known words) Prephonemic*

pains. He's growing up to be a big dog… Everybody, please stay in line!"

At one point, when a new team of doctors had taken over, I noticed small tufts of fur on the floor under the examining table. Cody, Twila, and Kristy had been "prepping" the animals before bandaging their cuts. I knew that, in reality, Twila's dog had undergone surgery recently and had been shaved in the area of the sutures. Although the children assured me they were only cutting off a little fur, I explained that they would have to just pretend to cut the fur, since it would not grow back on these animals.

Cheryl was thrilled with the children's response to the new play contexts. She carefully noted individual children's engagement in the activities, using a stamp and ink pad to date each written piece. Table One describes samples of writing produced by the children in Cheryl's class.

The left column contains information about the visual appearance, or form, of writing produced. These forms can be considered strategies employed by children who have not yet been taught conventional printing, or who have not yet mastered it. Youngsters who have not yet had formal writing instruction rely on their existing knowledge and individual perceptions of writing. For example, several children produced scribbles that mimic the fast, fluent writing of adults. Other children relied on well-rehearsed, known words (such as names of family members), while others used the letters in their own names, not necessarily in order, to signify words and phrases. This strategy can be called using "name elements," and is a common phenomenon in early writing.

Of equal importance, Cheryl began to recognize her own influence as a subtle, yet highly effective model in the children's play. Many early childhood teachers struggle with their own role in children's play, but Cheryl soon discovered that she did not need to play an overt "teacher role." She understood that her mere presence was enough to entice children to participate.

Cheryl: My decision to take on the role of facilitator in two thematic play settings, and to model some functions of writing in those situations, has produced changes that have amazed me. I have seen thematic play sustained for much longer periods than earlier in the year, and play with greater purpose, intensity, and energy. I have seen more cooperative play. I have seen writing activity grow from only one or two children producing a few pieces, to at least two-thirds of the class becoming involved at one time or another. I know much more about the children as writers now: what forms they are using, what principles of writing they understand. I see them as writers, and it seems as though they are beginning to see themselves that way also.

Just as Cheryl was drawn into the writing process by observing her students, and reflecting on her role in these play-based activities. Cynthia continued learning from the children in her class—not only about their growing interest in and development of storybook dramatizations, but also about her own role in the classroom.

Cynthia: I introduced the new library center during a Monday circle time. I explained that I would be reading stories about children and people from different places in the world, and that, if they liked these stories, they could listen to them again in the new center. I encouraged the children to "be the characters" in the story, too, and formally introduced them to all of the new materials. The stories I read in the following weeks included, among others: *Abiyoyo* (Seeger, 1986), *Mama Do You Love Me?* (Joose, 1991), *Mufaro's Beautiful Daughters* (Steptoe, 1987), *On Mother's Lap* (Scott, 1992), *The Story About Ping* (Flack, 1933)—an old favorite—and *Tikki Tikki Tembo* (Mosel, 1992).

As the children began to dramatize the stories they heard me read and that they listened to in the new literacy center, I observed evidence of "narrative competence" (Heath, in Vukelich, 1991). Narrative competence is defined by Heath as "the ability to comprehend and produce characters' actions, motives, goals, and language [that] is consistent with the story line." The story of Ping was repeatedly reenacted. Martin wanted to be the "boat man." Theresa looked for a duck in the puppet basket and found a bird. "This could be the duck," she stated. Garrett, playing nearby, remembered having seen rubber ducks in another classroom; he went off to borrow them for the play. Then Nicky joined the group and all four climbed into the rocking boat, from which one proceeded to fall overboard "just like in the story." Together, the children called for the boat man: "LA LA LA LA LA LAIEE!" Then, they pled with the boat man not to spank Ping for being late! Surely these actors found empathy for the character of this story.

Along with improved narrative competence, I observed more cooperation, sharing, and collaboration as the children dramatized the stories. One day, five of the children joined together for a spontaneous reenactment of *The Little Band* (Sage, 1991). As the illustrations for this story depict children wearing brightly colored outfits, the actors found costumes for themselves in the dress-up basket. They all chose instruments from the available selection, and they asked me to flip the rocking boat over to use as a bridge. They paraded around the classroom, playing to their hearts' content and stopping occasionally to exchange instruments. Other children, playing in different areas of the classroom, waved to the band as it passed by—just as onlookers in a busy town had done in the story.

In another example, the entire class became involved in a dramatization of *Tikki Tikki Tembo*, a story that became the class favorite. This story was being reenacted by a boy and a girl using stick puppets that represented family members of various ethnic groups. Other children sat nearby as the audience, chiming in on the repetitive chant: "Tikki tikki tembo, no sa rembo chari bari ruci pip pari pembo!" Before long, children playing independently throughout the class joined in the chorus. This sense of unity in the room pointed to the children's increased literacy involvement. As the children gained a continued sense of "mastery of the underlying conventions which govern the exchange between author and audience" (Applebee, 1978), they were truly absorbing the messages and values within the story.

It is clear from Cynthia's account that she was able to recognize many areas of student competence and achievement during these playful literacy-based activities. She was able to note instances in which the children employed features of written language—features that many of us take for granted, ignoring the important develop-

Table 2

LANGUAGE, LITERACY, AND LITERARY SKILLS PRACTICED IN DRAMATIC PLAY AND STORYBOOK REENACTMENTS

Language, Literacy, and Literary Skills	*Importance to the Development of Conventional Literacy*
Narrative Competence	Awareness of the *structure* of stories prepares children to anticipate and comprehend stories that are read to them or that they read on their own.
Knowledge of Written Language	Familiarity with storybook (in contrast to conversational) language prepares children to comprehend the special syntax, conventions, and decontextualized nature of conventions of written language.
Vocabulary	The vocabulary of storybooks is often highly descriptive, serving to introduce new words to young listeners. The richer a child's vocabulary, the easier it will be for her/him to decode new words in self-selected reading.
Print Conventions	As children reenact familiar storybooks (sometimes referred to as "pretend reading"), their attention gradually shifts from the illustrations to the text. With appropriate adult modeling and interaction, children begin to recognize such print conventions as spaces between words, punctuation, individual letters, directionality, and spelling.
Literary Perspective	By dramatizing stories, children learn to understand characters' points of view. This insight prepares students to understand stories with more complex characters and plots, and to give critical consideration to multiple interpretations of stories beyond the literal.

mental shifts that are signified by the use of such features. For example, children may begin using dialogue carriers to convey information about who is speaking. Or they may assume the role of different characters, demonstrating their sophistication in understanding multiple points of view. They may begin to incorporate, to a greater extent than before, the syntax of the written language in their favorite storybooks. All of these behaviors represent normal developmental progression for youngsters who are being raised in literacy-rich environments, and their presence indicates that the child should easily acquire conventional literacy skills in kindergarten and 1st grade.

Table Two summarizes language and literacy-related skills that can be developed and observed as children are engaged in the types of storybook reenactments and dramatizations described by Cynthia. This summary is based on the work of Sulzby (1985, 1991), Doake (1985), Martinez (1993), and other scholars whose work illuminates the development of language and literacy in early childhood.

Special Circumstances

Although Cheryl's and Cynthia's experiences, as described to this point, had gone very well, not all of their students responded with equal enthusiasm to these new literacy activities. Here, the teachers describe special circumstances that arose in their classes.

Cheryl: A few children did not join in playing at the veterinary center, but continued with writing in the housekeeping area. Ricky is still not interested in imaginary play, but he spends time at the writing center every day. He wrote several notes to his father, who would go away on business trips; he put these notes in a folder and saved them for his father's return. When his father came in as the parent helper, Ricky proudly handed over all the notes. His father promised they would read them together at home. I have begun to provide information to interested parents on enriching the home literacy environment by explaining what I am trying to do in the classroom. One parent has decided to build some shelves, modeled after our writing center, to hold her daughter's writing and drawing supplies.

Cynthia: At times, reenacting stories took on more of a personal, than a group, meaning. Jamal, a child who did not generally choose to play in the literacy center, was drawn to a dramatic reenactment of *Abiyoyo*. He alternated playing the threatening giant and the father who uses a magic wand to make the giant disappear. As the giant, Jamal pounded a drum with a rhythm stick to create the sound of the giant's approaching footsteps. The drum beats grew louder and faster as the giant danced closer and closer. Then Jamal took another rhythm stick and, switching to the role of the father, waved his "magic wand" to make the giant disappear. Within this literal interpretation of *Abiyoyo*, and emotional component arose for Jamal, who got to sort out his feelings about only seeing his father once a month. Jamal told his classmates about his dad who "lives far away but could still make a giant disappear." Similarly, Lisa was drawn to two Native Alaskan stories about mother-child relationships: *Mama, Do You Love Me?* and *On Mother's Lap*. Lisa, who had a baby brother at home, had been experiencing separation anxiety when her mom dropped her off in the morning.

Teacher Development

Although Cheryl and Cynthia worked independently on their projects, similarities appeared in their work. Both found themselves taking on new roles in the classroom, learning to facilitate reading and writing in ways that were previously unfamiliar to them. Both had taken deliberate measures to introduce new opportunities: Cheryl through "inside intervention"—by entering the play centers and assuming, very subtly, appropriate play roles; Cynthia through "outside" intervention—by introducing new stories, and deliberately and formally sharing with children the new props available for those who wished to "be the characters." Both observed substantial increases in children's engagement in literacy, and both reported evidence of collaboration, cooperation, and sharing. Children in Cheryl's class wrote for a variety of purposes. Children in Cynthia's class found numerous ways to dramatize new stories.

The reading and writing that sprang from the special centers spread to other parts of their classrooms. Both teachers began to consider additional changes they want to make.

Cheryl: I plan to continue modeling various functions of writing, such as story writing, and I want to try more thematic play centers. A visit from a veterinarian or veterinary technician will serve to extend the play in that setting. Barbara Schafer (in Strickland & Morrow, 1989) has

said that one of her goals is for the children in her class to have fun with the written and spoken word. My hope as a teacher-facilitator is that I will be able to encourage the enjoyment of writing I have seen emerge during this project, and that the classroom will become a place of discovery and excitement about literacy.

Cynthia: Martinez, Cheyney, and Teale (1991) describe two types of adult intervention in children's play activities: directive and facilitative. Although I began the new center with a more directive approach, I became more facilitative as time passed. If children asked me to enter their play, I would do so. I supported their efforts and, if asked, responded to their needs. The children heard new stories and were encouraged to listen to the recordings again and again. They had the freedom to use the materials in any way they chose. What I found most striking was that all of the materials were used to reconstruct and dramatize the stories. In fact, when we shared free time with two other classes, my students "taught" children from the other classroom to use the props and materials to reenact stories.

The question I posed at the outset of this project was, "Does a child's participation in story dramatization or reenactment enhance their emergent literacy behaviors?" Based on the examples provided above, I say that the more opportunities children have to reenact and dramatize the stories they have heard, then the greater propensity there is for language and literate behavior. Vygotsky (1978) tells us that children learn higher-order cognitive functions as they internalize social interactions. The types of interactions I observed in the new center never took place in my traditional library area. At first, I wondered if the children would be confused because, under normal circumstances, libraries are quiet places. But I truly wanted these experiences with books to be much more than they had been, and this is exactly what happened. In fact, before starting this project, only a few children had checked out books to take home. Now, all but one of the children have checked out at least one book.

This experience has encouraged me to pause and reevaluate my goals for the children with whom I work. The results I observed far surpassed my expectations. Creating awareness of other cultures was an important focus of this project. The other was watching for examples of literate behaviors that demonstrate the ability to comprehend, recall, and reconstruct stories, along with the cultivation of creativity in play. I saw evidence of this every day. This project has heightened my awareness of my students, as well as my ability to enhance a literature-based program through the use of multicultural books.

Conclusion

The changes created by Cheryl and Cynthia required little expense and effort. Yet these changes resulted in significantly increased levels of literacy engagement for the children in their classrooms. We encourage other early childhood teachers to take stock of the opportunities their students have for engagement in developmentally appropriate literacy learning activities and to make even small changes where necessary. The result will be remarkable development of language and literacy.

References

Applebee, A. N. (1978). *The child's concept of story*. Chicago: The University of Chicago Press.

Doake, D. (1985). Reading-like behavior: Its role in learning to read. In A. Jaggar & M. T. Smith-Burke (Eds.), *Observing the language learner* (pp. 82–98). Newark, DE: International Reading Association.

Galda, L. (1984). Narrative competence: Play, storytelling, and story comprehension. In A. D. Pellegrini & T. D. Yawkey (Eds.), *The development of oral and written language in social contexts* (pp. 105–117). Norwood, NJ: Ablex.

Isenberg, J., & Jacob, G. (1983). Literacy and symbolic play. *Childhood Education, 59*, 272–276.

Klenk, L. (in review). *The effects of play-based writing on kindergarten writing achievement*.

Martinez, M. G. (1993). Motivating dramatic story reenactments. *The Reading Teacher, 46*(8), 682–688.

Martinez, M. G., Cheyney, M., & Teale, W. H. (1991). Classroom literature activities and kindergartners' dramatic story reenactments. In J. F. Christie (Ed.), *Play and early literacy development* (pp. 119–140). Albany, NY: State University of New York Press.

Morrow, L. M. (1989). *Literacy development in the early years: Helping children read and write*. Englewood Cliffs, NJ: Prentice Hall.

Morrow, L. M. (1990). Preparing the classroom environment to promote literacy during play. *Early Childhood Research Quarterly, 5*, 537–554.

Moss, R. K. (1986). Transactions among teachers and children: Teachers' instruction and the writing process of kindergarten children. *English Quarterly, 19*(1), 22–38.

Neuman, S. B., & Roskos, K. (1990). Play, print, and purpose: Enriching play environments for literacy development. *Reading Teacher, 44*(3), 214–21.

Schrader, C. T. (1989). Written language use within the context of young children's symbolic play. *Early Childhood Research Quarterly, 4*(2), 225–44.

Strickland, D., & Morrow, L. M. (1989). *Emerging literacy: Young children learn to read and write*. Newark, DE: International Reading Association.

Sulzby, E. (1985). Children's emergent reading of favorite storybooks: A developmental study. *Reading Research Quarterly, 20*, 458–481.

Sulzby, E. (1991). Assessment of emergent literacy: Storybook reading. *The Reading Teacher, 44*(7), 498–500.

Temple, C., Nathan, R., Temple, F., & Burris, N. A. (1993). *The beginnings of writing*. Boston: Allyn & Bacon.

Vukelich, C. (1990). Where's the paper? Literacy during dramatic play. *Childhood Education, 66*, 205–209.

Vukelich, C. (1991). Materials and modeling: Promoting literacy during play. In J. F. Christie (Ed.), *Play and early literacy development* (pp. 215–231). Albany, NY: State University of New York Press.

Vukelich, C. (1994). Effects of play interventions on young children's knowledge of the functions of writing. *Early Childhood Research Quarterly, 9*, 153–170.

Vygotsky, L. S. (1978). *Mind in society: The development of higher psychological processes*. Cambridge, MA: Harvard University Press.

Children's Books Referenced

Flack, M. (1933). *The story about Ping*. Ill. by K. Wiess. Viking.

Joose, B. (1991). *Mama, do you love me?* Ill. by B. Lavalee. Chronicle.

Sage, J. (1991). *The little band*. Ill. by K. Narahashi. Simon & Schuster.

Scott, A. (1992). *On mother's lap*. Ill. by G. Coalson. Clarion.

Seeger, P. (1986). *Abiyoyo*. Ill. by M. Hays. Simon & Schuster.

Steptoe, J. (1987). *Mufaro's beautiful daughters*. Ill. by author. Lothrop.

Mosel, A. (1992). *Tikki Tikki Tembo*. Ill. by B. Lent. Holt.

Laura Klenk *is Assistant Professor, Reading, The State University of New York, University at Buffalo.*

Note: The author is indebted to Cheryl Beuchi and Cynthia Fofi for their contributions to this article.

SALTING THE OATS: USING INQUIRY-BASED SCIENCE TO ENGAGE LEARNERS AT RISK

Paddy Lynch

In a recent conversation about good writing, my third graders and I agreed that a well-written piece "hooks" us as readers at the beginning and "wows" us in some way at the end. Just as quality literature captivates the reader, quality instruction does the same for the learner by creating an atmosphere of curiosity, presenting challenges and anomalies that pique student interest. Increasingly, though, I find an abundance of children in my class who are hard to "hook" and even harder to "wow."

Teachers and students are under increased pressure to produce test scores that demonstrate at least a year's growth. Students who perform poorly face retention if they don't measure up, so school systems are scrambling for ways to improve student achievement in reading, writing, and math. As a result, a curricular hierarchy is being created that emphasizes the teaching of reading, writing, and math in isolation, and often excludes content area subjects, such as science and social studies. Low-performing students are pulled from their regular classes for one-on-one tutorial sessions, restricting their exposure to group discussions and activities that encourage higher-order thinking skills. In an attempt to "fix" what is "wrong" with at-risk children, are we inadvertently denying them opportunities to demonstrate their potential?

Barbara Means and Michael Knapps (1991) recognized a trend in education to bring at-risk students "up to snuff" academically. However, as they examined how schools attempted to meet the needs of these children, they concluded that "the most widely accepted prescription for compensatory education sought to remedy students' deficiencies by teaching 'the basics' through curricula organized around discrete skills taught in a linear sequence—much like the academic programs these students had previously encountered in their regular classrooms" (Clarizio, Mehrens, & Hapkiewicz, 1994, p. 180). The authors suggested a reshaping of remedial curricula based on the following guidelines:

- Focus on complex, meaningful problems.
- Embed basic skills instruction within the context of more global tasks.
- Make connections with students' out-of-school experiences and cultures.
- Model powerful thinking strategies.
- Encourage multiple approaches to academic tasks.
- Provide scaffolding to enable students to accomplish complex tasks.
- Make dialogue the central medium for teaching and learning.

These six guidelines would eventually provide the framework for the instructional design of my work with at-risk students.

Stepping Out of the Box

I teach in a year-round school where our academic year begins in July, we hold classes for nine weeks, then are off for three-week inter-sessions. Remediation for at-risk students occurs throughout the year during these inter-sessions. In the past, remediation consisted of five, half-day classes that ran concurrently with enrichment classes (open to all students) during the first week of each inter-session. Enrichment classes were designed with lots of hands-on activities and little, if any, pencil-and-paper work. Students who attended enrichment wanted to be there—those who came to remediation often did not. Although remediation teachers typically used games and computer-related activities to reinforce basic skills, the format remained a thinly veiled session of "skill-and-drill." Even changing the name from "remediation" to "mastery" classes didn't fool anyone. It seemed to me that we had fallen into the rut of compensatory education described by Means and Knapp, offering a slightly different version of what the students had failed at in the first place.

Context. That's what was missing in our remediation classes—a context, a purpose for learning. I suspected that the only purpose students might see in attending remediation was to shorten their vacation and reinforce their feeling of academic inadequacy. As a result, not only did these children have academic struggles to overcome, many harbored bad attitudes towards school as well. By creating a context for learning that would "hook" students emotionally and intellectually, I suspected that whatever walls students had built up against learning might begin to crumble. The hook for my remediation classes, I decided, would be science.

I approached my principal with some trepidation because what I had in mind did not target skills in isolation. Instead, I offered to design and teach two sessions of remediation in which reading, writing, and math were imbedded within the context of science. They were tools to be used in learning about something of interest to the children. He conceded that the idea had merit, and gave me permission to implement it for the December and March inter-sessions.

I knew my classes had to begin with lots of materials to manipulate. Not only would concrete activities reinforce scientific concepts, they would be the "hook" to cultivate curiosity and build confidence as well. I felt my remediation students could all be successful with the science process skills upon which these activities were based. Every child would be able to observe, predict, and classify successfully, and with help, they could learn to use numbers, measure, and communicate their findings. Some immediate success was essential for these children in order to create an atmosphere in which they could safety take risks.

As I explored ways in which I could make science come alive for my students, I encountered an article entitled, "Hands-on and First-Hand Experiences in the Context of Reading and Language Arts," by Valerie Bang-Jensen. (Bang-Jensen, 1995). I was intrigued. I had always used the terms "first-hand" and "hands-on" interchangeably. This article helped me see that there was a significant difference. Bang-Jensen believes children must have first-hand experiences with manipulatives—in other words, opportunities to explore, observe, ask questions, and make connections between what they know about the objects at hand and what seems new. Only after that initial experience of "messing around" with materials

would students be prepared for the "hands-on" use of manipulatives—to conduct formal scientific investigations or demonstrate their knowledge of concepts. My students would need time to simply play with materials first before I expected them to use those materials in specific ways.

Putting Faces on the Label "At-Risk"

It is so easy to lump students together under a label like "at-risk." I wanted to resist the temptation to refer to my children as a collective "they," so in order to learn something about each of them, I created surveys to find out how the children perceived themselves as learners, and how their parents and teachers perceived them. The results showed that, as a group, the ten boys and four girls with whom I would work were outgoing, creative, and active children. Reading-related difficulties, such as comprehension of written problems and directions, were the single most significant area of concern. I decided that during the inter-session, frequent discussions and whole-group shared reading would become daily rituals designed to provide the support my children needed to understand content and written directions.

Rock and Roll

Since the weather here in the mountains can be unpredictable in December, I wanted to find a theme that the children and I could explore indoors rather than out. Roller coasters came to mind. We could explore gravity, friction, velocity, and motion, and use cardboard tubes of various sizes to create roller coasters of our own by the end of the week. Thinking back on the six guidelines for revised compensatory curriculum, this theme would allow me to make a connection with the students' out-of-school experiences, since most of them would have ridden on a coaster or at least knew what they were like. Learning about, designing, and then building a roller coaster provided the complex, meaningful problem which lent itself beautifully to integrating reading, writing, and math.

Amazon.com and I became very good friends as I scoured the Internet for resources and ideas that would be appropriate for the class. Signs were plastered all over school pleading for cardboard paper tubes, which soon came pouring in by the bagful. I felt like Templeton the rat from *Charlotte's Web*, scavenging for anything I could get to make my class material-rich and engaging to my students.

For the first 20 minutes of each class, students would have the opportunity to explore six different centers. Each of these contained simple written directions and materials to manipulate that demonstrated concepts with which we would formally experiment later. Students were encouraged to visit all six centers, but were ultimately free to choose where they spent that time first thing in the morning. Sorting cardboard tubes for construction, working with stopwatches, and experiments with friction, gravity, and slope gave students the chance to do something they considered fun and easy. The success students experienced in this "first-hand" time helped put them at ease with themselves and with each other.

As the children began to discover that this remediation class was going to be different, I realized how careful I had to be in introducing the inevitable written tasks related to our topic. Any sign of written work and these kids were ready to bolt. So we talked. We'd experiment a little, then stop and talk. Go back to the experiment, mess around some more, then talk again.

My line of questioning was carefully worded in order to stretch their thinking or challenge them to observe more carefully. "Why do you think...?" "What would happen if...?" "Try that again and see what happens when..." became standard questioning procedure. I understood the need to make dialogue the primary medium for teaching and learning, but I didn't realize how many ways it benefited my students. Not only was it easier for them to talk about what they had done before writing about it, the discussion itself was adding to their knowledge base. With guidance, they were able to create working definitions of newly explored scientific concepts. Having that firm, first-hand foundation made reading about science so much easier for them because they already understood what they were reading about.

Discussion also provided a wonderful opportunity to showcase each student's insights. Instead of looking to me for answers, they began to realize they could learn a great deal from each other. The "smart" kids they depended on in the regular classroom weren't around, so these "at-risk" children became the experts. A "wow" experience if there ever was one!...

Although I believed in the effectiveness of inquiry-based remediation, I wasn't quite sure how it would work, so I planned in excruciating detail for the December session. Lesson plans were revised on a daily basis. As I reflected on that first class, a framework began to emerge that I would use to develop the March session, which focused on water. I came to recognize several crucial elements of successful classroom experiences:

- Daily first-hand experiences with materials we would use to explore scientific concepts
- Whole-group conversations about what students had discovered, then direct instruction to focus student attention on a specific concept
- Individual/small group experiments interspersed with whole-group discussions to share insights and profile student strengths
- Development of working definitions and oral articulation of how things work

- Shared reading of information which underscored the scientific principles students had explored and discussed
- Recording/demonstrating/using what was learned through a variety of tasks involving the written word, drawings, and numbers

A Second Experience

A few balmy days during March allowed us to do some of our activities outside. I filled a 20-gallon tub full of water, and we set about exploring standard liquid measurement. We made it "rain" inside our classroom, created condensation on our windows, explored the three states of matter, then built and acted out the behavior of water molecules in ice, liquid water, and water vapor.

We investigated the stream on our school property, collected samples of the critters who lived there, and graphed the results. No matter what scientific concept we were exploring, we always began with the tactile and the kinesthetic, and then we talked and talked. Only after I believed the students had internalized the concept did we read, write, and do math based on the subject we were studying.

Insights and Observations

"Is it time to go already? Ah, man!"

"This is just like enrichment!"

"Mrs. Lynch, can we do that whole thing again?" In looking back over my revised remediation experience, do I think my students made gains in reading, writing, and math? Absolutely. However, these children are years behind their peers, academically speaking, and anyone who thinks five half-day sessions three times a year will significantly increase test scores is naive. Changes, however, did occur. The content-based, first-hand science program "hooked" these reluctant learners in ways that helped them take academic risks they had previously avoided.

Since I was charged with remediating academic weaknesses in my students, I needed to know if this remediation approach had improved the academic as well as the emotional life of these children. I took notes and some photographs during the course of the week, wrote personal observations in my journal, and tried to step back from the flurry of activity to observe what and how the children were doing. As I sifted through the documentation, questions began to surface. Was there evidence that students were fully engaged in inquiry activities? Were students able to demonstrate their understanding of scientific concepts? Did students demonstrate higher-order thinking? Upon examination of student work and my notes and observations, I could respond with a resounding "yes"! Although there are many examples that demonstrate the successes of my children, the experience of one child in particular stands out. Let me introduce you to Jessica.

Jessica was 20 minutes late to our first class in December. When she entered the room, there was a scowl on her face, and her first words to me after I had greeted her were, "My mom says I don't have to come back if this class is boring!" Fair enough, I thought. She remained aloof and distant from the rest of the class, observant but reluctant to join in. When it came time to write about the day's experiences, she whined that she couldn't think and didn't know what to write.

The next day, Jessica entered the room promptly and more willing to participate than the day before. I could see by the look on her face that she was beginning to enjoy herself. By our third day together, she was really hooked. In her review of the day, she wrote in her learning log, "Scienice is the funiest thing. Scienice is good for your brain." At the end of our first week together, I asked the children to talk about their experiences with this "new" kind of remediation. They immediately compared it to the "fun" enrichment classes that were going on around us, as I had hoped they would. In talking about their successes, Jessica offered, "When you make a mistake, you always learn something. You learn what you did wrong, and then you won't make it again." What incredible insight, coming from a child whose many academic mistakes had landed her in an extra week of school. I only hoped that the confidence reflected in this statement would last.

I didn't see much of Jessica when school began in January because she was not in my regular classroom. But when we came together again in March, the first thing she did was give me a big hug. In her hands, was her new favorite book, *The Big Book of Why*. I heard not a peep of complaint about writing from her this time. Later in the week, I overheard her explaining the results of an experiment to a classmate, using vocabulary we had learned in December. "I'm good at science," she said. The next day, she reported that she had replicated one of our experiments at home. As we worked in our learning logs, Jessica was intent on her task, self-correcting and rereading as she worked. These were "baby steps" to be sure, but for a child for whom any academic task was an obstacle, the progress I saw in Jessica made me proud....

Personal Lessons and Conclusions

Looking back on this wonderful experience with at-risk children, I realized that I was like them in more ways than I cared to admit. Although I was excited about doing something different and hooked on the idea that inquiry-based science could work in remediation, I was afraid of the risk I was taking, of the uncertainty of its outcome, and of the changes I knew I would have to make in myself. By becoming a learner along with my students, I experienced first-hand the insecurity they lived with day after day. I felt as if I were turning my instructional practice inside-out in order to make something fresh from what was old and stale. It was hard work. I had to fight every day to remind myself that process, not product, was the goal, and that change and progress come slowly and in their own time. I learned to look for inspiration and "teachable moments" in the most unlikely places, to be patient, and to look beyond the appearance of a thing to its potential. Just like my students, I had to learn that sometimes even my frustrations could lead to opportunities if I would allow them.

There's an old, familiar expression that says you can lead a horse to water, but you can't make him drink. You can, however, salt his oats. That's what I think science inquiry does for remedial education. It flavors the learning process with an authenticity that is hard for children to resist. It's time-consuming, material-intensive, and messy, but for my third-grade students, it was worth every bit of effort.

Pass the saltshaker again, will you, please?

References

Bang-Jensen, V. (1995). Hands-on and first-hand experiences in the context of reading and language arts. *Language Arts, 72*, 352–358.

Clarizio, H., Mehrens, W., & Hapkiewicz, W. (1994). *Contemporary issues in educational psychology*. Burr Ridge, IL: McGraw-Hill.

Means, B., & Knapp, M. (1991). Cognitive approaches to teaching advanced skills to educationally disadvantaged students. *Phi Delta Kappan, 73*, 282–289.

Paddy Lynch, third-grade teacher, Hendersonville Elementary School, Hendersonville, North Carolina

UNIT 6
Trends

Unit Selections

Key Points to Consider

- Do you know the ABCs of exploring the Internet for early childhood Web sites? How comfortable are you with logging on, clicking around on a Web site, searching for information, participating in a chat room?

- It has been proven that smaller class sizes improve the quality of education for K-3 children. Can you think of any negative consequences of reducing class size?

- In this age of accountability, what five priorities would you choose for allocating funds and staff in K–3 classes?

- What is the problem with the belief that "all children can learn"?

 **Links: www.dushkin.com/online/**
These sites are annotated in the World Wide Web pages.

Awesome Library for Teachers
http://www.neat-schoolhouse.org/teacher.html

EdWeb/Andy Carvin
http://edweb.gsn.org

Future of Children
http://www.futureofchildren.org

National Institute on the Education of At-Risk Students
http://www.ed.gov/offices/OERI/At-Risk/

Prospects: The Congressionally Mandated Study of Educational Growth and Opportunity
http://www.ed.gov/pubs/Prospects/index.html

We begin this unit on trends with a primer on uses of the Internet for the early childhood professional. The first article starts with definitions, such as *bookmark* (a way to store Web site addresses), *listserv* (running dialogue for subscribers), and *icon* (graphic used to represent a link or operation). This professional development report includes a step-by-step guide for accessing the Internet for the first time. It also describes a variety of uses of the Internet in early childhood education, such as shopping for supplies, marketing a program, educating parents, and exploring a professional association Web site.

One trend to watch for across America is the move in some states to reduce class size in primary grades. California has led the way in lowering the number of children in K–3 classrooms, with largely rewarding results. The standardized test scores of these children are slightly better than those of children in larger classes. However, not all results have been positive. "Class-Size Reduction in California" highlights the consequences of statewide legislation and offers advice to other states that are entering into reduction moves.

The cost of class-size reform is high, as are many of the accountability measures that have been enacted by school districts across America. How priorities are set and how resources are allocated—these are the issues discussed in "Putting Money Where It Matters." Every decision made to increase the quality of early childhood education costs money. If schools want to continue making choices based on quality, they must rethink their use of resources. The author of this important policy article leads us to consider five significant ways to realign spending and staffing with quality reforms.

Scientists are changing their assumptions about human learning as they come to understand that the brain is an adaptable organism. The problem is, our theories of educational practice are not changing fast enough to keep up with new information on the way the brain processes information. This is the premise of "Learning to Go With the Grain of the Brain." Passive learning is no longer sufficient. The focus of pedagogy must be on helping children learn-by-doing so they can become masters of a wide range of skills.

"'All Children Can Learn': Facts and Fallacies" is the type of reading that must be done slowly and thoughtfully. The authors offer reasons for their skepticism with the central tenet of the effective schools movement—that children's learning will improve if schools adopt a certain set of effective practices. Their premise is that children in America do not have equal opportunity to learn or succeed. If disadvantaged children do not receive the resource-rich support they need, inequality in the nation's schools will continue. This provocative article deserves a careful read.

Two things are clear: the academic gap between disadvantaged and advantaged children is widening and preschool is unable to close that gap. The nation has excellent federally funded programs such as Even Start and Head Start, in addition to a myriad of state-funded initiatives and a smorgasbord of private programs. However, these efforts do not make up a national system that guarantees equal access and even quality. The author of "Time to Talk of Early Childhood" summarizes several recent

reports that clearly define the standards needed for high-quality preschool across America.

"Early Learning, Later Success: The Abecedarian Study" is a summary of preliminary outcomes of an early childhood educational intervention for poor children. Long-term results of this program are startling. Not only was the children's cognitive development greatly enhanced, enabling them to succeed in school, but they also successfully adapted in adulthood. The most significant policy implication of the study is that high-quality early childhood education improves academic achievement and social adjustment even into early adulthood. The Abecedarian model is a developmentally appropriate, individualized program with particular emphasis on language. It is a prime example of excellence in education.

Of all the issues facing early childhood education and child care today, none is as important as eliminating the barriers to quality. The trend in many states is toward a mediocre level of child care services, coupled with underpreparation and low wages of caregivers. This trend needs to be reversed. We can make an impact by continuing to read, think, and act on behalf of the young children in our care.

DEVELOPMENT

ABC's
of the Internet for
Early Childhood Professionals

BY SUSAN BOWERS, PH.D.

In the last decade, use of the Internet has exploded in all fields including early childhood (A to Z, 1998; Larson, 1998; Osborne, 1998; Rothenberg, 1998). As early childhood professionals, we can use the Internet for many purposes, including communicating with others via chat rooms and list-serves; gaining knowledge through web-pages, libraries, and public/private records; learning about organizations such as NAEYC and NACCP; purchasing supplies; finding curriculum ideas; and looking up journal research. Benefits of the Internet include increased opportunities to connect with other professionals (Hinchliffe, 1996; Stahl, 1999), to find new programming/curriculum ideas, to reach and educate parents (Eder, 1997; Goldstein, 1998), and to be better informed as we work to advocate for children and their families (Andrews & Jordan, 1998; Levy, 1997).

DEFINITIONS

Along with the Internet, there have been a number of new terms introduced. These include *Internet Browser,* which is the software used to look at, or browse, a web page. A *Search Engine* is a tool that helps the user search for particular topics, and an *Internet Service Provider,* ISP, is a company which offers or sells access to the Internet. "When you pay money to an ISP, they provide you with software for your computer and a password so that you can dial into the Internet" (Family Center of Washington County, 2000).

A *link* is "a connection from one location to another" while an *icon* is a "small illustrated image used to represent a link or operation". "An address on the web is called a 'Uniform Resource Locator', or URL". A *bookmark* is "a way to store a website address... so that you do not need to retype it every time you want to open that page" (Family Center of Washington County, 2000).

Person-to-person discussions often occur in a *chat room*. Chat rooms provide a discussion among individuals all logged into the same chat program at the same time. A *listserv* is a running dialogue in which "participants subscribe to a listserv and then receive all e-mail sent to the listserv by any other subscriber of the listserv". "Listservs are organized around topic areas and provide opportunities for sharing... information and in-depth discussions..." (Family Center of Washington County, 2000).

FINDING A PLACE TO LOG ON

If the computer at your worksite does not have Internet access, you still have lots of options. The public library is a great place to start since Internet access is usually free and there are people around to provide assistance. Other options include: your local community college, which may offer classes or seminars; a copy store or copy service center, such as Kinko's; and organizations whose mission is community service like local parks and recreation districts.

Another strategy is to ask your director or supervisor to schedule a tutorial at your workplace. Many individuals are willing to come in and give a session for little or no money.

Finally, be sure to take advantage of sessions at local, state, and national early childhood conferences. These are an excellent source for learning what you need to know, and often offer "hands-on" practice and demonstrations.

STARTING OUT

1. Find a quiet place free from distraction.
2. When you first log on, be sure you have plenty of time (so you won't get frustrated). For example, surfing the web between children's nap and wake-up is probably not a good idea—you won't get very far before you will need to quit.
3. Have someone with you the first couple times, since you might find you have questions you didn't anticipate—even if you have spent a lot of time "watching" other people surf.
4. Write down the sequence you use to log on and off, so you can refer to it the next couple of times.

YOUR FIRST SESSION

The NAEYC webpage is an excellent place to start practicing your Internet skills. You can get there two ways:

1. By typing "http://www.NAEYC.org" in the address window at the top of your search screen. This is usually a light-colored horizontal window that allows you to enter addresses (URL's). You usually have to click it to use the cursor there.
2. Or, by entering "National Association for the Education of Young Children" in a key word search.

A FUN TREASURE HUNT

Below is a short "treasure hunt" to get you started on the NAEYC page (skip ahead if you are an experienced user):

FIND 1: Accredited centers in your area

To find accredited centers in your area, use your mouse to click "parents" on the index running along the left side of the NAEYC homepage. This should bring up a new page designed for parents of young children. On the new page, one of the choices will be "find an accredited center". Use your mouse to click this option. Next, you should get a screen with an option "find programs". Use your mouse to click this option. This should present you with a template for entering information. Use your mouse to click the first and subsequent lines of the city/state in which you live. One mouse click gets you "in" to the template box in order to enter your information. When you have finished entering the information, click "start searching". Shortly, you should get a list of accredited early childhood programs in your area.

FIND 2: Neat things to buy

To find official NAEYC items, return to the NAEYC homepage. You can do this by clicking the "return home" box on the top of the left index bar, or by clicking back on the horizontal toolbar to retrace your previous steps. To find NAEYC merchandise, click "Week of the Young Child" (WOYC) on the index running down the left of the NAEYC homepage. Occasionally, you will need to scroll down to read the rest of a page. Scroll by clicking the vertical bar on the right side of the screen and dragging the graphic down along the edge of the screen. When you have reached WOYC, use your mouse to click "Week of the Young Child Resources". This should present you with an array of NAEYC merchandise, such as scarves and totebags.

FIND 3: Different websites with a place to "play"

Leave the NAEYC website by typing in a new URL in the box running horizontally across your toolbar, or by clicking "search" on your toolbar and entering a term. A fun place to go is "www.pbs.org," a site which offers an array of information based on PBS shows. Visit Mr. Rogers by using the mouse to click "PBS Kids," which leads you to "Mr. Rogers' Neighborhood". By clicking "house," you can take a tour of Mr. Rogers' house.

SHORTCUTS

1. Find a site which has links to other sites and use these.

2. Play with the options available on your machine. These include buttons across the toolbar at the top of the screen, such as "stop," which will halt your search.

3. Make effective use of bookmarks. Bookmarks, or "favorites" can usually be added/deleted through the toolbar.

4. Remember there's great diversity in the speed of computers. Experiment among the computers available to you or in your community until you find one that can search relatively quickly.

LATER SESSIONS

If you're an experienced user and a member of NAEYC, try logging on to the website as a member. To do this, you'll enter your name, etc. and be sent information for gaining access as a member. This will lead you to information provided only to NAEYC members. Similarly, other sites have information accessible only to "members" or "registered users". In general, visit a site first and become familiar with your computer and software before logging on as a user, as the registration process can sometimes be complicated.

In addition, learn to anticipate whether or not a site is going to be helpful to you. As one author put it, "The bounty of math and science resources available on the Internet can make you feel like you're driving in circles on the Information Highway" (Lindroth, 1996, p. 78). After you're an experienced user, you'll probably find you are drawn to certain kinds of sites, or that you like the kinds of information you can get from a particular source. Some sites, such as Earlychildhood.com are continuously updated and provide a variety of services, including discussion boards and job listings.

RECOMMENDED SITES FOR EARLY CHILDHOOD EDUCATORS

http://www.nncc.org
National Network for Child Care, sponsored by Cooperative Extension. Includes information for child care providers and others. This site also has informational clips and curriculum ideas presented by extension specialists across the nation.

http://zerotothree.org/
Homepage of Zero-to-Three, a national non-profit organization which seeks to "advance the healthy development of babies and young children." Offers information on child development, developmental activities, and a bookstore. Also includes a page specifically for professionals.

http://www.iamyourchild.org/
"I Am Your Child" is a national public awareness campaign about young children. Includes resource materials to share with parents, and national initiatives in early child development.

http://childrensdefense.org
Homepage for the Children's Defense Fund. Offers information on child law and policy, and serves as a center for children's issues.

http://www.nsaca.org/
National School-age Care Alliance. Offers information and resources for providers of before- and after-school care.

http://www.nafcc.org/
National Association for Family Child Care. Offers support and information for family care providers.

http://nrc.uchsc.edu/
Homepage of National Resource Center for Health and Safety in Child Care. Includes links to information about health and safety, including childhood diseases, and food preparation.

http://www.project-approach.com/
Homepage for the project approach, sponsored by Sylvia Chard. Describes the project approach and gives examples.

http://www.state.vt.us/srs/fcwc/frameset2.html
The Family Center of Washington County (VT) and the Vermont Department of Social and Rehabilitation services sponsor a computer tutorial for early childhood providers. The tutorial describes how to send email, join a listserv, participate in a chat room, and search the Internet.

http://www.earlychildhood.com
Earlychildhood.com offers articles, tips, and curriculum ideas for early childhood professionals; discussion/sharing boards; child care information for parents; classified advertisements; shopping; and links to other early childhood sites.

http://www.ParentSoup.com
This parenting site offers advice, chat rooms, and opinions by experts on a wide range of topics.

http://www.crayola.com
The Crayola website includes activities, ideas for art projects and information for children, educators, and parents.

http://dole5aday.com/
The website for the Dole Food Company is a fun resource for children and adults to learn about nutrition.

USES FOR THE INTERNET

Shopping for Supplies on the Net

One of the main advantages of purchasing items through the Internet is the ability to shop around. Visit several sites and compare prices, and look for bargains and special promotions. When pricing the item, be sure to add in shipping and tax. Often, it is helpful to read the details of the pricing carefully, and write them down or print for future reference.

Another good idea is to preview products on publishers' websites. This is particularly good for software purchases, as you can often access clips of them prior to purchasing (Haugland, 1997).

Finally, be careful when providing personal information, such as credit cards and names/addresses/statistics of your employees or co-workers. Check or ask to see what kind of security is offered on the computer you're using. Some worksites block information from coming in or going out. Be sure to look for disclaimers and notices on the site itself regarding the privacy of your information.

MARKETING YOUR PROGRAM THROUGH A WEBPAGE

Making a webpage is a great and fun way to learn about the Internet. For the most part, you will need a class or at least a more experienced partner to get started on your site. Elements to consider when designing a webpage include design, accessibility, and ease of use. There is an expanding body of research on what makes a user-friendly site, including the adaptability of the site for individuals with special needs (e.g., visually impaired, color blind).

When marketing your program, consider including phone numbers, which allows prospective parents to reach you if email fails. Other key points include asking for and security permission before posting photographs, particularly of children, and adding a counter to record the number of visitors to your webpage.

EDUCATING PARENTS

Haugland (1997) suggests early childhood professionals can provide leadership for families who are new to computers. There are five areas in which families may need our guidance. These include: 1) Finding software; 2) Deciding how long and how often children should use the computer; 3)

Finding and accessing helpful websites; 4) Finding "good" ways to use the computer; and 5) Deciding how and when children should be supervised (Haugland, 1997; Magid, 1996). Of these, Haugland (1997) stresses an important role is introducing parents to the concept of developmentally appropriate software [software which "matches children's current level of understanding and skills" (p. 133)]. Haugland suggests it is important to emphasize to parents that quality of the products is more important than the quantity of products they own. "Typically, a home library is a combination of one or two programs children like best from school and the remainder are different products which stimulate thinking" (p. 133).

In addition, we can lead families to use the Internet for meaningful interaction. Suggestions include family projects, such as recording events through a webpage (which is something like an electronic scrapbook), and/or planning a vacation (Haugland, 1997). As early childhood professionals, we can insert computer activities such as these in our regular newsletters and/or bulletin board displays, and model such projects in our own classrooms (e.g., Kristovich, Hertzog & Klein, 1998; Wright, 1998).

CONCLUSION

As early childhood professionals, we can use the Internet for many purposes including communicating with others, gaining knowledge, learning about organizations, purchasing supplies, finding curriculum ideas, and looking up journal research. By trying the sites listed here, and adding in some of your own, you are already well traveled on the information super-highway!

REFERENCES

A to Z: The early childhood educator's guide to the Internet (Revised). (1998). (ERIC Document Reproduction Service No. ED 433 141).

Andrews, J. & Jordan, D. (1998). Multimedia stories for deaf children. *Teaching Exceptional Children*, 30(5), 28–33.

Eder, S. (1997). Marketing a resource and referral resource room to child care providers and parents. (ERIC Document Reproduction Service No. ED 409 997).

Family Center of Washington County, VT. Creating on-line linkages in the early childhood community throughout

Vermont. Accessed: July 29, 2000 www.state.vt.us/srs/fcwc/glossary.html.

Goldstein, A. (1998). Child care consumer education on the internet. (ERIC Document Reproduction Service No. ED 425 866).

Haugland, S. (1997). Children's home computer use: An opportunity for parent/teacher collaboration. *Early Childhood Education Journal*, 25(2), 133–135.

Hinchliffe, L. (1996). Helping early childhood teacher education students learn about the Internet. (ERIC Document Reproduction Service No. ED 395 714).

Kristovich, S., Hertzog, N. & Klein, M. (1998). Connecting families through innovative technology in an early childhood gifted program. (ERIC Document Reproduction Service No. ED 425 019).

Larson, J. (1998). Making connections: Navigate the Internet for early childhood sites. *Texas Child Care*, 21(4), 16–21.

Levy, A. (1997). Culture in the classroom. *Early Childhood News*, 9(1), 28–30.

Lindroth, L. (1996). Internet connections. *Teaching Prek–8*, 26(4), 78–79.

Magid, L. (1996). Protecting your child on the information highway: What parents need to know. *Montessori Life*, 8(1), 26.

Osborne, J. (1998). Internet basics for early childhood educators. *Dimensions of Early Childhood*, 26(1), 5–8.

Rothenberg, D. (1998). Early childhood education in a technological age. (ERIC Document Reproduction Service No. ED 425 842).

Stahl, S. (1999). Developing Internet communication and peer support in a statewide child care community for participants in a child development associate (CDA) training program. (ERIC Document Reproduction Service No. ED 430 693).

Wright, J. (1998). A new look at integrating technology into the curriculum. *Early Childhood Education Journal*, 26(2), 107–109.

Susan Bowers, Ph.D., is a professor of early childhood studies at Northern Illinois University, and a child care consultant in the Chicago area. She has experience as a preschool teacher and director, as a parent counselor for child care resource and referral, and as a researcher in medical diagnostic settings.

Class-Size Reduction In California

A Story of Hope, Promise, and Unintended Consequences

The overall impact of class-size reduction in California will not be known for a few more years. Nevertheless, much has been learned in the first three years that can inform the national conversation on the topic, the authors point out.

BY BRIAN STECHER, GEORGE BOHRNSTEDT, MICHAEL KIRST, JOAN McROBIE, AND TRISH WILLIAMS

IN JULY 1996, the California legislature passed S.B. 1777, an education reform initiative that committed more than $1 billion a year to a class-size reduction (CSR) program of unprecedented magnitude. The measure—though voluntary—provided a powerful financial incentive for school districts to reduce the number of students in K-3 classes. This financial incentive, coupled with strong public support, catalyzed school districts to implement CSR with astonishing speed. By the time students started school in the fall of 1996—just six weeks after the measure's passage—the vast majority of California's school districts had already begun to shrink their first-grade classes from a statewide average of nearly 30 students to a new maximum of 20. By the end of the third year, 98.5% of eligible school districts and 92% of eligible K-3 students were participating in CSR.

Shortly after S.B. 1777 was signed into law, representatives from a group of research and policy organizations in California met to discuss the importance of planning for an evaluation of the new law's impact. This group, called the CSR Research Consortium, was headed by the American Institutes for Research (AIR) and RAND; it also included Policy Analysis for California Education (PACE), WestEd, and EdSource. The authors of this article are the leaders of the CSR Research Consortium, but many other researchers from the five institutions contributed directly to the project.[1]

The speed and enthusiasm with which California implemented CSR underscored a shared optimism on the part of legislators, educators, and parents that smaller classes would quickly improve the quality of education and lead the state's K-3 students to achieve higher scores on standardized tests. To some extent, this optimism has been rewarded: evaluations after the second and third years of CSR in California confirm that students enrolled in smaller classes do perform slightly better on standardized tests than students in larger classes. Educators hope these gains will increase as the program matures and students have longer exposure to smaller classes.

However, these small gains have had large costs. Indeed, class-size reform in California has had a profound unantici-pated consequence: in its first three years, CSR exacerbated existing inequities within the state's education system. The teacher work force increased by 38% in just two years, causing a drop in teacher qualifications that disproportionately affected school districts already struggling with overcrowding, poverty, and language barriers. The overall costs to implement CSR were also considerably higher for these school districts.

To be sure, the program is young, and its full effects—positive and negative—may not be realized for several more years. However, as class-size reduction programs gain momentum across the nation, educators and legislators would be well advised to learn from California's experience and keep equity foremost in their minds when planning their own programs. This article reviews the history and status of CSR in California, reports results from comprehensive evaluations of the program's first three years, and derives a short set of lessons from the state's experience. These lessons are intended to help inform the debate about class size in other states and in the nation as a whole.

Class-Size Reduction in the U.S.

The strong political support for CSR in California was based on the belief that reducing class size would produce significant improvement in student achievement. This belief, in turn, was based on the positive results of a class-size reduction experiment in Tennessee, the Student/Teacher Achievement Ratio, or STAR, program. Students who participated in reduced-size classes in the STAR program during the primary grades made statistically significant achievement gains in all subject areas tested. The achievement gains were equal for boys and girls. Also important from the perspective of some California legislators, the achievement gains were largest for minority students and students attending inner-city schools.[2]

STAR's success has inspired many states and the federal government to support policies to cut the size of primary-grade classes. In addition to California and Tennessee, Indiana, Nevada, North Carolina, Texas, Virginia, and Wisconsin have implemented class-size reduction initiatives. At least 18 other states are also reported to be involved in or considering some type of class-size reduction program.[3]

The federal government is also investing heavily in class-size reduction. In fiscal year 1999, Congress appropriated $1.2 billion to help school districts hire new teachers in order to drive down the size of primary-grade classes to 18 students or fewer. Congress appropriated an additional $1.3 billion for class-size reduction in fiscal year 2000. Federal class-size reduction assistance is targeted to districts with the highest concentrations of children in poverty as well as to those with the highest overall enrollments. Consequently, large urban school districts have received a significant portion of the federal funds. Within these districts, funds to hire teachers are generally targeted to schools with the greatest need or with the largest classes. The federal policy was designed specifically to avoid creating further inequity in the education system.[4]

Enacting CSR in California

By 1996 a 10-year decline in student achievement in California had reached the point of alarm—classrooms were overcrowded as a result of a 12% increase in K-12 enrollment over the previous five years; qualified teachers were in short supply; and minority students, low-income students, and those whose native language was not English (designated "EL" for "English Learner" students) were falling steadily behind. Public confidence in the state's education system was further eroded by the results of the 1994 National Assessment of Educational Progress (NAEP) reading assessment, in which California's fourth-graders tied for last place out of the 39 participating states.

At the same time, the California economy was booming, and the legislature found itself with a rare budget surplus. Because state law requires that a fixed percentage of surplus revenues be spent on the public schools, the legislature had substantial funds to invest to reverse the educational decline. Then-Gov. Pete Wilson and the legislature agreed to spend up to $1.5 billion a year to reduce K-3 class size. CSR is a voluntary program, but it provides an almost irresistible financial incentive for school districts to participate. In 1996–97, the first year of the program, districts were reimbursed a flat rate of $650 for each child in a reduced-size class. In 1997–98, the per-student rate was raised to $800, and it was increased to $832 for the third year of the program. During the first year of the program, the state also provided $200 million to help overcrowded school districts install portable classrooms (up to $25,000 per classroom), and in the second year it reallocated any "unused" CSR funds for additional facilities grants.

Although California's confidence in class-size reduction was based in large measure on Tennessee's STAR program, CSR and STAR are vastly different programs. STAR was a controlled experiment, albeit a large one involving more than 12,000 students during the course of its four-year intervention. CSR, by contrast, is a statewide program, not a controlled experiment. It is also being implemented on a vastly larger scale—1.8 million California K-3 students were in reduced classes by the end of the initiative's third year. The scale of CSR reform posed unique problems. In particular, many California schools confronted a profound shortage of qualified teachers and adequate teaching facilities. By contrast, all the teachers in the Tennessee experiment were fully qualified. In addition, the curriculum in Tennessee was standardized, while California's curriculum standards were still in development when CSR was implemented. Furthermore, California is culturally diverse in ways that Tennessee is not. While nearly all students in the Tennessee experiment spoke English, almost one-third of California's students live in households in which primarily other languages are spoken.

From its earliest meetings, the CSR Consortium agreed that the evaluation of California's program needed to be comprehensive. The group proposed to consider the effect of reduced class size on student achievement, but it also resolved to examine the impact of the reform on all aspects of the education system. The Consortium believed—correctly, as it turns out—that some of the most important effects of CSR might not relate directly to student achievement.

Effects of CSR: Anticipated Gains and Unanticipated Losses

The Consortium has now completed two evaluations of California's CSR reform, the first covering the first two years of the program (1996–97 and 1997–98), and the second covering the third year (1998–99).[5] The data suggest that CSR is having positive effects on parent attitudes and student achievement. However, the gains to date have come at a substantial cost in terms of equity. School districts serving most of the state's historically disadvantaged students—those who are minorities, those from low-income families, and EL students—have received fewer benefits and may even have been hurt by CSR. These districts found it more expensive to implement CSR, they saw a disproportionate decline in their average teacher qualifications, and they were forced to take more facilities and resources from other programs to create additional classroom space.

Winners and losers in the race to implement CSR. As mentioned above, California's CSR program was implemented very quickly. However, not all school districts were positioned to respond with equal speed. Urban districts—which have high percentages of low-income, minority, and EL students—were significantly slower to implement CSR than suburban and rural districts. Schools in urban districts were already dealing with shortages of space, teachers, and financial resources, all of which contributed to delays in implementing the program. CSR exacerbated these problems. Because funding was linked to the speed of implementation, districts that were slower to reduce class size received proportionally less CSR revenue from the state.

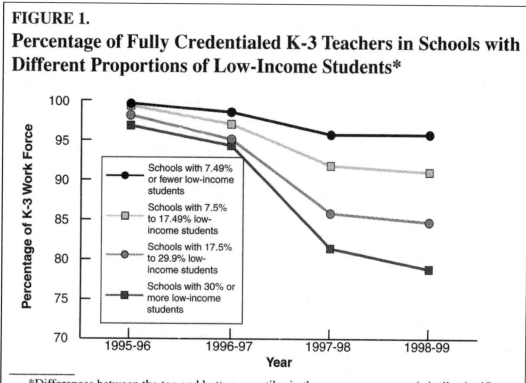

FIGURE 1.

Percentage of Fully Credentialed K-3 Teachers in Schools with Different Proportions of Low-Income Students*

*Differences between the top and bottom quartiles in the same years are statistically significant at the .01 level.

Source: CSR Research Consortium analysis of California Department of Education, CBEDS-PAIF (California Basic Educational Data System-Professional Assignment Information Form) data.

While all districts earned the same amount of revenue for each student in a reduced-size class, districts with smaller classes and more available space prior to CSR needed fewer new teachers and less additional space to implement it, so their overall costs were lower. In the first year of CSR, a majority of superintendents in the state reported that CSR funds were inadequate to cover the cost of implementation. Even after per-pupil funding was increased, more than 40% of superintendents still reported fiscal shortfalls. Districts serving the greatest number of low-income, minority, or EL students were more likely than others to report that the cost to implement CSR was greater than the revenues generated by the initiative. Districts also found that the cost of installing portable classrooms was usually greater than the allocation provided by the state.

Small gains in test scores, individual instruction, and parent/teacher communication. Data from the first three years of CSR do provide some cause for optimism. Test scores have improved for students in smaller classes, teachers say that they are spending more time teaching students and less time disciplining them,

and parents and teachers report having more contact with one another. It is possible that these positive results will increase as CSR matures and teachers learn how best to take advantage of smaller classes, thereby further increasing student achievement.

Third-grade students enrolled in reduced-size classes performed better on the Stanford Achievement Test (SAT-9) than did students in regular classes. This was true both after the second year of CSR, when third-grade students had little or no prior exposure to reduced classes, and after the third year, when third-grade students had been in smaller classes for one or two years. These small achievement gains persisted after students moved to larger fourth-grade classes. However, unlike the case of Tennessee, achievement gains were similar among all students in reduced-size classes, regardless of their family income, fluency in English, or minority status. In other words, there is no evidence that class-size reduction in California is serving, as it did in Tennessee, to close the achievement gap between poor, minority children and others. Furthermore, the test-score improvements made by California students were only a fraction of those

achieved by students in Tennessee's STAR program.

However, teachers of reduced-size classes were optimistic about the effects of CSR in their classrooms. They reported devoting more time to instructing small groups and to working with individual students on mathematics and language arts lessons than did teachers whose classes were not reduced in size. They also provided comparatively more extended attention to poor readers, and they were more positive about their ability to assess and meet student needs and to provide students with quick feedback and individual attention. Teachers of reduced-size classes also reported spending less time disciplining disruptive students. Still, classroom instruction in small classes was generally no different from that in larger classes; regardless of class size, teachers covered about the same number of mathematics and language arts topics, devoted about the same amount of time to each major curriculum element, and used similar teaching strategies.

Parents of children in reduced-size classes echoed the teachers' optimism. These parents rated all aspects of educational quality higher than did parents of children in non-reduced-size classes. Parents of students in smaller classes also reported having more contact with teachers and higher overall satisfaction with schools.

Unanticipated consequences for the most vulnerable districts. CSR's negative effects are more dramatic than its modest gains, and school districts that were already struggling have been hit the hardest. The most devastating consequences have been sharp declines in the average educational level, experience, and credentials of teachers. CSR caused the K-3 teacher work force to grow by at least 25,000 during its first three years, forcing school districts to compete for qualified teachers not only with one another but also with other sectors in the booming state economy. Consequently, a smaller proportion of California's current K-3 teachers have full credentials, education beyond a bachelor's degree, or three or more years' teaching experience.

More disturbing, the decline in teacher qualifications has been greater for elementary schools serving minority, low-income, or EL students. As Figure 1 shows, elementary schools serving the fewest low-income students saw the proportion of fully credentialed K-3 teachers drop 2% from 1995–96 to 1998–99, while schools serving the most low-income students experienced a 16% drop. In the third year of California's CSR program, the rapid decrease in qualified teachers slowed for schools with fewer low-income students but continued for schools with more low-income students. Although better-qualified teachers are not automatically more effective—some teachers on emergency permits may be very hard-working and creative and may produce higher achievement among their students—the uneven distribution of teacher qualifications is hard to justify on any ground.

The speed and scope of CSR implementation challenged district and school administrators to balance existing needs with new demands. Prior to CSR implementation, a small percentage of schools were already taking space that had been dedicated to other activities and converting it to classroom space. This intensified with the implementation of CSR. By 1997–98, more than one-quarter of schools had taken space away from special education, childcare, and music and art programs, and more than one-fifth had converted library space and computer labs. Because schools serving higher proportions of low-income, minority, and EL students were experienc-

ing overcrowding and facility constraints prior to the CSR reforms, those schools suffered a disproportionate blow as they scrambled to find space in which to house new, smaller classes.

CSR also affected the education of special-needs and EL students. As the CSR program grew, many teachers switched from teaching these two groups of students to teaching in regular K-3 classes; in 1997–98 alone, about 1,000 teachers moved out of these programs and into general education classes. Although the proportion of teachers certified to work with bilingual students has increased since CSR began, schools serving more EL students have received proportionately fewer of these specially trained teachers.

Interpreting the Results: Lessons for the Nation

California's CSR program is still young. The small achievement gains evident during the program's first three years may increase as students spend more time in smaller classes and as new teachers gain more experience. No other state has implemented a class-size reduction reform on this scale, and statewide gains—even small ones—are cause for optimism. Additional time and experience are needed before the cumulative effects of reduced-size classes can be measured and a reasonable standard of success established.

Teachers in reduced-size classes did not vastly alter their teaching.

However, other states hoping to implement class-size reduction can learn from California's experience, particularly from the unanticipated consequences of CSR. The overarching lesson is this: when planning for class-size reduction, policy makers and their education advisors should keep a keen eye on the issue of maintaining equity within the education system. Administrators, superintendents, teachers, and other educators should also consider three additional lessons to help maximize the benefits of CSR: the first is aimed at formulating effective policies, the second at improving teaching strategies, and the

third at ensuring that there will be enough qualified teachers.

1. *Design a more thoughtful policy.* As discussed above, several elements of California's CSR reform contributed to its unanticipated consequences. In their race to implement CSR, state legislators unwittingly rewarded the school districts that could implement it fastest—those that were already among the most advantaged. Other states could avoid this pitfall by designing programs that begin slowly. An ideal program would build enough time into the planning process to adequately assess the capacity of schools statewide to increase classroom space. In California, large urban school districts not only received a smaller proportion of state funds for CSR because they found implementation difficult, but they also ended up with the largest proportion of unqualified teachers. In retrospect, the program would have had a more equitable effect if it had

- relied on a cost-based formula for allocating funds,
- targeted funds first to districts with the neediest students,
- included a long-range plan for helping school districts cope with facilities shortages, and
- been rolled out with a staged and controlled implementation.

2. *Learn how to get the most out of smaller classes.* While there is a strong perception that more learning goes on in smaller classrooms, little is known about why smaller classes might be better learning environments. Teachers in California's reduced-size classes did not dramatically alter their teaching strategies or the amount of content they covered, although they did spend more individual time with students, including individual conferences of five minutes or more with students who were having reading problems. Teachers in reduced-size classes also spent less time managing disruptive behavior. Our study design did not link teachers with students; thus we were unable to determine directly if the teacher behaviors we observed corresponded to higher achievement for a teacher's own students. Educators and researchers need to learn more about why class-size reduction works in order to maximize the benefits of this reform through targeted staff development and teacher training. Currently, teachers in smaller classes have an unprecedented opportunity to develop more effective classroom prac-

tices and to contribute to the research base on this subject. Researchers need to continue to develop a theoretical perspective that may help to explain the classroom processes that uniquely apply in smaller classes and affect student achievement.

3. *Attend to issues of teacher supply and teacher professional development.* Before class-size reform begins, states should think about how implementation will change the balance of teacher supply and demand. The key questions are how many additional teachers will be needed to cover reduced-size classes and what is the capacity of the state's higher education institutions to train new teachers. Although most states have a reserve supply of credentialed teachers who are not currently working in schools, California found that its CSR program quickly exhausted this supply. A more thoughtful policy would estimate changes in the demand for teachers and take actions to increase the supply before shortfalls occur. Teacher-training institutions can increase their capacity to prepare new teachers to match the anticipated increase in demand created by CSR. States might also consider reforming their credentialing requirements to create alternative paths to certification for experienced professionals from other fields. In addition, incentive programs can be created to help recruit and retain effective teachers for underperforming schools to counteract the inequities in teacher qualifications that occurred in California.

In addition, administrators at the school, district, and state levels should develop programs to help new and inexperienced teachers succeed. There is a need for more mentoring programs aimed at helping new teachers deal with day-to-day problems, as well as formal workshops designed to broaden their general knowledge

about teaching. Universities will also be called on to provide new forms of training and support to help class-size reduction programs work. The most successful inservice training programs in California are those that provide immediate, problem-specific, and personal support on a continuing basis.

The overall impact of CSR in California will not be known for a few more years. Nevertheless, much has been learned in the first three years that can inform the national conversation about class-size reduction. In fact, early results from the CSR Consortium's evaluation in California played an important role in crafting the federal class- size reduction policy that is currently in effect. Other states can learn from the California experience, as well. Smaller classes do seem to have positive effects on student achievement, and they definitely increase the amount of individual contact between students and teachers. In these ways, CSR has the potential to improve education. Yet the reform also places large demands on schools for extra facilities and additional staff. Unless great care is taken to design and implement CSR reforms thoughtfully, these added demands can fall unevenly on rich and poor districts, leading to greater inequities and undermining the reform's potential.

Notes

1. Contributors to the research include Dominic Brewer, Elizabeth Burr, Delia Burroughs, Lisa Carlos, Tammi Chun, Eric Derghazarian, Marian Eaton, Gerald Hayward, Mette Huberman, Tessa Kaganoff, Victor Kuo, Roger Levine, Daniel McCaffrey, Tor Ormseth, Thomas Parrish, Robert Reichardt, Cathleen Stasz, Carol Studier, Jackie Teague, George Vernez, and Edward Wiley. Rachel Hart was instrumental in the development of this article.

2. Jeremy Finn and Charles Achilles, "Tennessee's Class Size Study: Findings, Implications, Misconceptions," *Educational Evaluation and Policy Analysis*, vol. 21, 1999, pp. 97–109.

3. Class-Size Reduction Program home page, U.S. Department of Education, www.ed.gov/offices/OESE/ClassSize/index.html.

4. U.S. Department of Education, "The Class-Size Reduction Program: Boosting Student Achievement in Schools Across the Nation," September 2000, available online at www.ed.gov/offices/OESE/ClassSize/reports.html.

5. George Bohrnstedt and Brian Stecher, eds., *Class Size Reduction in California: Early Evaluation Findings, 1996–1998* (Sacramento: California Department of Education, 1999); and Brian Stecher and George Bohrnstedt, eds., *Class Size Reduction in California: The 1998–1999 Evaluation Findings* (Sacramento: California Department of Education, 2000).

BRIAN STECHER is senior social scientist at the RAND Corporation, Santa Monica, Calif.; GEORGE BOHRNSTEDT is senior vice president for research at the American Institutes for Research, Palo Alto, Calif.; MICHAEL KIRST is a professor of education at Stanford University, Stanford, Calif.; JOAN McROBBIE is senior policy associate at WestEd, San Francisco; and TRISH WILLIAMS is executive director of EdSource, Palo Alto.

Putting Money Where It Matters

In this age of accountability, school and district leaders must set priorities and make tough decisions about how they allocate funds and staff.

Karen Hawley Miles

The focus in the United States on creating accountable, standards-based education is pushing districts and schools to more clearly define their goals and priorities for student learning. Districts and states make headlines with bold proclamations about the importance of academic achievement for all students. But the gap between rhetoric and reality threatens hopes for improvement. While teachers scramble to help students meet more ambitious academic targets, school and district spending patterns and organization structures have changed little in the past three decades (Miles, 1997a). No matter what school leaders and communities say is important, the way schools and districts use their dollars, organize their staff, and structure their time dictates the results.

> **While teachers scramble to help students meet more ambitious academic targets, school and district spending patterns and organization structures have changed little.**

As public institutions, schools and districts try to do everything for everyone—and do it all without making enemies. New dollars come to schools in small increments over time usu-

ally tied to specific purposes. We add new priorities and programs on top of the old. Instead of restructuring and integrating school and district organizations, we create specialties and departments to meet newly defined needs. Schools and districts now spend significantly more to educate each pupil than ever before (Snyder & Hoffman, 1999). Taking advantage of these resources to meet higher academic standards requires a political will and singleness of purpose that is difficult to sustain in public schools. Such action also demands an attention to organizational and budget details that does not come naturally to many educators and policymakers.

> **If the district declares that all students will read by 3rd grade, then staff, dollars, and time should support more effective literacy teaching.**

If we hope to meet our seemingly unreachable goals, districts and schools must define priorities for student performance, make choices about how to organize to meet them, and then move the dollars and people to match those commitments. If school leaders give priority to improving academic achievement, for example, then the district staff and budget should shift to support that

goal. If the district declares that all students will read by 3rd grade, then staff, dollars, and time should support more effective literacy teaching. Districts and schools should expect to give up some long-standing and useful programs to support these choices.

Matching Dollars to Priorities

For the past 10 years, I have helped districts and schools rethink their use of resources to support their reform efforts. In partnership with New American Schools and with support from Pew Charitable Trusts, I have worked with four large urban districts to analyze their district and school spending and then consider ways to reallocate dollars. My colleagues and I have discovered that, in many cases, the dollars needed for reform efforts are there, but they are tied up in existing staff, programs, and practices. We have found that schools need help shifting their use of resources to take advantage of what they already have and that districts often lag behind schools in changing their own spending and organization structures. To support schools in raising student performance, most districts need to realign spending and staffing in at least five ways.

Restructure salaries to attract and retain high-quality teachers. It is no secret that U.S. teaching salaries lag behind those of other professions.

The discrepancy is especially great for two types of teachers needed in schools: high-performing students from top colleges who have many other career options and teachers trained in math and science (Mohrman, Mohrman, & Odden, 1995). The earnings gap grows wider over a teaching career (Conley & Odden, 1995). Maximum teaching salaries fall well below those in other professions, meaning that the most talented individuals sacrifice much higher potential earnings if they remain in teaching. Districts need to reconsider their practice of paying all teachers the same regardless of subject area. In addition, they must find ways to restructure teacher salaries and responsibilities to provide the most talented, productive teachers with the opportunity to earn more competitive salaries during their careers.

Increasing salaries significantly without bankrupting districts means taking a hard look at the way salary dollars are spent. Since the 1920s, virtually all districts have used a salary structure that applies to every teacher regardless of grade or subject. Teachers can move up the salary ladder either by logging more years of teaching or accumulating education credits. Most districts increase salaries far more for experience than they do for education (Miles, 1997b). Boston Public Schools, for example, spent 36 percent of its 1998–99 salary budget to buy years of experience (29 percent) and education credits (7 percent).

For this investment to make sense for students, both teaching experience and accumulated credits would have to be clearly linked to student achievement. But research shows that after the first five years, the quality of teaching does not automatically improve with either course credits or years of teaching (Hanushek, 1994; Murnane, 1996). Experience and coursework have value, but neither is a fail-safe investment without coaching, hard work, and systems that reward and encourage good teaching. Many districts are currently experimenting with increasing teacher salaries on the basis of more direct measures of teaching quality. Most of these plans give bonuses to teachers who meet certain

criteria or student performance targets. These extra dollars are nice symbols, but the plans that have the most promise for significantly raising teacher salary levels redirect existing salary dollars even as they seek to add more.

Redirect district staff and spending from compliance efforts to provide schools with integrated support and accountability. Using standards to measure school performance changes the role of the district office. If schools do not have to report student performance, schools and districts are only held accountable for whether they do as they are told and keep children safe. As a result, curriculum offices issue guidebooks and sometimes check whether they are used, and districts create departments to monitor whether dollars from each funding source are spent as stipulated.

When schools become accountable for student learning, the district role must shift to helping schools measure student learning and supporting the changes in teaching and organization that best support improvement. Most districts need to focus more on four purposes: defining standards and targets, supporting schools and teachers, creating accountability, and restructuring school organizations.

Supporting these four goals is often possible by reallocating existing resources. In many large districts, the traditional compliance focus has resulted in a structure that spreads resources thinly across many schools and priorities. For example, one district was surprised to find that it devoted nine experts to supervising services across 30 schools. Each expert was responsible for making sure that schools met program requirements in one specific area, such as special education, Title I, bilingual education, literacy, or technology. Because these nine individuals focused on only one issue in multiple schools, they could conduct only superficial reviews of effectiveness, and they certainly couldn't provide support to underperforming schools. Even though the district devoted $24,000 in salaries and benefits to each school, the schools barely felt an impact. Instead, the schools needed deeper, integrated school support in

specific areas where improvement was most needed.

Shift more resources to teaching literacy in grades K–3. Research consistently shows that smaller group sizes matter most in early grades when students learn to read (Wenglinsky, 2001). It also shows that when students don't learn to read by 3rd grade, they continue to fall farther behind in school and are more likely to be assigned to costly special education programs and to drop out of school. Research suggests concrete ways to improve reading achievement:

- Class size reduction in grades pre-K–2 can make an important, lasting difference in student achievement.
- Small reductions in class size make little difference; only when class sizes get down to 15–17 students does achievement increase predictably.
- Even smaller group sizes, including one-on-one instruction, are crucial for developing readers, especially those from disadvantaged homes.
- If teachers don't change their classroom practice to take advantage of class size reductions, they can't expect improved student performance.

To incorporate these lessons, both districts and schools need to shift their use of existing resources. U.S. school districts average one teacher for every 17 students—with the ratio much higher in many urban districts—and one adult for every nine students. Yet, elementary school class size averages in the mid-20s (Miles, 1997a; Snyder & Hoffman, 1999). Most districts allocate more staff and dollars per pupil to high schools than to elementary schools.

To focus resources where they matter most, districts need to look first at how much they spend at the elementary school level compared to the high school level. Next, they need to invest to ensure that teachers have access to powerful professional development in teaching literacy. Third, they must actively support school-level changes that shift resources toward literacy instruction.

Districts will need to be prepared to defend school leaders who abandon popular, but outmoded or less important, programs and staff positions to support literacy efforts.

This active support of school-level changes in the use of resources creates special challenges for districts. For example, many schools have found ways to create small reading groups for part of the day by making group sizes larger at other times of the day. Others have reconsidered the role of each teacher, support person, and instructional aide to ensure that they support the focus on literacy. In some schools, this may mean changing the role of physical education, art, and music teachers or making these class sizes larger. It may mean hiring a highly trained literacy specialist instead of a traditional librarian. And redirecting resources toward literacy will mean integrating bilingual, Title I, and special education teachers more fully into a schoolwide literacy strategy. Schools need help making these shifts, which require changes in district policy, contract language, and staff allocation practices. Districts also need to be prepared to defend school leaders who abandon popular, but outmoded or less important, programs and staff positions to support literacy efforts.

Invest strategically in professional development for teachers. To take advantage of smaller class sizes and to improve literacy instruction, districts need to offer teachers high-quality professional development. The assertion that districts invest only a small percentage of their budgets in professional development has become a cliché among education reformers. Although some districts may need to invest more money, the priority, for many, will be to refocus existing efforts to create more effective professional development and more useful teacher time. Research shows that professional development that responds to school-level student performance priorities, focuses on instruction, and provides coaching for individual teachers and teams over time can have a powerful impact on

teacher practice. But professional development doesn't follow this model in most districts. And providing teachers with more professional time and intensive coaching support can seem expensive to districts that use a few traditional workshops as their "training."

In a detailed analysis of four large urban district budgets, we found that districts spend more than they think on professional development (Miles & Hornbeck, 2000). In these four districts, spending on professional development from all sources ranged 2–4 percent of the district budget. These figures are much larger than those districts traditionally report and manage. For example, one district reported $460,000 spent on strategic professional development, but the district actually spent nearly 20 times this amount when professional development efforts by all departments and sources were included. Worse, our analysis showed that professional development spending is often divided among many fragmented, sometimes conflicting, programs managed by different departments. Spending to support improved academic instruction represented only a fraction of total dollars in these districts, and the amount aimed at literacy instruction was even smaller. Harnessing these dollars requires district and school leaders to challenge the status quo and to abandon worthwhile initiatives in order to support more integrated models of professional development.

Reduce spending on nonacademic teaching staff in secondary schools. The traditional comprehensive high school often employs more teaching staff in nonacademic subjects than it does in English, math, science, and history. Traditional high schools devote only about half of each student's school day to courses covering academic skills, resulting in more than half the high school resources being aimed at goals that are not measured by the state and district standards. This allocation of resources also means that class sizes for the core subjects are usually 30 students or more, with teachers responsible for a total of more than 125 students.

But changing the balance of staff to make a meaningful difference in

student loads and academic time would require some high schools to double the number of academic staff. And shifting more resources toward academic subjects means reducing staff in other areas and challenging the structure—or even the existence—of such cherished programs as band and athletics. Given the number of the changes and their sometimes painful nature, it is unreasonable and impractical to expect principals or school-based decision-making groups to make them on their own. Until districts take steps to change the mix of staff, many high schools will make marginal improvements at best.

Making Choices

Organizing resources to act on urgent priorities, such as teaching all students to read in urban schools, requires leaders to take politically difficult stands. Union, district, and school board leaders need courage and strong community support to say:

- Even though all subjects are important, literacy is most important.
- Even though all teachers are important, those who bring deep subject knowledge and can integrate across disciplines or programs are worth more.
- Even though band, sports, and other electives can be a crucial part of a balanced education, the community must find new ways to pay for and provide them.
- Even though student readiness and social health provide a base for student learning, schools cannot be held accountable for providing all services to students, and they aren't staffed to do so.
- Even though investments in teacher professional development and technology may mean an extra student in your class, we can't build and sustain excellent schools without more of such investments.

Ensuring Adequate Funding

Regardless of overall spending levels, district and community leaders need to articulate priorities and direct spending to support them. But they must also ensure that schools have enough money to begin these tasks. There is no one way to define how much money is enough, but a few test questions can help put district spending in perspective: How does spending per pupil in your district compare to spending in other districts with similar student populations? How do teacher salary levels compare? How does the community's tax rate compare to the tax rates in similar districts?

If the community is underinvesting in education, leaders need to make the case for increased spending. But a community may be more likely to support increases in spending if citizens see that leaders have clear priorities and are willing to make difficult choices to ensure that new dollars get to the heart of improving student achievement.

References

Conley, S., & Odden, A. (1995). Linking teacher compensation to teacher career development: A strategic examination. *Educational Evaluation and Policy Analysis, 17,* 253–269.

Hanushek, E. A. (1994). *Making schools work: Improving performance and controlling costs.* Washington, DC: Brookings Institution.

Miles, K. H. (1997a). Finding the dollars to pay for 21st century schools: Taking advantage of the times. *School Business Affairs, 63*(6), 38–42.

Miles, K. H. (1997b). *Spending more on the edges: Public school spending from 1967 to 1991.* Ann Arbor, MI: UMI Press.

Miles, K. H., & Hornbeck, M. J. (2000). *Reinvesting in teaching: District spending on professional development.* Arlington, VA: New American Schools.

Mohrman, A., Mohrman, S. A., & Odden, A. (1995). Aligning teacher compensation with systemic school reform: Skill-based pay and group-based performance rewards. *Educational Evaluation and Policy Analysis, 18,* 51–71.

Murnane, R. J. (1996). Staffing the nation's schools with skilled teachers. In E. A. Hanushek & D. W. Jorgenson (Eds.), *Improving America's schools: The role of incentives* (pp. 243–260). Washington, DC: National Academy Press.

Snyder, T. D., & Hoffman, C. M. (1999). *Digest of education statistics 1999.* Washington, DC: National Center for Education Statistics, Office of Educational Research and Improvement, U.S. Department of Education.

Wenglinsky, H. (2001, June). The effect of class size on achievement [Memorandum]. Available: www.ets.org/search97egi/s97_cgi

Karen Hawley Miles is president of Education Resource Management Strategies, 3705 Euclid Ave., Dallas, Texas 75205; karenhmiles@cs.com.

Learning to Go with the Grain of the Brain

IF YOUNG PEOPLE ARE TO BE EQUIPPED EFFECTIVELY TO MEET THE CHALLENGES OF THE 21ST CENTURY, IT IS SURELY PRUDENT TO SEEK OUT THE VERY BEST UNDERSTANDINGS FROM CURRENT SCIENTIFIC RESEARCH INTO THE NATURE OF HOW HUMANS LEARN BEFORE CONSIDERING FURTHER REFORM OF THE EDUCATION SYSTEM.

By John Abbott and Terence Ryan

An analogy; humans have been eating and using their brains since the beginning of time. We think we know how to do this—it is all a matter of common sense. Yet, with the breakthroughs in the understanding of diet in the last 30 years, we are eating better and now live longer. That analogy is useful when we look at the brain and the opportunities that now present themselves to expand its capabilities. We are now in a position to understand the brain's adaptive functions—learning—far better.

Researchers in the 1990s have uncovered massive evidence in the cognitive sciences, and in neurobiology, evolutionary biology, evolutionary psychology, and even archaeology and anthropology, which shows us in great detail how it is that humans actually learn. We now can see why learning is much more than just the flip-side of good teaching and schooling. Much of this evidence confirms what many people have always intuitively thought; learning involves far more than schooling. People are quick to recognize that

many successful public figures were either school failures or removed themselves from formal schooling at an early date. Conversely many successful people in school seemed to have disappeared without a trace. Why? Not surprisingly, long-term studies show that the greatest predictors of success at university are:

1. the quantity and quality of the discussion in the child's home before entering school;
2. the amount of independent reading, regardless of subject matter, which the child does;
3. the clarity of value systems as understood and practised;
4. strong positive peer group pressure; and
5. the primary school. Further down the list is the secondary school. Formal schooling is only part of what fires up the inquisitiveness in a child's mind.

Children's learning is the most natural and innate of human skills; humans are born to learn—we are

better at that than any other species. Brain imaging technologies enable researchers to literally watch learning occur as specific patterns of brain activity within the brain light up on a computer screen. The unprecedented clarity this technology reveals about brain function is causing scientists to revise many of their earlier assumptions about how individual learning takes place. These findings have undermined the behaviourist metaphor of the brain as a blank slate waiting for information. The brain is now seen as a far more flexible, self-adjusting, biological metaphor—the brain as a living, unique, ever-changing organism that grows and reshapes itself in response to challenge, with elements that wither through lack of use. The evidence now emerging about learning and brain development has spawned a movement towards educational practice which confirms that thinking skills (metacognition), as well as significant aspects of intelligence, are learnable.

The prestigious Santa Fe Institute noted in a 1995 collection of essays,

The Mind, the Brain and Complex Adaptive Systems, the mismatch between emerging learning theory and dominant educational practice. "The method people naturally employ to acquire knowledge is largely unsupported by traditional classroom practice. The human mind is better equipped to gather information about the world by operating within it than by reading about it, hearing lectures on it, or studying abstract models of it."

As children get older, their **learning** must be integrated into the broader life of the community with **real tasks** for young people to do , and real responsibilities for them to shoulder.

These new understandings about human learning and the brain question the long-term effectiveness of plans among many governments to place even more reliance on the role of the school and the classroom in young people's learning.

Most school reform movements have been within the existing paradigm of pupils/teachers/schools—what we need now is out-of-the-box thinking which starts by focusing on the brain's ability to learn and how we become more effective humans. Only then can we think about how to develop and nurture appropriate learning environments.

We are, who we are, in large part because of our species' evolutionary experience over millions of years. Those experiences are firmly encapsulated in all of our brains, with each of us carrying all those predispositions that previous generations found useful to their survival. The

work of the Dartmouth cognitive neuroscientist, Michael Gazzaniga, shows that life is largely about discovering what is already built into our brains. He warns that, "All the ways that human societies try to change minds and to change how humans truly interact with the environment are doomed to fail. Indeed, societies fail when they preach at their populations. They tend to succeed when they allow each individual to discover what millions of years of evolution have already bestowed upon mind and body."

Evolution, we now understand, has provided humans with a powerful tool kit of predispositions that go a long way in explaining our ability to learn language, co-operate successfully in groups, think across problems, plan for the future, and how to empathize with others. Predispositions provide individuals with a whole range of skills that enable them to relate flexibly to their environment. Yet, because for most of human history man tended to live in relatively small groups, these skills have to be developed collaboratively as very few people ever possess all these attributes. The speed with which our predispositions evolve seems to be incredibly slow, and it is thought there have been no major changes in the last 30,000 years.

By melding neurological discoveries in an evolutionary framework, researchers can see how, within a single generation, the influences of millions of years of evolution mingle with the priorities of a particular culture. The *Harvard Business Review* stated graphically in late 1998, "You can take man out of the Stone Age, but you can't take the Stone Age out of man." We are enormously empowered by an array of evolved predispositions which enable us to adapt to vastly different sorts of circumstances, yet these evolved predispositions inhibit us as well.

We have to be cautious to devise learning environments that take such predispositions beyond "what

comes naturally,"—in doing this we must go with the grain of the brain.

That "grain" we can now begin to understand far better. The relationship between nature and nurture is well summarized by the English professor of psychobiology Henry Plotkin in his 1996 book *Evolution in Mind.* Plotkin notes, "Nature has itself evolved. Nurture can only be fully understood in light of historical causes. Nature has nurture." This goes a long way towards explaining just why humans learn the way they do.

Harvard's Howard Gardner uses his theory of multiple intelligences to show that, deep within our minds, we have multiple survival strategies that include an ability to look at any situation from a number of different perspectives. Link this with the emerging understanding of how the neural structures of the brain grow, and we begin to get an understanding of how these different forms of intelligence enable each of us "to make sense of our environments in very different ways." These "different ways" are critical to our species survival, and help provide insight into the origins of creativity. The balance between emotion and logic, the role of intuition, and the relationship between intrinsic and extrinsic motivation are all part of the "complex adaptive system" that best describes the brain's ability to deal with the messiness of ordinary everyday life situations.

Now, consider what we know about the brain and effective learning in light of the many systems developed over the past 150 years to organize individuals within an industrial economy. Prosperity meant organizing people into factories where their broadly-based skills were not needed and, very quickly in support of this, school systems were built which emphasized functional transactional skills that only utilized a small proportion of each individual brain. Such underused brains had to find their satisfaction elsewhere, and factory owners were quick to replace intrinsic motivation with extrinsic reward. Our present "crisis in schools" relates partly to the collapse of the old factory system and the recognition that successful workers now have to have more than just basic skills and an amenable attitude, which is largely what was required of their parents and grandparents.

Things are now very different. Author Daniel Yergin, winner of the Pulitzer Prize, recently observed, "Companies are being forced to think differently.... That means fostering a culture that encourages alertness, responsiveness, and flexibility, and the speeding up of the cycle time of processes and decisions. In the aftermath of re-engineering and restructuring, competitive forces now demand a rediscovery of employees and of the knowledge they command.... The high-rise pyramids of hierarchical corporate structures are being transformed into the low-rise of the flatter organization—less bureaucracy, more teamwork, and a greater dispersion of responsibility, information and decision making." In short, we need people who are competent problem-solvers, creative, flexible and personally responsible for their welfare and the welfare of those in their family and neighborhood.

Research from the evolutionary sciences show that these collaborative higher order skills and attitudes are indeed largely innate. Thus, with continuous and progressive stimulation at an early age (as would have been the case in pre-industrial times) they quickly develop. Despite six, eight or ten generations of such limited demands being placed on our sense-making skills, our genetic inheritance has not yet been modified a jot. Children are still born with latent predispositions, as it were, equipping them to take on the world. During much of this century, formal schooling has struggled to provide appropriate simulation of real-life situations. It has met inevitably with only limited success. For those who have been able to succeed in abstract terms, there are as many

for whom schooling has been a disaster because they are more practically orientated. Industrial society had no place for children in the world of adult affairs—children were seen to be in the way. So we are stuck with a system which has progressively turned childhood into an extended virtual holiday; in reality we have trivialized adolescence by denying adolescents the opportunity of learning from their own experiences, and making them good processors of information provided by other people.

However, it is only very recently that researchers have come to understand this. Learning theory in the late 19th and early 20th centuries was generally behaviourist—people needed rewards to do tasks; our brains were blank sheets awaiting instruction; and intelligence was dimly thought of as being completely innate and inherited. As England and its territories developed an education system for the masses (initially as much to keep children off the streets as to give them useful skills), it rapidly came to reflect the industrial factory model. When universities were asked to advise on the curriculum, they did so by suggesting a highly reductionist model of learning. The study of learning was a strictly academic affair to such early educational experts. They measured what happened in classrooms when people performed abstract tasks, but they hardly ever deigned to study the calculating ability of an apprentice working on the job such as Benjamin Franklin, or a street trader on the Whitechapel Road in the East End of London.

This late 19th century compromise between the scientific understandings of the day, the needs of industry and the desire to give all children basic skills, increased productivity and raised standards of living significantly. But this came at a cost. With so much of their latent predispositions untapped by the daily routine of instruction, many children became deeply frustrated. Instead of the daily challenge of

making sense of their environment, they now waited to be told what to do and how to do it.

Societies now stand at a very exciting time in human history—at an evolutionary crossroads. Will we be able to capitalize on these understandings and reverse what is now seen as an upside down and inside out system of education?

Everything that we understand about our intellectual development suggests that below the age of seven or eight, particularly below the age of three, we are heavily dependent on external encouragement and stimulation to develop the brain in ways survival skills (the ability to collaborate and see across issues) can be learned. In today's society, the functional skills of reading, writing, and numeracy are survival skills. If they are not learned at an early stage, learning them later on is far more difficult. Every youngster needs to make great demands on adults in order to master these basic survival skills. Although adults may be ambivalent about their roles as parents and caregivers, good parenting is utterly essential to a child if his or her mental faculties and social skills are to develop.

When they move into puberty, the natural tendency of young people is to reverse their dependency on adults. They want to be in control; not because they want to be bloody minded, but because all the hormonal changes going on within are pressing them to show they can now use what they learnt earlier to become fully functional, independent people. If they are not equipped with basic survival skills, adolescents are ill-prepared to deal with the physiological changes of adolescence and end up mentally, emotionally and socially adrift.

Now, consider the current model of schooling. In the elementary schools of many countries, class size is largest when children are very young. When children's predispositions are at their most fertile, we place them in classes of 30 or more. However, in secondary school we decrease class size—which clashes with the increasing desire of adolescents at about 14 or 15, to be independent. Many, for the most natural reasons, get completely turned off by schooling at this stage because it simply does not seem real in comparison to the emotionally-charged environments they experience away from school with their peers.

These new understandings about **human learning** and the brain question the long-term effectiveness of plans among many governments to place even more reliance on the role of the school and the classroom in **young people's** learning.

To remedy this upside down and inside out model of learning, we've got to go back to the way the brain developed through continuous interaction with its environment before the introduction of the industrial model of schooling interrupted the natural flow of learning. Such a brain-friendly model of learning would be based on a set of arrangements that mirrors, as far as possible, the biological process involved in weaning. It requires the development of a pedagogy that emphasises the young child's mastery of a range of skills, and that child's embryonic but growing ability to take responsibility for directing their own work and realizing that they'll be doing this for a lifetime. As early as possible, the system must aim to get the child to be a worker. It is no longer

enough for them to simply be recipients. As children get older, their learning must be integrated into the broader life of the community with real tasks for young people to do, and real responsibilities for them to shoulder.

Elementary schools should provide classes for five-year-olds of no more than ten or 12. Teachers should construct learning programs that combine—in the child's mind as well as theirs—an understanding of both content and process in ways which make children's thinking visible to themselves. This will significantly change the role of teachers, making it essential for them to model the very techniques of good learning that children need to acquire. Although good teachers will remain essential, successful learning requires more than just teacher, chalk and talk. As a policy, investment in the technologies of learning should increase with the child's age.

Let's briefly turn to the inside out part of the current model of learning. Young people spend no more than 20% of their waking hours between the ages of five and 18 in a classroom. However, within the community at large, an increasing number of people have many professional skills and attitudes to share with young people. For example, many individuals who have taken early retirement would be interested in sharing expertise and help young people's learning. These are the people adolescents need to be able to relate to— almost surrogate grandparents. The human resources of the community need to be recruited to work with young people.

If current education budgets were not increased but we began the formal education of young children in classes of ten or 12, we might think classes of 40 or more would be required in secondary school. But that need not be the case. If schools do

their job properly and children get intensive support in the earliest years, it would actually be better for adolescents, probably before the age of 16, to have little more than half their classes formally taught. It would be more helpful to them if they learnt to work on their own, and accessed the rich learning resources that schools and community mentors would then be able to provide. Too much instruction makes adolescents too dependent on the teacher and the classroom.

We now have it within our power to construct models of learning, at no greater cost than at present, which go with the grain of the brain while at the same time reconnecting adults and children outside the formal setting of a school.

John Abbott is President of the 21st Century Learning Initiative. He has been both teacher and principal and introduced Britain's first fully-computerized classroom. Director of the Education 2000Trust since 1985, he has been involved in the development of techniques and environments that enable young people to have confidence in their ability to become lifelong learners. In 1997 he was invited by Mikhail Gorbachev to join the State of the World Forum.

Terence Ryan is Senior Researcher at the 21st Century Learning Initiative.

The 21st Century Learning Initiative is a transnational program aiming to synthesize the best of research and development into the nature of human learning, and examining the implications of this for education, work and the development of communities worldwide.

For more information and resources, please refer to the Initiative's web site at http://www.21learn.org

The 21st Century Learning Initiative 11739 Bowman Green Drive Reston, VA 20190-3501 Ph: (703) 787-4020 Fax: (703) 787-4024 info@21learn.org

First published in *Education Canada*, Vol. 39, No. 1, Spring 1999, pp. 8-11. Permission to reprint granted by the authors and the Canadian Education Association.

'All Children Can Learn':

Facts and Fallacies

BY M. DONALD THOMAS AND WILLIAM L. BAINBRIDGE

A FEW decades ago, leaders in the field of school reform introduced the concept of "effective schools" as a way to identify what works best in educating children and to provide models for struggling schools to use for improvement. The effective schools movement is frequently attributed to the work of the late Ronald Edmonds. In a speech delivered to the National Conference of the Teacher Corps in 1978, Edmonds defined the five characteristics consistently evident in effective schools: strong leadership, clear emphasis on learning, positive school climate, regular and appropriate monitoring of student progress, and high expectations for students and staff.[1] From these straightforward principles, an entire belief system has evolved that offers a variety of solutions that are designed to improve schools.

However, the effective schools movement, like most other reform efforts, has developed philosophical and political schisms along its major fault line: the central tenet that children's learning can be improved if schools adopt effective practices. At its heart, this belief is positive, useful, and practical—but it does engender strong opinions and political reactions.

The initial understanding that school practices and policies can make a difference, even for children from homes in which parents have few educational or financial resources, has now been translated into the popular mantra "all children can learn." This phrase sometimes confuses the public and deters the possibility of substantially helping disadvantaged children obtain a high-quality, resource-rich education. In our view, because of the simplistic acceptance of this phrase at face value, the effective schools movement as currently promoted is contaminated with a series of fallacies and a number of unintended consequences. We offer the following ideas as a starting point for further, in-depth discussions that can lead to more thoughtful school policies.

The Fallacies

When we look at many of the potentially harmful policies and practices being implemented in schools today, we can only assume that they have been inspired by the following fallacies, which do not bear careful scrutiny:

- the fallacy that all children can learn—at the same level and in the same amount of time;
- the fallacy of the principal as sole instructional leader;
- the fallacy of setting standards on the basis of exceptions; and
- the fallacy of uniform standards for all children.

The fallacy that all children can learn—at the same level and in the same amount of time. All children *can* learn, at some level, and most children, as Ronald Edmonds stated, can learn the basic curriculum if sufficient resources are provided. The fallacy, however, is the belief that all children can learn the *same curriculum, in the same amount of time, and at the same level.* The problem with such an unexamined belief is that it may be used to deny differential financial support for those who come to school with environmental disadvantages. Not all children have high-quality nutrition, stimulating homes, and extensive learning opportunities prior to entering school.

Research in cognitive brain development shows that formation of synaptic contacts in the human cerebral cortex occurs between birth and age 10,[2] and most of the brain gets built within a few years after birth. Environment matters greatly in brain development. The period of early childhood is critical in brain development, and those who have high-protein diets and lots of sensory stimulation tend to have more synaptic connections. Brains that do not get enough protein and stimulation in their environments lose connections, and some potential neural pathways are shut down.[3] These facts help to explain what educators have long observed: children from impoverished environments, in which they do not receive good nutrition and stimulating experiences, generally achieve at lower levels than children from more enriching environments.

This concrete evidence should be enough to convince us that we should concentrate on improving the lives of children before they come to school and not simply proclaim that "all children can learn" without enacting proper public policy to provide economic opportunity for families, health care for all children, and parenting education for young mothers.

If we as a society can summon the courage and will to do these things, then maybe all children can learn at higher levels and the gap between low-income and more privileged children can really be narrowed.

The fallacy of the principal as sole instructional leader. Promoting the principal as the sole instructional leader may demean teachers. The principal may be a leader, but accountability for effective instruction belongs to *teachers*. Principals should understand instruction, and they can support it in many ways (for example, by hiring excellent teachers and by promoting effective professional development for them), but they do not teach the curriculum.

If teachers cannot teach effectively, then principals must carry out their major accountability duty—evaluating employees and dismissing ineffective ones. This is the most effective way that principals can improve instruction.

Principals have many responsibilities for managing the school: introducing best practices, implementing policies, protecting the ethics of the profession, staying within budget, and promoting a belief system in support of public education, to name just a few. Principals have more than enough to do without taking over responsibilities that belong to teachers.

The fallacy of setting standards on the basis of exceptions. Often, proponents of the effective schools philosophy cite a student who rose out of poverty or a school in which low-income children achieve at unusually high levels. These exceptions are then used to tell the world that all children can "pull themselves up by their bootstraps" or that all schools can reproduce the results achieved by the one cited.

Certainly, examples of success can provide lessons and models if they are considered thoughtfully. However, we must be careful that this kind of thinking does not lead to standards that are set on the basis of exceptions. Such standards imply that all children can achieve at high levels if they choose to do so—one child did it; so can others. No additional help is needed!

The hard truth is that exceptions occur under special circumstances that cannot usually be replicated or that may be partially replicated only if sufficient resources are available.

The fallacy of uniform standards for all children. Of all the fallacies being promoted, this is probably the most bizarre. Decades of history and mountains of research indicate that childhood development is unique for each individual. The idea that children and schools should be evaluated by a uniform criterion—usually a test score—has the potential to do untold damage.

Uniformity of measurement leaves out human judgment—the most critical element in decision making. Those who promote uniform standards (often state legislatures) promote a false system of evaluation that will probably disappear as rapidly as it has been established.

Although it is difficult to accept and even more difficult to admit, children in the United States do not have equal opportunities to learn, nor do they have equal opportunities to succeed. In time, with enough effort and money and solid social policies, the achievement gaps between the advantaged and disadvantaged can narrow. Until then, however, it is unfair to treat all children and all schools "equally" by setting standards that are not equitable. The assumption that all can meet these standards—without our providing educationally disadvantaged children with the extra support they need to achieve at high levels—perpetuates injustice.

As Edmund Burke stated, "The equal treatment of unequals is the greatest injustice of all." This statement has been inscribed on our national documents and should be chiseled into the hearts of all school personnel and those who enact education policy.

Unintended Consequences

Next, let us discuss the unintended consequences of the simplistic "all children can learn" approach. These include:

- establishing accountability based on state-developed tests;
- downplaying the need for early intervention for children who live under conditions of poverty; and
- using punishment as a motivator to improve schools.

Establishing accountability based on state-developed tests. The belief that "all children can learn" has spawned a movement of testing as the basis for student promotion, student graduation, evaluation of school personnel, and state and federal funding. Our experience with state-developed criterion-referenced tests leads us to the conclusion that most of these tests are either too simple or too difficult. In either case, they are inappropriate measures of school effectiveness. Not one study in the school literature can correlate a test score with either student success or teacher effectiveness. Tests created at the state level and imposed on schools may appear to be "politically correct," but their educational value is highly questionable.

As Linda McNeil points out, forcing arbitrary punitive standards on schools undermines both teaching and learning and results in "growing inequality between the content and quality of education provided

to white middle-class children and that provided to children in poor and minority schools."[4] In Texas, for example, McNeil found that, even though scores on the state-mandated Texas Assessment of Academic Skills were going up in many disadvantaged schools, teachers reported that students' ability to use the skills that had been drilled into them for the test was actually declining. In fact, she claims, "this system of testing is restratifying education by race and class."[5]

Downplaying the need for early intervention for children who live under conditions of poverty. The "all children can learn" mentality is dangerous because it may lead us to assume that all children can meet the same standards no matter how well or ill prepared they are to start school. This assumption in turn excuses us from addressing the need for better early childhood programs. To claim that "all children can learn" without recognizing that some children start school on a very unequal footing burdens our schools and teachers with daunting and perhaps insurmountable barriers.

An enormous amount of time, effort, and money must be spent to "reclaim" and "remediate" children whose skills lag behind those of their more advantaged peers. Yet there is a widespread attitude that, if students and teachers cannot overcome the obstacles created by poverty and poor nutrition in the short amount of time available in the average school year, they have "failed." This pressure is especially strong when children and their teachers are expected to achieve some arbitrary standard established by a state-mandated proficiency test.

The result of this attitude is that students rarely catch up, and teachers become demoralized. Sadly, this is the current situation in many of our nation's public schools. Even more alarming is the tendency of the news media to leave an impression that gaps in performance among student groups are related to skin color or ethnicity.[6]

Public policy in the U.S. is not as child-friendly as it is in many other countries, such as Sweden, Canada, Japan, or Israel. What is needed most to help children is for politicians to make good on their promise that "all children will be ready to learn" by the time they start school. Enacting public policy that establishes educational programs for very young children should be the major strategy for helping children achieve at higher levels and reducing the achievement gap between children of high and low socioeconomic status. Early intervention stimulates cognitive development, improves sensory development, and increases motivation to learn. It offers the best chance for all children to be ready to learn when they begin kindergarten. Providing good early childhood education is a big and costly responsibility, but this strategy is just, extremely cost-effective in the long run, and a measure of the character of a nation.

Using punishment as a motivator to improve our schools. Frederick Herzberg is dead, and with him the sensible notion that punishment never motivates nor serves as an effective way to improve our schools.[7] The punishment mentality spawns takeover laws, zero-tolerance policies, threats to administrators of losing their jobs, and decreased funding for those schools whose students most need additional support. Whatever happened to "due process of law" and "positive reinforcement"?

Herzberg, Maslow—wherever you are—we need you now more than ever!

Time for Change

If Edmonds were still with us, we believe he would be appalled at what has happened to the effective schools movement. Unfortunately, what began as a noble process to help low-income children achieve at higher levels has become an educational albatross that punishes both teachers and students and declares that schools are ineffective when all children do not learn at arbitrary levels predetermined by individuals external to the schools.

The thinking behind a simplistic interpretation of "all children can learn" suggests that there is no need for adequate resources and child-friendly public policy. Assuming that all children can reach the same high standards through the heroic efforts of educators, without major changes in education and social policy, is similar to assuming that doctors can make all children healthy even though many do not receive adequate home care and appropriate nutrition.

We fervently hope that all children will be treated as individuals, achieving at various levels appropriate to their development, and that they will not be treated as learning at the same level at the same time—all marching to the arbitrary beat of a state proficiency test. It would be much better for all of us to accept differences and provide sufficient resources so that each boy and girl has an opportunity to achieve at the maximum level congruent to whatever gifts or limitations each may have.

The time has come for educators to reexamine the slogan that "all children can learn." Let's return to the basic research and stress the facts instead of the fallacies that have hurt so many of our teachers, schools, and children.

Notes

1. See Ronald R. Edmonds, "Some Schools Work and More Can," *Social Policy*, March/April 1979, pp. 23–32; and idem, "Making Public Schools More Effective," *Social Policy*, September/October 1981, pp. 56–60.

2. Peter R. Huttenlocher and Arun S. Dabholkar, "Regional Differences in Synaptogenesis in Human Cerebral Cortex," *Journal of Comparative Neurology*, vol. 387, 1997, pp. 167–78.

3. John T. Bruer, "Neural Connections—Some You Use, Some You Lose," *Phi Delta Kappan*, December 1999, pp. 264–77.

4. Linda M. McNeil, "Creating New Inequalities: Contradictions of Reform," *Phi Delta Kappan*, June 2000, p. 730.

5. Ibid., p. 731.

6. William L. Bainbridge, "Is the Test Score Gap Really Color-Based?," *School Administrator*, August 2000, p. 50.

7. Frederick Herzberg, *The Managerial Choice: To Be Efficient and to Be Human* (Salt Lake City: Olympus Press, 1982).

From *Phi Delta Kappan,* May 2001, pp. 660-662. © 2001 by Phi Delta Kappa International. Reprinted by permission of the author.

TIME TO TALK OF EARLY CHILDHOOD

ANNE C. LEWIS

EVEN THOSE given to betting on long shots would not accept the odds facing thousands of kindergarten and primary school teachers these days. Before they complete the first lessons—and certainly before they give the first tests—these teachers know that they have signed up to perform the difficult juggling act of bringing all their young charges up to the same level, while sticking to the standards local definitions of accountability demand of them.

It is sad to admit that the inequality allowed to exist in the richest nation in the world means that children enter kindergarten with backgrounds that differ widely in the preparation they provide for learning. These gaps are present on the first day of school, and, so far, most schools have not figured out how to close them.

The recent report on mathematics achievement from the National Assessment of Educational Progress (NAEP), for example, did find higher performance since the early 1990s in the fourth and eighth grades. But NAEP also found that, because skills had improved in all racial and income groups, the academic gap between disadvantaged and more advantaged students hadn't closed. Indeed, in some cases, it had even grown wider.

The realities of a serious learning gap at the beginning of formal schooling, coupled with our failure to deal with it, might sour the whole school year for some readers. But something significant is on the verge of happening in public policy and understanding that could change the picture. We may be headed for an acceptance of universal preschool.

Certainly, some of the framework exists already. Even Start, Head Start, early education services for the developmentally delayed, programs such as Parents as Partners, and a variety of state-funded initiatives make opportunities available to some families in an effort to compensate for what more affluent families can do for their children. When we also take into account the array of private early childhood programs, we can see that the pattern of early childhood education in the U.S. seems to be a patchwork of programs. It has never really been a system. Certainly, the problem of unequal access has plagued U.S. early childhood education, but, more important, there has been no public commitment to quality.

The U.S. is one of the few industrialized nations that does not offer public support for universal preschool programs. This failure to give priority to the preparation of our youngest citizens means that we have no clear standards for the environments that best stimulate their learning. Moreover, we do not expect those to whom we entrust the care and education of young children to be extraordinarily well prepared, and we pay them accordingly.

The lack of universal standards and the inadequate levels of investment are now on a collision course with the findings of research about what high-quality early childhood education can accomplish. And standards need not here mean conformity. A good Head Start program can do as much for young children as the most exclusive suburban Montessori school and still be very different. The National Association for the Education of Young Children (NAEYC) represents all sorts of programs and providers, but for a long time it has supported certain standards for programs and for the preparation of caregivers and teachers.

Federal policy is now moving cautiously toward changing this situation. President Bush has emphasized more attention to cognitive preparation in Head Start programs. Unfortunately, such moves fall far short of promoting quality throughout the early childhood experiences of those children who will fill the K-12 classrooms of the future. Without some means of improving teacher preparation and knowledge of child development, a move toward more academic instruction in the early years could restrict young children's capacities for deep learning, a skill they will need as they enter school.

Yet, if policy makers and educators want to do better, the research community can guide them. Several recent reports, primarily from the National Research Council (NRC), summarize what is known about high-quality programs and interventions for preschool and provide the standards for preschool programs that local and state educators ought to embrace.

Eager to Learn: Educating Our Preschoolers, the NRC's review of the literature, finds substantial support for certain features of high-quality programs:

- active attention to all of the developmental needs of young children—cognitive, social/emotional, and motor;
- teachers' well-informed (and supportive) responses to how a child approaches learning;
- low child/adult ratios;
- well-planned and well-implemented goals in each cognitive domain, such as rich vocabulary and listening experiences;

- formal training in early childhood education for all teachers; and
- active, reflective engagement of teachers in their practice under high-quality supervision.

The NRC further argues that any curriculum, no matter the type of program, needs to be grounded in the common principles of learning. If children are to become engaged in learning in later years, for example, then the curricula they are exposed to in preschools should encourage them to reflect, predict, question, and hypothesize. Just because they are young doesn't mean they can't do these things....

In her annual address to the American Federation of Teachers' Quest conference this past summer, AFT President Sandra Feldman called for universal, voluntary preschool throughout the country. Citing some of the same reasons mentioned above—in particular the unequal readiness of children for learning when they enter formal schooling—Feldman proposed building onto the existing Head Start system to help create a national system of early childhood education that would be accessible and affordable to any family that wishes to use it. Public funds from a variety of sources could be combined to provide for poor families, and other families would be able to participate on a cost-sharing basis.

A major advantage to universal preschool, according to Feldman and others, is that high-quality teachers would become a necessity. The work can be intellectually challenging, and, if the salaries were competitive with those of other teaching jobs, the field might attract better-quality teachers, both new and experienced. Feldman suggests bringing back a strategy once used during teacher shortages: family day-care and preschool centers in schools so that teachers can bring their own children to participate.

What is needed right now, according to *From Neurons to Neighborhoods: The Science of Early Childhood Development*, another publication of the National Research Council, is a national dialogue on our shared responsibility for giving all children a chance to develop fully. "The time has come," the report says, "to stop blaming parents, communities, business, and government and to shape a shared agenda to ensure both a rewarding childhood and a promising future for all children." A dialogue—in schools, in communities, and even at broader levels—requires simply a few people to start talking about that agenda.

ANNE C. LEWIS is a national education policy writer living in the Washington, D.C., area (e-mail: aclewis@crosslink.net).

From *Phi Delta Kappan,* October 2001, pp. 103-104. © 2001 by Phi Delta Kappa International. Reprinted by permission.

Early Learning, Later Success: The Abecedarian Study

Early Childhood Educational Intervention for Poor Children

Executive Summary

Frank Porter Graham Child Development Center
(University of North Carolina at Chapel Hill)

Background

- Poverty in early childhood has long-lasting negative consequences for cognitive development and academic outcomes, as shown by numerous studies. Comparisons among different groups of school children find that poor children fare worse academically than those raised in more advantageous circumstances. Poor children begin to lag behind in the earliest school years, suggesting that they enter school not adequately prepared for success.[1]

- In an effort to overcome the negative academic odds for poor children, early childhood education has been provided both in rigorous, University-based model programs and at the state and national levels. Such endeavors were generally based on the theory that providing early intellectual stimulation would enhance cognitive development, thereby allowing children to enter school better prepared to learn. This should in turn increase the probability of early school success, lead to later scholastic success, and eventually, result in vocational achievement and successful social adaptation in adulthood.

- Unfortunately, few early childhood programs have been sufficiently well controlled to permit scientists to evaluate the extent to which long-term outcomes are attributable to the program itself. Low numbers of participants or high attrition among samples reduced confidence in findings from some University-based programs. Many state and local programs lacked the degree of scientific control necessary for firm conclusions.

- From pooled long-term results of other early childhood programs, investigators concluded that such programs were associated with reductions in the degree to which treated children were placed in special education and retained in grade during the public school years.[2] Short-term gains in cognitive

development were also found along with boosts in academic performance. However, both kinds of gains tended to erode 3 to 6 years after participants entered school.

- The Abecedarian Project differed from most other early childhood programs in that: 1) it began in early infancy whereas other programs began at age 2 or older, and 2) treated children had five years of exposure to early education in a high quality child care setting whereas most other programs were of shorter duration.

The Abecedarian Project

- The Abecedarian Project was a carefully controlled study in which 57 infants from low-income families were randomly assigned to receive early intervention in a high quality child care setting and 54 were in a non-treated control group. This degree of scientific control gives investigators greater confidence that differences between the treated and untreated individuals can be attributed to the intervention itself, rather than to differences among treated and untreated families.

- The treated children received full-time educational intervention in a high-quality childcare setting from infancy through age 5. Each child had an individualized prescription of educational activities consisting of "games" that were incorporated into his or her day. These activities addressed social, emotional, and cognitive development but gave particular emphasis to language.

- The treated and untreated children were initially comparable with respect to scores on infant mental and motor tests. However, from the age of 18 months and through the completion of the child care program, children in the intervention group had significantly higher scores on mental tests than children in the control group. Follow-up cognitive assessments completed at ages 12 and 15 years showed that the intervention group continued to have higher average scores on mental tests. The treatment/control group gap narrowed but the trajectories did not converge. Effect sizes remained moderate.

- Treated children scored significantly higher on tests of reading and math from the primary grades through middle adolescence. Effect sizes for reading were large; those for math were large to moderate.
- The investigators have now completed a young-adult follow-up assessment of study participants. At age 21, cognitive functioning, academic skills, educational attainment, employment, parenthood, and social adjustment were measured. One-hundred-four of the original 111 infants (53 from the intervention group and 51 controls) were assessed.

Major Findings of the Young Adult Follow-Up Study

- Young adults who received early educational intervention had significantly higher mental test scores from toddlerhood through age 21 than did untreated controls. Averaged over the age span tested, the mental test score effect size for treatment was moderate and considered educationally meaningful.
- Enhanced language skills in the children appears to have mediated the effects of early intervention on mental test performance (i.e., cognitive skills).
- Reading achievement scores were consistently higher for individuals with early intervention. Treatment effect sizes remained large from primary school through age 21. Enhanced cognitive skills appeared to mediate treatment effects on reading achievement.
- Mathematics achievement showed a pattern similar to that for reading, with treated individuals earning higher scores. Effect sizes were medium in contrast to the large effects for reading. Again, enhanced cognitive functioning appeared to mediate treatment effects.
- Those with treatment were significantly more likely still to be in school at age 21—40% of the intervention group compared with 20% of the control group.
- A significant difference was also found for the percent of young adults who ever attended a four-year college. About 35% of the young adults in the intervention group had either graduated from or were at the time of the assessment attending a four-year college or university. In contrast, only about 14% in the control group had done so.

- Young adults in the intervention group were, on average, one year older (19.1 years) when their first child was born compared with those in the control group (17.7 years), although the youngest individuals in both groups were comparable in age when their first child was born.
- Employment rates were higher (65%) for the treatment group than for the control group (50%), although the trend was not statistically significant.

Policy Implications

- The importance of high quality, educational childcare from early infancy is now clear. The Abecedarian study provides scientific evidence that early childhood education significantly improves the scholastic success and educational attainments of poor children even into early adulthood.
- The Abecedarian study began treatment in early infancy, emphasizing the importance of providing a learning environment for children from the very beginning of life. Every child deserves a good start in an environment that is safe, healthy, emotionally supportive, and cognitively stimulating. Welfare reform means that, more than ever, poverty children will need early childcare. The educational stimulus value of these early caregiving years must not be wasted.
- Childcare officials should be aware of the importance of quality care beginning in infancy.
- Quality care requires sufficient well-trained staff to ensure that every child receives the kind of appropriate, individualized attention provided by the Abecedarian model.
- Future research should concentrate on identifying the specific learning techniques most effective for all groups and types of young children.
- More and more of America's children will need out of home care. This is especially true for poor children. We must not lose this opportunity to provide them the early learning experiences that will increase their chances for later success.

Notes

1. Alexander, K. L., & Entwisle, D. R. (1988). Achievement in the first 2 years of school: Patterns and processes. *Monographs of the Society for Research in Child Development, 53* (Serial No. 218).
2. Lazar, I., Darlington, R., Murray, H., Royce, J., & Snipper, A. (1982). Lasting effects of early education: A report from the consortium for longitudinal studies. *Monographs of the Society for Research in Child Development, 47* (Serial No. 195).

Index

Index

Test Your Knowledge Form

We encourage you to photocopy and use this page as a tool to assess how the articles in *Annual Editions* expand on the information in your textbook. By reflecting on the articles you will gain enhanced text information. You can also access this useful form on a product's book support Web site at *http://www.dushkin.com/online/*.

NAME: DATE:

_____

TITLE AND NUMBER OF ARTICLE:

_____

BRIEFLY STATE THE MAIN IDEA OF THIS ARTICLE:

_____

LIST THREE IMPORTANT FACTS THAT THE AUTHOR USES TO SUPPORT THE MAIN IDEA:

_____

WHAT INFORMATION OR IDEAS DISCUSSED IN THIS ARTICLE ARE ALSO DISCUSSED IN YOUR TEXTBOOK OR OTHER READINGS THAT YOU HAVE DONE? LIST THE TEXTBOOK CHAPTERS AND PAGE NUMBERS:

_____

LIST ANY EXAMPLES OF BIAS OR FAULTY REASONING THAT YOU FOUND IN THE ARTICLE:

_____

LIST ANY NEW TERMS/CONCEPTS THAT WERE DISCUSSED IN THE ARTICLE, AND WRITE A SHORT DEFINITION:

We Want Your Advice

ANNUAL EDITIONS revisions depend on two major opinion sources: one is our Advisory Board, listed in the front of this volume, which works with us in scanning the thousands of articles published in the public press each year; the other is you—the person actually using the book. Please help us and the users of the next edition by completing the prepaid article rating form on this page and returning it to us. Thank you for your help!

ANNUAL EDITIONS: Early Childhood Education 02/03

ARTICLE RATING FORM

Here is an opportunity for you to have direct input into the next revision of this volume.
We would like you to rate each of the articles listed below, using the following scale:

1. **Excellent: should definitely be retained**
2. **Above average: should probably be retained**
3. **Below average: should probably be deleted**
4. **Poor: should definitely be deleted**

Your ratings will play a vital part in the next revision.
Please mail this prepaid form to us as soon as possible.
Thanks for your help!

RATING	ARTICLE	RATING	ARTICLE
	1. The Mission of the Movement to Leave No Child Behind. What You Can Do		28. "But What's Wrong with Letter Grades?" Responding to Parents' Questions About Alternative Assessment
	2. Eager to Learn—Educating Our Preschoolers: Executive Summary		29. The Silencing of Recess Bells
	3. Preschool Perspective, Èn Français		30. Children and Post Traumatic Stress Disorder: What Classroom Teachers Should Know
	4. How Do Education and Experience Affect Teachers of Young Children?		31. Reinforcement in Developmentally Appropriate Early Childhood Classrooms
	5. Wired for Thought		32. Use the Environment to Prevent Discipline Problems and Support Learning
	6. The 20th Century's Best and Worst Education Ideas		33. "Teacher! He Hit Me!" "She Pushed Me!"—Where Does It Start? How Can It Stop?
	7. Look Who's Listening		34. Promoting the Emotional Development of Preschoolers
	8. Our Window to the Future		35. Integrating the Visual Arts—Building Young Children's Knowledge, Skills, and Confidence
	9. Gender Expectations of Young Children and Their Behavior		36. Blocks as a Tool for Learning: Historical and Contemporary Perspectives
	10. No Time for Fun		37. Make the Most of Learning Centers
	11. Too Sexy Too Soon		38. Using Documentation Panels to Communicate With Families
	12. The New Summer Break		39. Children and Computer Technology: Analysis and Recommendations
	13. Talking to Kids About Race		40. Children Are Born Mathematicians: Promoting the Construction of Early Mathematical Concepts in Children Under Five
	14. Fathers' Involvement in Programs for Young Children		41. Playing With Literacy in Preschool Classrooms
	15. Children of Divorce: 25 Years Later		42. Salting the Oats: Using Inquiry-Based Science to Engage Learners at Risk
	16. For America's Infants and Toddlers, Are Important Values Threatened by Our Zeal to "Teach"?		43. ABC's of the Internet for Early Childhood Professionals
	17. 10 Signs of a Great Preschool		44. Class-Size Reduction in California
	18. Who Cares for Kids?		45. Putting Money Where It Matters
	19. Teaching Principals, Parents, and Colleagues About Developmentally Appropriate Practice		46. Learning to Go With the Grain of the Brain
	20. Italian Import Creates Preschools Where Kids Shape Agenda		47. 'All Children Can Learn': Facts and Fallacies
	21. Creating Culturally Responsive, Inclusive Classrooms		48. Time to Talk of Early Childhood
	22. All They Do Is Play? Play in Preschool		49. Early Learning, Later Success: The Abecedarian Study, Executive Summary
	23. Service Learning in Preschool: An Intergenerational Project Involving Five-Year-Olds, Fifth Graders, and Senior Citizens		
	24. Parent Involvement: It's Worth the Effort		
	25. Applying Brain Research to Create Developmentally Appropriate Learning Environments		
	26. The Child-Centered Kindergarten: A Position Paper		
	27. Ordeal With a No. 2 Pencil		

(Continued on next page)

NO POSTAGE
NECESSARY
IF MAILED
IN THE
UNITED STATES

BUSINESS REPLY MAIL
FIRST-CLASS MAIL PERMIT NO. 84 GUILFORD CT

POSTAGE WILL BE PAID BY ADDRESSEE

McGraw-Hill/Dushkin
530 Old Whitfield Street
Guilford, Ct 06437-9989

ABOUT YOU

Name _____   Date _____

Are you a teacher? ☐   A student? ☐
Your school's name _____

Department _____

Address _____ City _____ State ____ Zip ____

School telephone # _____

YOUR COMMENTS ARE IMPORTANT TO US!

Please fill in the following information:
For which course did you use this book?
_____

Did you use a text with this ANNUAL EDITION? ☐ yes ☐ no
What was the title of the text?
_____

What are your general reactions to the *Annual Editions* concept?
_____

Have you read any pertinent articles recently that you think should be included in the next edition? Explain.
_____

Are there any articles that you feel should be replaced in the next edition? Why?
_____

Are there any World Wide Web sites that you feel should be included in the next edition? Please annotate.
_____

May we contact you for editorial input? ☐ yes ☐ no
May we quote your comments? ☐ yes ☐ no